D1083233

Alliances and Small Powers

INSTITUTE OF WAR AND PEACE STUDIES

OF THE SCHOOL OF INTERNATIONAL AFFAIRS

OF COLUMBIA UNIVERSITY

Alliances and Small Powers is one of a series of studies sponsored by the Institute of War and Peace Studies of Columbia University. *Defense and Diplomacy* by Alfred Vagts; *Man, the State, and War* by Kenneth N. Waltz; *The Common Defense: Strategic Programs in National Politics* by Samuel P. Huntington; *Strategy, Politics, and Defense Budgets* by Warner R. Schilling, Paul Y. Hammond, and Glenn H. Snyder; *Political Unification* by Amitai Etzioni; *Stockpiling of Strategic Materials* by Glenn H. Snyder; *The Politics of Military Unification* by Demetrios Caraley; *NATO and the Range of American Choice* by William T. R. Fox and Annette B. Fox; *A World of Nations* by Dankwart A. Rustow; *Asia and United States Policy* by Wayne A. Wilcox; and *The American Study of International Relations* by William T. R. Fox are other volumes in the series. *Theoretical Aspects of International Relations*, edited by William T. R. Fox; *Inspection for Disarmament*, edited by Seymour Melman; and *Changing Patterns of Military Politics*, edited by Samuel P. Huntington are all volumes of essays planned and edited by Institute members. The Institute of War and Peace Studies jointly sponsored the publication of the following: *Political Power: USA/USSR* by Zbigniew Brzezinski and Samuel P. Huntington, with the Russian Institute of Columbia University; *Foreign Policy and Democratic Politics* by Kenneth N. Waltz, with the Center for International Affairs, Harvard University; *To Move a Nation* by Roger Hilsman, with the Washington Center of Foreign Policy Research, Johns Hopkins University; *Western European Perspectives on International Affairs* by Donald J. Puchala and Richard L. Merritt, with the Yale Political Data Program; and *How Nations Behave* by Louis Henkin, with the Council on Foreign Relations.

Alliances
and Small Powers

ROBERT L. ROTHSTEIN

COLUMBIA UNIVERSITY PRESS

NEW YORK AND LONDON

1968

Mr. Rothstein is Assistant Professor of Political Science at The Johns Hopkins University.

To My Mother and Father

Foreword

S TATE BEHAVIOR, like "war," appears to be a category much too broad to be analytically useful. Just as an understanding of the causes of one kind of war may lead to prescriptions for the avoidance of that kind of war but not some other, so propositions about the behavior of one kind of state may have predictive and prescriptive implications for that kind of state but not for states in general.

Even the category "small states" may be too broad for many analytical exercises. The poverty of power and the tyranny of weakness are well-worked themes, but not ones which make it easy for the analyst to focus clearly on actors in the international system who have modest goals and limited means. Small states in Europe during the last three centuries have generally been actors of this kind. Their survival record from the defeat of the Habsburg bid for European hegemony to the rise of the Third Reich has been a source of wonder. More and more the survival of the small states has become the subject of systematic investigations.

European small states, since the Peace of Westphalia, like small and great states everywhere at all times, will use all available means to get what they want. But European small states have not characteristically wanted the same things as other states in other times, or on other continents.

Robert Rothstein has addressed himself to the study of the foreign policy behavior of some of these European small states since the Congress of Vienna as they have used one distinctive means to promote their goal of national security, namely, alliances. He has assembled relevant historical data and has also examined in detail two important twentieth-century cases. To appraise this and other bodies of data, he has developed a theoretical framework of analysis. Finally, he has raised questions concerning the applicability of his empirical and theoretical approaches to the understanding of the alliances and small powers of the post-World War II period.

Europe's "old" small states may or may not be able to teach the "new" small states of the developing world how to find the road to security, or at least to survival. The new small states may or may not be able to teach the old ones how to extract concessions from competing great states in fields other than security. Both the old and the new have much to teach the student of world politics. Professor Rothstein's contribution will be useful in helping to answer the first of these questions. He undoubtedly would welcome, as I would, further studies by other scholars which will help answer the second.

WILLIAM T. R. FOX

Acknowledgments

IT GIVES me great pleasure to acknowledge my debts in writing this book. I would be remiss if I did not first mention Professor William T. R. Fox, whose patient, detailed, and incisive criticisms of earlier and later drafts of this work have removed many obscurities and improved it in countless ways. That, however, constitutes only part of my debt to Professor Fox and I should also like to acknowledge my gratitude for the financial support he provided through the Institute of War and Peace Studies and, above all, for the intellectual and personal friendship and support he has provided over the years.

Professor Warner Schilling took time from an impossibly crowded schedule to provide me with another set of perceptive and extremely helpful comments. His insistence on clarity, on the removal of unnecessary ambiguity, were very much appreciated, and I can only hope that I have approximated his very high standards. At an earlier date, Dr. Annette Baker Fox not only provided me with many useful comments about my manuscript but also encouraged me to turn it into a book. Professor Leland Goodrich was also extremely helpful, particularly when parts of this book first appeared as part of my doctoral dissertation at Columbia. Finally, my colleagues at Johns Hopkins University, Professors George Liska, Robert E. Osgood, and Robert W. Tucker, provided useful comments on the chapters on nonalignment and nuclear proliferation.

I should like to thank the editors of the *Political Science Quarterly* for permission to reprint a substantial portion of my essay

"Nuclear Proliferation and American Policy," which appeared in March, 1967, Vol. LXXXIII, No. 1. I should also like to thank the editors of *International Organization* for permission to reprint substantial portions of "Alignment, Nonalignment, and Small Powers, 1945–65," which appeared in the Summer, 1966, Vol. XX, No. 3.

With so many fine critics, it is obvious that I alone am responsible for any errors, misconceptions, or stylistic inadequacies which may be discovered.

Robert L. Rothstein

Washington, D.C.
February, 1968

Contents

Alliances and Small Powers

Introduction

THIS BOOK is concerned with establishing one central proposition: that Small Powers are something more than or different from Great Powers writ small. If true, the point is both theoretically and practically significant. For the theorist, evidence that the Small Power is different in kind, and not merely in degree, provides a clear warning against the dangers of generalizing about the behavior of all states. Small Powers think and act differently, and any analysis which fails to take that fact into account is bound to be simplistic and inadequate. The practitioner may also find the analysis helpful, if only indirectly. The reminder, implicit and explicit throughout the ensuing pages, that a particular Small Power's behavior cannot be understood unless the distinctive perspective with which it operates is understood is, perhaps, a useful corrective to the notion that all "rational" or "right-thinking" states will perceive international problems in the same way "we" (i.e., Superpowers, Great Powers, or even differently placed Small Powers) do.

The argument throughout this book revolves around the security problem which confronts most Small Powers. An examination of the entire range of policies open to Small Powers intent on buttressing their own security is clearly impossible. Thus the focus of this study is narrowed by concentrating on the problem of achieving security via an alliance policy. Differences between Great Powers and Small Powers, both in general and within specific historical systems, are illustrated by indicating the different ways in which they think about and utilize alliance policies.

The decision to concentrate on alliance policies may require some justification. For the most part, Small Powers have entered alliances reluctantly. The decision to ally obviously involves significant disadvantages as well as advantages. As a result, the rationale for each decision has required a degree of explicit articulation frequently lacking in discussions of other policy options (e.g., supporting international organizations). The analyst benefits, in the first instance, merely from possessing a focal point for an examination of Small Power behavior. On a more significant level, he also benefits by virtue of the fact that the decision to ally has normally been controversial enough or significant enough to elicit debate and discussion.

The possibility that Great Powers and Small Powers are very different kinds of entities has been obscured by the traditional literature of international relations. That literature tended to grade or rank states in terms of tangible power factors and since Small Powers obviously occupied the lowest ranges of that hierarchy, they were normally conceived as negligible factors in the play of European politics. The rare occasions upon which Small Powers were actively courted by the Great Powers hardly qualify the basic point: they were courted only because the apparent imminence of a general war seemed to increase the value of even minor increments of power.

It was improbable, given the prevailing method of calculating power relations, that Small Powers could be regarded in any other way. The assumption that they might be something more than inferior entities scarcely able to affect the balance of power (unless that balance was so precarious that even minor additions to either side could unsettle it) rarely arose. The contention that Small Powers might be unique entities with unique patterns of behavior would surely have been dismissed if it had occurred to anyone.

If Small Powers were nothing more than less powerful Great Powers, there was surely little point in attempting to study them as a distinct kind of unit: the rules of behavior devised for Great Powers also presumably comprehended the behavior of Small Powers, once certain obvious adjustments for size had been made. Small Powers clearly differed in degree from Great Powers; the compelling and irrefutable nature of that fact tended to obscure the possibility that they might also differ in kind.

The contemporary status and influence of Small Powers apparently signifies a major revolution in their role in world politics. "Apparently" is used advisedly, since their position in the nineteenth century relative to the Great Powers was neither so bad, nor is their position now so good, that we can accurately postulate a complete reversal in stature. Nevertheless, the change, whatever its exact dimension, has been decisive enough to warrant a reexamination of the behavior of Small Powers in different international systems.[1] At the very least, contemporary developments indicate the necessity of analyzing Small Powers on the basis of something other than traditional power factors.

There has never been, of course, a historical period in which a *completely* adequate analysis of Small Powers could have rested on a simple examination of basic power factors. Small Powers have been as powerful as their "capacity to achieve intended effects"; the results they have achieved, not the power they presumably possess on an analytical scale, is the decisive consideration. However, in earlier historical periods, the results achieved and the power possessed seemed to bear some reasonable relationship to each other. It is no longer true. The status and prestige of Small Powers has risen, while their relative strength in the traditional elements of power has actually declined. That hardly means that they are "powerless," for they are obviously able to achieve some very significant intended effects. But the wide disparity between

[1] Two contrasting quotations may illustrate the point. In 1831 the assembled Great Powers could decree to Belgium and the Netherlands that "they [the Great Powers] had the right, and events imposed upon them the duty, to prevent the new Belgian provinces, in their new status of independence, from endangering general security and the European balance. . . . Each nation has its particular rights, but Europe also has her rights." Quoted in Sir Charles Webster, *The Foreign Policy of Palmerston, 1830–1841* (London: G. Bell & Sons, 1951), p. 89. In 1961, Tito hosted a conference of Small Powers—a change in itself —and welcomed his guests with the declaration that "the fate of the world should not be left to a few big states." The Iraqi Foreign Minister, in reply, noted that "the world is no longer governed by the big powers . . . they must accept the influence of the nonaligned nations." *The New York Times*, Oct. 7, 1961, p. 2.

their material power and those effects illuminates the necessity, previously obscured by a relatively close relationship between material power and achievements, of defining and analyzing Small Powers according to wider criteria.

This book is not by any means a history of the evolution of the role of Small Powers since 1815, though inevitably it mentions and discusses factors which would form a part of that history. Nor is it an examination of the behavior of *all* Small Powers. The Small Powers to which any of the ensuing generalizations apply must assume that they are either directly involved, politically and geographically, in relations with Great Powers or very likely to be affected by the outcome of intra-Great-Power struggles.[2] They must feel that they are potentially or actually threatened by the policies of the Great Powers. Small Powers which feel that they are free to choose their own policies independent of Great Power actions are, by definition, excluded from the analysis which follows.[3]

It is worth emphasizing again that the essential quality which distinguishes the Small Powers which are being dealt with in this book from other Small Powers is the fact that they feel threatened, in some significant and immediate sense, by the play of Great Power politics. Obviously a good many Small Powers fail to meet the qualification: they either act as if or actually are (because of the circumstances of the time) unaffected by the actions of the larger states. Another group of Small Powers fits the category of "threatened" only fitfully and occasionally, as their perception of the significance of Great Power struggles for themselves undergoes change.

[2] For some discussion of the general point concerning involvement in Great Power conflicts, see George Liska, *International Equilibrium* (Cambridge: Harvard University Press, 1957), p. 33.

[3] None of the Small Powers which fall within the range of the ensuing theoretical propositions could state, as the Swedish Social Democrats did in 1923, that "We calculate that international relations would be bound to deteriorate for a period before the threat of war could become imminent [for Sweden] and that period would be sufficient to allow of adequate preparation." Quoted in Herbert Tingsten, *The Debate on the Foreign Policy of Sweden, 1918–1939* (London: Oxford University Press, 1949), p. 159. It hardly needs emphasis that the quotation is not an adequate description of Sweden's point of view at other periods; nor was it a universally held view at the time. But it does illustrate the point in the text.

For the most part, the necessary qualifications about exactly which group of Small Powers fit within any set of generalizations will be made in the course of the discussion. Nevertheless, two points are worth mentioning at this stage. The first concerns the fact that from 1815 to 1939 the Small Powers under examination, except for a few exceptions which will be noted, are European. The second point refers to a major limitation of this study; the states of Latin America are excluded from the analysis throughout the *entire* period covered. It is possible that many of the generalizations are applicable to some or all of the Latin American states. However, proof would require a much more detailed study of Latin American history than has been attempted, in particular to indicate whether the unique nature of the Western hemisphere system, a nature composed of one Great Power and a multitude of Small Powers, has led to a unique kind of Small Power behavior. It is necessary to keep these qualifications in mind in reading the text, for many misunderstandings about the range of various propositions may thus be avoided.

An assumption by a Small Power that the external situation is threatening has certain implications which ought to be noted. It suggests that there is very little time in which to rectify previous deficiencies during the interval between the perception of a potential threat and its materialization. It may also involve the necessity of maintaining a large standing army, of determining policy under great pressure, and even, in certain extreme circumstances, of threatening to strike or actually striking quickly to avoid granting the enemy the intiative—all of which may engender the disasters they are designed to avoid. It means, in sum, that the margin of error is small or nonexistent: to choose incorrectly may end the possibility of free choice. A lapse in vigilance can be fatal. Procrastination or "muddling through" appear to be ruled out. Security requires one to act as *if* all changes may be threatening, even if an artful and deliberate policy of procrastination seems the wisest course. The threatened Great Power and the threatened Small Power are superficially similar actors, but in reality, as will be argued in the first chapter, their actions rest on a substantively different foundation.

Most of the Small Powers which will be discussed in this book are essentially "satisfied" states, more concerned with enjoying what they have than with getting something new (or regaining something old). More significantly, perhaps, even when they seek to alter the status quo (as several Balkan states did in the 1860s and in the wars of 1912–13), their goals tend to be limited; they seek only to adjust the old order, not to undermine it or to alter it drastically. This point has to be modified in reference to many contemporary Small Powers. The number of revisionist or "unsatisfied" Small Powers has risen, and their concern for the stability of the international system has declined, though this is clearly not a blanket indictment of all the nonaligned states. Historically, with the possible exception of the Latin American states, the range of policy alternatives available to "satisfied" Small Powers has been wider than that available to revisionists. A Small Power intent on changing the existing distribution of benefits could do so only by becoming a satellite of a revisionist Great Power. The degree to which revisionism has become a relatively more attractive or successful policy in the Cold War will be discussed in Chapter 8.

This book is also not concerned with Small Power behavior before 1815. The period chosen coincides with the emergence of a state system which is essentially modern in terms of its organization and operation. In contrast, earlier systems tended to be less structured and more informal. Moreover, the idea and perception of a "systemic" interest, of an interest which might in some circumstances be more significant than a narrowly conceived national interest, did not begin to exert even a moderate amount of influence on the behavior of the members of the international system until after 1815. This is a point of some significance for an analysis such as this one which uses the idea of the international system as a framework for much of its research. The behavior of Small Powers during the course of major Great Power wars has also not been analyzed. The extent to which any generalizations would remain valid during wartime would require further research.

Some states describe themselves as "middle-range Powers". As such, they are not dealt with in these pages. In a theoretical sense, it would complicate an already complicated situation, perhaps beyond recall. It is worth noting that the category itself is of relatively recent derivation.[4] It did not exist before 1919, and the record since then has been ambiguous. Where such states—usually self-styled—do seem to exist, it is normally the result not of their own achievements but of the weakness, disappearance, or disinterestedness of neighboring Great Powers (e.g., note Poland's situation after 1919); or because the Great Powers cannot use their power superiority effectively and seek the political support of the most prominent uncommitted states (e.g., India in the Cold War period). A "middle-range" status implies a degree of external recognition: for example, continual reelection to the executive organs of international organizations or excessive deference on a wide range of regional and extra-regional matters. However, tangible proof of significant differences between Small Powers and middle-range Powers would have to rest on evidence that, when threatened, middle-range Powers do in fact possess a wider range of choice than Small Powers. That evidence does not yet exist. Until it does, the assumption that the distinction is formal and peripheral, not substantive and central, will prevail.

The organization of this book may require a word of explanation. The three parts into which it is divided are connected to the extent that they all reflect a common concern with the differences between Great Powers and Small Powers. Nevertheless, each part is also self-contained and represents a somewhat different way of examining Great Power-Small Power relationships.

Part I is the most abstract and analytical of the sections: it attempts to derive propositions about Small Powers which are valid for any historical period. The generalizations which result are essentially extrapolations from the historical record of the last one hundred and fifty years. Two case studies of alliances have also been included to illustrate in a specific way the significance and range, and to some extent the origin, of many of the abstractions in the text.

[4] Thus John W. Holmes, "Canada and the United States in World Politics," *Foreign Affairs*, XL (October 1961) 110–11, notes that the idea of middle range states is "ill-defined because the middle powers are by their diplomacy in the process of putting meaning into the term."

Part II discusses Great Power-Small Power relationships in specific historical systems of international relations. The generalizations in this section are much more concrete and specific than those in the preceding one, and they attempt to indicate the extent to which Great Power-Small Power relationships alter in response to changes in the international system. Part III discusses various aspects of Great Power-Small Power relationships in the contemporary world. It is, inevitably, the least theoretical and the most policy-oriented section of this book.

This book does not contain a single concluding chapter which either summarizes the preceding material or attempts to offer Small Powers advice on the basis of it. The fact that each of the three parts reflects a somewhat different approach to Small Powers is perhaps justification enough for not attempting a general conclusion. More fundamentally, the decision to let each part speak for itself rests on the assumption that the material covered is so complex and variegated that any attempt to draw it together is bound to be premature and simplistic.[5] In any event, many of the propositions which emerge in the course of the analysis relate to specific situations and would lose much of their force if detached from those situations.

This analysis covers a very long and complex historical period. It also attempts to generalize about a group of states which have rarely attracted the attention of theorists. When they have been analyzed, the normal result has been a series of truisms or platitudes which offer little guidance.[6] The best that this book can hope to be, in the circumstances, is a stationary target for future investigations. It will be a better target if one point which has already been made is kept clearly in mind: the ensuing generalizations refer *only* to Small Powers which are within an area of Great Power confrontation or which fear that that confrontation will affect their interests significantly.

[5] For a brief discussion of this point, with some illustrations of the difficulties involved in attempting an inclusive conclusion, see the introduction to Chapter 9.

[6] There are a few exceptions. The most notable works on Small Powers would include the following: Liska, *International Equilibrium*; Arnold Wolfers, "In Defense of Small Countries," *The Yale Review*, XXXIII (Winter 1943); Arnold Wolfers, "The Small Powers and the Enforcement of Peace" (privately) circulated, 1943); and Annette Baker Fox, *The Power of Small States* (Chicago: The University of Chicago Press, 1959).

PART I

Alliances and Small Powers:
A Theoretical Statement
and Two Case Studies

CHAPTER 1

Great Powers and Small Powers:
An Introduction

THE FORMAL distinction between Great Powers and Small Powers first emerged during the last year of the Napoleonic Wars. Previously, as Harold Nicolson noted, "the assumption had been that all sovereign and independent states were in theory equal, whatever might be their responsibilities or physical strength." [1] The presumed equality of all states did not, of course, prevent the Great Powers from treating weaker states instrumentally.[2] Small Powers threatened by neighboring Great Powers, or intent on securing benefits for themselves in the course of Great Power conflicts, were forced to play a perilous game: moving quickly from the lighter to the heavier side of the balance as soon as an apparent victor in any contest could be discerned.[3] If power corrupts, so does the lack of it. The unfavorable image of Small Powers which

[1] Harold Nicolson, *The Congress of Vienna: A Study in Allied Unity, 1812–1822* (New York: The Viking Press, 1961), p. 137.

[2] Thus, Walter Dorn, *Competition for Empire, 1740–1763* (New York: Harper & Brothers, 1940), p. 3, notes that ". . . international affairs had been controlled by a small group of great powers which applied the doctrine of the balance of power only to themselves, not to their relations with smaller and weaker states."

[3] Sir Charles Petrie's description of the policy of the House of Savoy is illustrative: "In short, the traditional policy of the House of Savoy, as indeed of all the Italian states, was to throw its weight first into this scale and then into that, with self-preservation as the immediate, and territorial acquisitions as the ultimate, goal. Too weak to stand alone, the House of Savoy could only achieve its purpose by being always on the winning side in the international controversies of the time." Cf. *Diplomatic History, 1713–1933* (London: Hollis and Carter, 1947), p. 167.

prevailed among the Great Powers undoubtedly emerged as a response to these practices. Small Powers were conceived as scavengers, forever seeking the crumbs left over from a Great Power settlement.[4] *All* Small Powers, of course, did not behave so badly (badly from the point of view of the Great Powers). Nevertheless, those which came to the attention of the Great Powers inevitably did, for they were noticed only when they became an object of desire for a Great Power, or when they intruded too noticeably in the diplomatic game.

The Problem of Definition

While the distinction between Great Powers and Small Powers was implicit in the political practice of earlier centuries, it was not raised into a formal principle until the exigencies of the struggle against Napoleon made it convenient, even necessary to do so. Small Powers were simply not powerful enough to fulfill the obligations the Great Powers had accepted in the Treaty of Chaumont—and the responsibility to act still rested on the power to do so effectively.[5] In itself, this fact might not have led to a formal and institutionalized distinction between Great Powers and Small Powers. However, it coincided with the clear realization by a num-

---

[4] Castlereagh reflected the traditional Great Power conception of Small Powers when he contemptuously noted in 1815 that: "There is not a Power, however feeble . . . that is not pushing some acquisition under the plea of security. . . . They seem to have no dread of a kick from the lion when his toils are removed, and are foolish enough to suppose that the Great Powers of Europe are to be in readiness to protect them in the enjoyment of these petty spoils." W. A. Phillips, *The Confederation of Europe* (London: Longmans, Green and Co., 1920), p. 138.

[5] One historian explained the situation this way: "How did it come about that the 'Great Powers'—the term had just begun to be current in diplomatic phraseology—arrogated to themselves the right to speak for the whole of Europe? The excuse seems to have been the dimensions reached by the Napoleonic Wars. For the main obligations of the Treaty of Chaumont, concluded in March 1814, were such as only Great Powers with large resources could undertake." H. G. Schenk, *The Aftermath of the Napoleonic Wars* (London: Kegan Paul, Trench, Trubner and Co., 1947), p. 127. The primary obligation was the promise to provide 60,000 men each for the next twenty years in the event of another French aggression.

ber of Great Power statesmen that the Congress of Vienna could not function effectively unless the actual differences between Great Powers and Small Powers were institutionalized so that the Great Powers could arrogate to themselves the right to act for all of Europe.[6]

The result was that the ascendancy of the Great Powers was henceforth both formal and substantive. While there were serious disagreements between the so-called "Eastern" and "Western" Great Powers about the treatment of Small Powers, they never reached the extent of invalidating the general assumption that the international politics of Europe was too important to be dealt with by all its inhabitants. In theory, and with a number of exceptions in practice, the formal operating principle was clear: the Great Powers, in concert, were to decide; the Small Powers were to obey. This distinction seemed all the more natural and inevitable, at the time, because it rested on what appeared to be an eminently clear foundation: the ability to fight a successful war against a recognized Great Power.

The Industrial Revolution began to affect military technology in the second half of the nineteenth century. Now, it seems clear that the criteria by which war capabilities were estimated should have been adjusted. Nevertheless, there was a considerable lag between the development of that military technology and its appreciation by decision-makers. Thus the test of a Great Power, and inversely of a Small Power, remained much the same throughout the century, the technological revolution notwithstanding. That test, as A. J. P. Taylor noted, was "the test of strength for war . . . this test was a simple one. Despite the development of artillery, infantry determined the outcome of battle. . . ."[7]

In any case, for the statesmen of the nineteenth century, and for most historians since, there was no problem in distinguishing

---

[6] As Sir Charles Webster noted, "to have brought all the Small Powers into the Alliance, as Capo d'Istria and the Tsar at one time thought of doing, would clearly have been to make the machine unworkable." *The Foreign Policy of Castlereagh* (London: G. Bell and Sons, 1958), II, 500.

[7] A. J. P. Taylor, *The Struggle for Mastery in Europe, 1848–1918* (Oxford: The Clarendon Press, 1954), p. XXIV.

between Great Powers and Small Powers—counting the number of available infantrymen sufficed. The fact that it still made a great deal of sense to discuss power in "zero-sum" (or relative) terms facilitated the categorization of states in terms of their military strength. Nothing as revolutionary as nuclear weapons intruded to make traditional calculations of power *partly* non-sensical. The other characteristics which supposedly distinguished the two groups of states were primarily reflections of the original military distinctions. Small Powers did have a narrower range of interests and less freedom of activity, but only because they were militarily weak. In sum, the distinction between Great Powers and Small Powers seemed so obvious that it was seldom discussed or questioned. As Harold Nicolson noted, in the nineteenth century "it was assumed that the Great Powers were greater than the Small Powers, since they possessed a more extended range of interests, wider responsibilities, and, above all, more money and more guns." [8] However, the conditions which created and fostered this situation have been continuously undermined by a series of historical developments, many of which seemed to emerge (or come to maturity) just before or just after the First World War. As a result, it is no longer accurate to distinguish Great Powers and Small Powers primarily on the basis of military power.

A brief enumeration of several of the more critical factors which enabled a number of Small Powers to assume an increasingly important role in world politics may illustrate the point. The breakdown of the Concert system, particularly after 1890, was especially significant. As the Great Powers assembled in two opposing alliance systems, the Small Powers were presented with a unique opportunity. If war was imminent, and many assumed it was, minor accretions of strength and the added security of more territory might provide the margin of victory. The prevailing power configuration made the support of various Small Powers *seem* necessary. As one observer noted, "The wavering allegiance of Roumania, a matter of slight importance in normal times, assumed great significance because the balance of power in Europe as a

[8] Harold Nicolson, *The Evolution of Diplomatic Method* (London: Constable and Co., Ltd., 1954), p. 73.

whole was so even that a small Balkan state might well bring down the scales on one side or the other." [9] Because the relative strength of the two alliance systems appeared equivalent, each side felt the need of securing for itself, or denying to its enemy, any amount of real power that was still nonaligned. This tendency was accelerated by the habit of making power calculations in traditional terms. As A. J. P. Taylor noted, the statesmen of the Great Powers "still thought in terms of a casual accumulation of man-power and failed to recognize that war had become a struggle solely between Great Powers. Every alliance with a small state meant an additional liability, not a gain. . . ." [10]

In addition, the fact that the Great Powers were marshaling their strength for a major conflict disinclined them to intervene forcibly when the Small Powers struck out on their own.[11] Since an aggressive Small Power might have a Great Power patron, the other Great Powers were reluctant to impose their will for fear it might set off a larger conflict.

As the solidarity of the Great Powers crumbled, the status of Small Powers rose, and rose far beyond any relationship to their *apparent* power. No other war, nor any previous political configuration, between 1815 and 1914 had offered them this opportunity—and many, though clearly not all, were quick to take advantage of the situation in the most unscrupulous ways (particularly, as in the Balkans, to settle scores with other weak powers in areas where the Great Powers seemed reluctant to intervene). The Small Powers were the unintended beneficiaries of a major structural alteration of the international system. The behavior and the tactics forced upon the Great Powers by the new configuration —the attempts to bribe the Small Powers into alliances, the failure to punish their transgressions, and so forth—further undermined the legitimacy of the Concert system. Once freed of the constraints of that system, the Small Powers were to prove increasingly re-

[9] Nicholas Mansergh, *The Coming of the First World War* (London: Longmans, Green and Co., 1949), p. 211.

[10] Taylor, *The Struggle for Mastery in Europe*, p. 551.

[11] For example, note the successes of the Balkan League in 1912 and 1913— after similar ventures had failed in the 1860s. See Ch. 6 below.

luctant to accept any vestiges of the inferior status it had conferred upon them.

The intellectual environment of the years after 1848 also slowly eroded the legitimacy of the hierarchical principle implicit in the Concert system. National self-determination,[12] liberalism, democracy, internationalism, and equality all served in various ways to dilute the acceptability of a distinction based solely on power calculations. Of course, the influence of these ideas was more formal than substantive. It primarily affected the ways in which statesmen were required to justify their policies. *Realpolitik* had to appear akin to disinterested idealism:

Where expediency had formerly determined the extent to which the lesser states were to be brought into consultation with the larger states, so as to facilitate the policies of the latter, the democratic ideal seemed to demand that all, great and small alike, participate as a matter of right. Equality, instead of being a convenient legal fiction, became in many quarters an article of faith. Thereafter the statesman had not only to devise policies according to self-interest and expediency; he had also to implement those policies in such a way as to acknowledge the values of democracy. So long as relations between states followed the traditional channels of diplomacy this problem did not become acute. Only when diplomacy entered a new phase—specifically that of international organization—did the elements of power, expediency and democracy have to be formally reconciled.[13]

While it is probably true that the impact of these essentially egalitarian ideas on the position of Small Powers was peripheral, it is equally true that they justified the increasingly influential status Small Powers enjoyed and sought. These ideas became the intellectual substructure of a new kind of international system. It might also be argued that the revolution in social and political thought that occurred after 1890 facilitated the rise of Small Powers. Perhaps the shift from positivism to an emphasis on unconscious elements of thought had its political counterpart in the shift from an

---

[12] In particular, national self-determination served to justify and rationalize the destruction of the old empires during and after the First World War. See Alfred Cobban, *National Self-Determination* (Oxford University Press, 1945).

[13] William W. Kaufmann, "The Organization of Responsibility," *World Politics*, 1 (July 1949), 512.

emphasis on "real" power factors alone to an emphasis on broader, less material, criteria by which to judge influence and importance (i.e., from the quantitative standard of the old diplomacy to the at least partly qualitative standard of the "new diplomacy," the League of Nations, and the theory of collective security).[14]

The reaction against the old system also increased as casualty figures mounted during the First World War. Clearly the world needed safeguards against a return to its most pernicious practices. The Small Powers could not fail to benefit from these changes since they could hardly be in a worse position, in terms of power and influence, than they had been before 1890. Moreover, the destruction of Austria-Hungary and the temporary elimination of the Soviet Union and Germany as effective Great Powers as a result of the First World War enhanced the position of many Small Powers. Not only did the destruction of the Hapsburg Empire serve as a catalyst for the proliferation of new states —which, by mere number, might have drowned out the voices of the remaining Great Powers—but also the unique power vacuum in Europe gave added opportunities to a variety of Small Powers to make their voices heard and their desires known.

The emergence of the League of Nations also tended to obscure the simple distinctions which had previously served to separate the Great from the Small Powers. In theory, it sought to provide for their security and to justify their presence and their influence. The Small Powers in the Assembly were formally equal to the Great Powers, and they ultimately exercised significant and occasionally predominant influence, even in the Council. In addition, the League offered some of their statesmen a unique opportunity to be heard, and an even more unique opportunity to display and experience some amount of international responsibility. The League also fostered the growth of an internationalist ethic which, by making wars and aggressions seem more barbaric, may have indirectly facilitated the survival of those states which were most defenseless.

[14] For the intellectual revolution see H. Stuart Hughes, *Consciousness and Society: The Reorientation of European Social Thought, 1890–1930* (New York: Alfred A. Knopf, 1958).

The attempt to stabilize the international environment by devising a system of what came to be called collective security had important implications for the role of Small Powers in world politics. Collective security, in theory, involved an international commitment for *all* states. Both Great and Small Powers alike engaged to concern themselves with an extended range of interests and responsibilities. Collective security involved the renunciation of force, except in narrowly circumscribed cases. To a certain extent, this decreased the utility of merely possessing more infantry and more guns. Furthermore, it was assumed that the balance of power, an inadequate protector of Small Powers,[15] would no longer serve as the ordering principle of international politics. Small Powers were no longer to be evaluated in terms of their instrumental relation to an always precarious balance. On the contrary, the force of great and small alike was to be indistinguishable in the massive force that would be unleashed against an aggressor. The theory of collective security consequently had the potential of altering the traditional behavior of the Great Powers in a direction which would insure the security of even the weakest state. Conversely, perception of this potential benefit offered a Small Power the opportunity, for the first time, of altering its own pattern of behavior to conform to the dictates of a new kind of international system—if collective security could work, the indignities of the scavenger and the supplicant could be replaced by the dignity of true and secure independence.

The military technology of the twentieth century has also tended to obscure the clarity of the old distinction between the great and the small. The emphasis shifted from mass unmechanized armies to mass mechanized armies, although the speed with which this change was appreciated varied considerably. It was possible for certain small but heavily industrialized countries like Belgium and Czechoslovakia to possess, or appear to possess, a significant amount of real power (which only partly and certainly inadequately compensated for their increasing indefensibility

---

[15] "It was apparent that the balance of power system, though intended as an instrument of peace, might easily be invoked to justify the absorption of smaller states. . . ." Dorn, *Competition for Empire*, p. 3.

in relation to the impact of the new technology on the factor of geographical extent); and for certain "Great" Powers, like Italy, to be great only in a formal (but still important) sense. It became, that is, more difficult to employ purely military factors of power in analyzing real strength, since merely knowing the number of infantry a state could put in the field was insufficient. It was now also necessary to weigh considerations of industrial potential, geographical position, and internal viability—all of which should have been considered, perhaps, in earlier periods, but were either ignored or underrated. The development of nuclear weapons *may* reverse this process. Though the initial effect of nuclear weapons was merely to confirm and enhance the already superior power of the Superpowers, their ultimate effect may well be to diffuse significant military power to an ever-widening group of states.

The newer Small Powers have achieved, in some instances, a kind of negative security based on their own weaknesses. Since they lack an industrial base and possess only a rudimentary governmental framework, they also lack the opportunity to develop their own power structure to even the level of nuisance value (short of an outside power *giving* them nuclear weapons and other advanced weapons). Nevertheless, the most modern weapons are seldom used against them since they do not seem to represent an appropriate target (in a psychological, political, or military sense) for enormously powerful and sophisticated military hardware. Their Great Power antagonists, once forced to intervene, are required to use weapons only slightly more advanced than those of earlier generations. The new states, in effect, may achieve some security merely by virtue of the fact that the cost of defeating them seems too high—surely a traditional calculation, but one resting in this instance on the unique fact that the Great Power is restrained by its own nonmilitary weaknesses, or by the strength of its Great Power enemy, and not by the military strength of the Small Power.

At any rate, it might be argued that the tangible elements of strength, in particular military power, have become a good deal less useful in the twentieth century than ever before. They must, of course, still be maintained by all states, as a hedge against all sorts of contingencies. But merely possessing a larger army, more advanced weapons, or a modern economy does not guarantee the ability to achieve desired ends—the relationship between tangible power and the achievement of national goals has become more and more indirect and obscure. The less tangible elements of strength have become progressively more important, ranging from a good historical "record" to belief in the correct vision of the good life or merely to an unusual ability to foresee the opportunities in passing events. The factors which have created this state of affairs are well known: the revulsion against war, the slow growth of norms which restrict the legitimacy of using force, the unique fears and patterns of behavior engendered by nuclear weapons, and, perhaps, a growing inwardness and concentration on domestic concerns by the advanced industrial states. Taken together, they have made it progressively easier for many Small Powers to survive and prosper.[16]

The point of the preceding analysis seems clear. By 1919, and increasingly since then, the traditional relationship between Great Powers and Small Powers had been altered beyond recognition. Arnold Toynbee even argued that "as a result of the war, the balance of moral influence, and even the balance of material power, as between Great Powers and states of lesser calibre, had shifted, on the whole, perceptibly in favor of the lesser states." [17]

Toynbee is wrong in suggesting that the "balance of material power" was shifting in favor of the lesser states. If anything, their military strength relative to the Great Powers was declining sharply. Nevertheless, Small Powers were in a better security position than ever before because other factors outweighed their military weakness. The continuing growth of an internationalist ethic was of some significance. The exhaustion of the Great Powers after the war was also important. So, too, was the increasing number of Small

---

[16] Some of these concerns will be discussed again in the final chapters of this book. But see Klaus Knorr, *On the Uses of Military Power in the Nuclear Age* (Princeton: Princeton University Press, 1966); Stanley Hoffmann, *The State of War: Essays on the Theory and Practice of International Politics* (New York: Frederick A. Praeger, 1965), pp. 236–37; Robert L. Rothstein, "Power, Security and the International System" (paper delivered at the American Political Science Association Convention, Chicago, September 1967).

[17] Arnold Toynbee, *Survey of International Affairs, 1926* (London: Oxford University Press, 1927), p. 21.

Powers and the decreasing number of Great Powers. Finally, as the last point suggests, the peculiar nature of the power configurations which prevailed just before and just after the First World War should not be forgotten: for different reasons, each granted many Small Powers a new status which was difficult to rescind.

The preceding factors simultaneously illustrate some of the reasons why Small Powers have become increasingly influential and why a definition of Small Powers based on tangible "elements of power" is unsatisfactory. The traditional definition is simply unable to explain the influence Small Powers have come to exert in world politics. In reality, it has never amounted to much more than a device to explain a *lack* of influence. It should be emphasized that the point is not that the traditional definition is wrong but rather that it is insufficient. Small Powers can not fight a successful war against a Great Power; but neither can several states to which Great Power status is granted. Italy could not defeat France; France could not defeat Germany; and Germany could not defeat the United States. Yet very few would deny that any of the above (except, perhaps, Italy) are Great Powers. Moreover, the introduction of nuclear weapons into world politics adds a further complication. A Small Power with a minimal, but protected, nuclear force *may* be able to at least deter hostile aggressions against its territory. And, if the possession of nuclear weapons becomes the standard by which Great Power status is judged, the situation becomes further confused. Would Egypt with a nuclear force be a Great Power, and Germany without one something less than a Great Power?

As a result of these difficulties, "Small Powers" are not defined but rather the weaker state in any given situation. If Small Powers are something different from, rather than merely weaker than, Great Powers, this definition does not indicate it. It contains no explanation for the increased influence Small Powers exert in world politics, and in a situation where their relatively declining strength *ought* to yield less influence. This attempt at definition merely confirms the commonplace proposition that the power of a state is relative to the power of its enemies.

Escape from this dilemma might be sought by foregoing any attempt to define Small Powers as such (i.e., as unique entities) and by accepting a definition based essentially on institutional representation. Thus George Liska has argued that:

. . . a definition of what constitutes a great and a small state might rest on primary power differentials or, derivatively, on the scope of interests and forms of institutional representation. To be a Great Power, a state must then be admitted to a concert of Powers or occupy a permanent seat in the League of Nations or United Nations council, have more than limited interests, and be able to assert them by means that include the threat or act of war.[18]

However, while this definition indicates the results and effects of being a Small Power, it does not define them as a separate category. It merely raises the problems created by defining Small Powers in terms of relative power to a new level. Rather than defining Small Powers, some of the effects of being relatively weaker than the Great Powers are indicated. Nor does this definition remove any of the confusions previously noted. It would, for example, consign the Soviet Union and the United States after 1919, and Communist China now, to the role of secondary states: obviously an unacceptable conclusion. In addition, the criteria in Liska's definition may be so intermingled that the result is confusion and not clarity. For example, Nationalist China is a permanent member of the Security Council, but its interests are limited, and so is its ability to assert them by forcible means. Any criteria involving the ability to threaten or use force, at least in our time, is bound to be ambiguous. The threat of retaliation against the Great Powers, should they use force, is such that it may even be true that *some* Small Powers are *relatively* freer in their ability to pursue their goals by forceful means. In addition, in the interdependent political system existing now, the criteria of general interests is unsatisfactory. Small Powers, even without nuclear weapons, can have an impact on international relations which extends beyond their regional subsystems.

The problem, again, seems to be that any definition which relies

[18] George Liska, *Nations in Alliance: The Limits of Interdependence* (Baltimore: The Johns Hopkins Press, 1962), p. 24.

solely on objective or tangible criteria ends by aligning states along an extended power spectrum so that it can only be said that B is stronger than A but weaker than C. The result is that the significance of the categories "Great" and "Small" is effectually denied —though the categories are still used as a kind of shorthand denomination—in favor of "more powerful or influential than x" or "less powerful or influential than x." In itself that hardly represents a major calamity, for in the majority of practical circumstances it seems to make very little difference whether the analyst is discussing "Great Powers vs. Small Powers" or "the more powerful vs. the less powerful."

Nevertheless, the fact that it does not seem to make very much difference which description is chosen does not mean that it does not make *some* difference. If there is a unique category of states called Small Powers, which possess distinct patterns of behavior, then it is clearly inadequate to describe them merely in terms of being less powerful. The problem of comprehending the behavior of Small Powers involves more than noting their weaknesses. It also involves understanding that the inferior power status of Small Powers, which they tend to imagine as a permanent feature of their existence,[19] may have created consistent patterns of behavior as a response to that situation. Those patterns of behavior cannot be understood unless the statement that Small Powers are only relatively weaker Great Powers is used as a starting point rather than an end of analysis. They are that, but also more. In addition, if this argument is correct, it has significant theoretical implications: It becomes impossible to talk about the behavior of states without clearly indicating what kind of states are being discussed.

The essence of this discussion rests on the assumption that the categories "Great" Power and "Small" Power have a significance beyond relative power ratios: that both groups of states develop behavioral patterns which decisively separate them from non-group

[19] Note that I am not arguing that Small Powers (or Great Powers) cannot change their status: obviously the examples of Holland, Portugal, Sweden, Prussia, etc., prove the contrary. I am arguing that any state which accepts the status of Small Power *also* implicitly accepts the fact that it cannot change that status by virtue of its own actions: that it is, for all *immediate* purposes, "permanently" inferior.

members, and that therefore it does make sense to talk of the behavior of Small Powers in general or of Great Powers in general. The question, then, is what characterizes Small Powers as unique entities, as something other than merely weaker states?

The answer, one presumes, must rest on an analysis of patterns of behavior which remain the same for Small Powers, despite basic shifts in the international system. Factors are sought in the environment which have not only conditioned Small Power behavior but have also persisted whatever the system. The difficulty of this task should be obvious: corresponding factors are sought between states as varied as nineteenth century Belgium, Czechoslovakia of the interwar years, and contemporary Indonesia. The problem is that there is not only a difference between Great Powers and Small Powers but also a difference between various kinds of Small Powers. Nevertheless, it is possible to argue, or at least suggest, that there are certain factors which have led to similar patterns of behavior among nearly *all* Small Powers, despite their differences.[20]

One factor which has obviously remained constant for Small Powers is that the solution to any "security-dilemma" must come from an outside source. No matter what international system is posited, that outside support, by its very nature, must be ambiguous. The security of a Small Power is an absolute requirement only for itself: the partitions of Poland and the sacrifice of the Czechs in 1938 illustrate this point.

Small Powers must, therefore, rely on essentially ambiguous external aid for the accomplishment of the basic goal of all states: survival. If they have learned anything from history, it is that external support usually arrives late, and that it is given only in expectation of future benefits. Moreover, a Small Power is rarely in a situation where it can increase its *own* power sufficiently to affect

[20] The problem of the existence of different kinds of Small Powers will be discussed in Chapter 8. For the most part, it is a contemporary problem: it is only in recent years that we have found it necessary to deal with Small Powers indifferent to, or ignorant of, the European tradition of politics. See, in particular, pages 243–44, which discuss not only the differences between Small Powers but also certain overriding considerations which suggest that, at a general level, Small Powers can still be talked about as a single category.

the outcome. That rare instance usually occurs when its existence is of minor significance in the dominant Great Power struggle (and thus the increase in its own power has only transitory effectiveness, until the larger conflict is decided). The result, in any case, is that the Small Power has only peripheral control over its own fate. It has fewer realistic policy options than a Great Power and its spectrum of choice is more limited. It can do less, by itself, to counter a threat which may be more extensive than a similar threat to a Great Power. If a Small Power is threatened by a Great Power, that threat is a total threat to its independent existence (whereas a Great Power threat to another Great Power *may* concern only marginal values).

This combination of factors must be joined to another: the narrow margin of safety which a Small Power possesses. With a small territory (normally), with few resources, and with uncertain friends, it has very little time in which to correct mistakes. Fearing to take risks, caution is enjoined.[21] Yet the small margin of error available means that decisions cannot be safely delayed. As the Greek dictator Metaxas once noted, muddling through is a prerogative granted only to Great Powers. Consequently the Small Power is forced into an intense concentration on short-run and local matters to the exclusion of, or at least to the detriment of, any concern for long-run stability. The present is simply too dangerous to justify excessive concern for hypothetical future effects. In addition, few Small Powers enjoy the luxury of possessing enough strength to handle all the problems on their political horizons; at best, they may be able to confront and survive the most serious problems, provided that they perceive them accurately.[22] In some cases, foreign policy not only concentrates exclusively on short-run factors but also tends to consume the entire political process of a Small

[21] Thus van Karnebeek, Dutch Foreign Minister in 1922, after noting that a Great Power can correct its mistakes more easily, declared that "just because the conduct of the foreign policy of Small States is so much more delicate than for those who have at their disposal great instruments of power, a certain reserve and caution is required." Quoted in Amry Vandenbosch, *Dutch Foreign Policy Since 1815* (The Hague: Martinus Nijhoff, 1959), p. 28.

[22] See Hoffmann, *The State of War*, p. 138.

Power. The threat confronting it may seem so total and so imminent that discussion of anything else appears irrelevant.[23]

The distinction between a weak and fearful Great Power and a
weak and fearful Small Power is subtle, but nevertheless significant.
Both are inhibited from achieving a rational relationship between
ends and means in the sense that long-range perspectives tend to
be obscured and forgotten in the course of palliating an immediate
danger. The most frequent result is an attempt to ward off catastrophe by immediately allying with or appeasing the more powerful enemy, thus further aggravating the disruption of the balance
of power, followed by a quick reversal of policy as soon as the
balance of power begins to shift. They seek the boon Odysseus
sought so successfully from Cyclops: to be eaten last.

However, once one proceeds beyond the initial similarity in response, the reaction of Great and Small Powers to weakness tends
to diverge. The condition of the two kinds of states differs in that,
for Small Powers, the situation of weakness appears basically un-
alterable (barring some unforeseen consequences of nuclear weapons). Belgium and France both feared Germany but their policies
designed to meet that threat clearly diverged. One reason—a reason
which inheres in the nature of weakness itself—is that Small Powers tend to rely on the hope that they can be protected by their own
insignificance. If they can appear detached enough, and disinterested enough, and if they can convincingly indicate that they are
too powerless to affect the issue, they hope the storm will pass them
by (illustrations abound: note the flight into "neutrality" of various
European Small Powers in the 1930s). This may explain, at least
in part, the vaunted irresponsibility of Small Powers. Their refusal

[23] Karl Deutsch has argued that Small Powers have more time to devote to
foreign affairs, as Great Powers become increasingly preoccupied with internal
matters. However, my contention here is somewhat different: that the Small
Powers are more occupied with foreign than domestic affairs because the issues
of foreign policy are so significant. Small Powers cannot allow domestic affairs
to dominate because the *primat der Aussenpolitik* is so clear. The argument has
to be adjusted for contemporary "neutralist" states: for these states an argument
can be made for the reverse proposition (i.e., foreign policy is simply an extension
of domestic policy). See below, Chapter 8. See also Karl Deutsch, "Large and
Small States in the Integration of Large Political Communities" (paper delivered
to the International Political Science Association meeting in Stockholm, 1955).

to take sufficient account of international stability at the expense of immediate security considerations reflects the insoluble dilemmas confronting permanently weak entities. To a Great Power, the hope of evading a threat by appearing insignificant and disinterested is impossible and delusory.

If the existence of an imminent Great Power threat is presumed, a whole range of policy options which are rational for a Small Power are clearly irrational for a Great Power in the same position (e.g., neutrality, isolation, nonalignment, and appeasement). Moreover, the frightened Small Power tends to place exaggerated reliance on demands for formal recognition of its status. Weak and threatened Great Powers seldom turn in this direction. They usually possess a long history of equal status with other Great Powers. Furthermore, no matter how weak a Great Power is, it is still, by definition, stronger than the most powerful Small Powers. Until the era of Superpowers, the threatened Great Power also always entertained hopes of altering its inferiority, or at least narrowing the deficiency so that it could become a less attractive target.[24]

The Small Power has no such hopes. Clamoring for formal recognition of equality serves to bolster hopes which have been endangered by substantive weakness. But it may have dangerous consequences, beyond the irritation it inspires. It may, for example, inhibit or prevent the Great Powers from reaching a compromise solution which might inflict minor injury on the status of Small Powers: the controversy over the election of Germany to a permanent seat on the League of Nations Council in 1926 is a good

[24] I would agree with Raymond Aron's contention that Small Powers can have only defensive ambitions, but I am more doubtful about the obverse side of his argument: i.e., that Great Powers, by definition, "desire to possess the capacity we have called offensive. . . ." Weak Great Powers frequently seek an end no more exalted than the one Professor Aron consigns to Small Powers— "to survive *as such*." It is my argument that these kinds of simple distinctions must be transcended if a definition is to do something more than merely indicate the effects of being weaker in any particular situation. Ultimately, it is the set of psychological expectations about the limits of possible and effective action which distinguishes Great and Small Powers, not merely the possession of capacities of one kind or another. For Professor Aron's argument, see Raymond Aron, *Peace and War: A Theory of International Relations* (Garden City, N.Y.: Doubleday & Company, 1966), p. 83.

example.[25] This illustrates one problem clearly. The demand for equality may be in conflict with the desire for security. By hindering the quest for security among the Great Powers, in order to guarantee a formal principle, the Small Power ultimately endangers its own security. But, again, few Small Powers can accept immediate deprivations in hopes of future benefits. Keynes' dictum—in the long run we are all dead—sometimes seems to have become the first principle of Small Power statesmen (more accurately, of *some* such statesmen).

Thus the psychology of fear leads Small Powers in conflicting directions: to attempt to withdraw from imminent conflict and, simultaneously, to demand formal equality in all situations.[26] On the one hand, fearing risks, the Small Powers assert "nothing we do matters very much." [27] But balancing the tendency to withdraw from a crisis is the pervasive tendency to demand equal status, with, presumably, full rights and obligations to participate in a crisis, even at the expense of long-range security.[28]

[25] The history of the incident can be found in Erik Lonnroth, "Sweden: The Diplomacy of Osten Unden," *The Diplomats 1919–1939*, edited by Gordon A. Craig and Felix Gilbert (New York: Atheneum, 1963).

[26] Cf. Liska, *Nations in Alliance*, p. 100. See pages 293–95 below for some comments on how the situation Small Powers have found themselves in may color their decision to seek nuclear weapons.

[27] The diplomatic position which results is exemplified in this statement by an Estonian diplomat: "We do not take sides. Quite frankly, we do not want to be placed in the position of risk, which taking sides would involve. We tell both sides frankly that we will go with the majority." Quoted in Joseph Davies, *Mission to Moscow* (New York: Pocket Books, 1943), p. 182. This position seems distinct from that of most Great Powers who, in Hoffmann's words, "do not hesitate deliberately to engender new risks. . . . The main objective of a large power is to maximize gains (defined in a variety of ways) rather than to minimize risks." Hoffmann, *The State of War*, p. 138. I am not in complete agreement with Hoffmann's statement, since, again, difficulties appear to arise when one confronts Great Powers whose aims are essentially defensive and designed to minimize risks. I prefer a formulation of the distinction between the two kinds of states which does not necessarily rest either on their capabilities or on their choice of a particular kind of policy.

[28] All Small Powers, even those violently opposed to each other, advocate more voting power for themselves in international organizations and condemn unilateral Great Power solutions or interventions. Common policies occasionally assert themselves even within certain alliance structures. In SEATO, the Small Power members have all desired more aid, more opportunity to present *their* views, and a

Does any of the foregoing material prove that there is a real distinction between Great Powers and Small Powers, that they are unique groups? The answer, clearly, is no. The evidence is no more than suggestive. Obviously, a great deal more empirical research would have to be done before any convincing generalizations could be offered. Nevertheless, while not proved, the argument seems sound enough to justify taking account of it in any attempt to define Small Powers.

It is extremely difficult to devise a definition which reflects the preceding argument. It is possible, however, to suggest one which takes note of the fact that Small Powers are not simply weaker Great Powers and that they must be defined in terms of something other than their relative power status. Any new definition should also take account of the fact that there is a psychological, as well as a material, distinction between Great and Small Powers. The latter earn their title not only by being weak but by recognizing the implications of that condition. Thus, *a Small Power is a state which recognizes that it can not obtain security primarily by use of its own capabilities, and that it must rely fundamentally on the aid of other states, institutions, processes, or developments to do so; the Small Power's belief in its inability to rely on its own means must also be recognized by the other states involved in international politics.*

One virtue of this definition is that it is acceptable under any international system. The Small Power is not defined by specific qualities which it possesses (or lacks) but rather by a position it occupies in its own and other eyes. Whatever the differences between Belgium and Burma, this definition subsumes them both. It also excludes states such as the France of 1938. By emphasizing

---

more integrated command structure with specifically designated alliance forces (to deprive their Great Power allies of one element of flexibility: i.e., flexibility to leave their smaller allies in the lurch). Cf. *SEATO: Six Studies,* edited by George Modelski (Melbourne: F. W. Cheshire, 1962), p. 156. Note also Iran's efforts to increase the power of CENTO in the late 1950s, that is, when it felt itself immediately threatened by the Soviet Union. Dana Adams Schmidt reported that, *inter alia,* "Iran urged that headquarters of the alliance be shifted from Ankara to its geographical center in Teheran and that it be given a unified military command like that of the North Atlantic Treaty Organization." *The New York Times,* January 31, 1955, p. 3.

recognition of its status by other states, the relationship between that status and the kind of international system which exists will be more easily recognized.[29] It will, in theory, be easier to explain basic changes in the role of Small Powers in world politics.

This analysis is concerned with the alliance policy of Small Powers. There are obviously other policies open to Small Powers intent on protecting their security. The remainder of this chapter will examine those policies in a very general fashion, if only to illustrate the utility of concentrating on alliance policies.

The next section discusses policies open to the Small Powers themselves, policies which, used wisely, can increase their security and mitigate the effects of weakness. The concluding section discusses actions which could be taken by the international community as a whole, actions which are beyond the means of the Small Powers themselves. The possibility of weakening the Great Powers, of improving international organization, and of assuring the operation of collective security will be examined in turn. The distinction between the policies in the two sections is obviously arbitrary, and is used primarily for clarity and convenience. Small Powers can have a significant effect in insuring the success of external actions like collective security. But an individual Small Power is not likely to be critical. Conversely, it is clear that the policies of the Great Powers are vital determinants or limiting factors in the actions that Small Powers undertake. Nevertheless, the distinction is both useful and not unnecessarily unrealistic.

The Policies of Small Powers

Neutrality and nonalignment have always appealed to Small Powers. The possibility of withdrawing from the struggles between the Great Powers, and of enjoying a period of years devoted to peace

---

[29] For an interesting but not particularly revealing attempt to rank states in the international system, see J. David Singer and Melvin Small, "The Composition and Status Ordering of the International System: 1815–1940," *World Politics,* XVIII (January 1966), 236–82.

and internal development, is the eternal myth for most Small Powers.

In the nineteenth century, Belgium and Luxembourg had their neutrality guaranteed by all the Great Powers. However, the essential condition which had facilitated agreement on a policy of guarantee disappeared after 1919: the Great Powers were no longer in equilibrium. Without a relative equilibrium, guarantee would most likely degenerate into control by the most powerful neighbor.[30] With Russia, Germany, and Austria-Hungary temporarily or permanently *hors de combat*, guaranteed neutrality became impossible for Belgium and Luxembourg, at least in traditional terms. In addition, the League of Nations seemed to involve commitments which were antithetical to neutrality. Nevertheless, several European Small Powers described the policies they adopted after 1935 in terms of "neutrality." Yet these policies had nothing to do with the traditional concepts of neutrality, which involved the rights and duties of nonbelligerents in a war. The new concept simply reflected a desperate attempt to remain outside any future war. It was called neutrality, one suspects, in an effort to legitimize it in traditional terms.[31] It had nothing to do with the legal problems of nonbelligerents. And, of course, it differed from guaranteed neutrality in that it was, as it were, an attempt to avoid any guarantee at all in a period when being guaranteed decreased one's inde-

[30] That is, when the Great Powers are relatively equal, they can expect only relatively equal gains from any attempt to aggrandize—on the principle of equal compensation. Thus it may be the path of least resistance to simply eliminate (i.e., accept the neutralization of) Small Powers from the competition rather than to divide them or reach an agreed settlement on equitable compensation. This is particularly true in the case where the Small Power(s) is likely to resist its fate strenuously; or where the Small Power(s) has been able to carry on its political life without becoming a burden to the community as a whole. For a somewhat similar formulation of this idea, cf. Liska, *Nations in Alliance*, p. 24.

[31] Cf. Nils Ørvik, *The Decline of Neutrality, 1914–1941* (Oslo: Johan Grundt Tanum Forlag, 1953), p. 183: ". . . with the exception of Switzerland, the small European neutrals had ventured upon a course which was neither collective security nor neutrality in the old sense. They seemed to seek a position where they could have one foot in each camp. . . . In practice each of them had drawn a circle around its own territory, and declared its determination to stay within this as long as possible whatever might be going on outside."

pendence, and increased the possibility that one's homeland would become a battlefield.

In discussing the utility of the concept, it seems prudent to use one of the currently fashionable terms, like "noninvolvement" or "nonalignment" to indicate that the efforts of the Small Powers to extricate themselves from purely Great Power conflicts and, above all, to avoid war are being discussed.[32] A superficial similarity exists between the arguments used to justify guaranteed neutrality and the self-styled neutrality of the 1930s. The same sort of conditions prevailed. In both instances the Small Powers were to be removed from the struggle, in preference to the dangers involved in their choosing one side or the other. It is a commentary on the times that in the earlier period it was imposed by the Great Powers and in the later it was requested by the Small Powers. Moreover, the Small Powers evinced no interest in true impartiality. They merely wanted to stay out of war, even if their interests behooved them to join one side.

Neutrality or nonalignment is sensible only when certain basic conditions prevail: the Small Power must not be so potentially powerful as to threaten to shift the balance if incorporated by one side; and the citizens of the Small State must be willing to withdraw from world affairs. In effect, the Small Power must be strategically irrelevant and politically nonprovocative. When these requirements are joined to the fact that Great Power equilibrium is also necessary, it becomes obvious why nonalignment was so absurd and spurious a policy in the 1930s. Almost none of the conditions held for the European Small Powers of that era. Their "neutrality" was a concoction brewed in part from nostalgia for supposedly happier days, and, in part, from sheer desperation.

What other problems are involved in nonalignment? One concerns its military advantages; again its relevance is limited to the interwar years. In general, nonalignment was usually a military advantage to one Great Power, and, as one would inevitably suspect, a corresponding disadvantage to another Great Power.[33] It

[32] Chapter 8 discusses current nonalignment policies. As noted in the text, the remarks here refer to earlier political configurations.

[33] Alfred Cobban, *National Self-Determination* (London: Oxford University Press, 1945), p. 168.

always seemed more advantageous to one Great Power to have the Small Power independent and unavailable as a route into its own country; and thus an advantage to the other to be able to exert pressure by the threat of utilizing its small ally's territory. On the other hand, it was even more preferable to have the Small Power as an ally rather than as an independent, for it could always join the other side. Belgium was aware of the subtleties of this problem in the period when it opted for "independence". That was a choice obviously favorable to Germany, since it clearly eliminated France's ability to strike through Belgium into the exposed Ruhr—and destroyed the credibility of France's eastern policy, which rested on a promise to come to her allies' aid by invading Germany. As a result, Belgium began a campaign to prove to France that her (Belgium's) "neutrality" was also advantageous to France. Brussels contended that, since Germany would not strike through an independent and rearmed Belgium, she had to attack along the Franco-German border, which was guarded by the Maginot Line. France would thus have a shorter strategic frontier, and would also be fighting where it was best prepared. At any rate, the point at issue is that "neutrality" was an advantage to one Great Power, and the recognition of this factor forced the Small Power into some rather complicated rationalizations of its policy.

Nonalignment cannot be justified on the basis of its presumed moral superiority over a policy of alignment. Obviously a decision to remain unaligned rests on the same expediential calculations which determine any other policy choice. Arguments which contend that nonalignment is always either wise or stupid are incorrect. For example, Machiavelli maintained that there was no advantage for a Small Power in attempting to remain outside a major conflict, and that in fact there was little likelihood that it would be able to do so. If it did remain neutral, it aroused the enmity of the eventual victor. If it joined the war, it might earn a share of the spoils. Even if it joined the losing side, it was likely to be treated more leniently than its Great Power ally. Nevertheless, Machiavelli's argument is not universally valid. There are advantages for a Small Power in remaining neutral in a conflict (particularly in an era of modern military technology), and they have, in fact, managed to do so in several major conflicts. Conversely, the fact that an argument for alignment is not universally valid does not justify the assumption that nonalignment is. The choice of either policy is wholly expediential.

It seems fair to conclude that neutrality or nonalignment is a dangerous security policy for Small Powers which are exposed to a Great Power threat. It is undoubtedly more effective for Small Powers which find themselves on the periphery of political activity, but, even in these cases, geography seems a more critical factor than the choice of a particular policy. Moreover, the conditions necessary to make nonalignment a viable policy are seldom if ever present. The normal result is that it becomes a euphemism for a policy of indecision and fear. The impossible desire to be independent, in a world in which independence is an illusion even for the greatest, was finally achieved by some Small Powers by burrowing their heads in the sand so that the actual world disappeared—unfortunately, they inevitably left the larger parts of their political anatomy unnecessarily exposed to the rigors of the world they thought they had left behind.

If nonalignment is an only occasionally effective policy, Small Powers must perforce learn to operate successfully within the arena of Great Power conflicts. The strategy they have tended to adopt is usually described in terms of the balance of power. They attempt, insofar as it is within their means, to prevent the hegemony of any single Great Power, or any single group of states, in order to avoid the unpalatable alternatives which face any Small Power when the balance is out of equilibrium.[34] Whether reference is made to the classical periods of the balance of power (before 1914), or whether the term is simply used to indicate a preference for equilibrium among all the existing Great Powers at any particular time, it still remains clear that Small Powers are operating in a dangerous environment. The precept that the balance of power protects the independence of all states has been absolute only for the Great Powers. The survival of Small Powers in any

[34] For other comments on Small Powers and the balance of power, see Chapter 5. The remarks here are intended only to point out a few of its dangers and to note the continuing fascination of many Small Powers for the idea of balancing.

system which claims allegiance to the rules of the balance of power is inherently uncertain, since they may find themselves sacrificed in order to allow the weaker Great Powers to recoup their fortunes. The fact that, in numerical terms, the actual sacrifice of Small Powers in such circumstances has been rare [though the cases which do exist are stark: Poland (1772–95) and Czechoslovakia (1938–39)] should not obscure the reality of fears engendered by the realization that it has always been a possibility. Existence within a world operating according to the unalloyed precepts of the balance of power could be very unpleasant for a Small Power.

Nevertheless, the idea of the balance of power appears to be intrinsically appealing to Small Powers, despite its dangers. One suspects the reason may lie in the vision of a perfectly even balance in which the weight of the Small Power might be decisive—the thought of sitting astride the fulcrum of a level balance, and determining the destiny of world politics, may seem megalomaniacal, but it may also explain the peculiar attachment manifested for the balance by even the most internationalist of statesmen.[35] This is not, of course, to deny that there are legitimate reasons for paying close attention to the balance of power. It is rather to suggest that Small Powers may manifest a singularly large appreciation for it, considering its somewhat dubious record.

It may be *a propos* to point out that the very idea of Small Powers carrying the balance between divided Great Powers is more an imaginative construction than a description of the past. As Karl Deutsch has pointed out, the idea is much too crude. It is very unlikely that a Small Power can force or even initiate a solution which a Great Power has previously rejected.[36] The Small Power, however, may perform a useful function as a mediator or conciliator,

[35] Beneš and Paul Hymans are examples. For Beneš, see the remarks by Harold Nicolson in his *Peacemaking, 1919* (New York: Harcourt, Brace and Company, 1939), p. 103. For Hymans, see his *Memoires* (Brussels: Editions de l'Institute de Sociologie Solvay, 1958), *passim*.

[36] Karl W. Deutsch, "Large and Small States in the Integration of Large Political Communities" (unpublished paper delivered to 1955 meeting of the International Political Science Association in Stockholm), p. 7.

a position which their statesmen no doubt find personally satisfying.

In any case, to describe the policy of a Small Power in terms of the balance of power is not very illuminating. If one maintains that a state must follow such a policy since it is inherent in all politics, the idea is merely tautologous and explains virtually nothing. On the other hand, if the term is used in any other sense, the exact meaning must be specified. Still, in terms of a policy option, the idea contains a certain amount of conventional wisdom for Small Powers. Whatever else they may mean when they proclaim attachment to the principles of the balance of power, they nearly always are referring to a situation in which power is so distributed that they can retain their independence. Normally that required a relative equilibrium among the Great Powers. If such a condition prevailed, they retained some maneuverability. However, the power configuration, historically, has as often been in relative disequilibrium as it has been in equilibrium. Traditionally, then, Small Powers—at least those which are not bent on altering the status quo—have sought a particular kind of configuration, one which seemed both practically and aesthetically to offer them the greatest chance for security. The most elemental means open to them to achieve or maintain that condition has been the alliance. Although alliances may be used for other purposes beyond achieving equilibrium, they have always been used for that purpose.

Small Powers may also attempt to compensate for their weakness by emphasizing their qualitative virtues.[37] They may, for example, rely on the superiority of their statesmen or soldiers to carry them through a crisis. Or they may emphasize the modernity of their defenses or their equipment. In addition, they might provide proof of their determination to fight by supporting a heavy military budget. These kinds of actions do not constitute a policy: they are, rather, a preface to policy. They can influence, though they cannot determine, the fate of any particular policy choice. If concentration on improving internal strength and external reputation were enough by themselves to insure the security of a Small Power, a

[37] Cf. George Liska, *International Equilibrium* (Cambridge: Harvard University Press, 1957), pp. 25 ff.

contradiction in terms would exist. The Small Power cannot determine its own fate by its own actions: it must seek external support. If aid is not necessary, a different political world would exist composed entirely of equally powerful states. The assumption here is that a determination to build its own strength to a maximum level, while it may make the Small Power a less attractive target, is not enough by itself. Therefore, in speaking of policies available to compensate for weakness, policies referred to are primarily those by which the Small Power attempts to remove or isolate itself from power conflicts, or policies in which it chooses to draw on the strength of others to insure its own security.

The Mirage of Equality and the Security of Small Powers

It is undoubtedly unrealistic to discuss, in practical terms, efforts designed to weaken the Great Powers to the extent that they could no longer impose their will on weaker states. Nevertheless, it remains a theoretical possibility, and obviously one of great attractiveness to Small Powers, provided that one can identify the agent of change.[38] If it is presumed that such an agent exists—perhaps the Great Powers themselves as a reaction, say, to another major war —a number of policies suggest themselves. Disarmament, or an arms control scheme which included the destruction of "offensive" weapons, is only the most obvious example. Alternatively, an effort to develop legal procedures which prohibited the use of force, such as compulsory arbitration, and thus diluted the military distinctions between states, might seem more attractive to the Great Powers. The revision of strategic boundaries is another alternative in certain cases, on the debatable assumption that, for example, Italy might behave better if a Small Power controlled the Brenner Pass. In any case, the unattractiveness or unattainability of any of the policies noted should make one point clear: any attempt to weaken the strong is illusory. Even if it proved possible, there is no assurance that it would be wise.

To assume that disarmament by the Great Powers reduces them

[38] Cf. Arnold Wolfers, *The Small Powers and the Enforcement of Peace* (New Haven: Yale Institute of International Studies, 1943), pp. 5–6.

to the level of Small Powers is absurd. There is no way to reduce the other, more fundamental distinctions that separate the two kinds of states: the differences in industrial power, population, technology, wealth, and so forth.[39] The Great Powers would be weakened only to the extent that it would take them longer to impose their will, and to the degree that the new state of affairs required them to mask their control behind polite subterfuges.

Even granting the assumption that such a course of action is possible, its wisdom remains in doubt. Great power should involve great responsibility. Any attempt to dilute that power, however illusory it would be, might induce the Great Powers to feel that they no longer need concern themselves with anything but their own affairs. Whatever commitment they accepted to protect the weaker members of the community would be reduced according to the extent to which it was assumed all were equally powerful. After all, there is no particular necessity to protect one's "equals". The attempt to weaken the Great Powers seems likely to create more illusions, rather than more equality. In addition, it might induce the more adventurous Small Powers to act impetuously. As the Swedish Foreign Minister, Osten Unden, once noted:

If any friend of peace asserts that the work of peace must begin with changing the distribution of power between States or revising frontiers, his love of peace is very Platonic. This point of view comes very close to hoping for the next war as the Providence which will set the world in order for the just and final peace.[40]

The effort to improve security by weakening the strongest elements in the international system, in fact by weakening any elements, may be worse than utopian. It may, in reality, be self-defeating. Security, in the final analysis, does not rest solely on the existence or nonexistence of a particular kind of power configuration, although it is undoubtedly true that some configurations tend

[39] Moreover, the unique behavioral patterns which have come to characterize Great Powers and Small Powers, which were discussed in the preceding section, would not disappear: Small Powers would still tend to act according to the imperatives of being permanently weaker, at least until the new condition of *presumed* equality became or appeared to become substantively significant.

[40] Quoted in Herbert Tingsten, *The Debate on the Foreign Policy of Sweden, 1918–1939* (London: Oxford University Press, 1949), p. 81.

to be more stable than others. The dangers attendant on the existence of a particular situation depend primarily on the intentions of the actors within it. A hegemonial system run by a peaceful and prosperous Great Power may obviously be more stable than a system in which five or six equally powerful (or powerless) states rapaciously contend for supremacy. The critical problem, then, is not simply the existence of states possessing widely divergent capabilities; rather the problem, at least in terms of security, is insuring that the most powerful is also the most peaceful. Since the possibility of achieving general agreement on this point is, to say the least, quite small, one solution is to create an international organization by definition more just than any of its members and, by subscription, more powerful.

Surely the international organizations which exist, and have existed, are pale reflections of the preceding image. They are quite clearly neither more just nor more powerful than some of their members. Yet they at least possess the potential of becoming so, and of relieving Small Powers of many of the burdens of security. Accordingly, Small Powers normally are in the vanguard of efforts to improve and strengthen existing international organizations (the major exceptions are revisionist Small Powers). They can, of course, do no more than lobby for their views: Any realistic effort to strengthen the League or the UN requires at least the concurrence of all the Great Powers, and probably most of the Small Powers.

What accounts, in more specific terms, for the enthusiasm which most Small Powers have usually manifested for international institutions? The promise of formal equality, as well as the status attendant upon being consulted on a wide range of issues, plays a part. So, too, does the potential security inherent in the promises of the covenant or the charter. Moreover, the new institutions might perform another function: restraining or hobbling the Great Powers.[41] Small Powers have not even been required to profess loyalty to the new institutions as ends in themselves. Quite to the

---

[41] Thus the Dominions "looked on the League far less as a means of protection than as a restraint on the imperial adventures of the Great Powers." Gwendolyn M. Carter, *The British Commonwealth and International Security* (Toronto: The Ryerson Press, 1957), p. 100.

contrary, they have been able to season idealism with a strong dose of realism. It is at least possible to attempt to implement policies within the new institutions which were inconceivable within the framework of the nation-state system, without evincing any deep attachment to international organization.[42]

Unfortunately, international organization is hardly a panacea. It can, to some extent, by its insistence on peaceful procedures, dilute the distinction between the militarily powerful and the militarily weak. It may, by its availability, lessen the impact of sudden crises or revolutions. It may also, by its mere existence, provide inexperienced Small Powers with a forum in which it is possible to develop some diplomatic sophistication—perhaps widening a political perspective which has, necessarily, been extremely narrow and parochial. In addition, the prestige which accompanies participation in international diplomacy may aid in weathering the dangers of internal revolution. Finally, international organizations can help materially through their specialized agencies, and ideologically through efforts to develop and implement an internationalist ethic. But there are other problems which international organizations create or intensify which make it something of a double-edged sword.

The first problem is the distortion of the institution by Great Powers intent on using it for their own purposes. France's efforts to turn the League into an alliance against Germany, and the United States' effort to turn the UN into a coalition against the Soviet Union, are cases in point. The international institutions so perverted become a danger for the Small Powers rather than a protection. The decision to remain faithful to such institutions reverts to a mere policy of choosing sides. It becomes clear that the institution is no more than a euphemism for a traditional alliance, and that no one will take its ideals seriously when the balance of power shifts.

The Great Powers may also feel that their commitment to maintain peace is limited when they are in an organization which fails to reconcile power and responsibility effectively.[43] When there is

[42] Cf. Ernst Haas, *The Uniting of Europe* (Stanford: Stanford University Press, 1958), pp. 14–15.

[43] Cf. Kaufmann, "The Organization of Responsibility," *passim.*

confusion about who is required to act, the most likely result is that no one will act. Consequently a Small Power may lose some real security when a Great Power confines its promises of aid to those found within the Charter or Covenant.

The difficulty of reconciling principles, such as equality or democracy, with the need for security creates another problem. The imperatives of the latter may require the betrayal of the former—but this becomes difficult when both the principles and the procedures to implement security are intertwined in the same document. The result, again, may be the failure to act at all.

The weakness and dangers of international organization can be summarized by noting that it may create illusions of power where there is only confusion of responsibility. "But if institutions lose touch with realities, they are a greater threat to weaker non-aggressive states than no institutions at all. They give rise to expectations which fail to be met at the critical moment." [44] It may well be better to return overtly to the "old" diplomacy rather than to rely on institutions which weaken security by creating illusions of strength.

All of the foregoing criticisms of international organization are drawn from recent history. They are not necessarily in the nature of things.[45] It is this realization which makes international organization of so much potential value to the Small Power.[46] However, the effectiveness of the League and the UN has varied in direct proportion to the state of the relationship between the Great Powers—which, in some ways, makes it a tautology, since it is of least use when most needed. To the extent that international organization has facilitated compromise and promoted a new ethic, it has been useful. But it has not yet reached the point where it provides for any state's security, let alone that of the Small Powers.

[44] Liska, *International Equilibrium*, pp. 21–22.

[45] Thus a specific problem, such as the absence of the United States from the League, cannot justify an attack on international organization as such: only on the League.

[46] Something of the attitude of Small Powers toward the League can be garnered from this statement by a Dutch Foreign Minister to his Parliament: ". . . when there is darkness and a jump must be made into it, the question which this assembly must answer is: is it not better to jump with than without the League?" Quoted in Vandenbosch, *Dutch Foreign Policy*, p. 172.

Collective security is usually discussed within the framework of international organization. There is no necessary relation between the two—though an historical one exists—and it is possible to conceive of a collective security system independent of the institutional framework of, say, the League or the UN. Such a division would have the advantage of ending much of the debate on the purposes and functions of the larger organization: that is, whether it is to concern itself solely with conciliation and discussion or whether it is required to impose its collective will. It would present one potential way of avoiding the problems of a too exaggerated gap between power and responsibility. Nevertheless, the comments which follow will be drawn from the experience of the last forty years, rather than from a purely theoretical analysis of collective security.

One of the primary weaknesses of collective security, from the point of view of Small Powers, has been that it provided no guarantee against the Great Power guarantors themselves. When the Great Powers resumed their competition and quarrels, the system was unable to withstand the shock. As long as the Small Powers were sought as allies or satellites, it was the traditional rules of the balance of power which operated, not the newer, universal precepts of collective security. What came to be called "collective security" at any particular time was the alliance system operated by the strongest League (or UN) Great Power.[47] The Small Powers were forced into the position of either allying against an aggressive Great Power or remaining unaligned and facing accusations of undermining "collective security."

The operation of a collective security system has proved to have other hazards. In the Italo-Ethiopian struggle the Small Powers in close proximity to Italy were forced to pay an extravagant price. Those that followed the League's policy, like Yugoslavia, found

[47] Thus Chamberlain could say that "collective security does not differ from the old alliances of pre-war days which we thought we had abandoned." Quoted in Ørvik, *The Decline of Neutrality*, p. 192. This was just what the Small Powers hoped collective security would prevent. Thus a Dutch Foreign Minister argued that "Collective security . . . was a change of methods, not of ends. . . . There would be no question of members being drawn into the orbit of any one particular power or group of powers." Vandenbosch, *Dutch Foreign Policy*, p. 189.

their economic position irreparably damaged. It was, in fact, the application of sanctions against Italy which allowed Germany to develop its economic dominance over Southeastern Europe by replacing Italy as a market.[48] Fidelity to the League ultimately weakened international security by allowing the primary enemy of the League to establish itself in a new area. The problem was complicated by the blindness of the other Great Powers who failed to compensate countries like Yugoslavia for the disproportionate load they were required to bear—despite the fact that there were specific provisions in the Covenant applicable to the situation.

The implications of the Ethiopian episode were not lost on the other European Small Powers. A collective security system in which the support of the Great Powers was grudging and inconsistent, and in which the Small Powers were urged to accept burdensome duties which could only be justified if Great Power support was assured, was worse than no system at all. Allegiance to the ideals of collective security was safe under two conditions: if no threat serious enough to activate the system arose, or if the system met its first challenges successfully enough to warrant continued support. After 1936 neither condition held, and the European Small Powers desperately sought to dilute whatever commitments they still maintained toward the security provisions of the Covenant. Henceforth, for both Great and Small Power alike, the rhetoric of collective security was at least partially transformed. Allegiance to its provisos could no longer be justified solely on the basis of the promise they contained, but had to meet the same political criteria employed in judging other security policies.

The fact that a collective security system theoretically gives the Small Power worldwide interests and responsibilities has an obverse side also. A weak, exposed state can suddenly find itself propelled into action which merely aggravates its position. It may find that the decision to support a collective action will exacerbate internal divisions, particularly in periods when the international struggle is in part ideological. Several states have found themselves involved in explosive situations because the decision to support an

[48] Cf. Royal Institute of International Affairs, *South-Eastern Europe, A Political and Economic Survey* (London: Oxford University Press, 1939), pp. 111–203.

action might appear as a decision to fight an ideology which a minority of its population favors—France and Belgium both faced this dilemma in the 1930s. Moreover, a strategically located Small Power may be compelled to become a spearhead of a punitive action which it disapproves—or, conversely, does not consider justified enough to warrant the kind of risks forced upon it merely by virtue of geography. Belgian policy after 1936 provides a case in point. Collective action against Germany would inevitably be launched via its territory. Since Germany was powerful enough to resist successfully, or at least destructively, Belgium was bound to become a battlefield again. The only alternative seemed to be a renegotiation of the commitments accepted in an earlier period. The Belgians became furiously intent on regaining their "neutrality" in an effort to prove that no one could use their territory, even for a League action, without first receiving their approval—and without the participation of *all* the other relevant Great Powers.[49]

Clearly then, the operation of a collective security system can force a Small Power to participate in actions for which it is unprepared, or which it might disapprove. It can weaken its integrity by forcing it to dissipate its strength, and it can expose it to the retaliation of a neighboring Great Power. In addition, the unsophisticated Small Power can be trapped into assuming that the real world corresponds to the dictates of the theory, and the cynical Small Power can be led to the position where it assumes that the theory has no correspondence at all with the facts. Both attitudes are ultimately destructive of the potential security inherent in the idea of collective security. For it is probably true that "had it proved practical, collective security would have represented an ideal solution from the point of view of weaker countries." [50] Even operating below its full capacity, the idea had something to contribute; it was a civilizing agent in the field of international politics and it was the harbinger of a better future. Unfortunately, its defects

[49] Cf. the speech by Spaak on April 29, 1937, *Annales Parlementaires,* Chambre des Representants, Session Legislative Ordinaire 1937 (Brussels: Imprimeries de Moniteur Belge), pp. 1284–87.

[50] Wolfers, "The Small Powers and the Enforcement of Peace," p. 7.

submerged its virtues, and the Small Powers, as well as the Great Powers, were forced to look elsewhere for security.

Before turning to an examination of alliances, it may be appropriate to point out that all of the alternatives available to compensate for the weakness of Small Powers are ambiguous. None of them assures security; any one of them may facilitate it. The policy of alliance will prove no less ambiguous. However, it has always been the most obvious weapon for the Small Power, and the one most employed. But borrowing someone else's strength, like borrowing his money, has disadvantages as well as advantages. Both will be discussed.

CHAPTER 2

Alliances: A Preliminary Analysis

IT IS undoubtedly true that the specific character of alliances differs in various historical periods. Thus, alliances were primarily defensive in nature from 1815 to 1859, became offensive instruments designed to fight a war between 1859 and 1871, and became defensive again after 1871.[1] Similarly, the predominant form chosen may also depend on the nature of the period. For example, alliances created in the League era tended to be at least formally open to *all* states. At other times, technological and political developments may favor integrated, multilateral alliances rather than the more traditional bilateral form.

Nevertheless, despite specific differences between alliances of different historical periods, certain general features of an alliance policy remain constant. This is particularly true in regard to two points: the goals which states hope to achieve by means of an alliance and the factors which seem likely to condition the success or failure of an alliance. Both will be discussed in the next section.

The emphasis throughout this book is, of course, on various distinctions between Great Powers and Small Powers. That emphasis is somewhat muted in this chapter, since the discussion revolves around features which are common to the alliance policy of

[1] Cf. Ch. 6 for details. They began to alter again when Bismarck agreed to support Italian territorial demands when the Triple Alliance was renewed. These sentences may sound somewhat more mechanistic than they are meant to be; there is no imputation here that the alliances themselves were deterministic. Obviously, the character they assume in any particular period is the result of a pattern of individual decisions by various statesmen.

all states. Nevertheless, certain distinctions between Great Powers and Small Powers begin to emerge even at this level—a point, perhaps, of some significance for the contention that Small Powers are unique actors in world politics.

The Nature of Alliances

Alliances are instruments of statecraft; as such, they are morally neutral. The decision to ally rarely stems from principle. In the normal course of events, it simply reflects the expediential calculations at the root of nearly all decisions concerning the use of one means rather than another. The statesman pondering the decision to ally must ask and answer three questions. What are the relative advantages of alignment versus nonalignment? If alliance seems wise, what are the advantages of various alternative alignments? And, once a decision has been reached on who one should ally with, what form should the alliance take? This chapter will be concerned primarily with the first two questions; Chapters 3 and 4 will deal at greater length with question three.

Criticism of alliances, like criticism of diplomacy, covers a wide range, extending from accusations of immorality to accusations of ineffectiveness. It may be helpful to reiterate a few of the more cogent criticisms, if only to illustrate some of the potential dangers inherent in an alliance policy. To begin with, the ethos of the time may be unfavorable to alliances (e.g., note the situation from 1919–33), and the signatories may lose status, prestige and influence by their decision. At such times, alliances tend to be justified on spurious grounds (e.g., their supposed correspondence with the dictates of collective security), although their substance usually involves a very explicit military commitment (obviously only the perception of a significant military threat justifies the expected political losses). Moreover, alliances tend to freeze the status quo which existed at the moment of signing. Neither partner is absolutely committed to honor its pledge; either can plead extenuating circumstances. Nevertheless, it is clearly difficult—or at least embarrassing—to renege. Even if the situation has altered, it is easier to act as if nothing has happened. The difficulty arises from the fact that the situation frequently changes with an asymmetrical impact: one ally is affected more than the other. Accordingly, one also stands to benefit more than the other from the continuation of the original commitment. The partner who benefits least by the changes can attempt to persuade its partner to alter that commitment, or it can either continue the alliance unchanged or denounce it—any of which may involve substantial political costs.

In addition, alliances are usually met by counteralliances, and the latter, if effective, may exacerbate the threat the original alliance was created to meet.[2] Furthermore, if one ally intends to use the alliance as a pawn to win concessions from the enemy, and has no real intention of honoring its commitment (e.g., as in the Franco-Soviet pact of 1935), the ally who acts in good faith may suffer significant losses. Finally, at the risk of belaboring the obvious, the operation of an alliance involves certain costs which might have been avoided: the costs involved in rendering aid, in compromising conflicts of interest, in accepting a certain amount of internal interference and so forth.

The fact that alliances may involve dangers and disadvantages constitutes a negative reason for remaining unaligned. There are, however, also positive advantages inherent in remaining unattached. An unaligned state retains a free hand in disposing and developing the available power it possesses.[3] Armies need not be deployed in a mutually acceptable way, weapons need not be standardized, plans need not be integrated, numerical strength need not be agreed upon; in effect, the fewer ties, the more independence. Moreover, an unaligned state, in theory, may pursue a more flexible policy and it may even be able to assume the initiative. Allies need

[2] Thus William Langer notes that "the English made the agreement with Japan in order to prevent an understanding between Russia and Japan, which would have rendered the British position in the Far East almost hopeless . . . the important thing for England was not what was in *the* alliance, but the fact that there was *an* alliance." *The Diplomacy of Imperialism, 1890–1902* (New York: Alfred A. Knopf, 1935), p. 783.

[3] Holstein argued in the 1890s that "it is in our interest to keep our hands free, so that His Majesty will be able to claim appropriate compensation not only for eventual support, but even for remaining neutral." Quoted in A. J. P. Taylor, *The Struggle for Mastery in Europe, 1848–1918* (Oxford: The Clarendon Press, 1954), p. 4.

neither be consulted nor persuaded. Finally, one avoids adding entrants to a list of enemies: the enemy of a prospective ally need not, by definition, become your enemy. These considerations are obviously hypothetical and of varying degrees of significance in different periods. Nevertheless, even if upon occasion they are no more than a reflection of nostalgia for the presumed virtues of independence, they can and do color the decision to ally.

The preceding paragraphs constitute an impressive indictment of alliances. The indictment, however, has hardly been decisive, for alliances, in one form or another, are always present, if not always in style. Their disadvantages induce prudence, not abstention. The rationale is obvious: the advantages of allying appear to outweigh the disadvantages with enough frequency to make alliances an integral part of any international system.

Those advantages tend to fall into two groups, one military and the other political. In military terms, the primary advantage involves the hope of deterring an enemy by indicating as clearly as possible that an attack will have to contend with the combined forces of the alliance, not simply the isolated force of the intended victim. If deterrence should fail, it is assumed that the pooled forces of the alliance will constitute a more effective fighting force than the individual forces of the attacked state. The possibility that the means used to achieve deterrence and defense may be in conflict is a relatively new phenomenon. Before the advent of nuclear weapons, one defended with the same weapons with which one hoped to deter. The situation is much more ambiguous now: the weapons for deterrence and for defense at least tend to be different.

An alliance, even in wartime, usually offers significant political advantages to the partners. Most critically, each partner hopes to influence the policy of its ally in a favorable direction. A formal tie may be accepted in hopes of gaining the *right* to be consulted.[4] In addition, the acceptance of mutual obligations may prevent one

[4] For example, Sir Percy Lorraine declared that, in signing the "Pact of Steel" in May 1939, "Mussolini has bought the right to be consulted by Hitler, and the price is the pact." *Documents on British Foreign Policy, 1919–1939*, edited by E. L. Woodward and Rohan Butler (London: H. M. Stationery Office, 1946–1966), 3rd. Series, Vol. V, No. 598. Henceforth cited as *G.B.D.*

of the allies from following a policy which the other considers "adventurism".[5] One might also ally in order to use the alliance as a bargaining weapon against another power, offering to dismantle the new alliance in exchange for certain stipulated responses. Finally, an alliance with a powerful and prestigious state may involve political and psychological advantages—note, for example, the benefits attendant upon allying with France in the 1920s.

Virtually all of the specific goals sought by states by means of an alliance policy may be subsumed under one of the larger headings just noted. For example, when a Small Power allies with a Great Power to prevent a hostile Great Power from attacking or practicing a policy of "one by one," the hope is obviously to deter. Or, a Great Power may ally with a Small Power in an effort to restrain the latter from certain actions. The United States alliance with Nationalist China frequently appears in this light. This goal clearly fits within one of the political categories previously noted. It will be presumed, henceforth, that this is true for the majority of goals sought by means of an alliance.

The advantages of an alliance policy have been divided into two categories, one military and the other political. It is, of course, as difficult to find a purely military alliance, without political undertones, as it would be to find a political alliance from which some military benefits were not sought. It is safe to assume that most allies seek both political and military advantages from any alliance. Nevertheless, it is possible to make a relevant distinction between alliances which seek one goal more than the other. The distinction has both theoretical and historical utility. It may in fact be true that failure to recognize it, or failure to agree on which purpose is dominant, is at the root of many intra-alliance squabbles. The problems which arose between France and the Little Entente in the 1930s, when it became clear that each side had a different conception of its alliance commitment, are a case in point.

---

[5] Langer, in discussing the Triple Alliance, notes that "the treaty gave them [Germany and Austria] the assurance that Italy would not join a hostile combination, and that she would not attack Austria in the rear in case of war between Austria and Russia." William Langer, *European Alliances and Alignments, 1871–1890* (New York: Alfred A. Knopf, 1950), p. 246.

The first conception, a military one, envisages an alliance as essentially an element in a war policy; the essence of the alliance is the additional force it provides. It is an instrument, par excellence, of deterrence and defense. It deters war by making the threat of combined strength credible, and it facilitates combined defense if deterrence fails. This kind of alliance policy normally reflects a reaction to an external threat which is perceived as dangerous. The alliance is seen as an immediate necessity to implement security, and any political losses attendant upon it are downgraded or ignored. This kind of alliance also clearly facilitates the achievement of one set of goals more readily than the other. It is, for example, easier to remain competitive in an arms race, but more difficult to restrain an ally who may provide needed assets in an imminent war.

Alternatively, an alliance may be viewed primarily as an element in a political policy. The alliance is valuable in terms of the diplomatic support it provides for a particular policy: the defense of the status quo against *peaceful* revision. The criteria for evaluating the success of this alliance are clearly different; it is not whether one achieves more deterrence or defense, but whether one develops more influence in legitimizing the contemporary distribution of benefits. The relationship between the members of the Little Entente and France in the 1920s illustrates the point. The respective military conventions were unreal, since the potential enemy was powerless, but the alliances served to underwrite the territorial settlement achieved in 1919.

It might be argued that the fundamental distinction between kinds of alliances is not between alliances which are primarily military or primarily political but between alliances designed to cope with an immediate military threat and alliances designed to cope with distant or potential military threats. The contention here, however, is considerably different. Even if an alliance is in fact designed to forestall a potential military threat, until that threat takes form it must do so by concentrating on political goals. From the point of view of the allies, it remains a political and diplomatic instrument whose operation is basically conditioned by the nature of the immediate environment—not by the existence of a potential threat. Thus, though it must be conceded that the case is not perfectly clear-cut, the distinction between military and political alliances seems more relevant than the distinction between different kinds of military alliances.

A military alliance emerges from the perception of a threat which cannot be met with one's own resources. A political alliance emerges from the perception that a situation exists which can be exploited by an alliance. This kind of alliance also facilitates the achievement of one set of goals more readily than the other. It is, for example, easier to restrain an adventuresome ally or to achieve essentially internal purposes,[6] than to present a credible military threat.

In historical terms, this distinction parallels certain traditional differences between Great Britain and the Continent. Castlereagh once noted that "our insular position places us sufficiently out of the reach of immediate danger to permit our pursuing a more generous and confiding policy." [7] The significance of this point of view, in terms of any alliance commitment Britain was likely to undertake, was explicitly spelled out for Talleyrand by Palmerston:

We have no objection to treaties for specific and definite and immediate objects, but we do not fancy treaties which are formed in contemplation of indefinite and indistinctly foreseen cases. We like to be free to judge of each occasion as it arises, and with all its concomitant circumstances and not to be bound by engagements contracted in ignorance of the particular character of the events to which they are to apply.[8]

The reaction of the Continental states was predictable. They could hardly accept so limited a conception of an alliance. As Kissinger noted:

Living with the conviction of invulnerability Castlereagh could gamble on the reality of good faith. Living with a premonition of catastrophe, Metternich had to look for a more tangible expression of security . . .

[6] See Taylor, *The Struggle for Mastery in Europe,* p. 276, for remarks about the internal effect of the Triple Alliance on Italy.

[7] Quoted in Henry Kissinger, *A World Restored* (Boston: Houghton Mifflin Company, 1957), p. 219.

[8] Quoted in Sir Charles Webster, *The Foreign Policy of Palmerston, 1830–1841* (London: G. Bell & Sons, 1951), I, 386, taken from the Palmerston Private Papers at Broadlands.

the policy of the Continental powers was precautionary; their crucial battle was the first, not the last; their effort was to prevent an overriding danger from materializing. . . .[9]

An alliance was not only an instrument to control an immediate crisis, or to fight an imminent war, but also a part of a wider *political* strategy designed to avert the development of potentially dangerous configurations of power.

Any state may refuse to enter an alliance because the costs appear prohibitive. Historically, the calculations on which this decision rested were inevitably different for states which felt they were confronted by an immediate (or constant) threat. For such states —in effect, for all the Continental states—the goals sought by means of an alliance policy had to be wider and more encompassing than the goals sought by Great Britain, because the threat they faced was wider and more encompassing. Great Britain primarily sought goals of defense with an admixture of deterrence. The Continental states primarily sought deterrence, with a stronger admixture of political goals. The alliance policy of most Small Powers, at least until our own era, has tended to resemble that of the Continental Great Powers: a policy of deterrence, but with an even stronger admixture of political goals, since the Small Power normally sought more than military protection. However, a major difference separated the Small Powers from the Continental Great Powers. For a Small Power, the necessity to use an alliance to accomplish its stated military purpose usually reflected the failure of its alliance policy; for the Continental Great Powers this was not necessarily true, since the possibility of winning a military victory was not, by definition, foreclosed.

A variety of purposes may be served by joining an alliance. The conditional nature of the commitment hardly needs emphasis. The mere existence of an alliance does not guarantee that its purposes will be accomplished. An obvious question arises: if an alliance is

[9] Kissinger, *A World Restored*, p. 219. The difference persisted throughout the century. Thus Taylor notes that Lord Grey "could not understand an alliance as a security for peace; like most Englishmen, he regarded all alliances as a commitment to war." *The Struggle for Mastery in Europe*, pp. 511–12.

an admittedly uncertain and flawed instrument of international politics, why bother to ally at all? Much the same question was put to Bismarck in 1880. Asked whether he had much faith in Russian intentions, whether he believed that the Czar would remain faithful to the stipulations of their recent alliance, he replied, ". . . at any rate more with a treaty than without." [10]

Bismarck was at once indicating his awareness of the uncertain nature of an alliance commitment and his belief that its utility was not completely vitiated by that uncertainty. If we start with the basic assumption of a state system ruled by anarchy, the rationale is obvious. An alliance adds precision to an existing community of interests, facilitating common action in the future. It can also explicitly outline the steps to be taken to protect those common interests. Thus an alliance adds some element of order, as well as a degree of predictability, to the international arena. It may also accomplish several other things. For one, it may add credibility to a threat, since the willingness to join with another state in enunciating that threat reveals some measure of seriousness. It may also serve to stabilize a situation in that it affects the calculations not only of the allies but also of their enemies. By seemingly identifying the precise configuration of power, at least in the near future, it is no longer as easy for the enemy to gamble on a divided response. As Haas and Whiting point out:

Whatever pomp and circumstance attend the final agreement serve to symbolize an element of stability and permanence which the allies would introduce into the uncertain world of human behavior. The calculated risk of defection by a partner is preferable to the certainty of failure by unilateral action. Any degree of probability that can be introduced into the actions of other countries is a decided asset for the policy-maker. Alliances serve this purpose, reducing the freedom of action of allied elites by changing their status in the view of all outside as well as inside the system.[11]

[10] Taylor, *The Struggle for Mastery in Europe,* p. 269.
[11] Ernst Haas and Allen Whiting, *Dynamics of International Relations* (New York: McGraw-Hill Book Co., 1956), p. 161.
A recent statistical study of alliances in the years from 1815–1939 has compiled some evidence that alliance commitments are indeed meaningful: that is, that nations in alliances do tend to come to the aid of their allies, and do behave differently than nations *not* in alliance. While the conclusions are hardly a

To some extent, an alliance that works reasonably well may also reduce the instrumentality of international relations. The mere process of successfully living together for some period of time may have a positive "feedback" in terms of loyalty and friendship.

In sum, then, the policy-maker can hope to achieve a wide variety of goals through an alliance. The alliance commitment itself, uncertain as it may be, fosters the attainment of these goals by introducing into the situation a specific commitment to pursue them; to a certain extent, it legitimizes that pursuit by inscribing it in a treaty; and it increases the probability that the goals will be pursued because the alliance creates a new status which makes it more difficult for the partners to renege on each other, not only because they would be dishonoring their commitment and earning a reputation for perfidy, but also because their new status usually creates a response in the external world, such as a countervailing alliance, which would tend to strengthen the bonds in the original alliance; it may also stabilize a situation by forcing enemy decision-makers to throw another weight into the opposing scales.[12]

It is a truism to assert that the ultimate success or failure of an alliance depends on the way in which it is maintained. It involves translating the common interests and aims which unite the allies into effective operational policies. The ease with which this can be done depends on a wide range of factors, some relating to the general features of the era, others to more specific configurations.

These factors are of such generality, even when they presume to inform us of the correct method to handle specific kinds of problems, that they are of only marginal utility in comprehending the fate of any alliance. In the final analysis, an answer to any question

---

revelation, and may have somewhat confused the relationship between cause and effect, they at least add an element of confirmation to more traditional analyses. See J. David Singer and Melvin Small, "Formal Alliances, 1815–1939," *Journal of Peace Research,* III (1966), 18–19.

[12] In addition to Haas and Whiting, important theoretical analyses of alliances can be found in Hans Morgenthau, "Alliances in Theory and Practice," *Alliance Policy in the Cold War,* edited by Arnold Wolfers (Baltimore: Johns Hopkins Press, 1959); and in George Liska, *Nations in Alliance: The Limits of Interdependence* (Baltimore: Johns Hopkins Press, 1962).

concerning the ultimate success or failure of an alliance must rest on empirical examination, not theoretical hypothesizing. An examination of a few of the generalizations which pass for conventional wisdom in this area may be illustrative.

Even the most obvious commonplace—that the interests which unite the allies must be at least complementary, if not identical—is hardly of universal validity. The proposition itself is simplistic: only some of the interests of the two states must be complementary, and they need not be parallel. Each ally can be protecting a wholly different set of interests in joining an alliance. It may even be possible to posit successful alliances between states with predominantly antagonistic interests, such as an alliance aimed at the control of a state which one assumes is (potentially) hostile.

The other factors which presumably determine success or failure are much more ambiguous. Even if one grants their validity on a commonsensical level, they offer neither the analyst nor the policymaker much help in interpreting decisions made in the real world. One finds it hard to argue with the proposition that an alliance will be strengthened if each ally retains some measure of independent strength; or that there should be some equity in the distribution of benefits, risks and concessions; or that alliances with states possessing similar values, and similar conceptions of an acceptable distribution of power, stand more chance of success. But no aid is offered in making the discriminations which could give substance to these maxims. Similarly, the negative propositions offered to explain the failure of an alliance, such as constant concessions, the creation of counteralliances, and the freezing of the status quo, are of such generality that they too offer only minimal guidance.

Even if these generalizations were more than mere rules of thumb, their significance might still be vitiated by factors beyond the control of the allies. A change in the distribution of "real" power could take place. As Haas and Whiting point out, the transformation could occur in a variety of ways; for example, the basis of power could shift to a new element, like uranium, which would transfer power to those states which possessed it. The policymakers also might change, and the new leaders might pursue different goals. New Powers might emerge to threaten the interests of formerly hostile states.[13] All of these transformations could effect an alliance by making it useless or unnecessary or even dangerous.

As a highly contingent instrument of statecraft, alliances have proved very resistant to theorizing which proceeds much beyond translating common sense into political maxims.[14] Involved in a confusing and complex matrix of domestic and external policy, affected by the most specific as well as the most general events of any era, alliances seem fated to remain the subject either of generalizations which are too ambiguous to enlighten the analyst or of empirical studies which are too narrow to provide theoretical guidance. The gap between theory and history remains wide. The historians rarely generalize and the theorists rarely study the historical record accurately. It seems worthwhile, therefore, to attempt to narrow that gap by explicitly deriving generalizations from a wide range of empirical studies. On a small scale, something of that nature is involved in this book.

It may be appropriate to end this introductory discussion of alliances by returning to the general theme of this book: the differences between Great Powers and Small Powers. The way in which an alliance is maintained is, of course, by consultation between partners. In theory, each ally ought to be consulted according to the degree to which an issue affects it, and according to the amount of power it can bring to bear on the solution of the issue.[15] However, if the alliance is between unequal partners, for example, a Great Power and a Small Power, ambiguities arise from the fact that each ally will operate on the basis of different perspectives. The Small Power may be vitally affected by an issue, yet have only minimal amounts of power to affect its outcome. As a result, it em-

---

[13] Haas and Whiting, *Dynamics of International Relations*, pp. 160–85.

[14] Thus two leading theorists have recently concluded, *inter alia*, that an alliance minimizes the range of issues over which a state will conflict with an ally, and it minimizes the intensity of such conflicts as do exist. And it increases the range and intensity of conflicts with non-alliance actors. One is struck by the extent to which the conclusions are commonplaces of the much-derided literature of diplomatic history (although of course the language is considerably different). Cf. Karl Deutsch and J. David Singer, "Multipolar Power Systems and International Stability," *World Politics*, XVI (April 1964), 396.

[15] Liska, *Nations in Alliance*, p. 76.

phasizes one of the two criteria just noted, to the detriment of the
other: the Small Power insists on its right to be consulted, but de-
emphasizes the relevancy of the power contribution it can make.
There is, therefore, from the very beginning an intrinsic asymmetry between Great Powers and Small Powers on the question of
the proper way to maintain an alliance. The Small Power demands consultation as an absolute right, whereas the Great Power
prefers relating its willingness to consult to the ability of its ally
to contribute to a solution in material terms.

The problem of conflicting perspectives is only one part of the
asymmetry between unequal partners in an alliance: it can be
extended in terms of the power commitment itself. A Small Power
allied with a Great Power may commit a proportionately larger
amount of its available power to the goals of the alliance. If it did
not, its material contribution would be virtually nonexistent.[16]
But having committed nearly all of its power to the alliance, it must
seek an alliance commitment wide enough to cover all the threats
to which it might be exposed. It cannot afford to commit so much
of its power to one alliance, unless the alliance promises complete
protection. Its Great Power ally, with interests and responsibilities
in a variety of areas, may seek a narrowly conceived alliance in
order to be free to use its noncommitted (i.e., to that alliance)
power elsewhere. This divergent conception of the range the alliance is expected to operate in, resting as it does on a basic difference in the scope of interests, may lead to difficulties in making the
alliance operate. The Small Power, with limited capabilities but a
total commitment (in terms of the capabilities it does have and the
extent of the threat to it), seems bound to seek an alliance in which
its ally closes the gap between concern and capabilities; the Great
Power, with large capabilities but only a partial commitment,
seems bound to seek an alliance in which the gap between concern
and capabilities is narrowed, but not to the detriment of its other
interests.

The preceding generalizations are not universally valid. The
extent to which they are likely to lead to real problems depends,
for the most part, on the immediate nature of the external threat

16 *Ibid.*

the alliance is designed to counter. The more extensive the threat, the easier it is to narrow the gap; the less extensive or dangerous, the more likely the allies are to risk intra-alliance friction in order to attain their own goals.

Choosing an Ally

In general, all states tend to ally for the same reasons. The ends they hope to secure can usually be subsumed under one of the categories listed in the preceding section. The differences between Great Powers and Small Powers on this issue concern matters of emphasis rather than substance. The questions they ask and the factors they weigh are identical, but Small Powers may consider one set of answers more significant than another in a manner which sets them apart, to a degree, from Great Powers.

In a theoretical sense, the most decisive differences between Great Powers and Small Powers, in terms of alliance policy, emerge on two other questions: the choice of allies (which will be discussed in this section), and the choice of a specific kind of alliance (which will be discussed at the end of the next two chapters). Historically, the answer to both questions has been heavily conditioned by circumstance. The search for the "best" ally and the "best" kind of alliance can hardly be carried on without examining the nature of the environment in which the choice has to be made. Something of that sort will be attempted in Part II—the range of options open to Small Powers will be related to the specific nature of the international system.

In terms of the historical analysis, all that can be said with any degree of certainty is that the options open to Small Powers have changed in response to changes in the international system, and that those options have consistently differed, at least to some degree, from those open to Great Powers. If that is *all* that can usefully be said about Great Powers and Small Powers, beyond filling in the historical details, the possibility of generalizing about Small Powers as unique entities, or of defining Small Powers in general, is nil. If the historical record is binding, only definitions which are limited and specific can be established, that is, a Small Power between the years X and Y fulfills a certain condition. The only possibility of transcending this difficulty—and it is a difficulty *if* Small Powers are really unique entities, and not simply Great Powers writ small—is by deliberately seeking differences between Great Powers and Small Powers which persist over time, no matter what the nature of the environment may be. Rather than examining the relationship between Great Powers and Small Powers in specific systems, the order of analysis must be altered: differences must be sought on an abstract level.

The remainder of this chapter and the concluding sections of the next two chapters offer a number of general propositions about various differences between Great Powers and Small Powers; the propositions rest on the historically absurd but analytically useful assumption of *ceteris paribus*. They may sound more rigorous and, in a sense, Machiavellian than they are meant to be, but they are offered only to illustrate the possibility that on an abstract level Small Powers and Great Powers are different kinds of entities. The fact that specific circumstances may make any of these propositions unrealistic is beyond dispute. The essential question is whether the propositions are theoretically useful and internally coherent.

The qualities which a prospective ally ought to possess seem obvious enough, at least on the surface. An ally should be powerful enough to offer substantial material support; and not possess interests which preclude the use of that power on behalf of the alliance. A common ideology may facilitate matters, but it is not imperative since sufficiently important common interests can overcome the difficulties inherent in conflicting ideologies.[17]

This seems reasonable enough. It would be difficult, perhaps even pointless, to dispute the contention that prospective allies

---

[17] Haas and Whiting, *Dynamics of International Relations*, p. 168. Any other factors which could influence the choice of an ally seem of secondary importance —in a theoretical sense. For example, it seems impossible to forecast the influence geography should exert on any decision, short of knowledge of the specific circumstances. The point seems to be that all factors other than those noted in the text are idiosyncratic; they cannot be evaluated in any meaningful sense without knowledge of all the environmental conditions.

ought to be powerful and willing to use their power in behalf of the alliance. Nevertheless, even if these propositions are so obvious that they appear banal, they are less valid for Small Powers than they are for Great Powers. The perspective from which Small Powers view the problems of security may make them reluctant to ally *solely* on the basis of power and interest. The point holds true, at least to some extent, even in the limiting case: in the situation where a Small Power perceives the threat that it faces in an immediate military sense. In the circumstance, it appears bound to seek the aid of the strongest available Great Power. However, reluctance to accept the obvious criteria as decisive, a reluctance which probably perforce will be overcome in light of the nature of the threat, rests on a theoretical perception of ancient lineage. Alliance with superior power is inherently dangerous for a Small Power.[18] The outcome may differ very little from the effect of merely procrastinating. The Small Power may move not from insecurity to security, but from insecurity to the status of a satellite.

Therefore superior power may be an attraction in an ally only for a Great Power. Small Powers, insofar as they have a choice, may prefer to gamble on a less powerful ally or on a combination of lesser states. This qualification obtains even more acutely if the Small Power seeks primarily political goals from the alliance, or if it does not perceive the Great Power threat as immediate. For example, to earn political capital, the Small Power may prefer a weaker, but more distant, ally to a powerful neighbor. The latter offers military advantages, if only in being accessible, but political disadvantages in terms of intervention and accusations of dependency. Even in military terms, the Small Power may not gain very much. As the weakest link in the alliance, it may become the

---

[18] The danger of unequal alliances has been recognized from Machiavelli onward. However, the historical record does *not* yield as much proof of the validity of the warning as one might suspect: that is, Small Powers, alone or in unequal alliances, have tended to survive more readily than might be presumed. Although the theoretical perception probably requires qualification, it appears to be taken seriously by Small Power statesmen, perhaps because of the stark nature of the evidence which does exist (e.g., the partition of Poland), or perhaps because it is convenient to do so.

preliminary target of an enemy attack. Moreover, if a Small Power is primarily interested in the alliance commitment per se (as is frequently the case in unequal alliances), but fears the intervention that might go with it, it may prefer an ally whose interests actually preclude it from using *all* its strength on behalf of the alliance. In any case, from the point of view of a Small Power, the existence of apparently identical interests may be no more than a facade behind which the stronger enforces an identical foreign policy. Finally, a Small Power might prefer to align itself on the basis of ideology, to the detriment of power and interest, in order to avoid an internal crisis or external reprobation—at least until a threat dangerous enough to submerge ideological predilections appears.

These examples may appear somewhat strained, but only to the extent that they attempt to reflect the ambiguities of a complex situation. The point can be more easily summarized than it can be demonstrated. The traditional rules of power may run differently for Great Powers and Small Powers. A Small Power is forced by the nature of its situation to constantly appraise considerations which need not (though they *might*) affect a Great Power's decision to ally: considerations of status, intervention, independence, and so forth. An alliance between a Great Power and a Small Power may also involve an inherent difficulty arising from the extent of their interests. The Great Power tends to ally in terms of a threat to the balance of the whole system; the Small Power in terms of a threat to its local balance. Inevitably, conflicts in perspective emerge. If the local threat also happens to affect the wider balance, the Small Power may find its interests sacrificed or it may lose much of its ability to influence the situation. On the other hand, if the local threat does not appear to affect the wider balance, it may be ignored until it does. In both cases, the ability of the Small Power to achieve its goals by virtue of an alliance with a Great Power is considerably attenuated.

The extent to which Small Powers "read" the rules of power somewhat differently may also be illustrated by noting their reaction in certain crises. Maurice Ash has argued:

. . . that the degree of alliance between states will become greater, the greater is the tension of relationships—that is, the higher is the general level of armaments. For as conditions of high tension develop, the more difficulty will each state experience in maintaining any given level of power, and therefore the more resort there will be to alliances and the help which they afford.[19]

If this proposition holds true for Small Powers, its significance should be clear. As tension rises, Small Powers should be striving to make their military commitments more automatic, to increase their General Staff consultations with their allies, to improve their communications, and so forth. However, the historical record belies the theoretical forecast. Before both the First and Second World Wars, Small Powers reacted in a number of ways, but only rarely in the manner Ash has suggested. For example, in confronting the threat of Hitler after 1933, Small Powers made every effort to loosen their commitments, not tighten them. The reasons were obvious enough. They were either allied with Great Powers who were weak and about to be attacked, or with Small Powers who could offer no military support.[20] It is clear that Ash's proposition has to be qualified or amended since it does not accurately reflect the behavior of Small Powers, behavior which is unique because it rests on a perspective which is itself unique.

Theoretically, power and interest, with the qualifications noted, suffice as the criteria by which to choose an ally. Historically, availability must be added. Belgium had every reason to desire some formal tie with Great Britain after 1919. Great Britain and France had every reason to desire an alliance with the United States. But in both instances to no avail: Great Britain remained true to its traditional policy toward alliances, and the United States was bent on remaining uncontaminated by European politics. The result was that the "ideal" allies were unavailable, and alliance-seekers had to settle for second or third best. Technically, this point could be ignored in a theoretical analysis. Power, interest, and ideology tell us who *ought* to be allied with, not who *can* be allied with. Nevertheless, the unavailability (for whatever reason)

---

[19] Maurice A. Ash, "An Analysis of Power, with Special Reference to International Politics," *World Politics*, (Jan. 1951), p. 234.

[20] Cf. Nils Ørvik, *The Decline of Neutrality, 1914–1941* (Oslo: Johan Grundt Tanum Forlag, 1953), *passim*, for confirmation.

of the "best" ally, the constant necessity to seek the best *possible* partner, seems so recurring a feature of the historical record (particularly from the point of view of Small Powers) that it deserves mention even in a discussion concerned with abstract propositions.

CHAPTER 3

Belgium and France, 1919–1936, and the Nature of Unequal Alliances

T HE TREATIES OF 1839, by which Belgium had received its independence, had been conceived as a barrier to France. They had left Belgium virtually defenseless. The strategic decisions concerning Limburg, Luxembourg, and the Escaut had all been determined in favor of the Netherlands.[1] By way of compensation, and in hopes of stabilizing a dangerous situation, the Great Powers guaranteed the independence of both small countries. Though the Belgians accepted the *"diktat"* of 1839 with great reluctance, in the ensuing years they came to value a status which relieved them of the responsibilities involved in insuring their own security.

Belgium and the Security Problem, 1919–1936

In 1870, when France and Prussia were on the verge of war, Great Britain extracted a promise from both to leave neutral Belgium untouched. The Belgians were saved and the war passed

This chapter was completed before the recent publication of five volumes of Belgian diplomatic papers covering the years 1920–1940. I have, however, consulted the first three volumes, and have added various material to the text and notes from them. I was not able to find the last two volumes; at any rate, only the first part of volume four is directly related to this case study. Nothing in the first three volumes adds materially to a new understanding of Belgian policy in this period: for whatever reason, the volumes have apparently been edited to avoid controversy, and to confirm what is already known through other sources.

[1] See *Le dossier diplomatique de la question belge; recueil des pieces officielles, avec notes,* edited by Fernand van Langenhove. (Paris: Ministry of Foreign Affairs, 1917), *passim.*

them by. The guarantee had been tested, and it had not been found wanting. The Belgians' achievement of noninvolvement and non-immolation created a state of euphoria in the country. The necessity of maintaining a strong Belgian army disappeared, for clearly "the expense would be unnecessary, since the country would be defended by the Great Powers who had signed the treaty of neutrality." [2] The Belgians presumed that future challenges would elicit equally prompt support from the Great Powers. Their optimism was misplaced, for they failed to comprehend the significance of the changes which occurred in European politics after 1870.

Belgium's greatest fear was another war in which either France or Germany would use her territory as a corridor. For more than forty years, until they finally blundered into catastrophe, the two Great Powers coexisted in a state of latent or high tension. If war broke out, only a repetition of the miracle of 1870 could save the Belgians. That is, Great Britain would once again have to intervene to protect them. The Belgians assumed that this would happen. The possibility that Great Britain might not intervene was not considered, for all the alternatives were too painful to contemplate.

What the Belgians did not see, of course, was that the political situation in Europe was drastically altered when Great Britain and France drew together. The guarantee of the British could no longer be effective. They had chosen a side, and could no longer protect the Belgians by threatening to fight against *any* aggressor who violated her neutrality. They were tied to France; henceforth, Germany would lose nothing by attacking across Belgium. No matter where Germany attacked France, Great Britain would line up against it. This made it almost certain that the Germans would choose the preferred route over the Meuse.[3] The legal status of Belgium's guarantee continued unchanged, but the political equilibrium which had facilitated the original guarantee had so altered that a significant gap existed between the words of the treaty and

[2] Jane K. Miller, *Belgian Foreign Policy Between Two Wars, 1919–1940* (New York: Bookman Associates, 1951), p. 23.

[3] Henri Rolin, *La Belgique Neutre?* (Brussels: Maison Ferdinand Larcier, 1937), pp. 110–11.

the reality of a new distribution of power. The guarantee had been given by five Great Powers; by 1870, it had become a guarantee by one Great Power; by 1914, it was a useless, if not pernicious, anachronism from an earlier era.

Nevertheless, the Belgians acted as if the world had changed scarcely at all, at least since 1870. Neutrality, a viable policy only when a relative equilibrium existed among the Great Powers, became a millstone. It paralyzed Belgian military and foreign policy to an unbelievable extent. As Hymans, the Foreign Minister in 1919, maintained, it deluded the Belgians and hindered their ability to understand foreign affairs, so much so that efforts to improve the national defenses were inevitably delayed or defeated.[4]

This became clear only after the First World War began, for "as late as July 1914, the vast majority of Belgians continued to believe that however disturbed Europe might be, the treaties of 1839 would protect them from war."[5] They were sublimely confident of the virtues of a regime which had lost its utility. When they suddenly found themselves served with a German ultimatum in August 1914, they were shocked and outraged. After all, von Bethmann-Hollweg's infamous "scrap of paper" was the very foundation of their existence. Moreover, that treaty which had been conceived as a barrier to France now served as an access to Germany. The strategic decision to bolster the Netherlands against France by giving her Limburg, Luxembourg, and the control of the Escaut backfired. Belgium was hopelessly defenseless, for everyone had forgot to turn the barrier around.

Under the circumstances, it was inevitable that the Belgians would begin to ponder the question of security again. The long years of the war provided an opportunity for a "great debate" in

[4] Paul Hymans, *Memoires* (Brussels: Editions de l'Institute de Sociologie Solvay, 1958), p. 283. Not all Belgians were unperceptive about the significance of the formation of the Anglo-French entente. Some statesmen were very worried about England's intentions, and were fearful that England would not repeat the "miracle" of 1870—that in fact premature British intervention in Belgium in support of France would turn the country into a battlefield. See Jonathan C. Helmreich, "Belgian Concern over Neutrality and British Intentions, 1906–14," *The Journal of Modern History*, XXXVI (December 1964), 416–27.

[5] Miller, *Belgian Foreign Policy*, p. 23.

political circles. The old system of guaranteed neutrality was unreservedly condemned, and the servitudes imposed by the treaties of 1839 were excoriated for the harm they had done. But the question of what could replace them was not easily answered.

The Quest for Security During the War

The Belgians were forced to make a number of critical decisions early in the war years. The first concerned the position they ought to adopt toward their allies. Should they become a full-fledged partner in the coalition, or should they insist on their unique status and remain outside wartime agreements like the Pact of London? Technically, the Belgians felt they were still a neutral state, but one defending its neutrality. The King and government-in-exile at La Havre thus opted for a strictly legal position. They refused to sign any of the treaties or to bargain for any concessions.[6]

The decision to insist on a separate but equal status had very little to do with the legal requisites of neutrality; it was clearly politically motivated. The Belgians simply felt that they would gain more at the end of the war by retaining their unique status, a status which constantly reminded the observer of their injured innocence—or so it seemed at the time. Thus Baron Beyens, the Foreign Minister, maintained that Belgium ought to avoid alliances, for an alliance "aurait fait perdre à la Belgique sa situation de nation défendant sa neutralité violée, qu'il était si important de lui conserver . . . . Elle serait tombée au rang des belligérants ordinaires . . . ."[7]

These arguments were essentially spurious. Belgium, whatever its legal status, was an ally of the Entente Powers once the war began. Its fate was intimately tied to theirs and the absence of a formal treaty did not make it less so. The existence of an alliance would have endowed Belgium's initial war aims with a legitimacy they did not otherwise possess. Moreover, Belgium could have capitalized on the higher status it enjoyed in the first years of the

---

[6] Emile Cammaerts, *Albert of Belgium: Defender of Right* (New York: The Macmillan Company, 1935), pp. 245–46.

[7] Baron Beyens, "Deux Politiques," *Le Flambeau* (April 30, 1922), 410–11.

conflict. The Government committed a singular error of judgment, particularly for a Small Power: it failed to act when opportunity was greatest. When the war ended, none of the Belgian demands had been met. The Belgians were forced to negotiate everything—security, reparations, revision of the Treaties of 1839—with the dwindling capital of forgotten heroics.[8]

Belgium also had to decide what territorial demands it would make; and, having determined that, what form any future security arrangement ought to take. Overtly, they sought very little from the war: the reestablishment of the status quo, compensation for damages, and guarantees against a repetition of the disaster of 1914.[9] To the Allied Governments, their position was a trifle more specific. They demanded complete independence, as well as favorable decisions on the questions of the Escaut, Limburg, and Luxembourg, but not annexation.[10] In reality Belgium's war aims were more grandiose. By the time of the peace conference the Government was heavily committed to an annexationist policy.[11] However, the latter aims were denied or hidden because of divisions in the Government, fear of the Dutch reaction, and a desire to appear untainted by baser motives. Belgian war aims thus became a function of whom the Government was talking to, and not of what it really desired.

The result was that the discussion of security occurred in a strange kind of vacuum. On the one hand, it was obvious that the Government wanted favorable decisions on the three key issues of Luxembourg, Limburg, and the Escaut. They had sound arguments to support their case. The danger now came from the other direction, and the rationale for leaving Belgium defenseless had disappeared. More compelling still was the impossibility of compensating for Belgium's weakness by resurrecting the old guarantee. Only Great Britain and France could resume their role. Whether

[8] For an incisive critique of Beyens' position, see Baron Pierre van Zuylen, *Les Mains Libres: Politique Extérieure de la Belgique, 1917–1940* (Paris: Desclée de Brouwer, 1950), pp. 11–14.

[9] Cammaerts, *Albert of Belgium*, p. 260.

[10] Robert Fenaux, *Paul Hymans: Un Homme, Un Temps, 1865–1941* (Brussels: Office de Publicité, n.d.), p. 102.

[11] Miller, *Belgian Foreign Policy*, p. 72.

they did so or not, it was in their own interest to strengthen Belgium. However, the discussion of these issues had to be put off until the Peace Conference. And the Belgians were even forced to disavow to the Dutch any future territorial demands.[12] It was a patently absurd situation. As Hymans later pointed out, "La révision des traités de 1839 fut la politique de la securité." [13] But revision could not be discussed because the Belgians were unable to decide what and how they wanted it to come about, and so were then forced to disavow it completely.

Thus the wartime discussions of security were essentially irrelevant. They were concerned with form; the substance was left to the peace. There was complete agreement on only one thing: the necessity of abandoning neutrality and revising the Treaties of 1839.[14] As the Government noted, neutrality ". . . serait une diminution de leur souveraineté, un moyen de protection illusoire, enfin, un prétexte pour l'Allemagne de s'ingèrer dans nos affaires." [15] The difficulty was that France, and Great Britain to a lesser extent, was still partial to the idea of a neutral Belgium. As Cambon told Beyens:

. . . une Belgique neutre, c'était un moyen de défense contre l'Allemagne, un moyen qu'on pouvait renforcer après la guerre en exigeant de nos ennemis communs des garanties plus sévères et plus strictes pour le respect de cette neutralité.[16]

To France, any change in Belgium's status implied an independent Belgium which could follow any policy it wished, perhaps even a pro-German policy. To England, a neutral Belgium was removed from the power struggle. It was safe to guarantee it; whereas an

[12] Thus Baron Beyens assured the Dutch that "the government of the King energetically disapproves of the intrigues directed against the integrity of Netherlands territory." Quoted in Ibid.

[13] Hymans, Memoires, p. 296.

[14] Count Capelle, Au Service du Roi (Brussels: Charles Dessart, 1949), p. 176.

[15] Hymans, Memoires, p. 178.

[16] Ibid., p. 167: ". . . a neutral Belgium was a means of defense against Germany, a means that one would be able to reinforce after the war, by demanding from our common enemies stricter and more stringent guarantees that they would respect that neutrality." This translation is mine. I have provided a translation of major quotations. In other instances, especially where the sense of the passage is obvious from the context, I have left the original untranslated.

independent Belgium could follow an adventurist policy, and draw England after it. There were, nevertheless, many Belgians who were against neutrality in any form, though for a variety of reasons.[17]

If neutrality was undesirable, and self-reliance an illusion, there appeared to be only one alternative left. Monsieur de Bassompierre, Director-General of Politics in the Foreign Ministry, outlined it clearly in a note dated October 1917. Belgium, he said, could obtain unfettered independence, and some guarantee of security, only if the Great Powers:

> . . . sont certains qu'en cas de nouvelle guerre nous serons à leur côtes contre l'Allemagne. Cette certitude ne peut leur être donnée que si nous leur faisons savoir clairement que nous serons prêts à prendre des engagements précis à cet égard. . . . Des accords militaires avec la France et l'Angleterre sont la condition indispensable de notre libération de la neutralité.[18]

A military accord with London and Paris would assure Belgium support against a new German aggression. It would also assure the Great Powers that an independent Belgium could play a part in maintaining the European balance against Germany. Such an agreement would both satisfy the Great Powers and insure Belgium all the advantages of full sovereignty.

The discussions heretofore had concerned only the form which the future security arrangements ought to take. It was necessary to correlate them with the decisions which were to be taken on the question of security, and the closely related question of the revision of the Treaties of 1839, at the peace conference. Consequently the preliminary decision to rely on military accords to placate the Great Powers was very provisional. What ultimately resulted was bound to be heavily dependent on events and decisions over which the Belgians had little control.

[17] *Ibid.*, pp. 174–77.

[18] *Ibid.*, p. 170: ". . . are certain that in the event of a new war we will be at their side against Germany. That certainty can be given to them only if we make it clearly known that we are ready to make precise commitments in this sense. . . . Military accords with France and England are the indispensable condition of our liberation from neutrality."

Belgium and the Peace Conference

In January 1919, before the Peace Conference had met, the Belgian Government released a *Memoire* which outlined its principal demands.[19] It very definitely committed the Government to an annexationist policy, but it was not without its ambiguities. There could be no doubt, however, that the earlier policies, which had not gone much beyond adjustments in the antebellum status quo, were superseded.

The *Memoire* argued quite cogently that "La système a donc fait faillite et les motifs qui ont déterminé les Belges à accepter les traités de 1839 ont cessé d'exister. . . ." It pointed out the harm done by the strategic decisions of 1839 and declared, somewhat tendentiously, that "Ce simple exposé montre que la guerre a été la faillite de l'oeuvre de 1839 dans toutes ses parties." [20] Obviously, they had to be revised.

Unfortunately, the specific proposals which the *Memoire* outlined were not as sound and convincing as the general argument that revision was necessary. The ambiguity arose primarily from the continued division within the Government. The Socialists and the Flemish were staunchly antiannexationist, though for different reasons. They were reinforced in their objections by other factors, particularly the specific disavowal accorded to the Dutch in 1916, and the general ethos of the time which was hardly favorable to strategic demands. The Belgian demands were completely strategical, for the desired areas were manifesting no inclination to become Belgian. It was hardly surprising, then, to find the *Memoire* greeted in silence. A document which revealed so much of the confusion underlying Belgian policy was unlikely to elicit a serious response from the Great Powers.

The Belgians were even more disillusioned when they learned that they were to be excluded from the Council of Ten. If the war had proved anything at all, at least from the Belgian point of view,

[19] See van Zuylen, *Les Mains Libres,* pp. 29–35.
[20] *Ibid.,* p. 30: "The system has failed and the motives which led the Belgians to accept the treaties of 1839 have ceased to exist. . . ."

it was that the war ". . . avait porté la Belgique sur un plan nouveau: elle n'était plus un petit État." [21] It was disturbing, disconcertingly so, to find that this sentiment had not yet reached universal proportions. The Belgians responded vigorously, and led the fight of the states with "intérêts limités" against the arbitrary dictates of the Council of Ten (or, more correctly, the Council of Nine, Five, Four, or Three). They were more successful than their predecessors at Vienna in 1815, but not enough to make much difference.

The crucial question for which the Belgians sought an answer at the peace conference concerned the means by which their new independence could be guaranteed. The wartime discussions had evolved from voluntary neutrality to military accords with Great Britain and France. For the moment, these suggestions were all forgot. The debate had taken a different turn.

France and Belgium, in contrast to the United States, were unanimous on one point. Security demanded something more than affirmations of faith in the untested League of Nations. France, of course, did manage to extract some concessions from its allies: the Rhineland was to be occupied for fifteen years and permanently demilitarized, Germany's army was limited to 100,000 men, and Great Britain and the United States guaranteed her against renewed German aggression. The three Great Powers also agreed that in the event of a German attack Belgium was to be considered part of France. An attack on Belgium would call the guarantee into operation as surely as an attack on France.

Nevertheless, the Belgians were not entirely satisfied. By 1919, they were seeking stronger foundations for Belgium's security. More precisely, they demanded better strategic frontiers and the double guarantee of France and Great Britain.[22] The guarantee was to be direct, rather than indirect. However, only the question

---

[21] Fernand van Langenhove, "La Politique Internationale de la Belgique après la première Guerre Mondiale," in Henri Pirenne, *Histoire de Belgique* (Brussels: La Renaissance du Livre, 1952), p. 17: ". . . had lifted Belgium to a new level: she was no longer a small state."

[22] Van Zuylen, *Les Mains Libres*, p. 50.

of strategic revision requires discussion, for the idea of a Great Power guarantee assumed significance only in the months following the end of the peace conference.

The quest for revision can be quickly summarized. The Council of Ten created a "Commission des Affaires belges," comprising representatives of the five Great Powers, which was asked to study the possibility of various territorial adjustments. Despite a sharp reaction on the part of the Dutch Government, which insisted that it would not accede to any cession of territory, the Commission reached the conclusion that the treaties of 1839 had to be completely revised "supprimer . . . les risques et les inconvénients divers résultant des dits Traités." [23]

The apparent Belgian triumph was shortlived, for the substance of the revisions still remained to be negotiated—and neither the Dutch nor, to the surprise of the Belgians, the British and French supported the Belgian demands. Hymans' argument was quite simple. If neutrality was gone, the whole system of 1839 was gone with it. Belgium had accepted that system solely because her security had been guaranteed by the Great Powers. Now that security had disappeared: therefore, the strategic servitudes had to be eliminated. Moreover, since the danger now came from the north, and not from France, Belgium needed new frontiers.

The Dutch met Hymans' demands with a flat rejection. Belgium, the Dutch delegate insisted, could get its security from the League. The negotiations were at an impasse. Finally, for want of an alternative, the whole affair was sent back to the Supreme Council just before the Peace Conference was to terminate. Their hurried decision crushed Belgian hopes. The Commission was ordered to submit "propositions n'impliquant ni transfert de souveraineté nationale, ni creation de servitudes internationales." [24] The decision marked the end of any Belgian hopes that their security could be augmented by revision of their frontiers. Whatever the inequities of the territorial decisions of 1839, the Belgians would simply have to live with them.

[23] Hymans, *Memoires*, p. 380: "in order to suppress the various risks and inconveniences resulting from the said treaties."

[24] *Ibid.*, p. 487.

Why had Belgium failed to receive any of its strategic demands at Paris? One reason, of course, was the general unpopularity at the time of frontier revision, except on the grounds of self-determination: the cession of the Brenner to Italy notwithstanding. Some blame can be attributed to the diplomatic blunders of the Belgians themselves. They entered the Peace Conference with no commitments of support, their demands had not been sounded in allied capitals, and they soon found themselves forgotten and pushed aside in the hectic weeks of peacemaking.

Ultimately, however, the answer must be found in the attitudes of the other powers. Wilson was unfriendly, the Dutch were obdurate, and even Great Britain and France were ambivalent in offering support. The British opposed concessions on the Escaut, fearing that German submarines would be based there in any future war. Worse yet, they feared that a strong Belgium under French hegemony would help the latter to crush Germany forever. The French, on the other hand, favored Belgian demands on the Escaut and in Limburg, but opposed them in Luxembourg. They preferred to control the tiny Grand Duchy themselves. In addition, French support was always limited by a desire to entice the Dutch into their web of alliances. Faced with strong opposition from Wilson and the Dutch, and supported halfheartedly by its allies, Belgium came away empty-handed.[25]

Belgium's situation in June of 1919 was not satisfactory, but neither was it tragic. It was true that the guarantees in the Peace Treaty, particularly those in the Covenant, were still hypothetical. It was true that the tripartite treaty might not be ratified. And it was true that a renewal of the old guarantee by Great Britain and France was regarded as unsatisfactory on all sides: the Great Powers because they preferred to guarantee a neutral Belgium, and Belgium because it despised neutrality and feared domination by her two guarantors. But the environment was not immediately threatening. Belgium would have time to repair its losses, "le temps d'aviser."

[25] See *ibid.*, pp. 356–57; and van Zuylen, *Les Main Libres*, p. 75.

The Origins of the Franco-Belgian Military Accord

The concert of Europe was not restored after the First World War, as it had been after the Congress of Vienna. That simple fact enormously complicated Belgium's quest for security. The whole axis of its policy had to be shifted, and it had to be done in a particularly difficult period of history.

If the three fallen Empires, or even Germany alone, had been restored to their rightful status, the problem would have been less complicated. Belgium might still have rejected permanent neutrality, but it is unlikely that any new policy would have gone much beyond voluntary neutrality—a shift in form, but not in substance.

As it was, her position was difficult. A return to her old status was impossible, because of the absence of sufficient guarantors and because of the objections of popular opinion. Yet she was still constricted by the harmful stipulations of the old treaties. The first task at hand was the elimination of those servitudes, and much of the summer of 1919 was devoted to negotiations to revise the treaties of 1839. The negotiations were unsuccessful: the Dutch were still obdurate, her erstwhile allies still ambivalent.[26]

The Belgians had always been aware that revision of the treaties of 1839 was not, by itself, a sufficient guarantee of security. It might facilitate it, but it would hardly assure it. Therefore it was still necessary to seek a Great Power guarantee, whatever the fate of revision.

The two treaties between Great Britain, France, and the United States indirectly covered Belgium. However the Belgians would have no part at all in the operation of either treaty. Moreover, the United States appeared to have only a small stake in Belgium's security.

Thus the Belgians sought a parallel treaty of their own with the British and the French. It was to be, as the British Ambassador in Brussels reported, "a defensive alliance in the case of unprovoked attack upon Belgium . . . on the same lines as the arrangement

[26] See van Zuylen, *Les Main Libres,* pp. 88ff.

between Great Britain, France and the United States in regard to France." [27] Curzon, however, warned the Belgians "not to be surprised if serious difficulties were found to exist." [28] It is worth pointing out that Belgian policy had finally come full circle from permanent neutrality, through voluntary neutrality, to technical military accords, and finally to an alliance. It would soon begin to reverse itself.

By the late autumn several things were clear. Belgian boundaries were going to remain the same, except for the minor acquisitions of Eupen and Malmedy. The guarantee-treaty was unlikely to be ratified in the United States Senate. In addition, Belgian efforts to extract a defensive alliance from Great Britain and France seemed doomed. It was clearly necessary to try a new tack. For the Belgians, that meant taking advantage of the fact that the Treaty of Versailles had left the guarantee implicit in the system of 1839 still standing.

On October 18, 1919, Hymans called in the British ambassador and suggested that, while the revision of the treaties of 1839 was proceeding, Belgian security should be guaranteed by the British and French Governments. They would simply consent to retain as operative those clauses of the treaties of 1839 which guaranteed the independence and integrity of Belgium.[29] The Belgian suggestion was soon expanded. The guarantee was now to extend past the ratification of any agreement on revision until the League of Nations could provide fresh guarantees for Belgium's security. The Belgians declared that they would not agree to any new arrangements until they were satisfied on the question of security.[30]

[27] *Documents on British Foreign Policy, 1919–1939*, edited by E. L. Woodward and Rohan Butler (London: H. M. Stationery Office, 1946–1966), 1st Series, Vol. II, No. 36, July 26, 1919.

[28] *Ibid.*, No. 122, Sept. 9, 1919, p. 491.

[29] *Ibid.*, No. 196, Oct. 28, 1919, pp. 734–75.

[30] *Ibid.*, No. 228, Nov. 10, 1919, pp. 781–74. Belgium's efforts to revise the treaties of 1839 can be followed in the recently published *Documents Diplomatiques Belges, 1920–1940*, edited by Ch. de Visscher and F. Van Langenhove (Brussels: Palais Des Academies, 1964), Vol. I: 1920–1924, pp. 33–106. Henceforth cited as *D.D.B.* On Belgium's insistence on retaining the guarantee of 1839 until she received new guarantees for her security, see especially pp. 39–45, and p. 55.

The French were favorable, and so too were the British, initially at least. Curzon at first advocated an interim guarantee to the Belgians, since it added no new obligations and also because an Anglo-French guarantee was an essential part of the proposed Belgian-Dutch accord.[31] But Curzon suddenly reversed himself, and declared that an interim guarantee was possible only if "the Belgian Government will give a guarantee for the neutrality of Belgium." [32] The Belgian reaction was predictable. They angrily declared that any suggestion of neutrality "would be regarded as an invitation . . . to Belgium to renew friendly relations with Germany." [33]

What prompted the British to set conditions they full well knew the Belgians would reject is a matter of conjecture. It may be presumed, however, that London's preference for a neutral Belgium reflected its consistent desire to keep Belgium from falling under French hegemony. Their policy succeeded only in forcing the Belgians to turn toward Paris to insure their security. In any case, Belgium rejected the British conditions on January 9, 1920 and abandoned its demand for a new guarantee.[34] As Hymans noted:

En réalité, aucun des textes . . . ne nous donnait l'assurance que des garanties supplémentaires viendraient s'ajouter aux garanties générales données par le Pacte de la Ligue des Nations. Ces textes ne maintenaient à la Belgique une garantie provisoire de la part de la France et de l'Angleterre que pour une courte période, celle précisément pendant laquelle l'occupation inter-alliée de toute la rive gauche du Rhin nous protège efficacement contre tout danger . . . et ils nous obligeaient à prendre . . . des engagements contraires à la dignité du pays.[35]

The Belgians demanded two things from the revision of the

[31] *Ibid.,* No. 274, Dec. 1, 1919, p. 882.
[32] *Ibid.,* No. 281, Dec. 2, 1919, p. 885; also D.D.B., I, 56.
[33] *Ibid.,* No. 286, Dec. 4, 1919, p. 885.
[34] *Ibid.,* No. 343, Jan. 9, 1920, p. 967.
[35] Quoted in van Zuylen, *Les Main Libres,* p. 94: "In reality, none of the texts . . . gave us the assurance that any supplementary guarantees would be added to the general guarantees given by the Covenant of the League of Nations. These texts gave Belgium a provisional guarantee from France and England for a short period, precisely that period during which the allied occupation of the left bank of the Rhine would protect us effectively against all dangers . . . and they obliged us to accept . . . commitments contrary to the dignity of the country."

treaties of 1839. They wanted the Dutch to declare that they would treat any violation of their territory as a *casus belli* and they wanted London and Paris to maintain their guarantee until an adequate substitute could be devised.[36] That substitute, according to the Belgians, could not come from any arrangement which required a prior determination by the Council of the League.[37] The Dutch refused to accept the Belgian demand, and London refused its role unless the Belgians accepted neutrality; and even the French response was ambiguous.[38]

The peace settlement had left the Belgians disillusioned and desperate. It was followed by the failure to achieve anything in terms of security from the Dutch negotiations. The demand for a defensive alliance with Great Britain and France had also fallen by the wayside, particularly after the rejection of the guarantee pact by the United States Senate. And now Belgium had to refuse an offer for an interim guarantee, because its terms were unacceptable.

The Belgians could have left the security question temporarily in suspense, for they were not in any immediate danger. They did not do so. By January 28, 1920, they had already begun to seek a military accord with France. The origins of that accord will be traced in the next section.

Throughout the First World War, the Quai d'Orsay had attempted to impress on the Belgian Government the need for an intimate association in the future. The French envisaged a complete entente involving both a customs union and a military alliance. The Belgians, however, in addition to the desire to avoid discussing such issues during the war, and thus compromising their virtue, also feared the effects of association with a much more powerful neighbor. The war ended with nothing decided. But it seems safe to assume that the Belgian conversion to the idea of a technical military accord owed something to French pressures for an even closer alignment. It may also be assumed that France's

---

[36] D.D.B., I, 67.
[37] For Belgian suspicions about the League, see *Ibid.*, pp. 88–89, 100.
[38] *Ibid.*, pp. 68–69.

ambiguous support of Belgian war aims had its origins in a desire to force the Belgian Government into the French orbit.

The idea of a military accord had been ignored during the Peace Conference and in the months immediately after; the Great Powers had other things in mind. However, by the last months of 1919, the international situation had been transformed in a significant way. The repudiation of the guarantee-treaty destroyed the keystone of France's security. She, too, began to cast about for new guarantees of security. Under the circumstances, it was hardly surprising that the two countries began to move together, and to resurrect old ideas about military ententes.

On December 23, 1919, Hymans publicly noted that one of the crucial tasks facing the Government in the months ahead was the conclusion of military accords with both Great Britain and France. He added one qualification. Nothing would be signed until Belgium had received satisfaction on the three issues of reparations, revision of the treaty of 1839, and Luxembourg.[39] The military accord, as Hymans noted, would be "le couronnement" of the other negotiations, and not a separate package.

The issue of Luxembourg stalled the negotiations with the Quai d'Orsay. The French insisted on maintaining control of the Luxembourg railroad network. But the Belgians refused to begin military conversations until their demands in Luxembourg were met. Ultimately a compromise emerged. The two governments would carry on parallel negotiations, but the military accord would not be signed until there was agreement on all other issues.

The difficulty was obvious. Luxembourg needed a new status after the First World War. The Belgians were quite clear on what it should be: annexation to Belgium. The French were ambivalent. They would have preferred to control the Grand Duchy them-

[39] See Hymans, Memoires, p. 534; and D.D.B., I, 92–94, 302–3. The origins of the accord are traced on pp. 302–447, but the published documents do not eliminate many of the obscurities which exist about the history of the negotiations of 1920. This may merely reflect the fact that documents can only reveal some aspects of any political decision; or it may reflect the difficulties of editing contemporary documentary collections when many of the participants are still alive or the issues covered are still matters of concern.

selves,[40] but not if it meant unduly antagonizing Belgium. In any event, they clearly intended to use the Luxembourg issue as a lever in extracting concessions from the Belgians. The Grand Duchy itself preferred a customs union with France, not Belgium. That factor, combined with French ambivalence, undoubtedly explains Belgium's decision to give up the idea of annexation and to accept a customs union (à deux) with the Grand Duchy.

The action of the United States Senate in rejecting the guarantee treaty transformed the situation. Henceforth, Belgium became a desirable, perhaps even necessary, ally of France—and the French became much more amenable to concessions on the Luxembourg issue, even though the French still intended to use it as a bargaining device in the ensuing negotiations.

Formal military talks opened early in April 1920. The French had promised the Belgians that they would invite the British to the General Staff discussions, but they had not done so. For the Belgians, British participation was important for more than military reasons, since they wanted to maintain agreement among the allies vis-à-vis Germany, as well as safeguard the equilibrium of their policy.[50] Hymans intended to invite the British himself. However, by April 6 the French had occupied five German cities in response to various German violations of the Peace Treaty and they asked the Belgians to participate in the occupation. After a great deal of hesitation, the Belgians decided to support France:[51] but that ac-

[40] Thus Berthelot told the Belgian Ambassador in 1916 that "Une partie du Palatinat tout au moins nous est nécessaire pour nous mettre à l'abri d'un retour des événements de 1914. Quant à l'annexion de Luxembourg, elle n'a pas été examinée. Mais je vous le répéte, vous ne feriez qu'affaiblir votre cause, la gâter même, en revenant sur cette question. . . ." Hymans, *Memoires*, p. 190. On French concern for Luxembourg's railroad network, see D.D.B., I, 324–28.

[50] Van Zuylen, *Les Main Libres*, p. 112; also D.D.B., I, 304, 355–57, 374–79.

[51] The Belgians insisted that they did not want to see a treaty infraction go unpunished or the French left in isolation. The real reason was different: "Ne pouvions-nous, par un acte de solidarité, nous procurer du côté francais des benefices politiques et positifs?" Hymans, *Memoires*, p. 544. Belgium, that is, sought France's gratitude—and with some success, since the French shortly thereafter informed Luxembourg that it would have to turn to Belgium for economic support. The crisis caused by France's decision is traced in detail in D.D.B., I, 107–301. Hymans' explanation for the decision is on pp. 241–42.

tion so antagonized the British that Hymans never extended the invitation. In the months ahead, the Belgians did try to interest London in the proposed accord, but with very little success—the British cabinet saw little purpose in signing an accord when there was no immediate danger of war.

Under increasing French pressure, the Belgians finally capitulated and agreed to sign an accord once its details were worked out, irrespective of whether the British also signed or agreement had been reached on the other issues separating the two countries. No one is quite certain what prompted the Belgian decision. Perhaps it was merely the result of months of unrelenting French pressure combined with months of diplomatic frustration for the Belgians. Hymans later insisted that French irritation at Belgium for prohibiting the transshipment of arms to the Polish Government was critical—"la conclusion rapide de l'accord militaire fut la compensation alloué à la France." [52] But the point still remains obscure because the Government had already yielded to the French demands before the Polish issue arose.[53] In any event, the process by which the Government finally agreed to sign the accord was clearly unusual. Consultations were limited to the Premier and the Minister of Defense, though it was only in later years that those who were not consulted protested.

The Military Accord, which was finally signed on September 7, 1920, was a masterpiece of ambiguity. The Belgians insisted that one statement in the covering letter justified their continuing assertions that Belgium had not become a French satellite:

Il va de soi que la souveraineté des deux États demeure intacte quant aux charges militaires qu'ils imposeront à leur pays respectifs et quant à l'appréciation, dans chaque cas, de la réalisation de l'éventualité en vue de laquelle le présent accord est conclu.[54]

---

[52] *Ibid.*, p. 570. French "concessions" (which turned out to be spurious) to Belgium at the Spa Conference in July apparently provided the occasion for the decision to yield to French pressures for rapid conclusion of the accord. See D.D.B., I, 400–1.

[53] Moreover, Hymans' own Ministry had been consulted during the course of the preliminary negotiations; and Hymans was an obvious Francophile, and unlikely to oppose the accord on that ground alone.

[54] Quoted in General van Overstraeten, *Albert I—Leopold III: Vingt Ans de*

The text of the accord itself was sufficiently ambiguous to vitiate any contention that Belgium was still a free agent. At the very least it was clear that allies with different purposes could legitimately draw different inferences from a number of clauses.

The original draft of the accord contained an explicit *casus foederis*: "l'aggression non provoquée, dirigée à la fois contre la France et la Belgique." The official version of the accord eliminated "à la fois" ("at once"). Hence the accord would come into operation if either Belgium or France were attacked separately. The dangerous implications of this omission became clear to the Belgians only after the French alliance system had been formally constructed. They began to realize, or suspect, that France intended to use their territory as an invasion route into the Ruhr. But they also feared that Germany might some day attack France, without simultaneously attacking Belgium, in order to retaliate for French support of Poland and the Little Entente.[55] The Belgians never conceived the problem conversely: Germany attacking Belgium alone. Nor did they assume that they had a stake in defeating Germany and upholding France, whatever the merits of the dispute. The Belgians, in 1920 as in 1936, simply wanted to remain out of any war. Whatever benefits they expected to receive from signing the accord, it apparently never occurred to them that it was an instrument clearly designed to limit or obscure whatever possibilities of non-involvement were open to them.

The other clause of the accord which engendered major problems declared that: "Pour répondre à une prise d'armes générales de l'Allemagne, les deux puissances s'engagent à décreter la mobilisation générale de leur forces." [56] The difficulty arose from the

---

Politique Militaire Belge (Paris: Desclée de Brouwer, n.d.), p. 36: "It goes without saying that the sovereignty of the two countries remains inviolate in reference to the military expenses they will impose on their respective countries and in reference to the estimation, in each case, of the realization of the eventuality in view of which the present accord is concluded." This book contains the first published copy of the treaty. The General was an important advisor to Leopold III and a vigorous opponent of the accord with France.

[55] See Hymans, *Memoires,* p. 603.

[56] Van Overstraeten, *Albert I—Leopold III*, p. 36: "In order to respond to a general mobilization by Germany, the two powers agree to order the general mobilization of their forces."

French interpretation. The French assumed that a period of diplomatic tension would require their entrance into Belgium. The Belgians assumed that the French would enter their country only when war broke out or, perhaps, on the eve of war—but certainly not when "diplomatic tension" was the prevalent condition.[57] The French clearly conceived the accord as something wider than a mere technical agreement, in fact as an alliance to bolster her eastern allies and to insure a defense of France as far to the North as possible. Though the Belgians were aware of the French interpretation, and diametrically opposed to it, they apparently preferred to live with it—at least until a threat arose—rather than risk the difficulties involved in clarifying or removing obvious discrepancies.

There were three other clauses which worried the Belgians. In one, the French and the Belgians arrogated to themselves the right to develop a defensive position on Luxembourg's eastern frontier. The Belgians, somewhat belatedly, were concerned about the possible effects of an arbitrary disregard of the Grand Duchy's sovereignty. Another clause entrusted the defense of the Belgian coast to the French navy, which made sense only on the presumption that Belgium and France were fighting Germany without the support of Great Britain. That, however, was the one condition above all others that Belgium wished to avoid. Finally, another clause stipulated that Belgium and France would maintain their occupation of the Rhineland as long as the execution of the Peace Treaty required it. If France and Great Britain clashed over the question of an early evacuation of the area, Belgium had apparently already cast her vote for France. In sum, the accord began to instruct Belgium in the difficulties of performing a balancing act between two Great Powers, when committed to one of them.

The Belgians, it may be recalled, had set certain conditions to be fulfilled before a military accord was concluded. They demanded, at the very least, the participation of Great Britain, a com-

---

[57] For the French interpretation, see Paul Reynaud, *In the Thick of the Fight, 1930–1945* (London: Cassell and Company Ltd., 1955), p. 152; also General Gamelin, *Servir* (Paris: Librarie Plon, 1946), II, 25, where he notes that the accord "dépassait en fait le cadre d'un simple accord militaire et avait une portée politique générale."

mercial treaty with France, and a satisfactory settlement of the Luxembourg question.[58] Yet, when the accord was actually signed, they had received only partial satisfaction on the Luxembourg issue, and no satisfaction at all on the other problems.

The agreement with Great Britain was particularly critical for a Small Power bent on pursuing a policy of "equilibrium" or "les main libres." [59] Nevertheless, the accord was signed, against the specific advice of Lloyd George's Government. Even if all of the preliminary conditions had been fulfilled, the accord which was negotiated could not have been justified. It was an ineptly drafted document bound to have deleterious effects both internally and externally.

On the internal scene, it aroused intense bitterness and suspicion on the part of the Flemish and the Socialists.[60] It became a symbol and weapon to various groups united only by their opposition to its terms. On the external scene, it elicited an extremely negative reaction from the Dutch, who accused the Belgians "d'être inféodée à la France et de rapprocher le danger de guerre des frontières hollandaises . . . ." [61] Moreover, it complicated relations with Great Britain, as noted previously, since it appeared as if the Belgians had cast their lot with France. And with France, the accord led to sixteen years of controversy, suspicion, and bitterness.

The French looked ahead to the period when Germany would regain full sovereignty. They saw that the only way in which they could effectively threaten Germany, and thus protect their eastern allies, was by being able to riposte through the Ruhr. Since it was obvious that Belgium had no intention of going to war with Ger-

[58] See van Zuylen, Les Main Libres, pp. 109–10.

[59] Thus van Zuylen notes that "sans l'appui de l'Angleterre, il n'existe pas de sécurité vraie pour la Belgique; sans l'Angleterre, l'accord militaire avec la France compromet la liberté et nous expose au danger d'être entraînes dans les enterprises extérieures de la République" (p. 132). For Lloyd George's fear that the accord was premature and that the French would use it as a cover to intervene in Germany in order to insure the execution of the Versailles Treaty, see D.D.B., I, 398–99.

[60] See Miller, Belgian Foreign Policy, pp. 182–83.

[61] J. Wullus-Rudiger, Les Origines Internationales du Drame Belge de 1940 (Brussels: Etablissements généraux d'imprimerie, 1950), p. 117.

many to protect French interests in the east, the French were left with only the one sound alternative of tying Belgium to herself in such a way that it would at least appear as *if* Belgium had given France the right to use her territory as a springboard over the Rhine.

After months of intense diplomatic pressure, a suitable instrument emerged: the Accord of 1920. The essentials were all there: a *casus foederis* which involved Belgium in any French war; an exchange of letters which pointed up the political nature of the agreement; a confused clause on mobilization, which appeared to justify a peculiar French interpretation; provisions for continuing General Staff contacts; commitments for the defense of Luxembourg and the Belgian coast; and, finally, a secret document to enclose and enshrine all the ambiguities. The Accord of 1920 was, on the one hand, very difficult to sensibly criticize, and, on the other hand, offered the appearance to all concerned that there might be something—good or bad—in the accord which affected their interests.

If France had received the promised Anglo-American guarantee, the Accord of 1920 would probably have been unnecessary, but circumstances contrived to make the accord a necessary instrument of French policy. The question that remains to be answered is obvious. What prompted Belgium to accept an agreement which virtually guaranteed years of controversy?

There are many answers to the question, though none are completely convincing. To some people, the accord reflected the exigencies of internal politics. The Belgian Government needed a political success after a series of disasters, and the accord was the only means at hand.[62] Hymans insisted that it "repondait aux besoins et à l'esprit des lendemains de la guerre," [63] but never explained what those needs and spirit were. The King reportedly favored the accord for the "effet tonique sur notre armée, et . . . empecher la réduction excessive de notre état militaire. . . ." [64] Henri Rolin saw it as a deterrent: "On espérait ainsi obtenir un effet pre-

[62] Van Zuylen, *Les Main Libres*, p. 119.

[63] Hymans, *Memoires*, p. 629.

[64] Quoted in van Overstraeten, *Albert I—Leopold III*, p. 40.

ventif. . . ." [65] Others related it to memories of 1914 when Belgium had been caught unprepared.[66]

Yet it seems most likely that the compelling reason for the accord has to be sought in a combination of circumstances such as Belgium's desire for independence and security interacting with external developments which she could not control. The decisive event was the rejection of the guarantee treaty by the United States Senate. France, thrown back on its own resources, began to construct an alliance system in eastern Europe. Belgium became an essential link in that system, for only Belgian acquiescence guaranteed France access to Germany after the Rhineland was evacuated. Thus France began a diplomatic campaign to conclude a military accord, suitable to its commitments in both East and West, with the Belgians. By an intense and adroit application of various kinds of pressures, she achieved her goal.

Belgium was bound to yield to France in some degree. But the degree to which she finally yielded, in signing an unacceptable agreement, is a reflection of her own inept diplomacy. Belgium's wartime diplomacy was confused and uncertain; it resulted in a failure to press claims when they could have been obtained, and a failure to discover the moment they had become unattainable.[67] Belgian diplomacy during the Peace Conference was equally inept. All of Belgium's basic demands were ignored or postponed for later discussion.[68] After the Peace Conference, the Belgians sought to devise a foreign policy based on balancing between Great Britain and France. It became an unquestioned maxim presumably underlying all actions. Irrespective of whether the course was wise or foolish, it remains clear that it was vitiated by the decision to sign an accord with France alone.

[65] Rolin, *La Belgique Neutre*, p. 75.

[66] See the speech by Viscount Poullet in the Chambre, *Annales*, May 23, 1922, p. 888.

[67] Belgium's difficulties reflect a more general problem which confronts Small Powers in their relations with Great Powers when they are not armed with a specific commitment. The commitment does not guarantee anything, but it makes it much more difficult to ignore or injure the Small Power.

[68] For an attack on the quality of Belgian diplomacy in the preceding years by Sir Eyre Crowe, see G.B.D., Vol V, No. 199, pp. 737–39.

Could Belgium have resisted French pressure? Some kind of agreement was undoubtedly inevitable, but the one which resulted reflected a consistent failure to use whatever bargaining assets the Belgians did possess. After all, Belgium was as desirable an ally for France as France was for Belgium. And, in the final analysis, one crucial fact requires emphasis: the Accord of 1920 was not a necessity in the circumstances of the time, and both Governments were aware of it. Belgium could have extracted concessions from France by pointing out how peripheral and even dangerous an instrument the accord was from a Belgian perspective, which would have been a compelling threat because it was so clearly true. The Belgians never threatened, nor stood firm; they talked as if they were independent, but acted as if they were a satellite.

When the balance sheet is totaled, it appears as if necessity in the form of superior power prevailed; but Belgium never made use of the degree of freedom it possessed in order to resist the demands of its powerful ally. Conceived as a poor substitute for more desirable, but unattainable, forms of security; inspired by divergent purposes, drafted amid confusion, politically provocative and militarily unnecessary—these were the origins of the Franco-Belgian Military Accord of 1920.

The Road to Locarno

The five years that culminated in the Locarno Pact were filled with efforts to devise effective guarantees against any future aggressions. Yet, whatever the appearance might have been, the problem of security was not really preeminent; it was forced to share its position with the problem of reparations and economic reconstruction.

The question of security was a very academic one. It was quite obvious that France was too powerful to be directly challenged. It was necessary, of course, to shore up the European settlement of 1919 against the day when Germany was resurrected, but that day appeared a long way off. The sense of immediacy which usually prevailed in Continental Europe was dissipated and diluted. Even the Small Powers directly threatened by the potential power of Germany or the Soviet Union could afford to procrastinate on the problem of security, while they concentrated on rebuilding their own countries and extracting as much as possible from Germany.

Belgium was a case in point. Even its efforts to sign a military accord with Great Britain in 1922 were dominated by the desire to reestablish a balancing position, rather than by a felt need for security. And, a year later, when Belgium joined France in occupying the Ruhr, it was prompted by economic motivations. The action appears not to have been discussed in terms of its political and military implications.

There is no public record of any Belgian effort to initiate new talks on a security agreement with Great Britain during 1921. Apparently Curzon's sharp criticism of Belgium's actions in April, 1920, as well as the accord with France in September, prompted the Government to move cautiously. It was a French initiative in late 1921 which reopened the question. Briand ordered his Ambassador in London, Count Saint-Aulaire, to broach the question of a new pact between the two countries.

Saint-Aulaire indicated to Curzon that an alliance limited to the hypothesis of direct German aggression, such as occurred in 1914, would be useless. Great Britain's own security interests would force her to intervene anyway. Nor, for that matter, would the Germans repeat the errors of 1914. A new tactic was more likely: ". . . elle envahira la Pologne . . . Sans doute, la France ne le tolerait pas . . . . Mais elle serait isolée, une alliance defensive anglaise, limitée à l'hypothese d'une agression directe, ne s'appliquant pas . . . à l'agression indirecte." [69]

The Belgians only learned of these negotiations "par une indiscrétion" at the beginning of the Conference of Cannes in January, 1922. Apparently the accord with France had not even brought them the right to be consulted. Theunis, the Premier, immediately asked Curzon for a pact for Belgium also. After another unsuccessful effort to reconvert the Belgians to the idea of neutrality, Curzon relented and merely asked the Belgians to agree "de résister, comme en 1914, à toute attaque venant de l'est et de s'opposer au passage

[69] Quoted in J. P. Selsam, *The Attempts to Form an Anglo-French Alliance, 1919–1924* (Philadelphia: University of Pennsylvania Press, 1936), p. 65.

de troupes allemandes que se dirigeraient vers Paris ou vers la mer . . . ." [70]

The Belgians agreed. In fact they went even further and drew up an agreement providing for aid against an aggression "venant de n'importe quel côté." [71] The latter point was apparently an innovation designed to allay Flemish fears of French domination.

Curzon was favorable, but he subordinated signing the agreement to the successful conclusion of an Anglo-French pact. That upset the Belgians, but before they could do much about it the whole conference was wrecked by Briand's precipitate resignation. All the agreements which had been negotiated, including the Anglo-French security pact, were placed in suspension. The Belgians immediately pressed Curzon to save the draft Anglo-Belgian treaty from the debris. Curzon and Lloyd George at first agreed, but as Poincaré, who succeeded Briand, grew more and more intransigent, the cabinet decided to drop the proposed Anglo-Belgian agreement. Their reasoning was obvious. An agreement with Belgium "eut couvert indirectement la France et diminue la pression anglaise sur Paris." [72] Thus Belgium remained tied to France alone. The Quai d'Orsay and the Elysée apparently assumed that that meant a great deal more than their counterparts in Brussels thought reasonable. The Belgians were not happy to learn from the French Ambassador that "M. Poincaré désirait que nos conversations avec l'Angleterre ne se poursuivent qu'aprés que nous aurions été d'accord avec Paris sur ce que nous dirions à Londres." [73] The Belgians declined the offer.

[70] Van Zuylen, *Les Main Libres,* p. 185: ". . . to resist, as in 1914, all attacks coming from the east and to oppose any passage of German troops directed toward Paris or the sea." The negotiations at Cannes have been described by the incumbent Foreign Minister in Henri Jaspar, "La Conference de Cannes," *Revue Générale,* August, 1937, pp. 129–47. See also D.D.B., I, 448–51.

[71] *Ibid.*

[72] *Ibid.,* p. 141. The British wanted France to first settle several outstanding issues, particularly in the Near East; an Anglo-Belgian pact might lead the French to forego their own agreement with London or at least make them more difficult on the problems which London wanted settled. See D.D.B., I, 504–6.

[73] D.D.B., I, 472. "M. Poincaré desires that our conversations with Great Britain be pursued only after we have come to an agreement with Paris on what we will say to London."

The reparation settlement had awarded Belgium far less than she expected. The whole country was united in the feeling that the great sacrifices of the First World War had been poorly compensated. No government could have remained in power if it had overtly retreated on this issue. With a resounding unanimity, each Cabinet insisted that Belgium had not received very much in the settlement, but that every possible ounce of what she had been allocated was to be extracted. On this question, Paris and Brussels were united.

Theunis argued that "ces réparations il nous les faut, impérieusement, absolument." [74] It was also quite clear that no amount of reparations could solve Belgium's security problems; that required, above all, the maintenance of the Anglo-French entente. It was necessary to balance the desire for reparations against the need to maintain the entente. If French intransigence on reparations, or any other issue, created or exacerbated a split in the entente, Belgium was bound to suffer. The Belgians therefore constantly sought to mediate between the conflicting French and British positions. The ultimate success of these efforts was limited by the fact that the Belgian position on reparations, in substance, was identical to that of the French. They were somewhat more flexible in tactical terms than Poincaré, but equally rigid when it appeared that Germany was to be permanently relieved of reparations obligations.

The failure of Belgium's mediations was signaled by the occupation of the Ruhr in 1923. As the French and British positions veered more and more away from each other in late 1922, the Belgian Government was helpless to stay the drift. It was no longer a question of maintaining the entente and extracting reparations. It was now necessary to choose one or the other and Belgium chose to extract reparations.

Jaspar, the foreign minister, maintained the purity of Belgium's motives. The occupation, he insisted, was merely "un moyen de pression pour amener l'Allemagne à reconnaître et payer la dette." [75] Whether the Belgian decision actually rested on other grounds, and

[74] Chambre, *Annales*, I (Jan. 9, 1923), 360.

[75] Henri Jaspar, "La Belgique et la politique occidentale depuis le Traité de Paix," *La Revue Belge* (1924), p. 407.

was not simply an effort to collect an impossible debt which a rapidly recovering Belgium no longer needed, remains in dispute.[76]

Nevertheless, whatever the reasons, the decision was a mistake, for Belgium, in the eyes of all but its own leaders, became a satellite of France.[77] The decision gave some credence to the view that the Military Accord of 1920 was something more than a mere technical agreement. The decision alienated British opinion to the extent that the idea of a new guarantee was permanently dropped.[78] The decision antagonized and embittered the Germans, and it did not induce France to treat Belgium in a more friendly way. The decision also led to a reparations settlement which was not absolutely essential, which never provided Belgium with very much in the way of receipts, and which might have been achieved anyway by a policy which was economically and politically reasonable. A British member of the Reparations Commission, describing the results of Belgium's decision, wrote a fitting epitaph for the whole incident:

Now that the Belgians have definitely lined up with the French [by occupying the Ruhr], they have surrendered their position of "compromiser" which they held since the Armistice. They held a position enabling them . . . to reap considerable national benefits . . . Belgium is a small power and is now definitely relegated to the position of a small power.[79]

Whatever the contents of the Military Accord with France, and whatever influence it had on the Belgian decision, the accord suf-

[76] For an argument that Belgium's actions reflected an appreciation of relative military power, see Arnold Toynbee, *Survey of International Affairs, 1924* (London: Oxford University Press, 1925) p. 268; for an argument that Belgium did not want France in control of German industry, whence it could destroy the port of Antwerp, see Miller, *Belgian Foreign Policy*, p. 122. The Belgian documents are silent on the whole episode.

[77] For some indications of the Belgian Government kowtowing to France, see Jules Laroche, *Au Quai D'Orsay avec Briand et Poincaré* (Paris: Hachette, 1957), pp. 80–82.

[78] See Great Britain, *Parliamentary Papers*, 1924, Cmd. 2169, p. 172, for a note by Curzon on August 11, 1923, destroying the possibility of an Anglo-Belgian agreement. See also, D.D.B., I, 514–31.

[79] Quoted in Miller, *Belgian Foreign Policy*, p. 148.

ficed to limit Belgium's political maneuverability by making it appear as a less than disinterested conciliator. Belgium might just as well have signed a truly extensive agreement with Paris, in exchange for specific concessions, since it suffered from the fact that everyone, including its ally, acted as if it really had. Belgium was painfully learning the dangers of signing ambiguous agreements with an unscrupulous ally.

On February 9, 1925, Stresemann proposed to the French Government that the existing boundaries between the two countries be guaranteed. The proposal was not new, but the atmosphere had considerably changed since 1922, when it had been first broached. The failure of the Geneva Protocol, the Dawes settlement, and the electoral victories of McDonald and Herriot combined in various ways to make the idea of a treaty of mutual guarantee acceptable.

Belgium had nothing to do with initiating the idea. In fact, the original suggestion by Stresemann notably failed to mention the Belgian-German boundary—apparently because Stresemann hoped to recover Eupen and Malmedy during the negotiations.[80] Nevertheless, his efforts were unsuccessful, and the guarantee treaty which was signed included Belgium's boundary as it had been drawn after the Peace Conference.[81] In essence, the treaty provided that if either Germany or France attacked the other (or Belgium), England and Italy would go to their aid if they determined that the attack was an "unprovoked act of aggression."

Belgium would still have preferred a guarantee pact which excluded Germany. However, the British attitude made it clear that the inclusion of Germany was a necessary prerequisite for the conclusion of any guarantee treaty. The resurrection of another Great

[80] See Gustav Stresemann, *His Diaries, Letters and Papers,* edited and translated by Eric Sutton (London: Macmillan and Co., 1937), II, 113.

[81] For a discussion of the issue, see L. G. A. Detry, "La Belgique et les 'Papiers de Stresemann,'" *Revue Belge des Livres, Documents et Archives de la Guerre, 1914–1918,* VIII, 499. For a documentary record of Belgium's position during this period, see D.D.B., II, 31–369. There is a good summary of Belgium's point of view on pp. 165–68. The Belgian position on most of the critical issues, particularly as to when and how the guarantee would come into operation, was quite similar to France's; see pp. 289–94.

Power might also restore some of the maneuvering space Belgium had lost when it could only choose between an omnipotent and security-obsessed France and an ambivalent and conciliatory Great Britain—provided, of course, that Germany did not become powerful enough to challenge the entire peace settlement.

The Franco-Belgian Military Accord had been an issue at the beginning of the Locarno Conference. It seemed, on the face of it, to be out of joint with the Locarno "spirit." If the secret provisions of the accord involved something more than technical arrangements providing for cooperation against a new German aggression, it might well be out of joint with the pact itself. Thus the Belgian Government made every effort to indicate that the two agreements were really complementary. They were both, a Government spokesman noted, defensive in intent, and the accord was nothing more than "une simple modalité d'éxécution du Pacte rhenan." [82] If either ally conceived the accord in broader terms, its incompatibility would be evident. Belgium guaranteed Germany against France by the provisions of Locarno, and a Franco-Belgian accord not strictly limited to defensive cooperation would make a farce of Belgium's presumed impartiality. The problem was not acute in 1925, and the Government's arguments were accepted.

By 1925, the virtues of steering an independent course in European politics were much less apparent to most Belgians. A new status had not won Belgium any concessions on the major issues of the time. Belgium had only the League of Nations and the Military Accord of 1920 as guarantees against a future aggression. Neither was sufficient and both involved serious disadvantages. The mood of the country was amenable to new departures, even ones which harked back to earlier days.

The Locarno Pact seemed to restore all the advantages of the nineteenth-century guarantee, while avoiding most of its disadvantages. It would have been nearly perfect if Germany had been excluded, and if the Military Accord with France could have been

[82] Chambre, *Annales*, I (Jan. 20, 1926), 650. Vandervelde, the Foreign Minister at the time, argued that Locarno and the accord, "loin de se contredire, se complètent" since both were defensive agreements against unprovoked aggression. D.D.B., II, 339.

redrawn in a precisely limited fashion.[83] Nevertheless, it had done
two essential things. It resurrected the English guarantee, and it
gave Belgium room to maneuver between her three powerful neighbors.

For Belgium, Locarno meant a return to the past. Again, Belgium was guaranteed by her neighbors. Again, Belgium could concentrate on other matters, while security was left to the Great
Powers. Belgium began to *feel* as secure as under the aegis of the
treaties of 1839, and, again, began to make the same mistakes. King
Albert's warning that a neutral Small Power needed a strong army
to maintain its neutrality was forgot, an argument that should have
been even more compelling for a Small Power bent on maintaining its independence. In the end, Locarno was harmful for Belgium, not because its provisions were too extensive or too narrow,
but because Belgium used the Pact as a convenient excuse to ignore
the problems of security.

The Locarno Years

The Belgian Government had hoped that the discussion of the
Accord of 1920 during the debate on the Locarno Pact had finally
stilled its critics. They soon found that their hopes were in vain,
for the Flemish and the Socialists were only partly convinced that
the accord was harmless. They continued to ask a question which
the Government could not answer decisively: why wasn't the Accord superfluous? Was it that it contained secret clauses? Even
the apparently reasonable argument that a public discussion of an
agreement aimed at military cooperation would render the agreement useless was unavailing. The real problem, of course, was not
the accord as such. Rather, it was that it symbolized infeudation
to the French, according to the violently anti-French Flemish, or
that it represented, according to the Socialists, a return to the era
of military alliances. In the face of these positions, any rational

[83] The French efforts to construct Locarno in such a way as to allow her to
come to the immediate aid of her Eastern allies should have warned the Belgians.
France was forced to rely on the indirect guarantees implicit in Art. 15 and 16
of the Covenant; but that did not make the Belgian passageway any less necessary for her operations.

explanation of the accord had to prove ineffective. In any event, any Government might quail at the dangers of publicizing a document so full of ambiguities, particularly when clarification of the ambiguities would have antagonized the only ally it possessed.

Belgian military plans in the 1920s envisaged a defense at the Belgian frontiers. General Galet, Chief of the General Staff, stated the military goal foreseen in 1928: "Ecarter la guerre de notre territoire; ou bloquer l'invasion à la frontière." [84] Belgium's frontier with Germany ran for about 100 kilometres, but that was only part of the problem. If the weak or nonexistent Dutch and Luxembourg defenses were breached by the Germans, the Belgian defenses could easily be flanked. They were thus worried about the entire German boundary from Luxembourg to northern Holland—a distance considerably longer than the Franco-German border. The seemingly insuperable problem of manning a border so extensive was mitigated by the fact that France had agreed, in the Accord of 1920, to fortify the eastern frontier of Luxembourg. A large chunk of the border could be left undefended, since it would be protected by the French defenses in the Grand Duchy. But the French never got around to implementing this part of the accord.[85] Nevertheless, the difficulties and contradictions in the military policy of the General Staff never fully emerged in the 1920s. Since the threat seemed far off, it appeared to be a waste of time to attempt to reconcile even the obvious discrepancies which existed, particularly the one between a defense based on the frontier, requiring a large standing army, and Parliament's continuous efforts to cut back the army and decrease the length of service.

The recurring controversy over the nature and extent of Belgium's international obligations was a source of irritation to Hymans, the foreign minister. Finally, in 1928, he decided to have the problem studied by two senior members of his department. After pointing out some of the ambiguities in the text of the Military Accord, as well as several conflicts in interpretation between the two governments, their report concluded with the observation that:

[84] Quoted in van Overstraeten, *Albert I—Leopold III*, p. 47.
[85] *Ibid.*, p. 53.

En réalité, ce à quoi il faudrait arriver, c'est à faire reconnaître par la France que l'Accord est devenue inutile depuis Locarno et que le seul complément qu'appelle le Pacte rhénan, ce sont des conversations entre États-Majors sur des plans de défense communs.[86]

Hymans, however, decided that it would be inopportune to bring the question up in Paris, for he feared annoying a French Government which was itself beset with numerous difficulties.

Events conspired to force Hymans' hand. Domestic pressures, friction with the Dutch, and several controversial public statements by Marshal Pétain compelled the Belgian Government to seek agreement on a common interpretation of the accord. Moreover, by 1930, the Belgians had finally become aware of the dangers of being tied to an ally who needed its territory to render effective aid to other allies. Hymans' *Memoires* record a conversation with the King on October 28, 1930 which highlights the new fear:

Reçu par le Roi. Il est inquiet . . . . La France a conclu des alliances qui l'engageraient dans des guerres lointaines. Il faut veiller à ce que la Belgique ne soit pas entraînée dans des conflits étrangers à ses intérêts et si sa sécurité et son honneur ne sont pas menacés.[87]

The problem that now confronted the Belgians was one of means. What was the best way to clarify the accord without unnecessarily antagonizing the French? It was impossible to simply denounce the accord. As Hymans noted: "Répudier l'accord mili-

---

[86] Van Zuylen, *Les Main Libres,* p. 252. "In reality, it is necessary to make the French recognize that the Accord has become useless since Locarno and that the only aspect of the 1920 Accord still necessary is the conversations between General Staffs on the plans for common defense." In the course of the examination of the accord, M. Mélot, one of the analysts, asked what the accord really was: "Est-ce un traité? Non. C'est une entente technique sous certaines conditions," D.D.B., II, 474. There is further material on this episode on pp. 468–76.

[87] Hymans, *Memoires,* p. 602: "Received by the King. He is anxious . . . . France has concluded alliances which could involve her in distant wars. It is necessary to keep watch that Belgium not be involved in conflicts foreign to its interests if its security and its honor are not menaced." It was also at precisely this moment that Poincaré told the Belgian Ambassador that Belgium would have to aid France if France went to the aid of Poland—even if the Accord of 1920 did not literally encompass the situation. The combination of public indiscretions by Pétain and private indiscretions—or perhaps excessive honesty—by Poincaré did much to unnerve or irritate Belgium political circles. See D.D.B., II, 617.

taire serait une imprudence. Nous soulèverions contre nous le sentiment français et une partie de l'opinion belge. Nous semblerions
changer notre politique et renier nos amitiés." [88] Hymans decided
that the best thing to do was to define Belgium's obligations unilaterally during the course of a speech in the Chambre. But first
it would be necessary to discuss the matter privately with both
Paris and London, if only to limit the potential repercussions of
his statement.

After a few inconclusive meetings with the British Ambassador,[89]
Hymans met Briand at Geneva on January 12, 1931, and discussed
the entire issue with the French Foreign Minister. He submitted
the text of a letter, which he hoped would clear up all the confusions. Its critical part noted:

... le coopération militaire de la France et de la Belgique . . . est
exclusivement régi par les dispositions de l'article IV du Traité de
garantie mutuelle, fait à Locarno . . . . Il en est ainsi depuis l'entrée
en vigueur de ce traité qui a éteint, par novation, les engagements
primitifs, auxquels ont été substituées des obligations plus étendues,
plus précises et mieux définies.[90]

Briand, intent on maintaining the advantages of the accord, objected to the letter. He insisted, as had Claudel, the French ambassador in Brussels, that though the accord was more or less useless, since it had been superseded by Locarno, it would create a
very bad "moral effect" to denounce it publicly.[91] The two foreign

[88] *Ibid.*, p. 616: "To repudiate the military accord would be imprudent. We
would stir up French sentiment against us as well as a part of Belgium opinion.
We would appear to be changing our policy and denying our friendships."

[89] The British were not enthusiastic about the Belgium decision to attempt to
clarify the accord. They felt little was to be gained, even if the accord was as
useless as the Belgians insisted, because the French would be irritated and public
opinion would see more in the event than the facts justified. See D.D.B., 625–67.

[90] Van Zuylen, *Les Main Libres*, p. 258: ". . . the military cooperation of
France and Belgium . . . is exclusively regulated by the dispositions of article
IV of the Treaty of mutual guaranty, signed at Locarno. . . . The coming into
effect of this treaty has extinguished earlier commitments, for which have been
substituted obligations more extensive, more precise and better defined."

[91] For Claudel's views, see D.D.B., II, 641. The Belgian ambassador in Paris
was also against any action which would make it appear that a basic rift between
Paris and Brussels existed. See pp. 635–38.

ministers then agreed to have Alexis St. Leger and Fernand van Langenhove continue the discussions privately.

The negotiations between Leger and van Langenhove were inconclusive, but they did clarify the situation in at least one respect. The extensive interpretation of the accord which Leger sought clearly indicated that France hoped to use it for purposes to which Belgium could not consent. Thus when Hymans met Briand again in Geneva in February, he insisted on the need for a common statement by the two countries, rather than a unilateral interpretation by either. He also insisted that the French accept two amendments to the accord.[92] On the issue of the relationship between military cooperation and the Covenant of the League, he declared that the amendment should say that the principle was found in the Covenant, but that the obligation to implement the principle was not.[93] The French agreed to this nuance. The second amendment noted that Locarno "a defini les engagements qui seuls avec ceux du Pacte de la Société des Nations lient les deux gouvernments en matiére d'assistance mutuelle."[94] Once again the French agreed. The obscurity of the accord finally seemed to have been overcome.

That judgment was illusory. The two Governments exchanged letters ratifying their new agreement. The French letter indicated why the accord was not quite as dead as appearances suggested. It noted that "le gouvernement français . . . est heureux de constater que cette communication n'implique aucun changement dans les rapports établis entre nos deux pays et est, en consequence, d'accord avec le gouvernement belge."[95] The French were giving with one hand, and taking away with the other. Nevertheless, the Belgians had forced the French to make some definite concessions, in writing, which restored a degree of maneuverability to their policies. They had also taken their first major step away from the French orbit.

On March 4, 1931, Hymans analyzed the accord in a major

[92] Hymans, *Memoires*, pp. 625–26.
[93] Leger had sought Belgian agreement to a clause which implied that the Covenant involved an obligation to render military aid to League members.
[94] Van Zuylen, *Les Main Libres*, p. 261.
[95] *Ibid.*, p. 263: "the French Government is happy to affirm that this communication does not imply any change in the relations established between our two countries and is, consequently, in agreement with the Belgian Government."

parliamentary address. The accord, he declared, left each state free to determine its own military establishment, and to decide whether the *casus foederis* had occurred. The Locarno Pact, in any event, had subsumed the accord, and it was Locarno and the Covenant, and not the accord, which constituted Belgium's international statute. However, Hymans' analysis did not eliminate all the ambiguities. Once the two governments agreed that a German aggression against either had occurred, the accord "présuppose leur volonte commune . . . de résister en commun." [96] That is, each state was left free to determine whether its ally had been attacked, but, once that determination had been made, it was obligated to come to the aid of its ally. There the matter rested. It could not really be said that ambiguity no longer ruled, but henceforth both sides had some of the ambiguity to work with.

The Rhineland was evacuated in 1930, five full years before the date forecast in the peace treaty. One of the unintended effects of this decision, which had been aimed at prolonging the détente in European politics, was to complicate Belgium's military position. Heretofore, the protection of the occupied territory, plus the overwhelming superiority of the French army, had made military planning somewhat unreal. The French had finally passed the bill which authorized the creation of the Maginot Line in December 1929. Its army was bound to become increasingly defensive in outlook and structure. However, since the Maginot Line stopped at the point where it met the Belgian-Luxembourg frontier, it was necessary for the French army to be able to march quickly to Belgium's aid if Germany attacked—but the French army was too

---

[96] See Chambre, *Annales,* March 4, 1931, pp. 888–92, for the contents of the speech. See also the long note in D.D.B., II, 647–75, dated January 14, 1931, which details the Belgian position at great length. The note is of interest not so much for its analysis of the accord but rather for its brief but very revealing conclusions. The author points out the limited role which Small Powers can play in world politics and suggests that it is only prudential for them to stay out of Great Power affairs. He also alludes to 1870 again, where Great Britain guarantees Belgium and threatens *either* Germany or France if they attack, and in which Belgian forces are deployed in a neutral fashion. See pp. 671–74. It indicates the degree to which Belgium was already pulling away from France; and, also, how quickly Small Powers tend to abdicate their claims to equal status when it appears that they may be called upon to implement them.

defensive in scope to be able to achieve anything beyond a partial intervention in Belgium, if that. Consequently, Belgium would have to bear the brunt of a German attack by itself. It was obviously impossible to do so by spreading out all along the frontier. New military plans were necessary.

The alternative which the General Staff devised provided for a defense in depth based on the line Antwerp-Namur.[97] Whatever the virtues of the new scheme from a military point of view, it raised a political storm for it left a large area of the country, between the frontier and the fortified line, completely defenseless. The struggle which developed over the issue was further embittered because the area left uncovered was primarily Walloon territory.

The evolution in military policy had another serious effect. It turned a significant part of the General Staff against the French tie. If Belgium had to meet the brunt of an attack by itself, the accord seemed useless. Since France refused to prolong the Maginot Line, she was obviously directing the German attack through Belgium. By remaining tied to France, Belgium merely became the most likely target of a German attack, on the presumption that Germany would strike at the weakest link in the Franco-Belgian defenses. There was at least the possibility that Germany would not strike at a Belgium which was dissociated from France, particularly if it meant that England would join the war again.[98]

It is perhaps worth emphasizing that the Belgians had a rather singular point of view toward the French refusal to prolong the Maginot Line until it reached the English Channel. At first glance, it might appear as if the Belgians should actually have been pleased at the French decision. It meant that the French army could come to their aid, whereas the prolongation of the Maginot Line along the Franco-Belgian border would have forced the Belgians to confront the German threat alone. Yet the Belgians did not see the problem in this way. From their point of view, the absolutely dominant question concerned the possibility of avoiding war altogether. They were determined to prevent Belgium from becoming

[97] Van Overstraeten, *Albert I—Leopold III,* pp. 48–49.
[98] Private sources.

a battlefield, and all other issues were secondary. Failure to prolong the Maginot Line meant that the French and German armies would meet each other in Belgium; prolongation of it offered the possibility, however slim, that Germany would attack elsewhere, especially for fear of British intervention. The Belgian position may indeed be criticized, either because it continued to read the future out of the lessons of 1914 or because it was simply not the best way to confront the German threat, but it is not possible to understand the position without realizing the Belgians' desperate desire to avoid turning Belgium into a battlefield.[99]

French pressure on Belgium had been considerably attenuated by the agreement reached in 1931. Henceforth, the French would have to rely primarily on Locarno or the Covenant in order to achieve their aims. They would have to justify their actions to a large group of states—which seemed to mean that if Belgium was precipitated into a war with Germany, it was at the very least assured of the aid of Great Britain and various other states.

Satisfaction with this state of affairs rapidly dissipated after the ambassador in Paris reported another conversation with Pétain early in 1933. Pétain declared that France intended to send its troops through Belgium in case of war. The ambassador replied, "Si nous vous le permettons." "Avec ou sans votre permission," replied Pétain. "En ce cas, nous vous recevrons à coups de canon," was the ambassador's response.[100] He soon learned that Pétain's views were shared by the French General Staff. It seemed prudent, therefore, to once again seek a clarification of French intentions.

The Belgians decided to broach their case by eliciting an interpretation of the clause in the Locarno Pact which provided for immediate aid, without a preliminary decision by the League of Nations Council, in the event of a "flagrant violation" of the agreement. Belgium feared that France would use this clause to enter their country merely as a precaution. If France's actions were not upheld by the other signatories, Belgium would be at war with Germany without England's support. The French response was

---

[99] See especially D.D.B., III, 230–31.
[100] Van Zuylen, Les Main Libres, p. 276. See also D.D.B., III, pp. 35–36.

delayed until December, and it hardly served to clarify the situation.

It appeared to argue that in the event of a "flagrant violation" of the Pact, a preliminary accord between the guarantor and the guarantee was not necessary. The guarantor could impose its guarantee: France could intervene no matter what decision the Belgians made.[101] Later in the month, the Belgians learned that London apparently agreed with the French interpretation.[102] The issue was left unresolved. All parties concerned preferred to leave the matter in some confusion, for the conflict was obviously insoluble as long as France hoped to use Belgian territory in support of her other allies.

The Disarmament Conference had been thrown into confusion by Germany's withdrawal in October 1933. The "Locarno years" were clearly at an end, but what the future held was a subject of excited conjecture.

Amid the uncertainty and fear, the Belgian Cabinet met to determine its course of action. The results were inconclusive, though a decision was reached to side with Great Britain against France on the issue of disarmament negotiations with Germany.[103] Belgium was gradually moving out of the French orbit, a trend facilitated and encouraged by various anti-French and pro-German officers on the General Staff.[104]

Finally, in an effort to clear the atmosphere, de Broqueville, the leader of the Government, decided to analyze the situation in Europe in a major parliamentary address. His speech was delayed until March 1934 because of the untimely accidental death of King Albert, but its effect was sensational. De Broqueville had merely argued that he foresaw negotiations as the only solution to the impasse created by the failure of the Disarmament Conference.

[101] *Ibid.,* p. 283. For further evidence of Belgian fears of French intervention, see D.D.B., III, 39, 47, 53, 253–54.

[102] *Ibid.,* p. 284.

[103] Notes from a conversation with Count Capelle, who was present. See also the note by van Langenhove in December which clearly indicated a break with the French on this issue. D.D.B., III, 255–58.

[104] Private sources.

"Je suis partisan de negociations immédiates pour renforcer par de nouveaux éléments la sécurité de la Belgique." [105] It was Belgium's first overt and tangible move away from France. The Quai d'Orsay, under the guidance of Barthou, was clearly uninterested in new negotiations with Germany.

De Broqueville's speech might well have been aimed at another, and more devious, purpose. The deterioration of the international situation turned Belgium once again toward Great Britain. Perhaps the speech represented an effort to indicate to London that Belgium was not a French satellite, and that it could be a worthy ally.[106] In fact, Anglo-Belgian negotiations were already germinating. General van Overstraeten had indicated their desirability to the new King Leopold: "Nous devons tendre à rester indépendants, à chercher appui du côté de l'Angleterre qui comme nous, désire la conservation de la paix. . . ." [107] Hymans made much the same point in a conversation with the British ambassador. And the Belgian ambassador in Berlin, Count Kerchove, had urged a new effort to negotiate a military accord with Great Britain not only because of German rearmament but also because the German response had been consistently equivocal whenever he sought to elucidate Berlin's position on the continuing validity of the Locarno pact.[108] A new era was opening in European politics. Belgium's response was to seek the forms of security which had protected it in days gone by.

The Last Years of the Military Accord

The death of King Albert early in 1934, coupled with the in-

[105] Sénat, *Annales,* March 6, 1934, p. 562.

[106] Private sources. The French were not unaware of these currents in Belgian political circles. After Barthou's visit to Brussels in March 1934, one French officer noted that "the French must not count on immediate intervention on the part of Belgium in case of German attack." Quoted in William E. Scott, *Alliance against Hitler: The Origins of the Franco-Soviet Pact* (Durham, N.C.: Duke University Press, 1962), p. 165.

[107] Van Overstraeten, *Albert I—Leopold III,* p. 107.

[108] *G. B. D.,* Vol. VI, 1933–34, No. 342, March 10, 1934, p. 541. See also *D.D.B.,* III, 321–25. For earlier suggestions of a similar kind by Kerchove, see his dispatch of November 1933, pp. 238–42.

creasingly tense foreign situation, shifted the balance of forces within the Belgian Government.[109] Advocates of a central position for Belgium—that is, for a weakening or elimination of any ties with France—gradually began to prevail over those believing French support was indispensable. The accession of Leopold facilitated the new trend. He lacked Albert's insight, experience, and prestige. Moreover, the memory of Entente collaboration in the First World War seemed less relevant to the new King. His inexperience necessitated reliance on older advisors, virtually all of whom were anti-French.[110] Rumors of the deleterious influence of various "éminence grises" began to circulate freely and to undermine confidence in the King's judgment.[111] The situation did not augur well for a country already beset by internal conflicts.

France refused to disarm until it felt secure. As a result, the Disarmament Conference had ended in an impasse. The Belgians shortly thereafter proposed a solution to the dilemma. France's security could be enhanced by strengthening her northern boundary. This could be accomplished by an explicit British guarantee to Belgium, which would be an indirect guarantee to France. France, in return for the augmentation of its security, would then make significant concessions to Germany on the question of disarmament. If these efforts were unsuccessful, the British guarantee would attenuate the resulting crisis by making it more difficult for either Germany or France to use Belgian territory as a springboard. Belgium was returning to an old theme: the quest for a guarantee from London. Belgium still hoped thereby to increase its security against Germany, but it also hoped to prevent any French action which would precipitate a new war.

Sir George Clerk, the British ambassador, provided all the incentive the Belgians required. He informed Hymans that:

We are able to protect ourselves effectively, and assure the peace, only if Belgian territory is inviolable both to armies and airforces; for that,

---

[109] See Lucien Marchal, *La Mauvaise Carte* (Brussels: 1946), pp. 51ff.

[110] Private sources.

[111] For an interesting, and not flattering, picture of Leopold at the time, see Grigore Gafencu, *The Last Days of Europe* (London: Frederick Muller, Ltd., 1947), pp. 74–76.

it is indispensable that no doubt exist, in anybody, that England will intervene immediately if the Belgian frontier is threatened.[112]

The Belgians responded by dispatching Baron van Zuylen to London to make some preliminary soundings.

Hymans had already articulated Belgium's position in a long note sent to various diplomatic missions. Above all, Belgium wanted to remain out of any war. However, if war should come, it was absolutely essential to avoid a situation in which Belgium fought on the side of France but without the active support of Great Britain. Belgium would not fight unless *both* France and Great Britain joined in. If Paris and London could not agree, then Belgium's position was clear: "..nous devons garder notre liberté, ne pas nous engager dans un groupe contre un autre." [113]

After a short interval, Hymans was invited to London. He had two long meetings with Simon, Hailsham, and Chamberlain on May 16 to set forth Belgium's case. He noted the "vertu préventive" of an agreement with England: *both* Germany and France would think twice before acting. And he told Simon that "la Belgique ne cherche pas à provoquer votre intervention, mais à la rendre inutile, par la menace de cette intervention. L'example de 1870 est caractérisatique à cet égard, et c'est celui qui nous a inspirés." [114]

Hymans then submitted the text of an agreement which differed from the Locarno guarantee in two ways. First, Great Britain made an explicit promise to aid Belgium with all its forces. Second, Great Britain would renounce the need to discuss the necessity of immediate aid: action, not consultation, would follow a German aggression.[115]

The results of the talks were inconclusive, but the two governments agreed to meet again. In the interval, relations between Great Britain and France cooled, particularly after Barthou's violent attack on Simon during the Disarmament Conference. This probably accounted for London's decision to ask Belgium to con-

---

[112] Van Zuylen, *Les Main Libres*, p. 296.
[113] D.D.B., III, 349–63. The note is dated April 24.
[114] *Ibid.*, p. 305; see also the analysis in D.D.B., III, 366–76.
[115] *Ibid.*, p. 305.

clude a nonaggression pact with Germany as a preliminary to an Anglo-Belgian accord.[116]

The Belgians vigorously resisted London's entreaties. They were not willing to antagonize France quite that much. The Foreign Office then informed the Belgians that they would have to be satisfied with a declaration to Parliament, rather than a pact, since England did not want to antagonize Germany. On July 13, 1934 Simon told the House of Commons that: "the integrity of the territory of Belgium is no less vital to the interests and safety of this country today than it has been in times past. It is a geographical fact which nothing can change." [117]

Kopke, the Director of the German Foreign Office, told the Belgian ambassador that: "La déclaration de Sir John Simon devrait être gravée en lettres d'or et encadrée dans tous les édifices publics belges. . . ." [118] Germany was clearly warned; so, for that matter, was France. And Belgium had at least seen it affirmed once again that Belgian independence was a *sine qua non* of European stability.

By 1935, it was becoming quite clear that Belgium needed a new military statute. The increasing external threat, as well as the growing divergence from France, behooved Belgium to increase its army, strengthen its fortifications, and revise its strategy. An intensive effort was made throughout 1935 to educate the public to the exigencies of the situation. However, the Government's new military bill was rejected in February 1936. The van Zeeland Government decided that something had to be done to unite the country. Since the Military Accord of 1920 was the very symbol of that division, and since the Government felt that the accord was deprived of substance by the modifications of 1931, it decided that denunciation of the accord was the only way to regain the support of the dissident Flemish Francophobes and to pass the necessary military law.[119]

[116] Private sources; and D.D.B., III, 384–85.
[117] Parliamentary Debates, 292 H. C. Deb. 5 s., July 13, 1934, p. 698.
[118] Quoted in van Zuylen, *Les Main Libres,* p. 313.
[119] Private sources. The Belgian diplomatic papers for January 1936 reveal an

Thus the imperatives of internal politics provided the immediate reasons for seeking to end the accord. Several external factors, however, set the stage for the decision such as fears concerning French intentions, the weakness of the French and British armies, the failure of the League of Nations, Hitler's announcement of universal conscription and rearmament, and France's alliance with the Soviet Union and its internal difficulties.

The Government was probably right in its assumption that the passage of a military law in 1936 required the denunciation of the accord. It should have been equally clear that it was Germany threatening Belgium's existence, and that the support of France was absolutely necessary to counter that threat. The Belgian decision to denounce the accord was akin to throwing away one part of its security in order to develop another part. If Belgian military strength could be developed only at the expense of its external ties, the Government was in an untenable position. The blame can be attributed to a generation of Belgian statesmen who negotiated an unnecessary and unpopular agreement, who allowed it to persist despite its dangers, and who never educated public opinion to the necessities of external support, perhaps because they were too shortsighted themselves to comprehend it.

The French were reluctant to accede to Belgian demands, for they feared the effect that denunciation of the accord would have on their eastern allies. After a few weeks of preliminary sparring, during which the French attempted by various devices to maintain something of the original accord, van Langenhove was sent to Paris to reach an immediate agreement. He told the French that Belgium was going to make a declaration denouncing the accord. The only question left to discuss was whether it was to be

---

interesting initiative by General Riedinger, the French military attaché in Brussels. On January 17, he told the Minister of Defense that he thought the accord should be denounced for it did not have "aucun intérêt pratique." The Minister agreed, but added that it should not be done in a way which suggested any loosening of ties between Paris and Brussels. Riedinger returned a week later to say that his initiative was not approved either by the ambassador nor by his superiors in Paris. The Ambassador felt the time was inopportune because of rumors of an impending action in the Rhineland by Hitler, and the Ministry of Defense in Paris was negative because it feared denunciation of the accord would put an end to General Staff conversations. D.D.B., III, 451–53.

unilateral or bilateral. Belgium would accept only an exchange of letters between the two Governments.[120] France yielded. Two identical letters were exchanged on March 6, 1936. The key paragraph declared:

Les deux gouvernements, constatent tout ce qu'il y a de périmé dans cet arrangement, ont reconnu l'intérêt de n'en retenir que le seul élément aujourd'hui valable, à savoir l'accord existant entre eux et qu'ils tiennent aujourd'hui à confirmer, quant au maintien d'un contact entre Etats-Majors. . . . Il demeure entendu que semblable contact ne peut engendrer aucun engagement d'ordre politique. . . .[121]

Shortly thereafter, van Zeeland noted that "il en resulte que l'accord franco-belge de 1920, avec les clauses périmées qui l'encombraient et le caractere de mystere dont il s'entourait, n'existe plus. . . ."[122]

The Belgians had turned the tables on France and exercised strong diplomatic pressure to achieve their aim. In order to pass a stronger military law, and to create a favorable "psychological effect" internally, they threatened to take unilateral action which would further weaken the French diplomatic position. As a sop to French feelings, they offered to continue General Staff talks (under the aegis of Locarno) but only if the French acceded to all of their demands. The Quai d'Orsay reluctantly capitulated.[123]

[120] *Ibid.*

[121] Van Zuylen, *Les Main Libres,* pp. 339–40: "The two Governments, verifying that which has lapsed in this arrangement, have recognized their interest in retaining the only worthwhile element, that is to say the accord existing between them and which they today reaffirm, as to the maintenance of General Staff contacts. . . . It is understood that these contacts are not able to engender any political commitments. . . ." That French political circles were bitter goes without saying. Bargeton, a leading official at the Quai d'Orsay, even told the Belgian ambassador that: "Nous n'ignorons pas, ici, qu'une partie de la population désire non seulement la dénonciation de l'accord militaire franco-belge de 1920, mais même la dénonciation des accords de Locarno et le retour à la neutralité d'avant 1914. Si tel était le cas, nous devrions modifier, complètement, toute la politique française et nous devrions abandonner la Belgigue à son sort en cas de guerre. Nous devrions, immédiatement, proceder à la construction de fortifications au Nord prolongeant notre ligne de l'est." D.D.B., III, 478.

[122] Sénat, *Annales* (March 11, 1936), p. 437.

[123] See D.D.B., III, 451–95 for as much material as we are likely to get about Franco-Belgian negotiations on the denunciation of the accord in 1936, especially pp. 479–89.

Ironically, and symbolically, on March 7 the day after the exchange of letters, Hitler's troops marched into the Rhineland. The accord was finally dead, but the Belgian "victory" in finally achieving that end was very hollow. What should have been accomplished in 1925 or 1931 became a dangerous expedient in 1936.

Belgium was still protected by the Locarno Pact, which was the very foundation of its security. Of all the many clauses in the nine treaties that constituted Locarno, those that provided for the continued demilitarization of the Rhineland were the most important. They were, as Jaspar contended in 1933, "le véritable bouclier de son indépendance." [124]

Thus one would expect Belgium to react violently if any attempt was ever made to remilitarize the area. With German troops once again directly on its frontiers, the problem of defending Belgium would become impossible. Critical hours of warning time, hours in which allies could advance to Belgium's aid, would be irrevocably gone. Yet, when Hitler's troops marched in, the Belgian reaction was lukewarm. An action, whose consequences for Belgium were "les plus profondes et les plus redoutables," [125] found Belgium playing two of its favorite roles—an injured innocent and an honest broker. Neither reflected an adequate appreciation of the elements in the new crisis.

When the crisis cooled, Belgium found itself in an unsatisfactory situation. Locarno was dead. A key provision had been violated with impunity, Germany and Italy were obviously unreliable, and France and Great Britain were weak and ambivalent. That left Belgium with the provisional agreement of March 19, which had prolonged the Locarno guarantee until a new pact could be negotiated. That new treaty did not necessarily have to guarantee Belgium.

Therefore, in the months that unfolded after the Rhineland

[124] Henri Jaspar, "Les directives de la politique extérieure de la Belgique," *L'Esprit International,* VII (Jan. 1933), 17.

[125] Paul van Zeeland, "La Position Internationale de la Belgique," *La Revue Générale* (May 1939), p. 591. For a description of Belgium's behavior at this time, in which the Belgians agreed to "take any action if France and the United Kingdom joined in," see Anthony Eden, *Facing the Dictators* (London: Cassell & Company, Ltd., 1962), pp. 343–67.

coup, responsible political figures began to cast about for a policy which might somehow keep Belgium out of war. The factors which shaped their quest are obvious. The League had failed and collec‐ tive security had proved a myth. The Rhineland coup had revealed the military and political weaknesses of France and Great Britain —and the determination of Germany's leaders. General Staff talks with London and Paris were useless. As van Overstraeten noted "A l'alliance défensive avec la France et l'Angleterre, il n'est qu'une alternative: la neutralité." [126]

The trend toward "neutralism" continued to grow. The virtues of alignment with the Western Powers were sharply disparaged by Foreign Minister Spaak. He noted that:

We did not want an alliance, whatever our sympathy with our possible partners, for it would have made of us mediocre followers, it would have involved us in an international policy that we were not strong enough to apply; it would have led us irresistibly to war.[127]

Formal commitments were ruled out, for they seemed to increase risks rather than security. Only one policy seemed possible:

Donner l'assurance à tous ses voisins qu'en aucun cas, qu'en aucune circonstance, la Belgique ne permettre que son territoire serve soit de passage, soit de base d'occupation à une armée étrangère, qui en pro‐ fiterait pour attaquer plus facilement un autre de ses voisins.[128]

It meant that Belgium had to pass a military law so strengthening itself that no aggressor would dare use its territory. Inevitably, that could be done only if the military was committed to defend *only* Belgian soil. Belgium had to be independent of all foreign ties, particularly French ones, if it was to be strong enough to be a dangerous target.

The stage was thus set for King Leopold's address on October 14, 1936. The key sentences of the address contended that:

[126] Van Overstraeten, *Albert I—Leopold III*, p. 225.

[127] Quoted in *Belgium: The Official Account of What Happened, 1939–1940* (London: Evans Brothers Ltd., 1941), p. 93.

[128] Spaak in the Chambre, *Annales*, October 28, 1936, p. 371: "To give as‐ surance to all its neighbors that, in any circumstance, Belgium would not permit its territory to serve either as a passage or a base of occupation for a foreign army which would profit from it in order to attack more easily another of her neigh‐ bors."

An alliance, even if purely defensive, does not lead to the goal; for, no matter how prompt the help of an ally would be, it would not come until after the invader's attack, which will be overwhelming. To meet this attack we would be alone in any case. . . . After this stage is over, friendly intervention will certainly assure final victory; but the struggle will cover the country with destruction of which that of the 1917–1918 war would be but a feeble image.

For this reason, as the minister for foreign affairs said recently, we must pursue "an exclusively and wholly Belgian policy." This policy must aim resolutely at keeping us outside the quarrels of our neighbors. . . .[129]

The Cabinet approved Leopold's speech. Henceforth, Belgium sought to be released from the obligations of Locarno and the London agreements of March 19. As van Zeeland noted, "Belgium had no intention of pulling other people's chestnuts out of the fires. . . ."[130] The quest was successful. France and Great Britain released Belgium from its obligations, but maintained their own obligations to help it in the event of a German attack. The Government was delighted. Spaak went so far as to declare that "Je suis gêné de retenir tous les profits, sans prendre aucun risque."[131] Shortly thereafter an impressive new military bill was passed.

In practical terms, General Staff contacts with Paris and London were suspended. Paul Reynaud later commented bitterly that:

Before calling upon the French army, Belgium would henceforth wait until she herself was invaded. It was an ideal solution for Hitler. He knew that France would never enter Belgium by force. He could, therefore, with complete safety, strangle our allies in the east.[132]

Franco-Belgian relations continued to deteriorate. By May 1938, they had descended to the point where the French ambassador could be warned that "we have just carried out maneuvers on the French border to demonstrate that, if you enter Belgium to support the Czechs, you will run into the Belgian army."[133]

[129] The full speech may be found in Miller, *Belgian Foreign Policy*, pp. 226–30.
[130] Paul van Zeeland, "Aims of Recent Belgian Foreign Policy," *Foreign Affairs*, Oct. 1939, p. 142.
[131] Quoted in van Zuylen, *Les Main Libres*, p. 388.
[132] Reynaud, *In the Thick of the Fight*, p. 153.
[133] *Ibid.*, p. 183.

Belgium had been the very symbol of internationalism, of a wise and responsible Small Power. Her defection to the ranks of the *sauve-qui-peut* powers, like Beck's Poland, seemed sacrilegious. If Belgium had lost faith, and was desperately seeking to withdraw to the periphery of European politics, on what grounds could the rest remain faithful? As André Tardieu declared, with some exaggeration, "Ce qui vient d'arrive en Belgique surpasse en signification matérielle et morale tout ce qui s'est produit en Europe depuis l'armistice." [134]

Belgian policy can be criticized only in terms of the alternatives available at the time. The new orientation after 1936 was never conceived as a panacea. It was justified by Spaak on more limited grounds: "La politique d'indépendance n'est pas peut-être la politique idéal, mais elle est, j'en suis chaque jour plus convaincu, la meilleure des politiques possibles. . . ." [135] Several years later an official publication by the Government-in-exile reexamined the policy, and still found it the best available:

It is true that this policy prevented neither German aggression nor invasion. It could perhaps reduce the risk slightly, though it could not remove it. Only the foresight and armed force of the Great Powers could have done that. But Belgium's attitude . . . cemented national unity and strengthened the common will to resist at a time when the country was about to face one of the most terrible ordeals of its history.[136]

The argument ultimately rests on an appreciation of the power situation in Europe after 1936. Belgium was small, weak, and exposed. It was threatened by a powerful and aggressive Great Power and ambiguously supported by two weak and spineless allies; its only hope lay in avoiding war altogether. The only chance to do so seemed to lie in making itself an unattractive target, by being militarily strong enough to make conquest difficult, and that necessitated dissociation from allies who seemed headed for a war in

---

[134] Quoted in Jean de Richemont, *L'Europe devant L'indépendance Belge* (Paris: Les Editions Internationales, 1939), p. 23.

[135] Chambre, *Annales*, March 16, 1938, p. 59.

[136] *Belgium: The Official Account of What Happened 1939–1940*, p. 25.

which they could barely defend themselves, let alone Belgium. It is a compelling argument, so far as it goes.

Conditions had deteriorated by 1936 to the extent that all the options which confronted Belgium seemed dangerous and un-acceptable. However, Belgium had done nothing to avert the situation which had arisen in Europe. At best, it can be said only that Belgian foreign policy was no worse than anyone else's. Even in terms of the situation of 1936, Belgium probably chose the worst of several admittedly bad alternatives. Did the best chance of avoiding war lie in attempting to withdraw from the danger, rather than in confronting it? Probably not. The events of 1870, which continued to fascinate Belgian statesmen, could no longer be repeated. Britain and France were allies. A German attack on France alone would as surely bring British intervention as a German attack on Belgium. Germany would lose nothing by attacking Belgium, and it would gain strategic advantages from doing so, particularly since the French defensive line along the Franco-Belgian border was obviously weak.

Belgium's best hope lay not in a return to the past but in a renewed effort to reinvigorate the old entente. When its own vital interests were at stake, it should have insisted that a firm stand be taken—perhaps even threatening to act alone as a catalyst to insure Great Power support. Instead, in the face of a threat, Belgium ran away in the perennial Small Power hope of being eaten last. In deserting France, it accentuated the danger and emboldened Hitler. The sole benefit that accrued to Belgium was the passage of a military bill, but that was surely of secondary importance in comparison to the maintenance of a united front against Germany.

Belgium committed other errors. Its statesmen were too fascinated by the idea of equilibrium. Consistent efforts to play the role of an "honest broker" between London and Paris were futile and dangerous when the resulting decision involved the compromise of Belgium's essential interests, as in the Rhineland episode.[137] In

---

[137] Alexis St. Leger had bitterly castigated the Belgians for their attitude as early as May 1933. He told the ambassador in Paris that "à force de vouloir tenir la balance égale entre la France et l'Angleterre, à force de vouloir être impartiaux, vous devenez partiaux." He went on to note that Belgium was ac-

internal politics, succeeding Governments, without exception, lacked political courage. They chose to yield to Flemish extremists, rather than risk a fight even when that decision meant that Belgium would have to stand alone against an infinitely more powerful enemy. Later governments listened to the advice of an arrogant and inexperienced young King, who was himself under the influence of advisers notoriously anti-French.[138] And, finally, since the new policy made sense only on the assumption that it would be completely successful, that Belgium would remain out of the next war, Belgian statesmen chose to act as if the world would correspond to their desires. In the peculiar atmosphere which prevailed at the time, all contacts with Paris were forbidden. Fortifications facing south were begun and maneuvers against a potential French attack were held. Belgium acted as if the Pax Britannica of the nineteenth century had been resurrected because only thus could it be saved. What was really resurrected was "the disdainful, complacent ignorance in regard to external dangers that had characterized it up to 1914." [139]

As to the Military Accord of 1920, it was unnecessary; it was badly drafted; it divided the country; and it created external difficulties—in sum, it became an albatross around the neck of succeeding governments, each desperately striving to dilute its pernicious effects without simultaneously antagonizing the only ally Belgium possessed. And when the danger which the accord was designed to combat actually arose, and when its advantages might finally have begun to outweigh its disadvantages, Belgium chose to denounce it in the apparent hope that that act by itself would effectively exorcise the danger.

---

tually sacrificing its real interests, which were identical to France's, in an effort to please London. Leger perhaps goes too far in suggesting an identity of interests between a Small Power like Belgium and a Great Power like France, particularly as early as 1933. Nevertheless, he is right about Belgium's mania for "impartiality" and he may also have been right about an identity of interests between the two countries as the threat of war grew larger and larger. See D.D.B., III, 114–15.

[138] See G. B. D., Third Series, Vol. IV, No. 70, p. 66.

[139] Henri Rolin, quoted in J. H. Huizinga, *Mr. Europe: A Political Biography of Paul Henri Spaak* (London: Weidenfeld and Nicolson, 1961), p. 85.

On Forms of Alliance:
the Nature of Unequal Alliances

The kinds of alliance patterns that develop in any era depend on the interaction of a number of variables.[140] The most significant may well be the nature and number of the actors in the system: e.g., whether their values are symmetrical, whether there is a relative equilibrium of power among the leading states, whether the level of military technology and economic growth is stable, and, finally, whether the extent and kinds of conflict which occur can be handled by the prevailing political tradition. The existence of supranational and international organizations may also have a decisive impact on which alliances, and what kinds of alliances, seem most appropriate. The point to be made is that perception of changes within and between the foregoing variables inevitably leads to a new pattern of alliance.

Despite the fact that the general pattern of alliances varies in response to the conditions of each era, the specific forms which alliances may take have remained relatively static. That is to say, a state can choose between a bilateral or a multilateral alliance, composed either of states of relatively equal power or of states possessing disparate capabilities, and organized in either a relatively centralized or decentralized manner.

[140] It is worth emphasizing that the remarks which follow are *not* limited to an extrapolation from the Belgian experience with France: that case study serves as an indication of the relevance and application of *some* of the theoretical principles which follow. However, the ensuing generalizations frequently go beyond any lessons which could safely be drawn from the Belgian case, and they reflect an effort to deal with the problem of unequal alliances for Small Powers on the most general level.

This section, and the concluding section of the next chapter, are extrapolations from a wide range of historical material. There is some parallel here with Professor Haas's description of an analytical system: "An analytical system is a pattern of relations that may or may not exist in actual life. It is designed by the observer for purposes of projection, or for comparison with actual behavior patterns. An analytical system can even be used for purposes of prediction if nothing more elaborate and specific is sought than statements of the 'if . . . then' variety." Ernst B. Haas, *Beyond the Nation-State* (Stanford: Stanford University Press, 1964), p. 54. The material in Part II is comparable with Professor Haas's description of a "concrete system," since, as will be noted, the emphasis is much more on the actors within the system than the system itself.

The possibility of discussing the advantages or disadvantages of particular kinds of alliances in any international system, even though the system itself may create a bias for one particular form, may be illustrated by noting certain consistent responses to one or another form. Small Powers have been warned time and again not to ally with Great Powers. Machiavelli's injunction that "a prince ought never to make common cause with one more powerful than himself, unless necessity forces him to it" [141] has been graphically rephrased in recent years by Gamal Abdel Nasser: "An alliance between a big and a small power is an alliance between the wolf and the sheep, and it is bound to end with the wolf devouring the sheep." [142] Similarly, alliances composed solely of Small Powers have always been regarded as worthless, if not dangerous, by all commentators. Alfred Cobban has noted that "the combination of any number of weak states does not make a strong one," [143] and Annette Baker Fox has concluded that Small Power alliances failed "for the sum of their power was weakness, and the combinations were too insubstantial." [144]

If it is presumed that more than one potential ally is available, the first choice which confronts a state about to embark on a policy of alliance is whether the alliance should be bilateral or multilateral. In theory, a bilateral alliance between relatively equal partners has certain advantages over a multilateral alliance. It is likely to be more flexible, and each ally probably will retain more freedom in allocating its resources. The common denominator of action may be higher than in cases where it must be determined by a larger group. In addition, a bilateral alliance is more likely to be concerned with specific, local interests on which there is some consensus. And, if war should occur, it may be easier to keep it limited and confined to a local area. Thus the multilateral alliance system which existed on the eve of the First World War tended to

[141] Machiavelli, *The Prince* (New York: Modern Library, 1950), Chapter XXI.

[142] Quoted in Keith Wheelock, *Nasser's New Egypt* (New York: Frederick A. Praeger, 1960), p. 41.

[143] Alfred Cobban, *National Self-Determination* (London: Oxford University Press, 1945), p. 178.

[144] Annette Baker Fox, *The Power of Small States* (Chicago: The University of Chicago Press, 1959), p. 185.

turn each local crisis into a general crisis; it insured that any war which did come was bound to be European in extent; and it tended, over a length of time, to deprive each ally of a good deal of its diplomatic maneuverability.

A bilateral alliance between *unequal* allies seems to be an entirely different matter. It has, without exception, been regarded in a negative fashion in the literature of international relations. That alone justifies pointing out that it can offer the weaker partner certain advantages. Obviously an alliance with a friendly Great Power provides a Small Power with additional strength and a more effective deterrent posture. In some cases, the commitment itself, without any tangible manifestations, may suffice to protect the weaker state—certain Latin American countries have undoubtedly been shielded from intervention in the past, not so much by what the United States did, but by the promise that we would do something (with, of course, the tacit support of the British fleet).

The obvious dangers of an unequal alliance, for Small Powers, have inspired many commentators to offer tactical principles designed to dilute its worst effects. Unfortunately, virtually all such rules of thumb are ambiguous and of doubtful validity. For example, Richelieu suggested that Small Powers should always seek an alliance at the rear of their potential enemy, thereby pinning down some of its forces in a distant area. However, an alliance with a distant Great Power could prove less reliable: it may be more difficult to agree on a common response to local conflicts.[145] It might also antagonize a neighboring Great Power to a dangerous extent. A Belgian alliance with the Soviet Union would merely have exacerbated its problems with Germany. The latter point illustrates another problem. If the Small Power needs immediate aid, and it allies with a distant Great Power, it may be overwhelmed in the interval between an attack and the arrival of aid. In effect, Richelieu's *aperçu* is ambiguous. If it is valid at all, it is so only when the Small Power is not faced with a military threat.

Talleyrand, in the course of a difficult negotiation, offered advice which has since been added to the list of maxims for the

[145] Cf. George Liska, *International Equilibrium* (Cambridge: Harvard University Press, 1957), p. 29.

survival of Small Powers: "si ça va sans dire, ça va encore mieux en le disant." At first glance, the advice seems compelling. Surely, where there is small margin of error, ambiguity may be a dangerous luxury. It is clearly true that the weak can be hurt badly by relying on obligations left obscure enough to facilitate evasion. The most likely result of an uncertain commitment is that the Great Power will assume that the Small Power has agreed to do whatever is in the interest of the stronger; Belgium's experience with France from 1920 to 1936 is a case in point. Furthermore, the Small Power may find its domestic politics consumed by a virulent debate over the nature of its commitment to the Great Power, the latter's intention to intervene, the possibility of withdrawing the commitment, and so forth. In sum, a poorly drawn commitment may lead to a decay in effective self-government due to the distortions produced by the ensuing debate over just what one is obligated to do. However, there is another side to this coin. The Small Power surely can be hurt by an ambiguous commitment, but it may also be able to use it to delay taking actions which it feels are dangerous. It only takes one to evade, and it can be either partner who does so. It is true that the Small Power gambles more in this situation, but it does so in virtually all situations.

A Small Power may also profit from another factor which appears to be inherent in unequal alliances, a factor which might be called "reverse potentiality." [146] Once an alliance has been created, there is a positive value placed on continuing it, even if it seems to perform very few functions (e.g., SEATO). The allied nations may fear the propaganda and political losses attendant on admitting failure. The Small Power may regain some of its maneuverability in this situation. It can take the initiative when the continuation of the alliance, or the maintenance of a facade of unity, would

---

[146] For a discussion of this possibility in terms of France's alliance system after the First World War, cf. René Albrecht-Carrié, *France, Europe and the Two World Wars* (Paris: Librairie Minard, 1960), pp. 43–44. A. J. P. Taylor in discussing Louis Napoleon's papal policy also notes the same phenomenon: "When one state is completely dependent on another, it is the weaker which can call the tune: it can threaten to collapse unless supported, and its protector has no answering threat to return." A. J. P. Taylor, *The Struggle for Mastery in Europe, 1848–1918* (Oxford: The Clarendon Press, 1954), pp. 29–30.

seem more important to the Great Power than avoiding the momentary inconveniences which the Small Power's initiative may engender.[147] Again, however, as a tactical principle, qualifications must be made. It is most likely to be successful, that is, to give the Small Power some flexibility, if the Great Power is weak or forced to develop a consensus before it can act; if the prevailing conflicts are limited and nonmilitary; if the Great Power cannot turn to other allies for aid; and if the Small Power possesses a necessary asset such as a port or a base.

It has also been suggested that the Small Power may benefit from its very smallness. A Great Power allied with a Small Power *must* support it. It has to provide it with continuous aid, and treat it with a certain amount of deference, merely because it is an ally—and the disruption of an ally is a political, if not a military, loss.[148] Perhaps it is excessive to suggest that this idea consciously motivates Small Powers to ally with Great Powers, but it is difficult to deny that it probably has affected their decisions in some cases. In any event, it hardly constitutes a strong enough motive, by itself, to justify the risks which inhere in unequal alliances.

The primary advantage of an unequal alliance, from the point of view of the Small Power, is that it is likely to increase its defensive capabilities. That advantage may be vitiated by virtue of the fact that the Small Power may become the focal point of an enemy attack. By its relative lack of strength (even with the material

[147] Note the difficulties which the U.S. has faced in its relations with Cambodia because of our commitments to Thailand and South Vietnam. For example, when the U.S. tried to mediate the border dispute between Thailand and Cambodia in 1961–63, the negative reaction of the Thais limited U.S. freedom. And Cambodia became anti-American in part because we could guarantee her against Communism but not against the Small Power threats (Thailand and South Vietnam) which Cambodia really feared. Cf. Roger M. Smith, *Cambodia's Foreign Policy* (Ithaca: Cornell University Press, 1965), pp. 138–39, 215–16.

[148] For a discussion of this problem in the contemporary world, see Charles Burton Marshall, "Alliances with Fledgling States," *Alliance Policy in the Cold War,* edited by Arnold Wolfers (Baltimore: Johns Hopkins Press, 1959). The Great Power also has less excuse to plead nonsupport because of material weakness: whereas the Small Power can always claim it is too weak to be anything but passive. The psychological response to a condition of dependence should also be noted: the Great Power may be forced to overcompensate its lesser ally to satisfy its desire for status.

support of its ally), the Small Power may draw upon itself a concentration of forces that ordinarily would have been directed primarily against its ally. General Chauvineau noted this possibility during the debate in 1938 about France's commitment to Czechoslovakia:

Un pays n'entrera plus de son plein gré dans une coalition si, de tous le coalisés, il s'estime le plus faible ou le plus vulnérable par sa situation géographique, parce qu'il serait alors designé comme la prémière victime d'une concentration des moyens offensifs terrestres, maritimes, aeriens de la coalition adverse.[149]

The significance of this factor, for the most part, depends on geopolitical conditions. If the Small Power is centrally located in a strategic sense, and seems destined to receive the brunt of the attack anyway, as Belgium was in 1914 and 1940, the wisest course may very well be to gamble on whatever deterrent effect the alliance does provide. Nevertheless, a state located in a dangerous area must recognize that it cannot ally with one side without becoming a threat to the other. Some slight hope may exist of proving its impartiality to both sides, but that seems of limited utility unless both Great Powers favor the status quo. If one is aggressive, the impartiality of the Small Power is a hindrance.

For the Small Power which is in a peripheral position geographically, the costs of allying with superior power are easier to calculate. They need not be weighed against the costs of an expected invasion. The primary disadvantages in this case are political and psychological; military costs are obviously low if shooting is not about to start or if a country is considerably away from the target area. These generalizations seem valid irrespective of whether the military technology is conventional or nuclear.

An unequal alliance creates other difficulties. The weaker ally may resent the support it receives; the larger ally may assume that its aid entitles it to a disproportionate amount of the external benefits which the alliance provides. The Small Power may also

[149] General Chauvineau, *Une invasion est-elle encore possible?* (Paris: Editions Berger-Leurault, 1938), p. 183: "A country will no longer enter an alliance willingly if, of all the allies, it judges itself the weakest or the most vulnerable geographically, because it will then be designated as the first victim of the land, sea and air forces of the opposing alliance."

lose a certain amount of propaganda potential by allying with a Great Power, at least since 1919. There is little moral capital to be wrung from an alliance in which a state is defined as unjust merely because of size. Much more may be gained by remaining unaligned, or by aligning only with peers. None of the foregoing need be true, but the historical record indicates its relevance.

Alignment with one Great Power usually reduces the opportunity to ally with any other Great Power. A prior commitment, especially by a weak state, limits the possible extent of any future commitment, and the possible bargains to be struck with other powers. This tends to make the problem of maximizing goals within an alliance particularly acute for a Small Power, for if goals cannot be attained within an alliance, where can they be attained? However, an unequal alliance provides the Small Power with only a limited potential for achieving goals. It has little leverage to exert against its stronger ally. The goals the alliance is likely to pursue are bound to be closer to those desired by the stronger partner, unless the weaker partner can utilize its "reverse potentiality" to an unlikely degree. In turn, this puts a great deal of pressure on it because it has to play a double hand, seeking gains both against and with its own ally. It may also be true that an unequal bilateral alliance is inherently unstable unless it limits its goals to a very narrowly conceived defense of the status quo. If not, the alliance may run afoul of the potential conflict between local and general interests. In addition, those Small Powers which refuse to defend the status quo, or are hostile to the new alliance, may respond by creating a separate alliance aimed at altering that status quo.[150]

There are also tactical weaknesses inherent in unequal alliances. For example, if a Small Power allies with a Great Power, and the latter then allies with the enemy of the Small Power, what can the Small Power do? The problem is not fanciful. Note the problems Yugoslavia faced in 1935 when Italy and France appeared to be on the verge of alliance. If a Small Power located between two

---

[150] For discussion of some of these points in terms of one area, cf. Leonard Binder, "The Middle East as a Subordinate International System," *World Politics*, X (April 1958), 408–29.

Great Powers allies with the weaker of the two in order to retain its independence, and the two Great Powers subsequently come to an agreement, the result may be identical. The Small Power stands in grave danger of losing its independence, since it has no viable policy alternatives.

The case for and against an unequal, bilateral alliance can be rapidly summarized. Its primary utility lies in the military realm, since the promise or provision of added military support aids the Small Power in danger of attack. However, even in the military realm, disadvantages appear. The Small Power may merely insure that it will become a target in any attack. For the military support to be of any use, it must be provided before an attack or shortly thereafter; Small Powers rarely have much territory within which to retreat while awaiting aid. In effect, for the majority of Small Powers, the whole country is virtually frontier territory. Modern weapons have only increased their defenselessness. As a result, the stakes involved in an alliance policy are enormous: they amount to survival in the most basic sense. The importance of the decision, as well as the narrow margin of error, may impose a pernicious influence on the conduct of foreign policy. Emphasis must be on constant readiness and immediate response to provocation. The bargaining elements of politics tend to disappear. The alliance must deter threats by appearing as if it will respond to any provocation by total war. The situation is hardly comfortable for the Small Power. If it succeeds in deterring, it does so at heavy political and military expense; if it fails to deter, it stands likely to be devastated. Of course, this picture is a bit overdrawn. Obviously it holds true only for Small Powers faced with extremely dangerous threats. Nevertheless, unless they happen to be as large as Spain, all Small Powers, if they are not actually in so dangerous a condition, are on the verge of it.

Politically and psychologically the unequal alliance is clearly disadvantageous. A Small Power may still ally with a Great Power if it has no other acceptable alternative, but it ought to recognize the costs of its choice. If alliances are in disrepute, charges of immorality must be met, and it is not very likely that the Small Power will escape accusations of dependency, even if it is lucky enough to escape the reality. The sole political advantage of an unequal, bilateral alliance appears to reside in the fact that two allies are more likely to agree on a common policy than a group of allies. But it is likely to be a common policy close to, or identical with, the policy of the stronger partner.

It is appropriate to add one final injunction. If a world existed in which "all other things" were really equal, the unequal alliance could be consigned to a convenient political limbo. Since circumstances may arise, nonetheless, in which even an alliance as disadvantageous as this one is actually the best or only alternative, it is worthwhile to reiterate that the Small Power can still display political wisdom in choosing an ally, negotiating an agreement, and operating the provisions of the agreement.

A multilateral alliance offers its members a number of advantages. It has all the advantages that an alliance per se has over a unilateral commitment: more deterrence and defense, a precise commitment, and the political and material support of the other allies. A multilateral alliance also seems less aggressive and realpolitik than a bilateral alliance. For whatever reason, it appears to be less cynical and dangerous than the smaller bilateral alliance. All multilateral agreements tend to be described, at least in our time, as "collective security" instruments, presumably to dilute the political losses attendant upon negotiating a traditional collective defense agreement.

In theory, a mixed (i.e., containing at least two Great Powers and one Small Power), multilateral alliance appears to be the most attractive alliance alternative open to Small Powers. That fact has not escaped their attention. Baron von Zuylen, Secretary-General of the Belgian Foreign Ministry in the 1930s, argued that "autre chose est l'alliance avec une grande Puissance et l'alliance avec un groupe de Puissance: la prémière pese indisculablement sur la liberté de petit état; dans la seconde, les grands se neutralisent mutuellement." [151] In various ways, the expanded alliance maxi-

---

[151] Von Zuylen, *Les Main Libres*, p. 11: "An alliance with a Great Power is one thing and an alliance with a group of powers is another: the first weighs indisputably on the liberty of the small state; in the second, the great powers neutralize each other."

mizes the probability of achieving intended purposes. A number of the traditional disadvantages associated with alliances are also substantially diminished in effect in a multilateral agreement.

The theoretical advantages of an unequal, multilateral alliance are clear. If a bilateral alliance provides more deterrence and defense than a unilateral commitment, a multilateral alliance in turn provides more than a bilateral one. The aggressor's problems are increased substantially, if only by virtue of an increase in the number of targets it becomes necessary to attack. A Small Power allied with one Great Power may only increase the likelihood of an attack against itself. Allied with two Great Powers, the number of forces deposed against its territory may be diminished, and it may also receive additional support to counter an attack. And that presupposes that the deterrent effect of the alliance has failed.[152]

Increased membership may mean decreased effectiveness. The common denominator of mutual interests can diminish to the extent that meaningful actions are rarely taken by the alliance as a whole. Foch's celebrated aphorism inevitably comes to mind: "My admiration for Napoleon has shrunk since I found out what a coalition was." From the point of view of the Small Power, the possibility that the alliance will become a facade for the policy of one Great Power is considerably diminished. The Small Power's potential for influencing decisions is likely to increase in a situation where power is diffused. There is rarely one overpowering national interest which always prevails in a multilateral alliance—though there have been, of course, certain periods in the history of NATO and the Warsaw pact in which the writ of Washington and Moscow ran deep. In any event, more members normally means more bargaining and more compromise, and consequently more opportunity for the Small Power to express itself effectively. In a sense, the desire of the Benelux countries to see Great Britain in

---

[152] Since the military utility of alliances has declined, from the point of view of Small Powers, it might also be noted that the Small Powers in a mixed, multilateral alliance may find it easier to use the alliance for peaceful and/or political purposes and to preserve their own power (especially in light of the tactical considerations which are noted below). For efforts by some of the Small Powers in NATO in this direction, see, for example, Melvin Conant, *The Long Polar Watch* (New York: Harper & Brothers, 1962), p. 67.

the Common Market reflects, at least in part, recognition of the dangers implicit in Franco-German solidarity, presuming it is ever effectively achieved, and the addition of Great Britain, *inter alia,* restores some maneuverability to the Small Powers.

The preceding example illustrates another opportunity open to Small Powers in multilateral alliances, the opportunity to act as a balancer within the alliance. By seeking the basis for compromise between conflicting positions, a Small Power can increase its own prestige and influence, and also facilitate successful operation of the alliance. As long as there are alternate power centers, and as long as there is a measure of disagreement between them, the Small Power is under less necessity to accept unpalatable decisions silently and passively. The attractiveness of the idea of carrying the balance is surpassed only by the very real advantages it sometimes confers (but, to repeat, only when the Great Powers are in partial disagreement).

Alliances may be viewed as discreditable features of the international landscape, and they may be villified for treachery, immorality, or aggressive tendencies. This range of criticism is considerably attenuated when it is applied to multilateral combinations. Morality in this instance reflects a quantitative judgment. Alliances are justified only when more than two states sign an agreement. Additional justification rests on their supposed coherence with the tenets of collective security. The stipulations of the alliance count less, in terms of appeal, than the rhetoric with which it is described.

The case for a mixed, multilateral alliance can be readily summarized. It provides the Small Power with more deterrence, more defense (if the Great Powers do not use the presence of other Great Powers as an excuse to evade their own commitments), and less risk. The combined power of the partners may also increase their political influence. They are more likely to be listened to, and less likely to be dismissed as representing narrow or parochial interests. The fact that membership is varied probably means that it will be difficult to achieve a political consensus. The agreements negotiated may be nothing more than a defense of the status quo. Nevertheless, this may not be altogether displeasing to a Small

Power bent on retaining its independence. In addition, it may be able to exert a significant amount of influence within the councils of the alliance.

In historical terms, the opportunity to negotiate a mixed multilateral alliance has not always been available. For example, the weakness, elimination, or isolation of various Great Powers after the First World War precluded the possibility of forming an effective multilateral alliance. For all practical purposes, Small Powers could ally only with France or among themselves. Under certain conditions, multilateral alliances similar to the ones existing on the eve of the First World War might have reemerged—but an alliance even vaguely resembling the integrated structure of NATO was beyond the realm of political discussion. Nationalism and autarchy were still too powerful forces; the ideological struggle was not as clear as it became after 1945; and no state felt quite as defenseless as the European states did immediately after the Second World War—in effect, in terms of the history of alliances since 1815, NATO appears to be the somewhat unusual result of very unique, and perhaps transitory, historical factors.

An alliance with a single Great Power is undesirable. An alliance of several Small Powers and one Great Power is only marginally, if at all, an improvement.[153] An alliance with several Great Powers is desirable but difficult to achieve. The only alternative left, if an alliance policy is still to be pursued, is an equal, multilateral alliance, that is, an alliance composed entirely of Small Powers.[154]

[153] Note the difficulties France had in the interwar years in coordinating its alliance system: Paris was the hub; the spokes led into various capitals, but unfortunately there was no rim to hold the wheel together and make it function.

[154] A bilateral alliance between Small Powers will not be discussed separately for its advantages and disadvantages can be subsumed within the succeeding discussion: it appears to be a slightly less effective version of a multilateral Small Power alliance.

CHAPTER 4

The Little Entente and the
Nature of Small Power Alliances

I N 1920 and 1921, Czechoslovakia, Rumania, and Yugoslavia
formed a defensive alliance aimed at preserving and enhancing
their new status. *Pesti-Hirlap,* an Hungarian newspaper, derisively
labled the new grouping as the "little entente," because it was
pretending to act like a shadow of the wartime entente between
Great Britain and France.[1] The name stuck, but it soon lost its
pejorative connotation. In the years that followed the Little Entente
became a significant factor in European politics; its ultimate destruction in the late 1930s was all the more stark because of its
earlier success. This chapter will examine the history of the Little
Entente in an attempt to evaluate the potentialities of Small Power
alliances.

The Origins of the Little Entente

The Successor States of the Austro-Hungarian Empire were united
in a shared hatred of Hapsburg domination.[2] However, during the
First World War itself, and in the peace conference immediately
thereafter, cooperation was inchoate and sporadic. All of the new
states were too involved in expropriating their own independence
from the crumbling dual monarchy to worry very much about

[1] See Stefan Osusky, "La Genèse de la Petite Entente," *Revue D'Histoire
Diplomatique,* 46 (1932), 140–41.
[2] See Florin Codresco, *La Petite Entente* (Paris: Les Presses Modernes, 1930),
p. 151.

what their neighbors were doing. Moreover, there were serious bones of contention, usually in the form of a complicated border dispute, which vitiated any immediate possibility of alliance.

A rudimentary common front did begin to emerge. The overwhelming factor in this development was undoubtedly a common realization that they were more threatened by other states than by each other. None could stand alone against the myriad threats of Hungarian revisionism, Italian irridentism, Soviet revolution, and British and French indifference or indecision. Still, when specific problems arose, the new states invariably reacted in strictly nationalistic terms. It would take the threatening external environment of the first postwar years to create a felt need for alliance. Any alliance with a neighbor required a compromise settlement of at least one dispute, and the mood for compromise could only appear when the reality of weakness and danger became clear.

Despite its other failures, the Austro-Hungarian Empire had been something of an economic success. Its disintegration into a motley group of inexperienced and nationalistic Small Powers created a need to base the economic future of the area on a new arrangement. It was not inherently impossible, at least in 1919, that a reasonable alternative could be devised. Unfortunately, an excessive economic nationalism destroyed any possibility of rational cooperation.[3] Thus the possibility of creating a broad alliance involving economic and social cooperation was eliminated from the start. Some states had common political goals which could form the basis of agreement, but none had economic goals which were complementary—they all wanted to be self-sufficient, and inevitably at the expense of the others.

The Czech army was routed by the forces of Bela Kun's Hungary in the summer of 1919. However, Kun's successes frightened the Rumanians, and they successfully intervened in the war in August. The episode was important as it tightened the ties of friendship between Prague and Bucharest, both of whom were reacting to the dangers of Hungarian *revanche*. The Kapp Putsch in Germany in March 1920 also facilitated eventual cooperation, for the new

[3] For an excellent analysis, see David Mitrany, *The Effect of the War in Southeastern Europe* (New Haven: Yale University Press, 1936), *passim*.

states were united in their fear that a monarchist reaction in Germany might lead to *Anschluss* or the restoration of the Haps-burgs. By the spring and summer of 1920, a number of other ex-ternal events began to threaten the territorial settlement in eastern Europe. In rapid order, rumors of a Franco-Hungarian conspiracy, the Polish-Soviet war, and rumors of an attempt by Charles to recapture his old throne in Hungary created the conditions which led to the formation of the Little Entente.

The Soviet Revolution complicated France's security problems. Germany could no longer be balanced by a Franco-Russian entente. However, the disintegration of the Austro-Hungarian Empire offered the French new possibilities of maneuver. If they could create a Danubian federation under their own tutelage, they could encircle Germany, isolate the Bolsheviks from Europe (and Ger-many especially), and develop a valuable sphere of economic and political influence. The desirability of a French surrogate for the old Empire was considerably enhanced by extensive French in-vestments in the area.

Two alternatives were open to France. She could either support the successor states which had a direct and felt interest in main-taining the status quo, or she could attempt to create a wider arrangement, which would also incorporate revisionist states, but revisionists who saw the need of supporting France against Germany and the Soviets. A great debate between exponents of the two alternatives continued throughout the first nine months of 1920. During that period, Hungary had been called to Paris to negotiate its own peace treaty. It soon became clear that Paléologue, the secretary-general of the Foreign Ministry, was a partisan of the wider grouping, and that he favored modifications in the status quo favorable to Hungary.

France did not derive any advantages from the balkanization that characterized the Danubian area. On the contrary, she sought a general solution to the problems besetting eastern Europe.[4] Nevertheless, the Hungarians hoped that France's support would

---

[4] Thus the Hungarian envoy in Paris warned his superiors "not to expect the restitution of St. Stephen's Kingdom from the French, who were seeking to solve the problem of Southeastern Europe, rather than to restore Hungary's

lead to substantial modifications in the territorial settlement which had been worked out in 1919. The French, however, were cautious, for they feared antagonizing Hungary's neighbors. As a result, the terms which the Hungarians had to accept in June 1920 did not involve any territorial concessions. Nonetheless, it was quite clear that Paris was not unalterably opposed to revisions benefiting Hungary.[5]

The Polish-Soviet war intervened to confuse the situation. Hungary immediately offered to begin negotiations with Rumania, which was directly threatened by the Bolsheviks, and also offered the beleaguered Poles direct military support.[6] Poland, in turn, began pressing for a Hungarian-Rumanian-Polish alliance, supported by France, to cooperate against the Soviets.

The Hungarian initiative was fruitless, for it engendered a quick response on the part of Prague and Belgrade. The Czechs refused to cooperate in the efforts to aid Pilsudski, in part out of exasperation with the Poles because of the Teschen dispute, but primarily because of a fear that Hungary would enhance its status by aiding Poland and that France would reward the Hungarians by supporting revision.[7]

---

territorial integrity." Quoted in Francis Deak, *Hungary at the Paris Peace Conference* (New York: Columbia University Press, 1942), p. 296.

For a detailed study of French policy toward Eastern Europe in the period from 1919–1925, see Piotr S. Wandycz, *France and Her Eastern Allies, 1919–1925; French-Czechoslovak-Polish Relations From the Paris Peace Conference to Locarno* (Minneapolis: The University of Minnesota Press, 1962). Professor Wandycz uses many documents to which I have not had access (or could not read as they are in Polish or Czech). However, documentation for this period is still very incomplete and none of the new material which Professor Wandycz uses appears to vitiate or undermine any of my conclusions. Since so much source material is missing for this period, any analyst is presented with wide opportunities for personal interpretation of events. Professor Wandycz, in the circumstances, tends to give Poland the benefit of the doubt in most cases, and to treat Benes and the Czechs in a rather negative fashion. My own interpretation is, in general, much more pro-Benes: while it is very easy to criticize him, none of his detractors present very convincing alternatives which he could have realistically followed at the time. Interpretations of Benes and his policies in the light of the problems of Czechoslovakia in 1938 and after are not completely fair or useful.

[5] *Ibid.*, pp. 295 ff. and *passim* for the negotiations in general.

[6] *Ibid.*, p. 311.

[7] For some of the rumors of Franco-Hungarian negotiations, see R. W. Seton-

At the height of the crisis, in early August, Beneš set out for Belgrade. As one observer commented:

Dr. Beneš's journey to Belgrade and the signature of the alliance a few days after Czecho-Slovakia declared her neutrality in the Polish-Soviet war can hardly be regarded as sheer coincidence, being evidently timed to counter diplomatic measures looking to Hungary's participation in the fight against the bolsheviks.[8]

On August 14,1920, Yugoslavia and Czechoslovakia signed the first formal Little Entente treaty. The critical clause declared that "in case of an unprovoked attack on the part of Hungary against one of the High Contracting Parties, the other Party agrees to assist in the defense of the Party attacked. . . ."[9]

Beneš then set out for Bucharest, but his efforts there were only partially successful. Jonescu, his opposite number, was loath to commit Rumania to an arrangement which might destroy the possibility of a wider organization. Moreover, it was still uncertain whether the recent Polish victory at Warsaw had eliminated the Soviet threat.[10] If not, the Rumanians and the Poles might need Hungarian aid. Nevertheless, the Rumanians were willing to agree to reciprocal military assistance in the event of an Hungarian aggression, as long as that commitment was not embodied in a formal treaty.[11]

The initial French reaction to the Czech-Yugoslav pact was entirely negative. In fact, Peretti, chief of the Political Section of the Foreign Ministry, "remarked that the Little Entente may almost be regarded as directed against France. . . ."[12]

The French efforts to avert the creation of the Little Entente,

---

Watson, "The Little Entente," *The New Europe*, XVII (Oct. 17, 1920), 5–6. For Czech-Polish relations in general, see Wandycz, *France and Her Eastern Allies, passim.*

[8] Deak, *Hungary at the Paris Peace Conference*, p. 320.

[9] For the full text, see John O. Crane, *The Little Entente* (New York: The Macmillan Company, 1931), pp. 180–190.

[10] Deak, *Hungary at the Paris Peace Conference*, p. 321.

[11] See *Documents Diplomatique Relatifs aux Conventions D'Alliance Conclues avec Le Royaume des Serbes, Croates et Slóvenes et le Royaume de Roumanie* (Prague, 1923), p. 67. Henceforth cited as *D. D.*

[12] *Papers and Documents Relating to the Foreign Relations of Hungary* edited

and to keep Rumania out of it, came to an abrupt end in September. One reason was the end of the Polish-Soviet war, which allowed Rumania to forget about Hungary as a potential ally. In fact, Hungarian revision now seemed to be the most immediate threat. With the Polish-Soviet war concluded, with the Czechs and Yugoslavs applying intensive anti-Hungarian pressure, with Rumania turning toward the Little Entente, and with its own Foreign Office divided on the correct course, the French shifted their tactics. Instead of attempting to destroy the fledgling alliance, they attempted to channel it in acceptable directions. As the Hungarian envoy in Paris noted, "France . . . has endeavored to take away its specifically anti-Hungarian character by broadening the alliance. . . ." [13]

However, even this shift in French policy was soon to come to naught, for within a fortnight France completely reversed its policy. The Little Entente emerged as the French standard-bearer in eastern Europe. The factor which precipitated the diplomatic revolution was the replacement of Paléologue as secretary-general of the Foreign Ministry by Philip of Berthelot. Two weeks later, the Hungarian envoy sadly concluded that "there can no longer be any doubt that the policy adopted by the new personnel of the Quai d'Orsay is the support of the Little Entente." [14]

by Francis Deak and Dezso Ujvary (Budapest: Ministry for Foreign Affairs, 1939), No. 631, Sept. 4, 1920, p. 616. Henceforth cited as H. F. R.

Great Britain was no less annoyed. Harold Nicolson reports that "Lord Curzon regarded them [the Little Entente treaties] almost as a personal affront." *Curzon: The Last Phase* (New York: Harcourt, Brace and Company, 1939), p. 213. See also Wandycz, *France and Her Eastern Allies*, pp. 195–96.

[13] *Ibid.*, No. 650, Sept. 13, 1920, p. 630.

[14] *Ibid.*, No. 725, Oct. 17, 1920, p. 696. The French wanted, of course, an eastern European alliance which was much more anti-Soviet than the Little Entente appeared likely to be: Benes consistently opposed any effort to turn his country or the Little Entente into a French instrument against the Soviets. The French Governments in this period also probably felt that the Warsaw-Bucharest-Budapest axis offered better opportunities for economic control of the area by French finance than did the Prague-Belgrade-Bucharest axis. Hungary and Poland were both in more desperate straits in this period than their neighbors, and would have had to yield, and did in fact offer, economic concessions to Paris which Prague refused. Ideological factors may also have been somewhat significant, as the French Governments until 1924 were right-wing; the Czechs had left of center or center Governments. For an analysis of these factors, see Wandycz, *France and Her Eastern Allies*, especially p. 197.

The year 1920 ended with the Little Entente still in gestation. But in the abbreviated form of a defensive convention between Czechoslovakia and Yugoslavia, with the informal support of Rumania, it had already made its presence felt. France had been converted from a lukewarm and ambivalent power to a friendly power. Hungary's schemes to thwart the peace settlement had been rebuffed. The idea of a Polish-Rumanian-Hungarian pact, inevitably at the expense of the other Successor States, had been impeded and then destroyed. Rumania had been converted from an ambiguous and uncertain bystander to a staunch supporter of the status quo. And Poland, though it would not join an anti-Hungarian pact, at least stifled its antagonism upon learning that the French were now the unspoken third partner of the Czechs and Yugoslavs.

In this first confrontation of a Great Power, saddled with diverse and conflicting interests, with two Small Powers, bent on maintaining the status quo, the Small Powers won by precipitating a solution which the Great Power could only reverse by losing their support. Thus Beneš and Paschitch forced the French to choose between them and the Hungarians. Inevitably the Little Entente, stronger than the Hungarians, more democratic, and as a former ally of France, emerged as a French bastion. The Little Entente, in a real sense, therefore, was the reaction of two Small Powers to an attempt by a Great Power to intervene too actively in their affairs.

Charles, the last of the Hapsburgs, had never legally abdicated. He had merely declared a unilateral suspension of his powers, indicating that he would recognize as definitive the future decisions of the people of his domains.[15] His sovereign rights were theoretically still in existence since he had not signed the peace treaties which abrogated them. The ambiguous situation created by Charles' ambivalent actions worried the Little Entente states, all of whom stood to lose territory if a restoration succeeded.

Beneš and his colleagues also recognized that there was a strong current of support in France for a Hapsburg restoration, even

[15] See Baron Charles von Werkmann, *The Tragedy of Charles of Hapsburg* (London: Philip Allan and Co., 1929), p. 19.

though it might be unofficial. A new Hapsburg empire, politically modified and under French auspices was too obvious a solution to the problems of the Danube to be dismissed as impossible and visionary. Therefore, if the Little Entente states were to retain their independence and territorial integrity, it was necessary to react quickly and powerfully against any attempts by Charles to regain the crown of St. Stephen.

Information from many sources, as well as the interpretations Charles' followers lent to it, all seemed to augur well for an attempt to regain the throne. Thus in February, 1921:

A Frenchman of very great standing and authority sent word to the Emperor that the chances of a Restoration in Hungary were becoming worse by postponement; that at the moment the Powers would protest against his return, but that their protests would not alter a fait accompli.[16]

The King's aide-de-camp later insisted that "it must be fully realized, that His Majesty had absolute guarantees from Briand's Cabinet that he had nothing to fear from the Little Entente." [17] As a result, in the last days of March 1921 Charles suddenly reappeared on Hungarian soil, intent on recouping his losses.

On March 29 the Yugoslavian representative in Budapest declared that Charles' return constituted a *casus belli* for his country.[18] Beneš demanded the immediate removal of the ex-King, and threatened unspecified reprisals.[19] Rumania declared that the return was "contrary to Rumania's interest." [20] The Conference of Ambassadors, the body set up to administer the peace treaties, insisted that the return of the King could only have "conséquences désastreuses" [21] for Hungary.

Charles had already been warned by Horthy of the likelihood of a Little Entente attack, and of the weakness of Hungary's army.[22]

---

[16] *Ibid.*, pp. 130–31.
[17] A. Boroviczeny, "First Attempt of Karl," in Ellis Ashmead-Bartlett, *The Tragedy of Central Europe* (London: Thornton Butterworth Ltd., 1923), p. 252.
[18] H. F. R., No. 260, March 29, 1921, p. 285.
[19] *Ibid.*, No. 271, March 30, 1921, p. 292.
[20] *Ibid.*, No. 261, March 29, 1921, p. 286.
[21] Quoted in Codresco, *La Petite Entente,* p. 200.
[22] Boroviczeny, "First Attempt of Karl," p. 253.

In the circumstances, he decided to leave, rather than risk the consequences of intervention and war. The status quo remained intact.

It was a victory for the Little Entente. The Hungarian envoy in Paris reported that Berthelot actually believed that the restoration was in France's interest, since it would help forestall an eventual *Anschluss*. However, Berthelot noted that that interest had to be subordinated to the interests of the Little Entente.[23] Later in the summer, Briand told the Hungarians that "France would not adopt an independent policy in Eastern Europe, but would turn over this territory to the newly-created or enlarged countries who had been France's allies in the war." [24]

Beneš attempted to capitalize on the crisis by signing a formal treaty with the Rumanians. He was successful, for Jonescu felt that "le moment psychologique est proche." [25] The new convention was signed on April 23, 1921. It did not differ in any very significant way from the original Czech-Yugoslav pact.

The ring of alliances which constituted the Little Entente was completed on June 7. The Rumanians and the Yugoslavs negotiated an agreement, somewhat different from the two earlier alliances. Belgrade and Bucharest had a common interest in defense against Bulgaria as well as Hungary. Therefore the new treaty provided for common defense and consultation against both potential enemies. The Little Entente was now formally constituted.

Charles' first attempt to regain the throne had succeeded only in driving his opponents closer together, in revealing the strength of the Little Entente, and in weakening his own and his country's position.

Encouraged by the Little Entente's setback in the Burgenland affair, by the parlous condition of Hungary itself, by the urgings of his supporters, and by the imminent dispersal of Hungarian troops loyal to the Hapsburgs, Charles launched his second and final attempt to regain the throne on October 21.[26] He was not

[23] H. F. R., No. 343, April 10, 1921, p. 353.
[24] *Ibid.*, No. 502, June 14, 1921, p. 540.
[25] D. D., No. 46, April 2, 1921, p. 107.
[26] See Werkmann, *The Tragedy of Charles of Hapsburg*, p. 246. The Burgenland affair can be followed in Codresco, *La Petite Entente*, pp. 205 ff.

dissuaded by a letter from Horthy, dated September 4, 1921, which noted that:

Your Majesty is probably aware that Take Jonescu has laid before the Little Entente and Poland a plan for the complete partition of Hungary among her neighbors, in order that these states may be enabled to disarm. The Little Entente is constantly seeking a pretext to put this plan into execution. Your Majesty's appearance would supply just the excuse which they want. . . .[27]

The Czechs mobilized 300,000 men, and the Yugoslavs 200,000, within a week of Charles' new attempt. The Rumanians ordered the mobilization of eight divisions.[28] Beneš immediately announced that "La presence de l'ex-empereur sur le sol hongrois est un casus belli." [29]

The Conference of Ambassadors intervened, in hopes of forestalling an attack by the Little Entente states. Their note to Hungary asked that country "à proclaimer sans délai la déchéance de l'ex-roi Charles," and to provide for his immediate departure, failing which they would decline responsibility for the intervention of the Little Entente.[30]

The Horthy Government interned Charles with the help of troops loyal to the Government. The ex-King was subsequently deported to Madeira, where he died the following year.[31] The Hungarian Government was also compelled to issue a declaration excluding the Hapsburgs from the throne, and subordinating the future choice of a ruling house to preliminary consultation with the Great Powers.

The Little Entente had forced the Conference of Ambassadors to act quickly and conclusively in its behalf. Moreover, the Hapsburg question had been liquidated. The Little Entente had passed its first test. It had dealt with a threat from Hungary, which con-

---

[27] Ibid., p. 229.

[28] Albert Mousset, La Petite Entente (Paris: Editions Bossard, 1923), p. 60.

[29] Ibid., p. 61.

[30] Aurel Cosma, La Petite Entente (Paris: Jouve and Cio, Editeurs, 1928), p. 61.

[31] Werkmann, The Tragedy of Charles of Hapsburg, relates the tale in some detail.

stituted the specific rationale for the alliance, and it had demonstrated the utility of collective action.

Goals and Expectations

The Little Entente emerged as a response to the concrete dangers of an unstable international environment. Successive threats from the machinations of France, Hungary, and the Hapsburgs impelled the three successor states to conciliate their own differences and form a common front against the perils confronting them. The Little Entente was also, however, something more than a response to immediate threats. Its founders, particularly Beneš and Jonescu, viewed it as a means to achieve long-term goals which were independent of, though related to, each of the crises which provoked the formation of the alliance.

The preeminent purpose of the Little Entente was to maintain the status quo established by the peace treaties against all comers —Hungarians, Bulgarians, Hapsburgs, Frenchmen, Germans, or Italians. Jonescu phrased it most precisely in declaring that "notre but était de constituer autour des traités de paix un mur destiné à empêcher toute tentative . . . pour les démolir ou même les ébrecher, car la paix du monde . . . ne peut être basée que sur le maintien intégral de ces traités. . . ."[32]

It was easier to state the goal than it was to discover a means to achieve it. The three allies were united in their desire to control Hungary and permanently exile the Hapsburgs. They were also opposed to an *Anschluss* of Austria and Germany, although somewhat ambivalently: many felt that an *Anschluss* was less dangerous than the return of the Hapsburgs, and might actually help forestall it. Beyond that, their interests began to diverge. The difficulty of conciliating so many conflicting interests had a significant effect, as will be discussed, on Beneš' conception of the kind of alliance which it was possible to create in 1920 and 1921.

[32] Quoted in Codresco, *La Petite Entente*, p. 156: "Our goal was to establish around the peace treaties a wall designed to prevent all attempts . . . to demolish them or even to breach them, because world peace was able to be based only on the complete integrity of these treaties. . . ."

The second long-range goal of the Little Entente involved the desire to keep the Great Powers out of the area and retain control over their own destinies. The danger of Great Power intervention was not illusory. For example, one British ambassador argued that:

I am convinced that the only way in which the various States, forming part of the Empire, can be helped to extricate themselves from their appalling muddle is to take them all in hand and make them do what they are told. . . . It seems to me that we must for a time interfere boldly in the internal affairs of all these States. . . .[33]

If the Great Powers were to be excluded from the area, it was necessary to prove to them that the Successor States were capable of settling their own problems. Thus, as Jonescu argued, "ces accords ont surtout pour but d'éviter que des divergences naturelles entre voisins puissent s'aggraver et présenter une fissure aux intrigues ennemies." [34] Moreover, if the Small Powers could come to an agreement among themselves, the temptation to appeal to a Great Power for support would be diminished.

The desire to exclude the Great Powers, and to settle their own affairs, could only be achieved if the peoples of the Danubian area had faith in their own future, and if they could devise a viable alternative to the plans for confederation which attracted the Great Powers. But the problem of instilling confidence within the area was immense, for it was wracked with internal and external crises.[35] Without a feeling of security about the external situation, internal reforms were impossible. Since the League of Nations was inadequate and the Great Powers ambivalent, the only alternative seemed to be the creation of effective regional arrangements.

The final long-range goal of the Little Entente was particularly critical: to provide an alternative to the various plans for Danubian confederation. Whatever form the new arrangement took, the successor states were quite positive about one thing. They would not allow the old Hungary and the old Austria to be reconstituted.[36]

[33] G. B. D., First Series, Vol. VI, Nov. 7, 1919, p. 352.

[34] Quoted in Cosma, La Petite Entente, p. 32.

[35] For a description of the chaotic conditions, see Eduard Beneš, "La Petite Entente et la Reconstruction de l'Europe Centrale," L'Europe Nouvelle, Sept. 19, 1920, p. 1367.

[36] Cosma, La Petite Entente, p. 28.

In addition, they would not accept any plan which limited their economic independence.[37] The only acceptable solution, once again, seemed to be a regional arrangement which included only those states with similar or complementary interests.

The Little Entente states were in a very difficult situation after the First World War. The utility and wisdom of their independence still had to be proved. They were faced with real and immediate threats both from within and without the area. Their internal stability was precarious, their economies unsound, and they were unable to count on the assured support of any Great Power if their security was threatened. It was a situation in which something had to be done, but, more critically, it had to be done quickly.

It was thus that a debate developed between Jonescu and Beneš on the kind of alliance best suited to stabilize the area and preserve the status quo; for on these two things, everyone was agreed. The critical question involved the kind of alternative to Danubian federation which held most chance of excluding the Great Powers and reserving the right of decision to the victorious Small Powers.

In contrast to his domestic rival Bratianu, Jonescu's vision of the appropriate arrangement for Central Europe was not anti-Slav. It also rested on the exclusion, at least initially, of the old enemy states of Austria and Hungary. To this extent, his ideas paralleled those of Beneš. In other respects, their views were opposed or dissimilar.

Jonescu desired "contrebalancer le bloc germano-hongrois d'une part, et le bloc russe, d'autre part." The *cordon sanitaire* which he envisaged would have comprised the three Little Entente states plus Poland and Greece. The result would be "l'alliance de *tous* les vainqueurs de l'Europe central et oriental pour le maintien de tous les traités contres *toutes* les attaques." [38] Jonescu concluded an article, which had described the nature and extent of the cooperation he foresaw for the five allies, by noting that "We considered that these decisions represented the maximum that could

---

[37] Frederick Hertz, *The Economic Problems of the Danubian States* (London: Victor Gollancz Ltd., 1947), p. 65.

[38] Jonescu quoted in Mousset, *La Petite Entente,* p. 37.

be accomplished for the time being, and trusted the future to strengthen the relations between our states." [39]

But it was just that "future" that Beneš could not trust. The chaos and fear which characterized the area could not be allowed to subsist while extensive diplomatic negotiations were proceeding. It was clear that it was impossible to find a single objective which could immediately unite all five states. No common denominator existed, short of the sudden appearance of an overriding common threat.

It was obviously necessary to find some grounds to unite the area immediately, but that meant that only those states "who felt their security threatened from the same source could cooperate closely." [40] The one immediate and perceived threat was Hungarian revisionism. *Ipso facto,* it became the tie which could unite at least some of the Danubian states. The solution left much to be desired, but a united, powerful, and antirevisionist Little Entente did provide the Great Powers with a polar star by which they could set their courses in central Europe. It proscribed their intervention; it left Danubian affairs to the Danubians; and it dealt with some of the critical problems of the area. If the Little Entente was not a solution to all the problems of the area, it did at least offer the possibility of solution at some future date. By assuming a concrete and effective form by the summer of 1921, it had met the most critical imperative: it was, that is, a *timely* alternative to the threat of chaos.[41]

In place of Jonescu's scheme for an extensive alliance composed of all the victor states, united by indirect and diffuse goals, Beneš preached the virtues of a limited alliance united by identical interests. It was not, therefore, as later critics insisted, a foolish alliance. It was merely one of limited utility.

[39] Relevant parts of the article are translated in Robert Machray, "The Little Entente and Its Policies," *Fortnightly Review,* 1926, pp. 767–78.

[40] Curt F. Beck, *Eduard Beneš's Political Theory: Application of Democracy to International Relations* (Unpublished doctoral dissertation, Harvard University, 1950), p. 137.

[41] On Beneš' vision of the necessity of a democratic order in the future, *ibid.,* p. 134 and *passim.*

The Little Entente did not lack weaknesses. The most significant weakness, undoubtedly, was that it seemed to permanently divide the area into two groups of competing states, one supporting the status quo and the other urging revision. Moreover, the sense of strength which the Little Entente powers derived from their alliance, and from French support, disinclined them to negotiate minor revisions which might have pacified Hungary and prevented the Magyars from seeking Great Power support to achieve their ends. In addition, while the Little Entente was determined to suppress Hungary, it failed to broaden the range of common policies uniting the allies. This is true not only in economic and social terms but also in relation to the different Great Power threats that each of the three states faced.

Still, before the convolutions of the 1930s, the Little Entente was a potent and influential factor in European politics. Its political influence far exceeded that which any single member of the group could have wielded. It achieved none of its aims perfectly, but it did achieve most of them at least partially—and probably better than any conceivable alternative. It does not seem reasonable to condemn it for its failures in the Nazi era. It had never been conceived as an alliance capable of handling Great Power conflicts. In the circumstances, its failure was beyond its control.

The Little Entente in Evolution

The leaders of the Little Entente, flushed with the success of their venture against the Hapsburgs, began to expand the scope of their activities. The general tasks they set for themselves were quite simple. They hoped, on the one hand, to expand the Little Entente so that it would encompass all the status quo Powers in Central Europe. And, on the other hand, they hoped to render the alliance which they had already constructed into a stronger and more organic instrument. If these two aims should conflict—if, for example, the price Poland set for inclusion should be too high in terms of the original goals of the three partners—then, most assuredly, the emphasis on strengthening the alliance would prevail over the emphasis on expansion. The primary goal of the Little Entente remained the same: to safeguard its local interests against all threats, particularly the Hungarian one. But, insofar as they could accomplish this aim without remaining transfixed by it, they also hoped to develop close ties with Poland and Greece. Moreover, they hoped to develop a positive program for central Europe, the attraction of which would dilute the mistrust and suspicion the creation of the alliance had engendered in various circles in Europe. It was quite clear, as one observer was to note later, that "the scope of these aims clearly went beyond the terms of the treaties which had established the Little Entente. . . ."[42]

The Genoa Conference, scheduled for April and May, 1922, was one of the landmarks of interwar history. Occurring amid an enervating economic crisis, as well as deteriorating situations in the Near East and Germany, it brought together all the important European Powers, including, for the first time, the Soviet Union. The Genoa Conference failed in its purpose of economic reconstruction, at least in part because of the developing struggle between Poincaré and Lloyd George. It is perhaps symbolic of its real failure that the Conference is best remembered for the Rapallo pact between the two pariahs, Germany and the Soviet Union. But from one standpoint at least, the Genoa Conference was a significant success. The Little Entente emerged from it as "la quatrième grande puissance dans le concert européen."[43]

The common front essayed by the Little Entente (plus Poland) appeared particularly striking amid the chaos and uncertainty that characterized the rest of the Conference. They soon reaped just reward for their efforts, for after the stunning announcement of the Rapallo pact, the other Great Powers invited the Little Entente to send a delegate to the meetings of the Supreme Council. The distinction between "puissances principales" and "puissances à intérêts limités" finally seemed to have been obliterated. Parenthetically, it is not without significance that on all critical issues "la Petite Entente fit toujours cause commune avec la France, et dejoua la politique britannique. . . ."[44]

[42] Anonymous, "The Foreign Policy of the Little Entente," *Slavonic Review*, 1926–1927, p. 528.

[43] Cosma, *La Petite Entente*, p. 95.

[44] Codresco, *La Petite Entente*, p. 264.

Buoyed by success, the three allies extended the scope of the treaties which bound them, and agreed to meet in at least two formal conferences each year.[45] The Little Entente no longer limited itself to riding herd over Hungary. Henceforth it "adoptera incessamment sa politique à la situation internationale, crée par les évênements les plus récents de l'Europe entière et deviendra un veritable organisme international." [46]

Despite the close nature of the ties which bound them together, France had not yet signed a formal alliance treaty with any of the Little Entente countries.[47] Foch broached the subject to the Czechs in May 1923 but found Benes hesitant. He preferred a joint Anglo-French guarantee, since a bilateral pact might seem to put the Czechs permanently in the French sphere.[48] Friction between Paris and London precluded a double guarantee, and the Czechs finally agreed to sign a bilateral pact. The treaty, concluded in January 1924, was not unusual. It provided for consultation when common interests were endangered, but it did not bind either party to any automatic responses. General Staff conversations began in January 1924 but collaboration was never very active, and was soon nonexistent.[49]

[45] For the military agreements of the Little Entente, see Alfred Vagts, *Defense and Diplomacy* (New York: Kings Crown Press, 1956), p. 133.

[46] Codresco, *La Petite Entente*, p. 288: "would consistently adjust its policies to the international situation created by the most recent events in all of Europe and it would become a true international organ." Polish relations with the Little Entente, and especially Czechoslovakia, reached their high point in 1922, but cooperation declined after that. The Poles would not join an alliance which offered no protection against either Germany or the Soviet Union; and Beneš was unwilling to sign any agreement which appeared to align his country against any Great Power. Thus the Little Entente was never very attractive to a Poland which had nothing against Hungary; and the Poles were never very attractive allies to Benes, as they appeared "adventurist" and unstable (as well as right-wing and conservative). The Rumanians, however, who shared a common anti-Soviet position with Poland, would have liked the Poles in the Little Entente—the stumbling bloc was always Benes' refusal to take an anti-Soviet position. See Wandycz, *France and Her Eastern Allies*, pp. 250–64.

[47] France had military missions in each of these countries, and was also pursuing an active lending policy in the area. See Wandycz, *France and Her Eastern Allies, passim*.

[48] See Jules Laroche, *Au Quai D'Orsay avec Briand et Poincaré*, pp. 487–88.

[49] Vagts, *Defense and Diplomacy*, p. 135. Beneš always conceived the pact with

The logical conclusion of the French system rested on the creation of formal ties with Yugoslavia and Rumania also. The problem proved to be more difficult in each of these cases. The stumbling block with Yugoslavia was Italy. Rome had never been more than lukewarm to the Little Entente, though it had supported it in its efforts to exclude the Hapsburgs and prevent an *Anschluss*. Mussolini, like his predecessors, was worried about French domination of the area. He also wanted to settle the continuing crisis with the Yugoslavs over Fiume and the Adriatic. The French at first refused to sign a bilateral pact with Yugoslavia, and sought to devise a tripartite formula which would satisfy Mussolini, and also safeguard the peace settlement.[50] They were unsuccessful.

Italy's reaction to the Czech-French pact was to accuse the French of trying to isolate Italy and construct a new hegemony in central Europe.[51] According to the Czech minister in Rome, Beneš attempted to pacify Italy by personally expediting the conclusion of an Italian-Yugoslav agreement on Fiume (which was signed in January 1924).[52]

The Czechs also began negotiating with the Italians early in 1924. The French were unenthusiastic, for they feared that the Italians would use the agreement to infiltrate the Little Entente. Beneš insisted, nevertheless, arguing that it would bind Italy to preserve the peace treaties; i.e., Italy would not support revision. The pact was finally signed in May 1924, providing for mutual consultation in the face of a common threat, but it never amounted to much. In any case, the Franco-Italian conflict had, for the mean-

---

France in a limited fashion. He declared that it was "a very pliable instrument calling for frequent conferences on a basis of mutual equality but reserving complete liberty of action to both partners." Quoted in Wandycz, *France and Her Eastern Allies,* p. 300. Again, Beneš did not want to seem too tied to any Great Power—even France whose policies toward Germany he disapproved. Nor did he want to antagonize London, Berlin, or Rome. Contrary to rumors at the time, the pact did not contain a secret military convention; it only provided for General Staff consultations.

[50] Laroche, *Au Quai D'Orsay avec Briand,* p. 223.

[51] Vlastimil Kybal, "Czechoslovakia and Italy: My Negotiations with Mussolini," *Journal of Central European Affairs,* XIV (Jan. 1954 and April 1954), Part II, p. 66.

[52] *Ibid.,* p. 68.

time, set aside the conclusion of a Franco-Yugoslav pact. The French still sought a formula which would satisfy all the divergent interests. They all might be needed some day.

The Rumanian link in the French chain was delayed because of the Soviet problem. The Little Entente countries had agreed to disagree on their policies toward Moscow. Nevertheless, Rumania was determined to receive a French guarantee of Bessarabia. The French appeared willing, if Yugoslavia also agreed to come to Rumania's aid against the Soviets. Beneš interceded at this point, and promised Czech aid only if Hungary should aid the Soviets—an unlikely event. Beneš' intervention, as well as a disinclination to involve themselves with the Soviet Union, led the Yugoslavs to refuse the French condition.[53] Thus Rumania would also have to wait a few years before it could be formally enrolled in the French system.

In the meanwhile, the Little Entente had adopted a positive and constructive attitude toward most of Europe's problems. The alliance strongly supported both the Draft Treaty of Mutual Assistance and the Geneva Protocol. It also actively supported efforts to aid both Austria and Hungary. Toward the feuding Great Powers, the three states adopted a policy mediatory in form, but which usually supported France when any particular issue was brought to a head. The deleterious effects of extreme partiality for the status quo, and for French policy, seemed theoretical or uncertain. As long as its opposition was scattered and weak, still licking the wounds of war, success was assured. No one who wanted to was strong enough to challenge an alliance which, at the least, was quite sure about what it did not want to see happen.

Beneš and his partners in the Little Entente greeted the Locarno Pact with much overt enthusiasm. In defending the agreement in Parliament, he pointed out the ways in which it guaranteed French military aid in circumstances where it had previously been optional. And he concluded by noting that Locarno "est, pour une longue periode de temps, l'acceptation du status quo dans l'Eu-

[53] Felix John Vondracek, *The Foreign Policy of Czechoslovakia, 1918–1935* (New York: Columbia University Press, 1937), pp. 223 ff.

rope occidentale et central, ce qui a une immense portée politique. . . ." [54]

However, there is evidence that Beneš' public position was far
more favorable than his private one. The American chargé in
Prague cabled home on March 18 that:

The German offer is viewed as a dexterous effort to separate Poland
and this country from France and Belgium, or that failing France and
Belgium from Great Britain. It is interpreted as an admission that
Germany will not permanently accept her eastern frontiers and, consequently, as an inferential repudiation of the treaties which established
them. . . . [55]

Beneš also told the chargé that he did not believe the territorial
status quo in central Europe could be maintained in the long run,
but that he approved the German offer anyway, primarily because
he felt that the guarantee to France implied a guarantee to the
Czechs because of their alliance. Moreover, he did not feel that
Germany would be a real threat for twenty years. [56]

Yet there could be no denying that Locarno had certain implications which boded ill for the future security of the Small
Powers of Central Europe. As a result, for the first time in some
years, the Poles and Czechs began to move together, [57] even to the
extent of signing a treaty of conciliation and arbitration in 1926.
It could not be said, however, that the treaty heralded a new era
of cooperation between Prague and Warsaw. It was rather the

---

[54] Eduard Beneš, "Les Accords de Locarno" (Prague: Orbis, 1925), p. 24 and
passim. The Locarno pact consisted of five related treaties. The first was a Treaty
of Mutual Guarantee, limited to Germany's western borders, providing for
maintenance of the status quo and arbitration or conciliation of disputes: war was
illegal unless in self-defence or in support of the League. Great Britain and Italy
were the guarantors. The other four treaties were arbitration pacts between
Germany and France, Belgium, Czechoslovakia, and Poland.

[55] Quoted in Zygmunt J. Gasiorowski, "Beneš and Locarno: Some Unpublished
Documents," *The Review of Politics*, XX (April 1958), pp. 210–11.

[56] *Ibid.*, p. 215. Dispatch of April 3, 1925.

[57] *Ibid.*, p. 218. They had some reason to do so. Stresemann gloated that the
Czechs and Poles at Locarno ". . . had to sit in a neighboring room until we let
them in . . . such was the situation of states which had been so pampered until
then, because they were the servants of others, but were dropped the moment it
seemed possible to come to an understanding with Germany." Quoted in
Wandycz, *France and Her Eastern Allies*, p. 361.

ephemeral response of two enemies, wounded by a common enemy, turning to each other for solace until more suitable partners could be found.

In the final analysis, the Locarno Pacts did not have a great impact on the Little Entente. They affected only the Czechs directly, and, in any event, it was clear that the threats they might engender were still far off.[58] In the meantime, they ushered in a period when the political influence of the Little Entente would flourish, unhampered by any significant threats to the territorial status quo.

The ideal solution to the security problem in Europe, or so it seemed from the East, would have been a Great Power entente based on the French conception of the way to maintain peace. But whatever happened between the Great Powers themselves, the Small Powers could influence their decisions only if they confronted them with a determined, consistent, and nonprovocative common front. The Little Entente was meant, therefore, to operate on at least two levels. On the one hand, it served as the instrument of pacification and settlement in Central Europe. However, the Little Entente was also a political instrument to develop and maintain the influence of a united group of Small Powers who, in isolation, offered the Great Powers no clear signal as to future policy in Central Europe. With confidence bolstered by several triumphs, and a lack of powerful opposition, the Little Entente had gone a long way toward success by the end of 1925: Central Europe was pacified, the Little Entente powers were the *immediate* arbiters of its destiny, and it was to their united force that the Great Powers turned when Danubian questions arose.

But by 1925 the sense of immediacy which had characterized the foundation of the alliance had begun to dissipate. If it was to survive and prosper in succeeding years, its political horizons would inevitably have to expand. It did not appear impossible to do so— as long as the Soviet, German, and Italian threats remained sub-

[58] Their ultimate effect was very serious. As Professor Wandycz notes: "Eastern alliances could function only if France were determined and able to help Warsaw or Prague at the *casus foederis* by starting an offensive action across the Rhine. Locarno by creating an illusion of peace and security in the west, and by limiting French freedom of intervention against Germany, led naturally to a gradual abandonment of offensive strategy." (367–68).

merged, and as long as the economic system did not break down completely.

The Little Entente in the Locarno Years

Beneš was extraordinarily sanguine about the international situation in 1930. He declared that "notre Etat n'est réalement en présence d'aucune question internationale, ni d'aucun conflit, qui ne soient résolus. En un mot, tout a été fait." [59] However, before Beneš could even draft a new speech, the international order began to crumble under the accumulated weight of economic disaster and international aggression. The forces held dormant for ten years by the overwhelming power of the victor states, by the weakness of the dissatisfied, and by the temporary palliatives which were plastered on each succeeding crack in the new order, suddenly re-emerged to challenge the peace settlement of 1919.

The Little Entente, the prime benefactor of the new legitimacy, struggled manfully to remain afloat in the midst of each storm, and to retain all its gains intact. For some years, as Beneš' judgment indicates, they seemed to be successful. Hungary was still isolated, France still strong, the other Great Powers weak, disinterested, or occupied elsewhere; their economies were progressing, if fitfully, and they seemed to have proved their ability to function as independent entities. But the depression, the breakdown of constitutional government, and the reemergence of Great Power struggles contrived to weaken the ties which bound the successor states together. The most dangerous immediate threat which confronted them was the conversion of Italy to an avowed revisionist policy, after 1928, and its subsequent struggle for hegemony with France. Troubled by the effects of this conflict, always latent in Italian policy, as well as by developing economic and internal crises, the Little Entente states responded by reorganizing their alliance, perhaps in the hope that the strength which would not come from common interests and real power would come from formal ties.

In general, Italy's aims in southeastern Europe were quite clear.

[59] Eduard Beneš, *La Situation de L'Europe, La Société des Nations et la Tchecoslovaquie* (Prague: Orbis, 1930), p. 29.

She wanted to keep the French out, to isolate and destroy Yugo-slavia, and to establish a position of dominance in Albania and Austria.[60] The one thing she most feared was the creation of a strong pro-Slavic bloc, under French auspices, on her northern frontier.

Yugoslavia had made numerous efforts to come to an agreement with Italy. Several treaties had been negotiated, each hopefully sig-nifying the end of strife between the two countries, but each settle-ment proved provisional and unsatisfactory. The Albanian question remained insoluble. Neither Rome nor Belgrade could accept the other's control of Zog's little kingdom.

The Yugoslavs, unable to conclude an acceptable agreement with Mussolini, proceeded to initial a pact with France in March of 1926. The French, after pressuring the Rumanians to accept an extension of their pact with Poland, also signed a treaty of alliance with Bucharest in June. However, Mussolini had no intention of allowing French forays into Southeastern Europe to go unanswered. His first response was the conclusion of a treaty of friendship and collaboration with the Rumanians, an act which immediately gave rise to rumors of the imminent dissolution of the Little Entente. Rumania denied the rumors. At best she was undoubtedly only seeking to straddle all available fences.

Mussolini was not yet through. In November 1926 he signed a treaty with Albania, unilaterally guaranteeing the integrity of that small country. In April 1927 he signed a treaty of collaboration with Hungary, the arch apostle of revision. The die seemed to have been thrown: Italy apparently had decided to cast its lot with the discontented states (always, of course, on the assumption that Italy's own gains in 1919 would not be challenged).

The Yugoslavs decided, according to one source, that the Italians hoped to destroy the French system by isolating and destroying their own country. Rome apparently sought a bloc, under its con-trol, consisting of Hungary, Rumania, Bulgaria, and a weakened Yugoslavia. Marinkovic, the foreign minister, thought that he could

[60] See Martin Wight, "Eastern Europe," *The World in March 1939* edited by Arnold Toynbee and Frank T. Ashton-Gwatkin (London: Oxford University Press, 1952), p. 239.

end the "Italian game" by signing an open security pact with
France, thereby crushing Italy's hopes of isolating Yugoslavia. The
French reluctantly agreed, and in November 1927 the security
pact became official, though the French, undoubtedly fearing Yugoslav adventurism, refused to initial a military convention.[61]

Yugoslavia and Italy were now at sword's point. The French
were unhappy, for they would have preferred to draft both countries into their system of alliances. Mussolini's actions and threats,
however, destroyed any possibility of satisfying Italy without disrupting the Little Entente. Faced with the choice of alienating the
Little Entente, a faithful and consistent ally, or alienating Italy, at
best a risky and uncertain friend, the Quai d'Orsay lined up with
the Little Entente. Rumania was the uncertain factor, since it
gained virtually nothing from an anti-Italian policy.

The portents were ominous. Two camps had reemerged in one
part of Europe, and, as Toynbee noted, Franco-Italian rivalry:

. . . tended once again to turn the local troubles of South-Eastern
Europe into a danger to the peace of Europe in general. . . . Italy and
France seemed to be assuming the roles which Russia and Austria-
Hungary had played there in a previous act. . . .[62]

Hungary also now had an ally, an ally which the other Great Powers might some day consider more important than the Little Entente.

The Little Entente states were opposed to both the restoration of
the Hapsburgs and an Austro-German *Anschluss*. The French
position was somewhat different: Paris would not tolerate *Anschluss*, but its opposition to the Hapsburgs depended on the influence of the Little Entente and on the imminence of *Anschluss*.
That is, if the choice came to an either/or proposition, France
would opt for the Hapsburgs as the lesser evil. Since the calcula-

[61] The material in the foregoing paragraph comes from Jacob B. Hoptner,
Yugoslavia in Crisis: 1934–1941 (Doctoral Dissertation, Columbia University,
1958), pp. 16–18. This dissertation has recently been published, but my page
references are to the dissertation.

On Italian policy, see also M. H. H. Macartney and Paul Cremona, *Italy's
Foreign and Colonial Policy, 1914–1937* (London: Oxford University Press,
1938).

[62] Arnold Toynbee, *Survey of International Affairs, 1927* (London: Oxford
University Press, 1926), p. 153.

tions of the Little Entente postulated equal opposition to both alternatives, and *Anschluss* over the Hapsburgs, if forced to choose, the best solution for France was the maintenance of the status quo.[63] But the deteriorating economic situation in Austria and Germany was rapidly undermining the stability of both countries.

The announcement of an Austro-German customs union in March 1931 illuminated France's dilemma. Because Paris feared the political effects of a customs union, and because the Little Entente reacted vigorously against the idea, the maneuver had to be obstructed. France could not afford to antagonize the Little Entente for it had no viable alternative to it until Laval attempted to reach an agreement with Italy, at the expense of Yugoslavia.

The Little Entente was not completely unified on the question, but after some French and Czech pressures a common front did emerge.[64] Just as Rumania and Czechoslovakia were loath to embroil themselves in the Italian-Yugoslav crisis, and Yugoslavia and Czechoslovakia in the Rumanian-Soviet struggle, so now Rumania and Yugoslavia were reluctant to involve themselves in a situation which threatened the Czechs more than themselves. Nevertheless, the Little Entente as an alliance did offer some advantages: the negative advantage of diplomatic silence by two partners and the assurance that the prime enemy could not use either of the other allies as a wedge to infiltrate Central Europe.

In the years between 1929 and 1933, the international scene was shaken by a series of disasters. Japan had defied the League of Nations; the Disarmament Conference was floundering; the Italian threat to Yugoslavia was growing more menacing; fascism was threatening the internal stability of Rumania and Yugoslavia; and, finally, the economic situation was becoming increasingly desperate.

The compromise agreement among the Great Powers at the Dis-

---

[63] Beneš in particular feared a Hapsburg restoration: ". . . he preferred even an *Anschluss* to the restoration of the Hapsburgs." Quoted in William E. Scott, *Alliance Against Hitler: The Origins of the Franco-Soviet Pact* (Durham, N.C.: Duke University Press, 1962), p. 82.

[64] Arnold Toynbee, *Survey of International Affairs, 1931*, p. 305.

armament Conference, signed on December 10, 1932 undoubtedly provided the immediate incentive for the reorganization of the Little Entente. One of its clauses stipulated that "l'un des principes qui doit servir de guide à la Conference du désarmement devrait être l'octroi à l'Allemagne, *ainsi qu'aux autres puissances desarmées par les traités,* de l'égalité des droits dans un regime qui comprendrait, pour toutes les nations, la sécurité." [65] The italicized clause worried the three allies. The last thing they wanted was a rearmed Hungary, Austria, and Bulgaria.

At the annual alliance conference in Belgrade in December 1932, the Foreign Ministers announced that they had decided to strengthen their alliance. A new organizational pact was to be signed early in 1933. [66] In the interval, Italy was detected in a minor violation of the disarmament clauses of the Treaty of St. Germain. The Little Entente countries sought to bring the affair before the League of Nations, but their efforts were rebuffed by Great Britain and France, both of whom wanted to conciliate Italy.[67]

It is not surprising, therefore, to discover that the Pact of Organization, which the Little Entente signed on February 16, 1933, was more extensive than the arrangement foreseen in 1932. A Permanent Council and a Secretariat were established, and a new Economic Council was created. The key change was an agreement that every new pact of any one of the member states, as well as any economic arrangement, required the unanimous consent of the Permanent Council. Economic interests were to be progressively coordinated; the treaties which bound them together were indefinitely prolonged, and the views of the alliance were to be presented by a single delegation in the future.[68]

[65] Quoted in Lazare Marcovitch, *La Politique Extérieure de la Yougoslavie* (Paris: Societé Général D'Imprimerie, 1935), p. 9: "One of the principles which must guide the Disarmament Conference must be the concession to Germany, *as well as to the other states disarmed by the treaties,* of equality of rights in a settlement which includes security for all states." (My italics.)

[66] Robert Machray, *The Struggle for the Danube and the Little Entente, 1929–1938* (London: George Allen and Unwin, Ltd., 1938), p. 104.

[67] For the Hirtenberg affair, as it was called, see *G. B. D.,* Second Series, V, 58–59.

[68] Machray, *The Struggle for the Danube,* pp. 111–13 and 324–26 for details.

These efforts, of course, came too late. There was no way in which the alliance could be reorganized to counter the superior power of its enemies or the weakness of its friends. Nor could it do much about the erosion of constitutional government within Rumania and Yugoslavia. The fascist or reactionary governments which emerged found more affinities with Germany and Italy than they did with France or Great Britain.

The enthusiasm with which each of the three allies described the significance of the reorganization was spurious. Beneš revealed the substantive impact of the new arrangement when he noted that the obligations which each state accepted were "éssentielle-ment les mémes qu'auparavant," but "elles sont seulement for-mulées desormais et pour tout l'avenir en toute précision juri-dique." [69] That is to say, the Little Entente was running hard to stay in the same place.

The private rationalizations of the pact, as well as the public reactions of other states, were less sanguine. In Italy "it was re-sented as an offensively ingenious attempt . . . for the purpose of claiming, conjointly, the rank of a Great Power." [70] The Czech Ambassador told Neurath that "Italy's attitude toward Yugoslavia and Hungary had been the special occasion for this step by the Little Entente." [71] The Rumanian Minister, citing other factors as decisive, told Neurath that it was "a demonstration against the revision of the boundaries." He concluded with an expression of disinterest in Germany's revisionist aims, provided they left Ru-mania's spoils untouched.[72] And Benes told Simon that "the object of the reorganization was eventually to include Hungary." He then noted the pacific effect the new pact would have: "As none of the component parties could afford to be drawn into war with

[69] Eduard Beneš, Le Pacte D'Organisation de la Petite Entente et L'Etat Actuel de la Politique International (Prague: Orbis, 1933), p. 41.

[70] Arnold Toynbee, Survey of International Affairs, 1933 (London: Oxford University Press, 1932), p. 206.

[71] Documents on German Foreign Policy, 1918–1945 (Washington: U.S. Government Printing Office, 1957), Series C, Vol. I, No. 31, Feb. 22, 1933, p. 68. Henceforth cited as D. G. F. P.

[72] Ibid., No. 32, Feb. 22, 1933, pp. 69–70.

a great neighbor of another component, it followed that each party used its influence with its ally in a pacific sense. . . ." [73]

Out of the grab bag of motives and excuses which each of the Little Entente countries adduced as the rationale for the new pact, one fact emerges clearly. The idea of a narrowly conceived national interest was beginning to prevail over any wider conception, which might have placed more value on the alliance itself. Each state began seeking the policy which offered the best hope of buying off its prime antagonist. Titulescu, virtually the symbol of the status quo, reportedly told the Germans that "the Poles are a matter of complete indifference to Titulescu";[74] and "Rumania had no objection to the Anschluss of Austria with Germany." [75] And King Alexander allegedly told the German minister in Belgrade that "to have Germany as a neighbor would suit him quite well, for an understanding between Germany and Austria would finally solve the Austrian question." [76]

Yet, despite their apparent disinclination to rely on the Little Entente when the chips were down, the three allies had negotiated an extensive reorganization which appeared to attest to the continuing vitality of their alliance. There is no mystery here. To have refused to strengthen the alliance, or to have dissolved it, would have meant a significant loss of prestige and influence. It was, in any event, better to rely on a weak reed, for the time being, than no reed at all. The new pact might at least buy time to shop around for new partners. Moreover, a strengthened Little Entente promised each ally a stronger bargaining position: defection from a powerful alliance might be worth more than defection from an obviously weak alliance. Finally, none of the three states had an attractive alternative. It was still too early to jump aboard the German ship, or to jump off the French one.

Thus when the next crisis arose, the debate on the Four Power Pact, the Little Entente remained united. They successfully forced

[73] G. B. D., Second Series, Vol. V, No. 43, March 18, 1933, p. 64.
[74] D. G. F. P., Series C, Vol. I, No. 118, March 27, 1933, p. 220.
[75] Ibid., No. 328, June 21, 1933, p. 585.
[76] Ibid., No. 279, June 1, 1933, p. 509.

France to emasculate the Pact, until it was virtually useless. As St. Leger told Lord Tyrrell, "nothing less would satisfy the Little Entente, and, until the Little Entente had declared that their anxiety was allayed, no French Parliament would allow France to become a party." [77] It was an impressive triumph for the Little Entente—one of its last. Still, it would manage to exercise a little influence on the events to come, certainly more than each of the states could have achieved by itself.

The Disruption of the Little Entente

Italian pressure after 1926 had forced the Little Entente countries to tighten their ties with France. The French treaty with Yugoslavia in 1927, in particular, was designed to reinsure the Yugoslavs against the danger of an Italian-Hungarian alliance. However, the Italian threat clearly foreshadowed the preeminent danger which confronted the Little Entente: that is to say, the enmity of a Great Power directed solely against one of the entente partners. Henceforth, risks and gains were in disequilibrium, since neither Czechoslovakia nor Rumania were essentially endangered by the Italian threat, nor willing to enlarge the scope of the alliance merely to protect Yugoslavia. The only immediate common threat was Hungary, and the Little Entente limited its specific commitments to the threat represented by Magyar and Hapsburg revisionism. The aid they were willing to offer each other against the specific Great Power threats each confronted was provisional and contingent. They promised to forestall any Hungarian attempt to attack an ally beleaguered by a major threat, but beyond that each state could only offer diplomatic support or neutrality. Consequently, Yugoslavia was left to extricate itself from the Italian danger, though the Little Entente's efforts to revise and perfect the form of their alliance, but not to extend its obligations, indirectly aided Belgrade. The fact that the Yugoslavs were successful in maintaining their integrity may, in large part, be attributed to the weakness of the Italian threat.

[77] G. B. D., Second Series, Vol. V, No. 178, May 29, 1933, p. 281.

After 1933, however, Germany was the major threat. This time, it was the Czechs who found themselves exposed and endangered. Prague, already allied with France, sought to make assurance doubly sure by seeking Soviet support. Neither the Rumanians nor the Yugoslavs could accept this new departure in interwar politics: the Rumanians because they considered the Soviets as their prime antagonists and the Yugoslavs because their ruling dynasty was closely related to the Romanovs. Each turned elsewhere for support, leaving the Czechs to fend for themselves. Beneš could hardly complain, since he had previously refused to guarantee his allies against their Great Power enemies, but the situation was critically different in one respect. The Nazi threat to Czechoslovakia was very real, very immediate, and very powerful. The Soviet and Italian threats had been provisional, ambiguous and distant.

Every power in Europe saw some danger in German resurgence. Nevertheless, all but France and Czechoslovakia also foresaw advantages from Germany's full-scale return to international politics. For Italy, a powerful Germany presented an opportunity to resume its traditional balancing role, and the recurrent vision of determining that balance once again affected its policies. For Poland, a powerful Germany, bent on revision—a terrible threat to the owners of the "Polish Corridor"—also meant relief from the dangers of a Soviet-German pact. For Rumania, Germany's revisionism, which affected it only indirectly, converted the Soviet Union into a staunch defender of the status quo: Bessarabia was momentarily safe. And for the Yugoslavs, a resurgence of Germany relieved it of considerable Italian pressure in the Adriatic. Germany also offered all the states of southeastern Europe an economic market beyond their wildest dreams. Germany was both threat and promise, but the threat seemed long-range, the promise immediate. It was too much to ask the already bedeviled statesmen of southeastern Europe to refuse the promise in order to ward off the danger.

The French sought to counter the German threat by extending and improving their alliance system. The most obvious potential ally was Italy, since the Italians were equally fearful of *Anschluss*.

The Czechs were agreeable to the idea of a Franco-Italian pact, which would guarantee the independence of Austria, but the Yugoslavs were upset. They would have preferred Hitler in Vienna, rather than Mussolini. Any increase in Italian influence in Austria would have left the Yugoslavs encircled by hostile states. In addition, there was some indication that France favored a restoration of the Hapsburgs, if the only other alternative was *Anschluss*; but the Hapsburgs were still anathema to Yugoslavia. It was clear to Belgrade that any Franco-Italian pact could only be made at its expense. It was this threat which undoubtedly lay behind Alexander's ill-fated trip to France in October 1934.[78]

After the death of Alexander, Italy attempted to reach some sort of agreement with Yugoslavia. Such a pact would have bolstered the Italian position against Germany, and it also would have left Italy's northern frontier secure during her Ethiopian adventure. The problem was Italy's pact with Hungary. As long as Hungary threatened all of the Little Entente states, and Italy openly or tacitly supported her efforts, neither Belgrade nor Bucharest could arrive at an entente with Rome. The problem was somewhat diluted by the fact that the Hungarian threat to the Little Entente was asymmetrical. It was worse to Czechoslovakia and Rumania than it was to Yugoslavia. Prodded by Italy, Hungary was willing to forego its claims in Yugoslavia, provided she was assured of her part of the spoils in Czechoslovakia. The Yugoslavia of Prince Paul and Stoyadinovitch tacitly capitulated. They eventually signed a treaty with Italy, and assured the Hungarians they would not help the Czechs, provided the Hungarians were shrewd enough to let Germany strike the first blow. The conflict between Rumania and Hungary remained insoluble, and an effective Rumanian-Italian agreement was thus never achieved.

The Yugoslavs also sought German support. They hoped thereby to foil an Italian-German pact, which would have left them isolated and helpless. They sought reinsurance against French attempts to restore the Hapsburgs (which Germany opposed, since it would have proscribed *Anschluss*), and against Italian attempts

[78] Yugoslavia was also nervous about the implications of Barthou's negotiations with the Soviets. See Scott, *Alliance Against Hitler,* pp. 201–2.

to support Croatian separatists and achieve dominance in the Adriatic. The Yugoslavs thus tried to ride all the horses: formal ties with old allies were renewed; a new pact was signed with Italy; Germany was conciliated, and the Hungarian threat was directed elsewhere. It was a superficially virtuosic performance, but its success rested on the continuation of German-Italian friction. If that disappeared, so too would Belgrade's independence.

In sum, the German threat to Czechoslovakia, the Italian threat to Yugoslavia, and the weakness of Great Britain and France produced a situation in which the Little Entente states desperately sought security through the support of friendly Great Powers—but either without their allies, or at their expense. Revision could be denounced as fervently as ever, but the denunciations were insincere if it was clear that whatever changes were to take place would only deprive allies of territory.

The German Minister in Belgrade reported that:

The impression here was increasing that France would not hesitate to jettison Yugoslavia's interests if thereby she could gain Italian support in matters of disarmament and her own security. This feeling of impotent hatred for Italy and mistrust of France had produced the spontaneous desire of developing, if possible, closer relations with Germany. . . . There was a feeling of being abandoned, and a search for the support of a great power with whom no differences existed, such as Germany was and would continue to be. . . .[79]

Thus Yugoslavia was rapidly becoming disenchanted with the fruits of its traditional policies. Barthou had failed to convince them that rapprochement with Italy was a necessary prerequisite for European peace. In fact, Belgrade feared Italian intervention in Austria more than German intervention; German pressure was actually welcomed as a menace to Mussolini's designs.[80]

King Alexander, worried about the potential effects of an Italian-

[79] D. G. F. P., Series C, Vol. III, No. 39, June 27, 1934, p. 93.

[80] See G. E. R. Gedye, *Betrayal in Central Europe* (New York: Harper & Brothers, 1939), p. 122; also Arnold Toynbee, *Survey of International Affairs, 1934*, p. 557. However it ought to be noted that Barthou got strong support for his scheme for an "Eastern Locarno" in 1939 from *all* of the Little Entente states: they would agree to anything which promised support against revisionism. See Scott, *Alliance Against Hitler*, pp. 173–75.

French entente, visited France in October. Before leaving, he had informed the Germans that "I shall never take part in a coalition to settle Central European affairs, if it does not include Germany." [81] His assassination, along with Barthou's, left his ultimate intentions obscure. He was succeeded by a regency directed by Prince Paul. Pierre Laval inherited Barthou's mantle.

The Yugoslavs intended to publicly condemn Italy and Hungary—the countries responsible for sheltering the Croat terrorists who murdered Alexander and Barthou—before the League of Nations. Their efforts were forestalled by Great Britain and France, both of whom desired to appease Italy. They were forced to confine their prosecution to Hungary. Anthony Eden had already informed them that "if Yugoslavia insisted on pressing its case against Italy and Mussolini decided to go to war on that account, England would not help the Yugoslavs." [82] Laval took the same position.

The fact that they were left in isolation against Italy weighed heavily on Yugoslav calculations. The Little Entente had rallied to their cause,[83] but clearly only the unqualified support of a Great Power counted when the struggle pitted a Small Power against another Great Power.

The Franco-Italian accord in January 1935, and the military agreement which followed in June, were the linchpins of Laval's "grand design." He noted that:

Italy was the corridor which would permit us to rejoin the 100 divisions of the Little Entente armies. Italy was the corridor through Middle Eastern Europe towards Moscow, that is to say, towards the Soviet Army. I put into effect the policy of encirclement.[84]

[81] Quoted in Hoptner, *Yugoslavia in Crisis*, p. 31.

[82] *Ibid.*, p. 35. For Laval's position, see Scott, *Alliance Against Hitler*, p. 214. For Eden's version of the affair, which of course portrays Lord Avon as nothing but an "honest broker," etc., see Anthony Eden, *Facing the Dictators* (London: Cassell & Company, Ltd., 1962), pp. 108–19.

[83] Robert Lee Wolff, *The Balkans in Our Time* (Cambridge: Harvard University Press, 1956), notes that "The murder of King Alexander might well have opened southeast Europe to Mussolini . . . had not Yugoslavia been firmly linked to both the Little Entente and Balkan Entente and receiving full support from its Allies" (p. 158).

[84] Quoted in Arthur Furnia, *The Diplomacy of Appeasement: Anglo-French Relations and the Prelude to World War II, 1931–1938* (Washington, D.C.: The University Press, 1960), p. 131.

Laval had failed, however, to reconcile his other allies to his new policy. R. W. Seton-Watson reported that the effect of the Laval-Mussolini entente was so devastating in southeastern Europe that "French influence for a time sank almost to zero." [85] The Italians also apparently felt that the Rome accords had dealt the Little Entente a deathblow for Count Szembek of Poland reports the Italian Ambassador as saying "nous avons enfin réussi à couper la Petite Entente." [86]

The Yugoslavs were particularly bitter, and neither the Czechs nor the Rumanians were enthusiastic. Mussolini's support of the status quo was always expediential. Thus he was, even to Prague and Bucharest, an acceptable ally only of the last resort. Neither was sure it was quite that late.

For Belgrade, the Rome accords constituted a fatal thrust at the remnants of Alexander's traditional policy. Laval's efforts could succeed only if a Franco-Italian pact was preceded by a settlement of the Yugoslav-Italian conflict. Perhaps because he found the problem insoluble (because of Mussolini's conditions), the Rome accords were signed in isolation.

Inevitably, Yugoslavia was antagonized. The critical question was whether it was antagonized enough to completely reverse its former stance. Even if Belgrade was completely alienated, an argument could still be made for an Italian policy simply on the basis of relative power. Moreover, a Franco-Soviet pact might make the "Italian corridor" essential. But Laval lost on all fronts. The Italian entente did not survive the Ethiopian crisis and the Soviet pact, deliberately denuded of real force, still ended Laval's schemes for a Franco-German-Italian front; Yugoslavia, angered and fearful, attempted to conciliate both Italy and Germany.[87] Poland, angry at the Soviet pact, also moved toward Germany. The Little Entente could not fail to suffer. As Yugoslavia moved toward Germany and Italy, as Czechoslovakia remained tied to France, and as Rumania

[85] R. W. Seton-Watson, *Britain and the Dictators* (London: Cambridge University Press, 1938), p. 232.

[86] Count Jean Szembek, *Journal, 1933–1939* (Paris: Librairie Plon, 1952), p. 16.

[87] For details of the Franco-Soviet pact, see Scott, *Alliance Against Hitler*, pp. 246–48.

cast about for a guiding star, the ties of amity began to loosen. The alliance was gradually transformed into a battleground where Beneš fought for closer ties with Paris, and Stoyadinovitch for a Little Entente that was really "little,"that is, limited to the Hungarian threat as the only common denominator of action.

Fearing Italian retribution, doubtful of the ability or willingness of France and England to offer aid, and increasingly worried about Germany's economic dominance (which had been enhanced by the trade vacuum created by sanctions against Italy), Yugoslavia began reorienting its foreign policy. "For Yugoslavia, security became more important than loyalty to seemingly outworn systems of alliance." [88] A policy "as wise as a serpent and as soft as a dove" was necessary. At the end of 1935, when the British ambassador asked Stoyadinovitch for his country's support if war broke out between Italy and Great Britain, he was informed that:

We have followed English and French advice and have considerably improved our relations with Italy in recent months. A step of this kind, by us, would spoil all this work and expose us to the subsequent vengeance of Italy. Who will then defend us from Italy? [89]

The General Staff also urged a cautious and circumspect attitude in the future, and cast doubt upon the credibility of external aid.[90] The situation was still ambiguous, and no measure had been taken which overtly broke new ground. It was only after the effects of Hitler's Rhineland coup had been digested that Yugoslavia, and Rumania to a lesser extent, made a definitive break with the past. As Flandin noted, the events of March 7, 1936 meant that "the French alliance with the Little Entente was now valueless. In the future they could not hope to give effective assistance to Poland, Czechoslovakia, Yugoslavia, or Rumania, in the event of German aggression. . . ." [91]

At the next meeting of the Little Entente, Prince Paul rejected

[88] Hoptner, Yugoslavia in Crisis, p. 121.
[89] Ibid., p. 52.
[90] Ibid., pp. 55–58.
[91] Quoted in L. B. Namier, Europe in Decay, 1936–1940 (London: Macmillan and Co., Ltd., 1950), p. 11.

every proposal to strengthen the alliance. As Beneš sadly observed, "I was surprised to see that a rift was already clearly visible in the Little Entente's ranks." [92] Titulescu's fall from power in August 1936 constituted another grievous blow to the alliance. As Max Beloff noted, King Carol had apparently decided "that Titulescu's policy of overt friendship with France and Czechoslovakia, and tacit acceptance of collaboration with the Soviet Union, was too dangerous." [93] Rumania decided to move closer to Beck's Poland, and this meant accepting Beck's vigorous anti-Communist policy. It also meant, of course, that the Czech-Soviet pact of May 1935 was virtually useless, since Moscow was separated from Prague by the hostile capitals of Warsaw and Bucharest.

In the meanwhile, Stoyadinovitch was forging closer ties with Germany. In June, he noted that Germany "was willing to furnish us complete security against Hungary and Italy . . . . to secure Yugoslavia's future, we must as soon as possible obtain insurance . . . against Italy." [94] Hitler then attempted to mediate between Belgrade and Rome and to direct Hungary's irredentism against the Czechs. This situation left the Yugoslavs in an anomalous position: allied with France and fearing to take any action which would move this ally toward the still hostile Italy, yet unable to support France too much without disturbing the growing relationship with Germany.

The next meeting of the Little Entente in September revealed the extent of the fissures which had been developing. The Czechs were pro-French, anti-German, and anti-*Anschluss*. Belgrade and Bucharest refused to commit themselves to any of these positions, and had in fact become reconciled to the idea of an *Anschluss*.

Hitler had told Ciano in October 1936 that "Yugoslavia is concerned at aggressive intentions which Italy might have against her. It will suffice to give her assurance on this score to win her over to our system. . . ." [95]

[92] Eduard Beneš, *Memoirs* (London: Allen and Unwin, 1954), p. 30.

[93] Max Beloff, *The Foreign Policy of Soviet Russia, 1929–1936* (London: Oxford University Press, 1956), II, 71–72.

[94] Hoptner, *Yugoslavia in Crisis*, p. 63.

[95] *Ciano's Diplomatic Papers* edited by Malcolm Muggeridge (London: Oldhams Press Limited, 1948), p. 59. Henceforth cited as Ciano D.P.

After protracted negotiations, an Italian-Yugoslav agreement was finally signed on March 25, 1937. It provided for mutual recognition and respect of each other's territorial integrity, neutrality in the event either was the victim of unprovoked aggression, Albania's independence, and some economic concessions by Italy. The agreement to remain neutral was diluted by Italy's recognition of Yugoslavia's existing obligations. That is, Yugoslavia still remained, formally, in the French system.[96] For the Yugoslavs, the agreement meant the end of Italian irredentism and support for Croat terrorists and a new weight to balance French and German pressures. For Italy, it meant increased security in the north against both the French and the Germans, as well as recognition of its primacy in Albania, and a ringing diplomatic victory over France.

Stoyadinovitch outlined his new policy to Ciano in a conversation on March 26, 1937. He indicated his intention of refusing any closer ties with France, and his unwillingness to come to the aid of Czechoslovakia. As for the Little Entente:

. . . formally at least, it will not undergo any transformation. One thing is certain, that whereas relations between Yugoslavia and Rumania will remain unaltered, that is to say, firm and cordial, those between these two countries and Czechoslovakia will, on the contrary, be reduced to an empty formality.[97]

The Yugoslavs were touching all bases. As Kanya noted, Stoyadinovitch "intends to continue to have his fingers in a large number of pies." [98]

Beneš had attempted to compensate for the loosening of the Little Entente ties by perfecting his relations with Poland and, if the evidence is reliable, even Germany, unsuccessfully.[99] He had also toyed with the idea of entering the Rome-Vienna-Budapest entente, but was precluded from doing so by the necessity of receiving

[96] *Ibid.*, p. 97; cf. also Hoptner, *Yugoslavia in Crisis,* pp. 94 ff.

[97] Ciano *D. P.,* p. 99.

[98] Quoted in *Ibid.,* p. 66.

[99] On Czech-Polish relations, see Namier, *Europe in Decay,* pp. 283–84; on German-Czech talks, see Gerhard L. Weinberg, "Secret Hitler-Benes Negotiations in 1936–37," *Journal of Central European Affairs,* XIX (Jan. 1960), 366–74. Also Namier, p. 184.

the consent of Yugoslavia and Rumania.[100] Schuschnigg had the same idea, but Mussolini had forced him to break off talks with the Czechs. The Duce had decided to opt for Germany, and the elimination of Czechoslovakia was one of the essential objectives of the Rome-Berlin axis.[101]

The Little Entente had still not been formally abandoned by any of its partners, and it continued to function, if only fitfully and half-heartedly.[102] It did manage to maintain a common front against Hungary. Negotiations with Budapest were suspended until the Hungarians accepted the status quo. On other issues, however, the rift widened.

Thus Delbos' efforts to extract a mutual assistance pact from Belgrade and Bucharest in December 1937 came to naught. Stoyadinovitch in fact assured Ciano that "Yugoslavia will never be found in the camp hostile to Italy and that he would continue to resist French pressure to sign a pact of mutual assistance. . . ."[103] Nevertheless, Stoyadinovitch had renewed the old treaty of alliance with France, and had visited both Paris and London.

It was evident, as 1937 drew to a close, that the Czechs stood alone, unless one counted the French and British positions as pro-Czech. But the "old" Little Entente, for what it was worth, was still alive. When the peripatetic Stoyadinovitch visited Berlin in January, 1938, he told Hitler that "whatever action he took vis-à-vis Hungary must be within the framework of the Little Entente."[104] Neurath concluded that Stoyadinovitch "intends at all events to avoid being drawn into any possible conflicts. Nor will he for the time being break away from the Little Entente; but he is avoiding everything that might lead to its consolidation."[105]

Stoyadinovitch had also told Hitler that the Austrian question

---

[100] Toynbee, *Survey of International Affairs, 1934, op. cit.*, pp. 506–7.

[101] John A. Lukacs, *The Great Powers and Eastern Europe* (New York: American Book Company, 1953), p. 60.

[102] See Jozo Tomasevich, "Foreign Economic Relations, 1918–1941," *Yugoslavia,* edited by Robert J. Kerner (Berkeley: University of California Press, 1949), p. 332.

[103] Ciano D. P., pp. 150–51.

[104] D. G. F. P., Series D, Vol. II, No. 367, Jan. 18, 1938, p. 583.

[105] *Ibid.,* Vol. V, No. 164, Jan. 22, 1938, p. 231.

was "a purely German domestic matter." [106] When it finally came about, he could only note that he "had long foreseen the event and is completely undisturbed by German intentions. . . ." [107] But shortly thereafter he let Ciano know that he was not happy with the idea of Germany taking over the Sudetenland next, and that he feared a German *drang nach süd* toward the Adriatic.[108] He had no suggestions concerning what could be done about it.

If the Hungarians attacked the Czechs, by themselves or simultaneously with Germany, Yugoslavia and Rumania were dutybound to go to Prague's aid. Stoyadinovitch had impressed upon the Italians the necessity of inducing Hungary to wait until after Germany marched before it attacked the Czechs. The Hungarians agreed and, in hopes of compensation elsewhere, promised that they would "never take the initiative in the action against Czechoslovakia . . . but will, however, intervene shortly after the conflict had been begun by Germany. . . ." [109]

Both Belgrade and Bucharest, more and more fearful of the German danger, pressed the Czechs to settle the Sudetenland dispute. King Carol had even sent a message to Beneš expressing "Rumania's wish that solution of the Sudeten German problem, satisfactory to Germany, should be achieved." [110] However, as events were about to prove, the Little Entente was not completely dead— at least on Hungary, the minor issue which had once united them.

The Hungarians had been attempting for some time to reach an agreement with Yugoslavia which would allow them to attack the Czechs without fear of Yugoslav (or Rumanian) retaliation. Their quest was never completely successful, except insofar as they were insured against retaliation if they struck after the Germans did, i.e., after the battle was over.[111] Neither Bucharest nor Belgrade would go further; they possessed former Magyar territories which might be next on the list.

[106] Hoptner, *Yugoslavia in Crisis,* pp. 128–29.
[107] Ciano *D.P.,* p. 200.
[108] *Ibid.,* pp. 213–14.
[109] *Ibid.,* p. 228.
[110] D. G. F. P., Series D, Vol. II, No. 361, Aug. 15, 1938, p. 571.
[111] Ciano *D.P.,* p. 160.

At the last meeting of the Little Entente in Bled on August 21, 1938, the Hungarian effort to split the alliance failed. The three allies reaffirmed their obligations of mutual assistance if Hungary should attack.[112] The Bled meeting, contrary to Ciano's opinion, had not marked "a new phase in the crumbling of the Little Entente." [113] On the contrary, it marked a momentary reaffirmation of old ties—for what they were worth.

As the Czech-German crisis sped toward its denouement at Munich, the Rumanians and the Yugoslavs made last-ditch efforts to insure their own noninvolvement. They were both increasingly aware of the implications of Hitler's ambitions. Comnene, the Rumanian foreign minister, even noted that "it would be Poland's turn next and then that of Rumania. . . ." [114] Yet there seemed to be no immediate alternative to throwing the Czechs to the wolves, in the desperate hope that the wolves would be satiated or destroyed (by someone else) in the future.

The Czechs asked Stoyadinovitch his intentions in late September, when Hungary was mobilizing, but he asked for more information. Privately, he thought Yugoslavia should opt out on the principle of *rebus sic stantibus*, but he was aware that this would not be "a popular act". "Something," he said, "had to be figured out." [115] Neither he nor Comnene wanted to fulfill their obligations nor be caught evading them. Finally Stoyadinovitch sent a telegraph to Goring in Berlin urging him to oppose any action by Hungary.[116]

When the actual crisis came Hungary did not march, for Budapest had never received the preliminary guarantee of neutrality from the Yugoslavs which it felt was necessary before it could take any offensive action. Thus the alliance ended as it began, in a united stand against Hungary. Czechoslovakia's two partners warned the Magyars that "in case of an attack of Hungary against Czechoslovakia, they would be obliged to fulfill their engagements as

---

[112] G. B. D., Third Series, Vol. I, No. 690, Aug. 25, 1938, p. 157.
[113] Ciano D.P., p. 146.
[114] G. B. D., Third Series, Vol. I, No. 898, Sept. 15, 1938, pp. 354–55.
[115] Hoptner, *Yugoslavia in Crisis*, p. 166.
[116] *Ibid.*, p. 167.

members of the Little Entente." [117] It meant very little to the Czechs.

Conclusion

The Little Entente was dead. Rumania and Yugoslavia could not spare the time to grieve, for they were soon beset by the problem of avoiding their erstwhile ally's fate. When, in what must have been a wry moment, Gafencu discussed the old alliance with Stoyadinovitch, the German minister in Bucharest took him to task for doing so. Gafencu replied:

. . . that he had, to be sure, discussed . . . the possibility of keeping alive the fiction of the Little Entente. But if Germany held the view that the Little Entente had ceased to exist, he was completely in agreement and accepted the view as his own.[118]

The ultimate fate of central and southeastern Europe was determined by the Great Powers, not by the Small Powers who inhabited the region. Yet, having said this, it is also quite clear that some area of choice was always left open to the Small Powers. At best, in the early years of the interwar period, they had a strong influence on the shape of things to come within the territory once dominated by the old Empire. Bolstered by the weakness of the revisionists, aided by the power of France, supported by the new institution at Geneva, the Little Entente became a symbol of peace and stability. In an era when disputes were adjudicated peacefully, at least for the most part, an alliance composed solely of Small Powers was not, as is often claimed, a "multiplication of weakness." On the contrary, it represented a degree of strength far beyond the reach of any of the allies in isolation.

The best that the Little Entente could have done in the 1930s was to sink together, rather than separately. While that ending might have been more intrinsically appealing, it was precluded by the nature of the situation, particularly by the fact that each threat affected each ally with varying degrees of intensity. Those who

[117] Tomasevich, *Foreign Economic Relations,* p. 333.
[118] D. G. F. P., Series D, Vol. V, No. 289, Feb. 10, 1939, p. 388.

were not immediately endangered by a Great Power threat chose to ignore it or try and hide from it. It seemed merely quixotic to stand up to an indirect threat which the other Great Powers were conjuring away. Thus the Czechs were sacrificed, but not really by the Little Entente. That alliance, to the very end, remained faithful to its original, limited purpose. That the alliance was not expanded to meet a threat its creators never assumed it could meet, and that the alliance never took the lead in solving Great Power confrontations, is hardly surprising. An alliance of Small Powers is an instrument of limited utility. It neither can nor is designed to handle major military threats. When Small Powers are threatened by Great Powers, they must turn to other Great Powers for support. When they cannot get that support, necessity compels them to seek agreement with the powerful aggressor—not other Small Powers.

The great failure of the Little Entente lies not in its inability to cope with the Great Powers, but in its own domestic difficulties. Its constituent parts never became fully stable and democratic. Both Yugoslavia and Rumania fell victim to the forces of internal disruption, and were in constant turmoil. Too often defeated or weak leaders turned for support to ideological counterparts in other states. However, it is difficult to see what the Little Entente *qua* Little Entente could have done about it. No alliance could have been created which arrogated to itself the right to intervene in domestic affairs. The alliance also took too little account of economic problems. However, the economic problems of Central Europe would only yield to a European solution not a regional one, particularly because the reconstitution of the old Empire, even in an economic sense, would never have been freely accepted.

The Little Entente has also been accused of freezing the status quo in Central Europe and refusing to agree to even moderate changes, which might have removed the pernicious distinction between victor and vanquished states.[119] The indictment is generally true, but not necessarily decisive. It is difficult to conceive an alternative to the Little Entente which seems more viable. If it had

[119] See Arnold Wolfers, *Britain and France Between Two Wars* (New York: Harcourt, Brace and Company, 1940), pp. 115–22; and Lukacs, *The Great Powers and Eastern Europe*, p. 20.

been allowed to continue its development, unaffected by the resurrection of Germany, it *might* ultimately have been able to devise a general, and peaceful, solution to the problems of Central Europe. In any event, Beneš and a few other leaders were not unalterably opposed to minor revision of the settlement, as long as it came about by mutual negotiation.

The increasing power of Germany and Italy destroyed any possibility of peaceful change. As long as the Hungarians found support in Berlin and Rome, it seemed too dangerous to grant them concessions. Before they received that support, the Little Entente was too busy consolidating itself to worry about concessions. Perhaps the Little Entente states were correct in insisting that it was first necessary to prove that the peace settlement, in its main outlines, was inviolable, before any efforts were made to adjust it. If not, the result might have been a series of kaleidoscopic changes, instability, and chaos. By the time that the Little Entente was consolidated, their opponents already had other champions, more accommodating and more powerful.

The Little Entente offered, as nothing else appeared to do, at least the possibility of maintaining peace, protecting an inchoate independence, and restraining the Great Powers. It was a compromise between the necessity to unite against immediate threats and the ideal of a stable and prosperous substitute for Austria-Hungary. It failed, in part because it did not adjust quickly enough to changes in world politics, but primarily because it was overwhelmed by problems which only the Great Powers could have solved.

The Nature of Small Power Alliances*

In theory, Small Power alliances are condemned; in practice, they remain popular. The theorists are undoubtedly correct in the sense that Small Power alliances offer few military advantages, but wrong

---

* See footnote 140 on page 116 for a discussion of the range of the generalizations which follow: in brief, they are not limited to, though they significantly rely upon, the experiences of the Little Entente but rather attempt to generalize widely about Small Power alliances.

in inadequately evaluating their political utility. Statesmen are correct in attempting to utilize Small Power alliances for the limited tasks they can perform, but wrong in assuming that a combination of Small Powers is equivalent to a Great Power.

Small Power alliances are militarily useless, if not actually pernicious: therein lies the heart of the indictment against them. Complete integration of forces and strategy *might* modify the picture somewhat. The opportunity to pick one army off at a time would be reduced, and a more coherent strategy could be adopted. The "frontierness" of each ally would be reduced to the extent that it was effectively incorporated, in strategic terms, in a wider area. More breathing space, perhaps even the construction of a strategic redoubt, might also dilute the worst effects of the necessity of instant response to provocation.

Traditionally, alliance forces have not been integrated.[120] Each ally maintained an army sufficient for its own needs, and the alliance commitment itself imposed very little by way of innovation. Normal procedure simply involved an increase in General Staff contacts and occasional joint exercises (but never against Great Powers). Since each ally had barely enough troops for its own defense, at least against a Great Power threat, it had very little in military terms to offer its partners. As someone once said of the Little Entente, in case of danger they had equal doses of sympathy and neutrality to offer each other. In fact, a kind of tacit agreement usually existed about the proper response in case *one* partner was threatened by a Great Power: the unthreatened partners would neither attack you during a crisis, nor lend active support to your enemies.

It was hardly fair to expect more. Even if the partners promised each other armed support against *any* attack, the practical significance of the action against a Great Power was not likely to be large. If a Great Power had one hundred divisions, and each Small Power ten, the addition of another ten had only a very limited significance. Still, it might have *some* effect. Bargaining opportuni-

---

[120] The Little Entente did make some tentative but abortive steps toward political and military integration in the 1930s but they were forgotten as the crisis developed.

ties increased to the extent that the new divisions threatened the Great Power's timetable. Belgium and Holland effectively armed *might* have had a considerable impact on the way in which both World Wars were fought. In any event, some increase in bargaining potential, plus some decrease in anxiety to the extent that allies were written off as threats (which, contrary to the normal reaction, has always seemed of some value),[121] constituted the primary military advantages of a Small Power alliance against a Great Power. It could be a marginally significant factor. Thus the elements in Czechoslovakia which favored resistance in 1938 were bolstered by the support, official and unofficial, which they received from Yugoslavia and Rumania.

Small Power alliances are also criticized because the goals they must pursue are inevitably limited in geographic terms, and in that they can be achieved only (or primarily) against other Small Powers. The criticism, if true, is not decisive. Achievement of limited goals remains worthwhile. But the validity of the criticism itself is open to question. In practice, Small Power alliances have been able, upon occasion, to achieve wider goals than the criticism implies.

It is true, though hardly surprising, that Small Power alliances tend to be more effective in local areas. It is equally true that the primary goals of most Small Power alliances have been directed against other Small Powers. The "laws" of power would make even less sense than they do if the contrary appeared true. However, Small Power alliances can also achieve some goals against Great Powers, and they can exert some influence on an international scale.

If anything has facilitated these achievements, it has been the development of international organization. The importance attached to representation on the governing bodies of the League of Nations or the UN, and to the votes they record, has consistently increased the influence of voting blocs. Groups like the Little Entente, which always had a representative on the League Council and which always voted together, exerted an influence on world events dispro-

[121] This could also have a limited amount of military utility, in that it permitted troops to be relocated more effectively.

portionate to their actual power. The process also tended to be cumulative. Once consulted, a presumption about the right to be consulted again developed. The Small Powers thus favored enhanced their prestige, and developed some expertise in the process of diplomacy.

In its worst forms, the influence of Small Powers in international organizations[112] has led to a kind of international log-rolling contest; in its best forms, the combined influence of the Small Powers occasionally has served as a voice of moderation and sense. The result was and is obvious. For good or ill, Small Powers have the potential of thwarting a Great Power simply by marshaling votes rather than guns against it. They might even occasionally make their own case in the world arena in much the same way. Thus Small Power alliances possess some political potential in terms of enhanced prestige, influence, and bargaining capability. It is impossible to prove that the same results could not have been achieved without an alliance. Nevertheless, the argument that the alliance has at the very least expedited matters seems plausible, even convincing, until contrary evidence is presented.

If the Small Powers in an alliance can agree among themselves, if they can keep their own house in order, they can make it very difficult for the Great Powers to intervene in their region (at least without openly committing an injustice). Insofar as they are successful, a primary element of potential conflict is eliminated: not conflict itself, to be sure, but at least those forms of conflict associated with Great Power intervention. Beneš' decision to create the Little Entente in 1920 and 1921 explicitly reflected this calculation. If nothing else, the Little Entente might succeed in keeping the French and the Italians at an acceptable distance.

There is a possibility, then, that a Small Power alliance can be-

---

[112] Obviously other factors have also played a very significant role in the growth of Small Power influence; but on the specific point concerning the influence of Small Power *alliances,* the role of international organization seems very critical—though, of course, the nature of the new military technology, and the consequent reluctance to use it except in very major conflicts, has had an effect which can hardly be overstated. As alliances have increasingly been created to serve political purposes the importance of organizations like the UN was bound to rise; the point has been especially significant for Small Power alliances.

come an effective regional policeman. The essential weakness of this conception is that it must be based on the status quo. The alliance cannot pursue revisionist goals either against Great Powers or local Small Powers. To do so against a Small Power would undoubtedly force the latter to appeal to an external Great Power for aid. Inevitably, the other Great Powers would be forced to intervene and the autonomy of the area would disappear.

However, in defense of the status quo, the Small Power alliance may be very useful. It may even be able to perform a valuable, though limited, military function by restraining adventuresome Small Powers even if they are not members of the alliance. In addition, if the group is inclusive, it diminishes any opportunities open to the Great Powers to use an ostracized Small Power as a foothold for intervention. The experience of Bulgaria and the Balkan Entente in the interwar years is a negative case in point.[123] The members of a regional alliance are also more likely to understand the problems of their own area, not only in a political but also in an economic and social sense.[124]

Small Power alliances are a poor instrument if the immediate

[123] Cf. the discussion in R. J. Kerner and H. N. Howard, *The Balkan Conferences and the Balkan Entente* (Berkeley: University of California Press, 1936). Note also the statement by Toynbee about the dangers of a Balkan Pact without Bulgaria, since the latter would then "continue to offer a foothold for any Great Power which desired to intervene in Balkan affairs." Toynbee, *Survey of International Affairs, 1934*, p. 512.

The history of the Arab League offers several examples of the dangers of a Small Power alliance which is not truly unified on a wide range of issues— virtually everything except Israel—and which has thus yielded few of the advantages which, in theory, could have been achieved. A critical factor was the intra-alliance conflict between Egypt and Iraq. The existence of the League did not prevent its members from allying with outside Great Powers. Thus one analyst notes that Iraq's adherence to the Baghdad Pact "almost wrecked the Arab League." Robert W. Macdonald, *The League of Arab States* (Princeton: Princeton University Press, 1965), p. 233 and *passim*. And for difficulties with Cambodia (as a non-member of SEATO) and its attempt to use Chinese support to counterbalance U.S. support of Cambodia's Small Power enemies, cf. Roger M. Smith, *Cambodia's Foreign Policy* (Ithaca: Cornell University Press, 1965), pp. 130–31, 217.

[124] The anti-stability propensity of Small Powers may also be diluted by an alliance: it may give them more confidence in their ability to ride out a storm without seeking the first available harbor. Moreover, the mere fact that it can always point to the necessity of time to "consult with allies" may provide valuable breathing space.

goal is increased military strength. But they may very well be extremely useful instruments if the goal involves maintaining the
status quo and controlling or removing local grievances without
Great Power intervention. In effect, they have been a much underrated form of alliance. Nevertheless, to be fair, it is necessary to
admit that some criticism can be made of their role as regional
policemen.

Small Power alliances, it should be noted, may prove to be economically burdensome. In some historical instances, while the alliance cooperated on the political and military levels, the allies com-
peted vigorously and ruthlessly on the economic level. For the most
part, economies were competitive rather than complementary. They
fought for the same markets, rather than providing each other with
markets. The Little Entente stands as the classic example, but it is
hardly an isolated case. Since alliances tend to be (or so theorists
contend) only as strong as their weakest link, the economic disloca-
tion of any partner injures the whole alliance. But the problem
has usually been too broad to be solved on a regional level, even
with the best of wills, and the normal result has been an appeal to
a Great Power for aid. Yet if a Great Power was called upon, one
of the essential advantages of Small Power alliances was vitiated,
and whatever political unity had been achieved began to crack. The
problem could be solved on an international level, though it rarely
has been. If the idea took hold, the bloc votes of the alliance, and
its enhanced status, could be significant. There is no doubt that
the criticism is sound in the long run; in the short run the alliance
could still be useful. And, of course, the assumption that the situation would be better if no alliance existed does not hold. The problem would hardly disappear *pari passu* with the alliance.

It has also been suggested that a Small Power alliance under-
mines the sense of responsibility which the Great Powers have for
an area.[125] There is some validity to this idea. It is reasonable to
assume that the creation of a local alliance which claims the right
to deal with its own problems will dilute whatever interest other
powers might have in the area—particularly if it is successful in
its claims, and if the area is important to the Great Powers only

[125] Cf. Arnold Wolfers, *The Small Powers and the Enforcement of Peace* (New
Haven: Yale Institute of International Studies, 1943), p. 5.

when it threatens to provoke trouble on an international scale. However, the historical record is not clear. Did Great Britain's lagging interest in Eastern Europe have anything to do with the creation of the Little Entente? The opposite seems more nearly true. Even if formed, the Little Entente would surely have been a different instrument had Great Britain involved itself in the decision. If the Great Powers do withdraw, the price might still be worth paying but only if the Small Powers are able to handle their own problems.

Arnold Wolfers has also argued that Small Power alliances undermine the internal unity of each ally and entangle them in each other's quarrels.[126] The point, again, is ambiguous and inconclusive. Not all Small Powers have a great deal of unity to be undermined. The alliance may, in fact, help them through the stages in which they are trying to create unity. It is difficult to find evidence which indicates any cause and effect relationship between unity and participation in an alliance; which is not to say that the proposition is in error, but only that it is doubtful. It is true that an alliance inevitably entangles states in their allies' problems, if only indirectly. The problem, of course, is that non-alliance does not mean non-involvement. States are always involved in their neighbors' problems, and the only question is what form that involvement will take. An alliance at the very least may buy the prospect of consultation, as well as some opportunity to serve as a moderating influence.

Another argument holds that Small Power alliances are frequently directed against illusory threats, which become real as a response to the creation of the alliance. M. W. Fodor, for example, declared that the states of the Little Entente "allied themselves against a phantom, and thus succeeded slowly in creating a danger." [127] The problem is critical only when there is a military commitment in the alliance. Since that commitment is relatively useless against a Great Power, it is usually directed against a Small Power. However, the combined strength of several Small Powers is rarely necessary to coerce another Small Power. Yet the military commit-

---

[126] *Ibid.*

[127] M. W. Fodor, *Plot and Counterplot in Central Europe* (Boston: Houghton, Mifflin Company, 1937), p. 179.

ment tends to intensify the conflict between the alliance and its
enemies. If nothing else, it makes it very difficult for the alliance
to expand. The history of the Little Entente is illustrative. It retained an extensive military commitment against Hungary, even
though any of the allies could have defeated Hungary by itself.
Most significantly, it tended to inhibit the chance of reaching a
compromise settlement with the Hungarians, who were forced to
appeal to Germany and Italy for aid. In addition, it was one factor
which affected Poland's decision to remain out of the alliance; the
Poles had no quarrel with the Hungarians and saw no reason to
buy into one.

In any case, the criticism seems generally valid, though not decisive. The political lesson is clear: accept extensive military commitments only when confronted by a very immediate threat. A
military commitment may be necessary, but its cost must be recognized, that is, an alliance so frozen in form that political solutions
may be inhibited. Since the main virtues of Small Power alliances
are political anyway, caution in accepting a military commitment is
prudent and wise. A commitment can be justified only in major
emergencies.

If the *ceteris paribus* injunction really held, the preceding analysis could probably be "read" in the following manner. Small Powers
ought to prefer mixed, multilateral alliances. They provide the most
benefits in terms of security and political influence. If unavailable,
they probably should choose a Small Power alliance in preference
to an unequal, bilateral alliance, particularly if the Small Powers do
not fear an immediate threat to their security, and if their goals in
allying are primarily political. An alliance with a single Great Power
ought to be chosen only if all the other alternatives are proscribed,
and if the Small Powers fear an imminent attack—and even then
only in hopes of improving their deterrent stance.

In the abstract, the optimal alliance strategies for Great Powers
and Small Powers tend to differ. At least at this level of analysis,
what a Small Power "ought" to do is not necessarily what a Great
Power "ought" to do. Empirical verification of this judgment is
virtually impossible. It is too difficult to isolate the various factors
which have led to a particular decision, and thus impossible to
prove that any action resulted from behavior which can be uniquely

attributed to Small Powers. At the most the evidence, whether empirical case studies or inductive generalizations, can only be suggestive. But it is in no way inconsistent with the evidence to argue that Small Powers are not only the relatively weakest constituent in any situation but also a different kind of constituent.

One final word perhaps ought to be added about Great Power and Small Power perspectives on the problem of centralization— i.e., whether the alliance is to be highly organized and whether it is to contain an extensive commitment to respond automatically to various contingencies. An alliance so organized has obvious advantages of more efficient planning, a stronger political front, a more credible defense, and more opportunities for consultation. The willingness to concede more power to a central organ has a beneficial effect not only on the quality of the alliance itself but also on the more serious way in which the external world appraises it. However, a centralized alliance may also create intra-alliance frictions because of constant intervention in domestic affairs (e.g., in order to insure certain standards in equipment). It may tend to reduce flexibility, particularly in a crisis, because the tight commitment will require action rather than caution, and it will probably make any war general, since all the allies will be forced into it. It should be noted that there is an asymmetry between Great Powers and Small Powers in terms of the degree of disadvantage involved in the loss of flexibility and the likelihood of general war. In both cases the Small Power may prefer, not that these consequences come to pass, but that an awareness that they *might* come to pass spreads throughout the international system. Only thus can it hope to deter a major threat. From the point of view of the Great Power, with interests which transcend the alliance, flexibility and the ability to limit a war are prime advantages and both are more difficult to achieve within a centralized alliance. The point is not that one form is absolutely best for Small Powers and another for Great Powers. Rather that, again, there tend to be different perspectives underlying their decisions. Much the same point could be made in an analysis of the advantages and disadvantages of a decentralized alliance.

PART II

Alliances, Small Powers, and the International System, 1815–1939

CHAPTER 5

The Classical Period: 1815–1854

E ACH of the chapters in Part II attempts to sketch in the essential features of a particular historical system of international politics and then to analyze the different ways in which those features affected Great Powers and Small Powers. The emphasis is on specific Small Powers within distinct systems, and not on the general aspects of Small Power behavior in *any* system.

These chapters are much more concerned with the nature of the actors within particular systems than they are with the nature of the system itself. The two perspectives are obviously interdependent, but emphasizing one over the other has significant effects. A systemic perspective tends to overstate similarities in behavior and to ascribe similar motivations to the individual actors: their uniqueness and their eccentricities are diminished when viewed from "on high" (i.e., from the patterns downward). This is clearly an unacceptable result for an analysis such as this one which is attempting to illustrate differences in behavior between two groups of actors, Small Powers and Great Powers.

The systems which follow, therefore, are not only concrete (as distinct from analytical)[1] but also generally oriented toward the behavior of the actors themselves rather than to the patterns created by their interactions. However, it should be made very clear that systemic structures will not be ignored or undervalued. Great Powers, and Superpowers even more so, tend to be system-dominant

[1] See Ernest B. Haas, *Beyond the Nation-State* (Stanford: Stanford University Press, 1964), p. 54. See also the footnote above, p. 116.

actors. Their behavior is not so heavily conditioned by the structure of the international arena that all freedom and flexibility of maneuver is gone. Great Powers determine the nature of systemic patterns; as such, they can alter the system, or perhaps merely ignore its imperatives without suffering grievously. Small Powers, on the other hand, are much more limited in their freedom by the nature of the systemic structure. For the most part, they are dominated by the system, in the sense that the opportunities they have are dependent on the kind of system which exists. They can rarely create their own opportunities. This does not mean that there are *no* differences among Small Powers—Beck of Poland and Beneš of Czechoslovakia perceived their opportunities in a very different fashion. But both were dependent for those opportunities on the operation of the system, and its Great Power actors. What all of this implies is that while an analysis of Small Power behavior can be actor-oriented, it must also contain a much stronger element of systemic analysis per se (that is, of the patterns created by Great Power interaction) than might be necessary if the concern was only with Great Powers. The point is simple enough, but it is important enough to emphasize—examination of the behavior of Great Powers and Small Powers in historical systems indicates that one of the basic differences between them rests on the degree to which their behavior is conditioned, even determined, by the nature of the system itself.

Historical Systems

Any attempt to isolate distinct historical systems of international relations is bound to be arbitrary and relatively unsatisfactory. Behavioral patterns have altered in the past one hundred and fifty years, but they have done so slowly and erratically. The unwary ascribe too much significance to the immediate impact of long-range trends. In fact, of course, both an awareness of changes within an international system, and an estimate of their significance, tend to spread to the members of the system at widely differing rates. An analyst who assumes that all the statesmen within a particular period perceive their systemic environment in a similar way may merely distort the historical record.

Systems theory itself is a very imperfect instrument, if by it is meant something more than a mere description of a set of patterned interactions. If it is also intended to be used as an explanation for those interactions, certain qualifications ought to be kept in mind. Systems theory (as explanation) assumes that the behavior of statesmen is determined (or heavily conditioned) by perceptions about the general structure of the international environment. However, different statesmen can perceive different structures or draw different explanations from the same structure. Moreover, they may never perceive the existence of any system at all, at least in a manner which is substantively significant. They may order their behavior in response to "rules of thumb," or intuition, or the ad hoc and parochial factors which in any specific instance may seem more relevant than systemic imperatives. As a result, systems theory may obscure the historical record because it attempts to explain events in terms of a set of structural imperatives which may be unperceived, partially perceived, or ignored. At best, it is simplistic.

Systems theory can also be used as an approach to international politics, rather than as a description or explanation of events. In this sense, it could be argued that ordering the phenomena of international politics in terms of discrete and internally coherent structural models is a more (or differently) effective way to understand international politics. The models do clarify and simplify the interactions which actually occur in various international systems; and they have a didactic utility for a theorist intent on illuminating certain points which could be obscured by too much detail. But certain inherent and obvious limitations of this process ought to be noted. It is an approach which is essentially conservative, since it stresses the mechanisms by which each model maintains its stability. Even models extrapolated from particular historical periods tend to be static. A group of actors and a set of rules by which they operate confront the theorist, but how they got there and where they are going remains obscure. The mere statement that the system fails when the actors change or when they disobey the rules is not very helpful, for it hardly explains why they do so.

The idea of an international system will be used here simply in the sense of a variable which conditions or sets limits to the behavior of the actors within it. Patterns are created by the regularized interaction of actors. The system is the relationship among those patterns.[2] The behavior of an actor can reflect a response to factors such as type of regime, ideology, the personality of its leaders, pure chance, and the like. The system is merely another variable affecting behavior; its effect is strongest on Small Powers and, probably, on all actors when there is an absence of crisis.

Systems change and neither a single model, nor a set of continuous but discrete and isolated models, offers a completely adequate picture of international politics. If the purpose of this section was historical, or even if it was designed to remove or attenuate the difficulties systems theory must cope with in explaining transitions between periods (or models), an intensive and extensive examination of the ways in which the objectives and the means open to international actors have changed would be imperative. For the purposes of this section, to examine the behavior of Small Powers and to relate it and compare it with the behavior of Great Powers, the question of why and how systems change is not decisive. The different historical systems in the next few chapters are used to illustrate points about Small Powers, not systems per se. Thus the fact that systems do change is sufficient. The very real weaknesses of systems theory cannot be ignored. Nevertheless, for the limited purposes at hand, it is a useful instrument.

It may very well be, as noted earlier, that the apparent alteration of systemic patterns is never clearly perceived by the statesmen within a system. In effect, very significant and very salient changes may be necessary before behavioral patterns, as distinct from systemic patterns, begin to adjust, before "politics as usual" has to be even slightly altered. The point may hold with particular strength when the historical period which is on the verge of division into separate systems is stable and relatively peaceful.[3]

[2] For another definition, see Stanley Hoffmann, "International Systems and International Law," *World Politics* (October 1961), p. 207. I have attempted to deal with some of the ambiguities of systems theory in a more detailed fashion in a paper delivered to the American Political Science Association Convention, September 1967, entitled "Power, Security and the International System."

[3] As was the period from 1815 to 1914. For a distinction between stable and revolutionary systems, see Hoffmann, "International Systems and International Law," p. 208 ff.

It is possible to avoid the foregoing difficulties, as well as the general problems involved in isolating specific systems, by accepting a division based on events whose salience and significance is seldom denied: major war between at least two of the Great Powers in the system. There are obvious dangers in doing so, since it overemphasizes the significance of a single event and obscures the impact of long-term trends (such as the Industrial Revolution). However, since there is evidence to indicate that patterns do alter after each major war, even if the war is only partly responsible and even though that alteration may still be imperfectly perceived by the participants, the suggested division seems tenable.[4] In any case, by choosing an admittedly gross criterion, and extending each system over a rather long period of years, the theoretical purpose of this section may be facilitated. Differences between Great Powers and Small Powers may stand out more clearly than if the differences were compared within smaller and less contrasting periods.

This chapter will examine the years from 1815 to 1854, from the end of the Napoleonic Wars to the beginning of the Crimean War. Chapter 6 will cover the years from 1854 until the outbreak of the

[4] Richard N. Rosecrance, *Action and Reaction in World Politics* (Boston: Little, Brown and Company, 1963), provides a different breakdown of the years covered in this essay. Rosecrance contends that it is possible to distinguish several discrete systems within each of the periods emphasized in this study. Perhaps because of the perspecitve of this essay, the differences between some of Rosecrance's systems seem very slight—the behavior of the actors within the system changed very slowly, and only after the intervention of an obviously significant external event (like Great Power war). One of the great virtues of Professor Rosecrance's book is its emphasis on the significance of domestic factors in altering patterns of interaction on the international level. Although it has perhaps led him to see more change, or at least more frequent change, than others would credit, it is a perspective which provides a very useful corrective to traditionalists (who see very little change at all) or to abstract systems theorists (who see only the determinism of structural patterns and "rules").

Concentration on Small Powers forces one onto grounds somewhere between the two positions, although the exact position varies with circumstances. Certainly domestic changes within Small Powers are of limited significance for the whole international system (except for the contemporary world), and could hardly be the central focus in an analysis of Small Powers and the international system. A focus which emphasizes the compelling nature of the system itself is inherently more reasonable. However, it fails to attribute enough significance to the unique nature of the Small Power actor and, consequently, the unique way in which it interprets and responds to systemic imperatives.

First World War, and Chapter 7 will cover the years between the First and Second World Wars. It is perhaps appropriate to point out that these periods are in fact distinguished from each other by something other than the dates of Great Power wars, in particular, by the nature and number of conflicts which have the potential of transforming the system. Any system will be decisively affected by a quest for hegemony on the part of a powerful member, but each system may also have unique conflicts which can overturn it. In the multipolar system which operated from 1815 to 1854 no such conflict existed; from 1871 to 1914 the Franco-German conflict dominated world politics (though more fitfully and ambiguously than is normally presumed); and from 1919 to 1939 the same conflict remained dominant, though in a more virulent form, supplemented in the 1930s by a three-cornered ideological struggle. The nature of Cold War conflicts, and the potential impact of nuclear proliferation on contemporary events, will be discussed in Part III. It is at least possible that the revolution in the nature of weapons could thrust us into a new period of international politics, without any change in the nature of the dominant conflicts and without the occurrence of a major war.

The Survival of Small Powers

Small Powers have managed to survive, even to prosper, despite their weakness. Until recent years, they have also had to counter accusations not only of weakness but also of inefficiency, treachery, and "ahistoricalness." It seems legitimate, then, to preface an examination of their alliance policy with some attempt to explain how they have managed to survive at all.

The problem hardly existed for most observers of the "old diplomacy," for the answer seemed so obvious: Small Powers survived, perilously but persistently, because of the operation of the balance of power.[5] This proposition would be straightforward enough, if

[5] See Alfred Cobban, *National Self-Determination* (London: Oxford University Press, 1945), pp. 168 ff.; cf. also Quincy Wright, *A Study of War* (Chicago: The University of Chicago Press, 1942), I, 268.

the balance of power's primary function really involved the preservation of the independence and integrity of *all* the states within its compass. It is beyond doubt, however, that the balance was rarely, if ever, conceived in so impartial a fashion. It guaranteed the existence only of the primary members of the system, not all its constituents.[6]

Nevertheless, even if the balance of power never *directly* guaranteed the survival of Small Powers, in certain circumstances it could yield substantial indirect benefits. If there was an apparently equal distribution of power among the Great Powers, the Small Powers might be spared some of the worst effects of an unstable power configuration. It must be emphasized that the conception of the balance of power in this instance is very narrow. It reflects only one very unique distribution of power, a distribution which rarely occurred in the historical record. The point is more normative than descriptive: *if* only power could be so diffused, Small Powers might be more secure.

The rationale underlying this conception is quite clear. Historically, Small Powers have been most endangered when the balance has been unstable or askew. For example, when Great Britain concentrated on internal affairs, and ignored its continental interests, the normal result has been the destruction of one or more Small Powers.[7] If time is needed to reestablish an equilibrium against an aggressive Great Power, a Small Power may be sacrificed simply to buy the weak Great Powers a certain amount of time. The ultimate reestablishment of an equilibrium may be extremely small consolation to a Small Power eaten as an hors d'oeuvre in the interval.

An equal, or an apparently equal, balance of power also offers a Small Power another potential benefit. If the balance is level, minor amounts of power assume a large amount of importance. If a sig-

[6] See Walter Dorn, *Competition for Empire, 1740–1763* (New York: Harper & Bros., 1940), pp. 1–4.

[7] Note the correspondence between Britain's concentration on internal affairs and the partition of Poland (1772–1795), the tribulations of Denmark in the 1860s, and the disappearance of Austria in 1938.

nificant imbalance exists, the weight of a Small Power is irrelevant.[8] The ability to maneuver is also sharply circumscribed when the struggle has degenerated into a conflict between one or two over-powerful revisionists and one or two virtually impotent status quo powers desperately in need of time. Viable alternatives for the Small Power in this situation are scarce. Neither joining the re-visionists as a scavenger nor waiting sadly to be devoured by them constitute attractive propositions. General Syrovy, Beneš' successor, aptly illustrated the horns of the dilemma when he informed a group of Englishmen in October of 1938 that "we have run with the angels; now we shall hunt with the wolves." [9]

In a sense, the foregoing considerations made the Small Powers and Great Britain the only "true" defenders of the balance of power. For all other powers, security seemed to reside in a favorable *imbalance* of power. For both England and the Small Powers, an equal distribution of power not only enhanced the value of what power they did have, but also increased their sense of security—a considerable benefit, particularly for the constantly endangered Small Powers.

In any event, whether the attractions of an ideal (i.e., equal) balance are spurious or real, it has occurred so rarely that any dis-cussion of it is bound to appear somewhat academic. It is, however, possible to use the term "balance of power" to indicate several other power configurations, configurations which diverged in some essen-tial way from the ideal but which nevertheless possessed character-istics which historically have been identified with balance of power systems.

It is, for example, possible to postulate a situation in which the distribution of power is approximately equal but in which the Great Powers are momentarily more concerned with maintaining what they have than with attaining something new. In effect, the more competitive aspects of a balance of power system are diluted

---

[8] Note the situation on the eve of the First World War. See Sidney Fay, *The Origins of the World War* (New York: The Macmillan Company, 1949), p. 123.

[9] Quoted in John Wheeler-Bennett, *Munich: Prologue to Tragedy* (London: Macmillan and Company, 1948), p. 158.

or attenuated in an effort to stabilize the existing distribution of benefits. This conservative system parallels to a large degree the situation which has normally emerged directly after an exhaustive war (e.g., after 1815 and 1919) when the Great Powers have sought or been satisfied with a period of time in which to recuperate. The role of the Small Power is fundamentally affected by this development. On the one hand, since no one has much use for its meager resources, it is likely to be told what to do and how to behave—and not bribed, cajoled, or begged. On the other hand, its security is bound to be enhanced, since any accord on the distribution of benefits would have to involve a guarantee of the integrity of any Small Power by the Great Powers, an expediential guarantee but nonetheless a guarantee. For a satisfied Small Power, this situation is even more preferable than the ideal distribution of power previously noted. In the earlier case, all the traditional methods of inter-state competition were in full use; in the present case, the inertia of the Great Powers grants a certain, if momentary, immunity from danger to the Small Powers.

For a revisionist Small Power, a competitive situation, with power distributed either equally or unequally, is clearly more advantageous. One need only recall the benefits that Hungary and Poland foresaw in the reemergence of Germany as a power factor in the 1930s. The revisionist Small Power may also achieve minor alterations of its position in a conservative system simply because the Great Powers are disinclined to enforce their will, though the alterations are unlikely to be extensive enough to satisfy the Small Power's ambitions, particularly if it is opposed by several satisfied Small Powers (e.g., note Hungary's failures vis-à-vis the Little Entente in the 1920s). The conservative, postwar behavioral pattern rarely subsists for a long period of time and it is necessary to examine at least two other patterns of the balance of power, patterns which constitute the predominant cases with which we have to deal.

The first concerns the situation where any Great Power accord which may have existed has disintegrated, and international politics has reverted to a struggle among the Great Powers to insure their own security by establishing some minimal power superiority over all potential enemies. Walter Dorn described the imperatives of this situation when he noted that being a Great Power:

. . . signified the pursuit of an expansionist or imperialistic foreign policy. Every great power was a potential aggressor to its neighbor and, since it knew this neighbor to be inspired by similar motives, it could not but regard every subtle maneuver of the latter as a potential aggression.[10]

This power configuration differs from the cases already noted in that it is much more fluid. The assumption that a relatively equal balance already exists does not animate any of the actors. What role falls to the Small Power in these circumstances? In general, the Great Powers will tend to concentrate on perfecting their own strength internally, and on guaranteeing the support or neutrality of one or another of the Great Powers in a future conflict. Since the situation is fluid, it is clearly more advantageous to attempt to influence the behavior of the other, noncommitted Great Powers rather than to court Small Power support. Still, the very fluidity of the situation does grant the Small Power a degree of maneuverability, though only in a very peripheral sense: by definition, Great Power antagonisms have not become so intense that the Great Powers are unable to impose their collective will on impertinent or recalcitrant Small Powers.[11] Obviously the ability of any Small Power to decisively affect the operation of this kind of balance of power system is marginal. At best, it can accelerate or delay a process begun by others. Historically, this situation at least approximates the years which will be examined in this chapter.

The second pattern of the balance of power which requires discussion occurs when the balance rigidifies in direct proportion to the increasing dominance of one conflict: e.g., note the effect of the Franco-German struggle after 1871. The fluid competition which characterized the previous configuration is replaced by a progressively intensified struggle between monolithic groups. The extent to which some amount of cooperation and line-crossing, at least on less than critical issues, remains possible probably deter-

[10] Dorn, *Competition for Empire*, p. 1.

[11] A. J. P. Taylor, *The Struggle for Mastery in Europe, 1848–1918* (Oxford: The Clarendon Press, 1954), p. 147.

mines the extent to which the system can promise interim stability. It is in this situation that the Small Power finds itself most ardently courted either, as on the eve of the First World War, on the mistaken assumption that it would prove to be a valuable strategic asset or, as in the Cold War, as a kind of symbolic surrogate for Great Power war itself. In both instances, the belief that the increased influence of various Small Powers meant increased security is essentially illusory and ephemeral (nuclear weapons may, though probably not, alter this judgment), since it reflects the development of a situation which may be disastrous: an imminent or apparently imminent general war.

If the gap between the perceived power positions of the major blocs is small, the significance of Small Power support rises. However, even though its influence is momentarily quite extensive, the viable alternatives open to a Small Power in a bipolar world *in which conflict seems imminent* are scant.[12] In fact, it is clear that Small Powers lose a significant element of their security in a bipolar world, particularly one which is rigid and intensely competitive. When all the Great Powers have chosen sides, there is no additional risk in attacking a Small Power, since it will not involve an uncommitted Great Power in an ensuing war. Note the case of Germany and Belgium after 1905. If Great Britain was really committed to come to the aid of France if Germany attacked, the Germans incurred no additional risk by striking through Belgium since Great Britain would be in the war anyway. Moreover, a Small Power, unless it occupies a very peripheral position geographically, stands a poor chance of being left outside a war between the two blocs, and it may well be the initial sufferer in that war. In reality, then, a Small Power pays a high price for the momentarily increased status which it enjoys in a rigid two-bloc system: the price of a sharp decrease in its general security position. Unless a fortuitous

[12] Machiavelli argued that it was foolish for a Small Power to presume that it could stand aside in a Great Power conflict, and that, furthermore, it had nothing to gain by doing so: it becomes the enemy of the victor, whereas it could have shared in the booty. And, if it chooses the wrong side, it will probably receive treatment little different from what it would have received as a bystander. Machiavelli's argument may be of dubious validity; but it does reflect a clear appreciation of some of the dangers of a certain kind of power situation.

factor intervenes (such as nuclear weapons) to moderate the possibility of war, its best hope is to choose the winning side.[13]

Perhaps the preceding discussion will make one point clear: the balance of power is, at best, an uncertain protector of Small Powers. In theory, if it promised to preserve the independence of all states, it would of course protect Small Powers. But, while the theory was obscure on this point, in practice it was very clear that the Small Powers were forced to fend for themselves. None of the power configurations which were subsumed under the label of the balance of power ever granted the Small Power very much influence over its own fate. Perversely, Small Powers were most vulnerable precisely at the moment when they were most in demand. The fact that they were suddenly viewed as significant meant that the balance of power was unstable or that the Great Powers were on the verge of war. As a final irony, the most secure Small Powers were those who were protected, not by the operation of a balance of power, but by the hegemony of one Great Power, as the continued independence of the states of Latin America indicates.

A variant of the contention that Small Powers survived because of the balance of power maintained that it was the policy of Great Britain toward that balance which was crucial.[14] Small Powers presumably benefited, if only indirectly and inadvertently, from London's efforts to keep its continental neighbors on an even keel. Great Britain's policy hardly owed its origins to a sentimental attachment to "far off" little countries. Its roots lay in a solid appreciation of real interests, most clearly set forth in Sir Eyre Crowe's famous memorandum. However, from the point of view of the Small Powers, Britain seemed to have the distressing habit of periodically

---

[13] The point has been well understood by threatened Small Powers. For example, note the behavior of the European Small Powers in the late 1930s when Hitler's power was on the rise and France and England seemed weak. And one analyst notes that Thailand's decision to ally with Japan in 1940–41 was "consistent with previous Thai foreign policy in acting in time of danger to align Thailand with the strongest power in Asia." Donald E. Nuechterlein, *Thailand and the Struggle for Southeast Asia* (Ithaca: Cornell University Press, 1965), p. 107.

[14] Cobban, *National Self-Determination*, p. 168.

forsaking its role and leaving them exposed to the demands of aggressive neighbors. Moreover, detailed examination casts grave doubts on the contention itself. It is not clear that British policy alone, unsupported by other Powers and/or beneficial circumstances, would have sufficed to save many Small Powers from defeat or destruction. As Temperley noted, Canning (and his predecessors) desired to protect the weaker states, but ". . . he was not prepared to carry out his championship of small powers to quixotic lengths." [15] More than a century later Neville Chamberlain again illustrated the danger of relying on British power as a *deus ex machina* to preserve the independence of Small Powers:

However much we may sympathize with a small nation confronted by a big and powerful neighbor, we cannot in all circumstances undertake to involve the whole British Empire in a war simply on her account. If we have to fight it must be on larger issues than that.[16]

It has also been argued that Small Powers survived simply because they were indirect and unintended beneficiaries of the rivalry and jealousy of the Great Powers, a rivalry and jealousy which persisted whatever the system. Various Small Powers have occasionally found their independence guaranteed because their powerful neighbors were unable to agree on any other solution, short of a war they preferred to avoid. They have also been used as buffer states to provide breathing space between antagonistic Great Powers. However, before any Small Power could, in effect, be removed from the play of world politics, it had to fulfill several preliminary conditions, not the least of which was a promise to follow a truly unbiased policy. In addition, the balance had to be in a reasonable equilibrium for any of these policies to be viable. If none of the necessary conditions prevailed, the rivalry of the Great Powers was more likely to lead to subordination to one, rather than guarantee by all, of the Great Powers.

The slow but steady evolution of a number of intellectual movements—liberalism, democracy, national self-determination, inter-

---

[15] Sir Harold Temperley, *The Foreign Policy of Canning, 1822–1827* (London: G. Bell and Sons, Ltd., 1925), p. 462.

[16] Quoted in Wheeler-Bennett, *Munich: Prologue to Tragedy*, p. 158.

national law—has also been put forth as a partial or indirect explanation of the survival of Small Powers.[17] Whatever other effects these movements had, they all worked in favor of the weaker members of the international system, in the sense that it was necessary to justify actions by an appeal to something other than a narrowly conceived *raison d'état*. To some extent this merely fostered hypocrisy, since the Great Powers still acted according to what they conceived as the imperatives of security. The fact that they increasingly felt the necessity of obscuring their true motives behind a veil of liberal and legal rhetoric nevertheless presaged a day when that rhetoric might be transformed into a substantial operative factor. This trend was undoubtedly assisted and encouraged by virtue of the fact that the most eminent member of the European Concert, Great Britain, was a democratic and peaceful state intent on preserving the status quo. It may also have been encouraged by the spread of technology facilitating the diffusion of knowledge which, hopefully, would enlighten at least some opinions.

There can hardly be any doubt that the ultimate fate of Small Powers is determined by the policies of the Great Powers. All of the preceding discussion refers, in the final analysis, to indirect benefits which fall to Small Powers as a result of various actions by their more powerful neighbors. Small Powers survive because it is in the interest of the Great Powers that they do so, or because they are momentarily shielded by the fact that Great Power energies are concentrated elsewhere.[18] Nonetheless, it is not entirely irrelevant to point out that within certain limits the Small Power could affect its chances of survival, primarily by altering the expectations which the Great Powers held about its position and its likely response to external pressures.

If the Small Power followed a cautious and nonprovocative policy, it might be ignored and consequently uncompelled. If it appeared to represent a coherent national state without dissident minorities or irredentist neighbors, it was that much harder to jus-

[17] See Wright, *A Study of War*, p. 268; and George Liska, *International Equilibrium* (Cambridge: Harvard University Press, 1957), pp. 28–33.

[18] For a somewhat different formulation, see Georg Schwarzenberger, *Power Politics* (New York: Frederick A. Praeger, 1951), pp. 104–11.

tify its elimination. If it maintained a high level of military preparedness, and possessed a reputation for military virtues, it might
turn itself into an unattractive target, promising an aggressor costs
incommensurate with any potential gains. In sum, it could hope to
improve its chances by appearing to be a substantially stronger and
more unified state.[19]

The survival of Small Powers in the preceding century cannot be
attributed to a single factor. Any one of the factors or conditions
which have been mentioned might suffice. On the other hand, all
together might prove insufficient. The best that can be said is that,
ceteris paribus, some circumstances, some actions, some distribu-
tions of power were more favorable to the survival of Small Powers than others. Specific explanations require empirical examination, in particular in terms of the nature of Great Power—Small
Power relationships at any one moment. And it may be appropriate
to conclude by emphasizing that some part of the answer must inevitably remain obscure, either because the historical record cannot
be untangled, or because of variations in "the tides in the affairs of
men [which] promote consolidation, or fragmentation, respect for
smaller nations, or disregard of their right to independent existence." [20]

Alliance Policies, 1815–1854

The European system of the nineteenth century has been described
often enough to make its general characteristics well known. Above
all, that system was dominated in fact and thought by the policies
of the Great Powers. Those who had the power to act also had the
responsibility to do so. This section is concerned with the way in
which this pattern of politics affected the behavior of Small Powers.

To begin with, certain points require restatement. The distinction between Great Powers and Small Powers originally arose in
response to military necessities. States were first separated into for-

---

[19] For a discussion of some of these points, see Wright, *A Study of War,* p.
288; and Cobban, *National Self-Determination,* p. 169. This is a central thesis
of Fox, *The Power of Small States,* pp. 180 ff.

[20] Liska, *International Equilibrium,* p. 33.

mal categories according to their ability to guarantee 60,000 troops in the field against a new French aggression.[21] The inability of any Small Power to make such a commitment, coinciding with the assumption that the peace negotiations would be unduly hampered by granting them equal status, led to the creation of a formal distinction between superior and inferior states which persisted throughout much of the century. The Small Powers, of course, objected vociferously, but to no avail. If it had not been for the objections of Great Britain, their position would have been even more subordinate and more onerous than the one granted to them.[22] This situation had within it the seeds of future discord. On the one hand, it sharpened the conflict between the Eastern and Western wings of the Concert. On the other hand, the disaffection of the Small Powers toward a treaty and a system which lowered their status and influence created an area of potential discord should one condition arise.[23] That condition was the destruction of Great Power unity.

Nevertheless, despite dire predictions to the contrary, the Great Powers managed to maintain just enough unity, even when the Congress system deteriorated into an ad hoc Concert system, to limit the effects of Small Power discontent—at least until the end of the century. Bound together by similar values and similar procedures and limited by the military means at their disposal,[24] the Great Powers managed to limit their wars and control their disputes, primarily by removing the most refractory and dangerous ones from the operation of the balance. Moreover, until the eruption of the Franco-Prussian struggle, no single conflict dominated the scene. All states were free to move in response to the presum-

[21] See Chapter 1 above.

[22] See Sir Charles Webster, The Foreign Policy of Castlereagh (London: G. Bell and Sons, 1958), I, 69–73.

[23] Ibid., p. 500.

[24] Despite the emergence of mass armies during the French Revolution, the General Staffs of the various European countries, except for Prussia, simply ignored that development and returned to a military system in tune with 18th Century imperatives. See B. H. Liddell-Hart, "Armed Forces and the Art of War: Armies," in J. P. T. Bury, The New Cambridge Modern History, Vol. X: The Zenith of European Power (Cambridge: Cambridge University Press, 1960), p. 302.

ably objective imperatives of a balance of power system, free from the vices of too much friendship or too much hatred.[25]

In a system in which the Great Powers maintained their unity because they recognized the dangers of not doing so, in which they limited their goals in order to maintain the stability of the entire system, and in which military technology remained tied to obsolescent traditions in which counting infantry sufficed for determining power—what role could the Small Power play?

The answer is clear. Their role could only be peripheral in terms of the functioning of the whole system. But that did not mean that the system affected them in a peripheral way. Quite to the contrary, it could have a decisive impact on their existence. Several factors operated to reduce the maneuverability of the Small Powers. For one, since no Great Power had either the desire or the means to overthrow the whole system, wars were fought with less than a total resource commitment. In such wars the minor resources of a Small Power were irrelevant. If the force level was to be raised, the Great Power could raise the level or, preferably, bargain for the support of one of its peers. The fact that the system was fluid facilitated this since none of the Great Powers was irrevocably committed for or against any other. It was more worthwhile to concentrate on influencing intra-Great Power relations than on winning the support of any Small Power. Moreover, since the Great Powers were far superior to the Small Powers in military terms, certain tactical possibilities theoretically open to later generations of Small Powers were absent. They did not have the real power, or the political leverage which is willed to them in a bipolar system, to begin a catalytic war (à la Serbia in 1914) or to disrupt potential Great Power settlements (as the Czechs might have in 1938). The Small Powers were simply chattels of the Concert: as long as the latter functioned moderately well, their ability to influence events was virtually nil. They could not even expect the immunity in minor transgressions which inertia sometimes granted

---

[25] For a formulation of the "essential rules" of such a system, see Morton A. Kaplan, *System and Process in International Politics* (New York: John Wiley and Son, Inc., 1957), pp. 22 ff.

their superiors. As Palmerston noted: "Great Powers like Russia may persevere in wrongdoing, and other states may not like to make the effort necessary for compelling it to take the right course. But no such impunity in wrong is possessed by a small and weak state. . . ."[26]

In terms of alliance policy, this configuration of international politics had several significant effects. Since the Great Powers forswore attempts to overthrow the system, at least until the period of nationalist wars from 1859 to 1871, they concentrated on adjusting and compromising disputes as they arose.[27] They competed vigorously to secure results favorable to themselves but the results were kept within acceptable limits. Alliances performed an important but limited function in this situation. As the most familiar instrument of any balancing system, they were in full use. However, in conformity with the general pattern of relations, they too were conceived in a limited way, functioning simply as a means to redress slight alterations in the general equilibrium.

The new military technology did not begin to have a decisive impact on alliances until the last decades of the century. In this period, the old conception of the proper function of an alliance prevailed. As Langer noted:

The great coalitions of modern history were almost always made just before the outbreak of war or during the course of the conflict itself . . . the easy-going nature of warfare made advance arrangements quite unnecessary and the slowness of communication made it inadvisable to enter commitments of binding character. It was the greater pressure [of democracy] in international relations and the greater speed of military operations that gave rise to the necessity for permanent combinations and resulted in the gradual evolution of the great European alliance systems of the period preceding the World War.[28]

Thus before the onset of the mid-century wars, alliances were defensive instruments aimed at containing an actual (not a potential) threat to the balance of power. They were designed to main-

---

[26] Quoted in Taylor, *The Struggle for Mastery in Europe*, p. 147.
[27] *Ibid.*, p. 568.
[28] William L. Langer, *European Alliances and Alignments, 1871–1890* (New York: Alfred A. Knopf, 1950), pp. 5–6.

tain the existing system against any attempts to overthrow it. As such, they were obviously concerned with specific goals, and hence lacked the open-ended quality of the alliances constructed after 1871. Since military technology was still in a relatively undeveloped state, it was not necessary to lay out military commitments in great detail. There was still time, once a crisis erupted or a war actually began, to arrange explicit details of cooperation. The presumed "vice of immediacy" noted by Alfred Vagts was an accurate reflection only of the period immediately before the First World War, in which mobilization schedules began to determine political maneuvering. In the earlier years, a *relative* fluidity and flexibility characterized the system.[29] As a result, alliances were defensive, ad hoc, localized and specific, and limited. They were defensive in that they sought to maintain stability, not create a means of overturning it. They were ad hoc in that they were usually created only after a threat arose, and were not constructed beforehand to deal with potential threats. They were specific in that they were concerned only with the immediate crisis; and localized in that they concerned only neighboring states, since only neighbors could represent a real danger. And alliances were limited in that each ally still retained its ability to maneuver in the system at large. These characteristics reflected a political system in which there was a significant amount of agreement on values and methods, and in which military technology was still rudimentary enough not to conflict with the desire and need for flexibility. In turn, the alliance pattern bolstered and did not conflict with the system in which it operated.[30]

Small Powers operating in this system had a very narrow range

[29] The flexibility of the nineteenth-century international system has undoubtedly been overstated. Any system dependent on human perceptions and decisions is bound to be somewhat rigid because of limitations emanating from stupidity, error, prejudice, habit, and so forth. Nevertheless, in comparative terms, that system, at least before 1871, was flexible enough to deserve the description; or perhaps one should say that its obviously less than perfect flexibility was sufficient, given the nature of the environment it had to contend with.

[30] For an excellent analysis of the nature of alliances in these years, see Gordon Craig, "The System of Alliances and the Balance of Power," in Bury, *The Zenith of European Power*, pp. 266–72. See also Rosecrance, *Action and Reaction in World Politics*, pp. 165–66.

of choices open to them. If they became areas of contention between rival Great Powers, the best they could hope for was the uncertain security inherent in a momentarily stable balance of power. At worst, they could expect partition. The fate of Poland was not forgotten, even if it was not repeated. Occasionally, if conditions permitted it and no other solution seemed feasible, certain Small Powers had their neutrality permanently guaranteed, a status usually imposed upon them in spite of their protests. In effect, they became buffer states because the potential cost of making them anything else seemed too high. The opportunity to improve one's position by means of an alliance was virtually nonexistent. The power of the second-level state was simply not sufficient to make it worth any concessions on the part of Great Powers, who were, in any event, fighting wars clearly within their own capacity.

Many Small Powers heartily disliked their inferior status.[31] From the time of their exclusion from the Vienna settlement to the end of the century, when a variety of factors created new opportunities, they chafed at their condition. When the system which they found so onerous began to break down after 1871, they scarcely bemoaned its fate. In fact, they ignored the long-range implications of that breakdown and concentrated on securing whatever immediate advantages the new situation offered. This occurred despite the fact that their security was highest when their status was lowest. In the old system they had been indirectly protected by the overall equilibrium and by the fact that none of the Great Powers sought unlimited gains.

Since alliances were created only after a crisis erupted, the Small Powers had no opportunity to seek political goals by a peacetime alliance with a Great Power. Since they had very little material power, they were in an equally disadvantageous position in terms of gaining military advantages from a war alliance. Ignored in peacetime, except when they became trouble spots (in which case the Great Powers alone disposed of them), and irrelevant in a

[31] It is worth reemphasizing that here, as elsewhere, "Small Powers" refers only to those Small Powers who are within the area of Great Power confrontation: thus, e.g., this generalizations refers to the Balkan Small Powers, but not necessarily to, say, Portugal.

Great Power war which was to be fought for only limited gains, Small Powers interested in improving their political position or directly threatened by a Great Power were reduced to becoming scavengers. Once a war started, it was they, not the Great Powers, who were forced to make concessions in an effort to make sure they were on the winning side.[32]

If both bilateral and multilateral alliances with Great Powers offered few advantages, there still remained the possibility of creating an effective Small Power alliance. However, the inherent limitations of this kind of alignment were quite evident. For one thing, since there was no forum like the League of Nations in which their combined votes could be bargained for political concessions, one possible advantage was nonexistent. For another, the Great Powers were simply not constrained by the ideological bonds which, in later years, allowed Small Powers so much immunity. Great Power intervention to control refractory Small Powers was considered a normal and legitimate responsibility of their superior status, not a crime against law and justice. Finally, since the possibility of a protracted war or an unlimited one apparently never occurred to anyone, the military advantages presumably occasioned by a combination of weak Powers were nonexistent. This was, indeed, the era when the sum of weakness did not equal strength.

All of this may be illustrated by taking note of the contrary fate of the Balkan alliance in the 1860s and in 1912. In theory, at least, a Small Power alliance should be most effective when the Great Powers are engaged in another area. The wars of 1866 and 1870 should, then, have allowed the Balkan alliance to achieve substantial gains at the expense of Turkey, while the "sick man's" protectors were too busy to intervene. However, despite the crisis in Western Europe, the Great Powers were still able to cooperate sufficiently to thwart all efforts of the Balkan states to change their status. The system was fluid enough to permit the Great Powers to join together to suppress Small Power initiatives in one area,

---

[32] For various comments on the cynical and expediential nature of Small Power politics, cf., Sir Charles Petrie, *Diplomatic History, 1713–1933* (London: Hollis and Carter, 1947); W. A. Phillips, *The Confederation of Europe* (London: Longmans, Green and Co., 1920), p. 130; Webster, *The Foreign Policy of Castlereagh,* p. 500.

while they themselves were fighting in another area. The result was that the efforts of the Balkan League were unsuccessful in the 1860s because the Great Powers were not totally immobilized by their own frictions. By 1912, conditions had so altered that the Balkan League managed to reverse its earlier performance, although internal squabbles ultimately destroyed it.[33]

It has been argued that an alliance policy is most critical in a multipolar system in which no single conflict is dominant.[34] From the point of view of the Small Power, this is not necessarily true. The political system which existed from 1815 to 1854 was surely multipolar, and it would be difficult to isolate a single conflict within it as dominant. Yet, since the Small Powers were clients and objects of the system, and not equal partners, their alliance policies were either nonexistent, irrelevant, or ineffectual. In a real sense, it is difficult to discuss the alliance policy of weaker states in this political configuration. Even the traditional chess metaphor which equates Small Powers with pawns is ambiguous, for pawns at least have the potential of becoming truly significant as the game progresses. But in a system in which all contests ended no later than the middle game, the Small Power was a wasted asset since it did not have even the potential of becoming something greater than its power. The frustrating and dispiriting aspects of such a situation explain, at least in part, the avidity with which many Small Powers grasped the new and dangerous opportunities offered to them by the international system which began to emerge after the Franco-Prussian War. As illustrated by the failures of the Balkan League, a limited Great Power war within a balance of power system did not necessarily grant the Small Powers carte blanche to rectify local grievances. After 1871, but especially after 1890, even the possibility of a bipolar, Great Power conflict increased their maneuverability immeasurably.

[33] For an analysis of the Balkan League in both periods, see L. S. Stavrianos, *Balkan Federation: A History of the Movement toward Balkan Unity in Modern Times* (Northhampton, Mass.: Smith College Studies in History, 1944), Ch. V and pp. 168 ff.

[34] See Liska, *Nations in Alliance*, p. 16.

CHAPTER 6

The Disruption of the Old System: 1854–1914

THE MORE or less traditional balance of power system which operated from 1815 to 1854 was rapidly undermined and fundamentally altered in the course of the wars which erupted between 1854 and 1871. The unity in purpose and method, which had allowed the Great Powers to compromise their conflicts short of war, was challenged and destroyed by Napoleon III's effort to organize Europe on a national basis under French hegemony. Neither principle was acceptable to Napoleon's peers. They could hardly accept his pretensions to hegemony any more than they could countenance a Europe based on national states. The result of the ferment created by his machinations was hardly a Europe altered to his specifications. But, more to the point, the opportunities created by his disloyalty to the old system led to major revisions in the status quo. The most notable were the unification of Germany and Italy; almost equally significant was Russia's disaffection with the terms imposed upon her after the Crimean War. Great Power unity dissolved in the face of these developments, and the moderation and prudence of the past was succeeded by unalloyed power politics and a *sauve qui peut* atmosphere.

For the Small Powers, the situation had certain theoretical attractions. Since the Great Powers were fighting each other, presumably they would be too busy to control their Small Power neighbors. Moreover, not only would Small Power maneuverability increase in direct proportion to the degree of Great Power conflict but also the Small Powers might even be sought as allies by the various antagonists. After all, even if they had only minimal armies, they could still perform other services. In reality, however, the situation was quite different. Small Power immunity did *not* increase in direct proportion to Great Power conflict because the Great Powers still retained enough unity to cooperate against the peripheral threats of discontented Small Powers, and because the Great Powers did not conceive of the Small Powers as valuable military allies in an imminent war. It was wiser to concentrate on neutralizing or allying with another Great Power, rather than wasting time and effort on a Small Power. The failure of the Balkan League to achieve its goals in the 1860s is illustrative.

Even if the Small Powers were still limited to a subsidiary role, the chaotic period after 1854 ultimately had effects which decisively altered their position. For one thing, the unification of Germany and the decisive defeat of France in the Franco-Prussian War had a momentous impact on the balance of power system.[1] In fact, that system, as it had operated before 1854, could not be reestablished. The essential flexibility which must characterize a balancing system was proscribed by the fact that Franco-German hostility precluded any major alignment between them. Henceforth they would be on opposite sides of the balance, even if the objective situation required their cooperation. In addition, the relative equality in power which should characterize a balancing system, and had characterized the system before 1854, was gradually eroded by the rapid development of German power. After 1890, it became clearer and clearer that Germany was simply becoming too powerful to accept the constraints of the old system unless she did it voluntarily. The system was no longer sufficiently (i.e., obvious to all) stronger than one of its constituents, if that constituent attempted to assert its strength. The result of these developments was the gradual emergence of a system increasingly characterized by bipolar patterns of behavior, although with a strong alloy of traditional balancing techniques.

In terms of alliance policy, the wars of 1854 to 1871 also had a

[1] For a detailed examination of this period, see W. E. Mosse, *The European Powers and the German Question, 1848–71* (Cambridge: The Cambridge University Press, 1958).

decisive effect. Instead of an ad hoc, defensive arrangement designed to meet a perceived threat, alliances became aggressive instruments deliberately created beforehand in order to alter the territorial settlement of 1815, not to maintain it. In effect, they became instruments of war. Each ally expected tangible military support in a prospective conflict. Moreover, the specific territorial revisions which each sought were agreed upon beforehand. They were the inducements which persuaded hesitant states to opt for one or another alignment. The classic examples were Cavour's alliance with Napoleon in 1858, and Bismarck's Italian agreement of 1866.[2]

The factor which did most to facilitate the change in the nature of alliances, beyond the specific policy decisions of Napoleon III and Bismarck, was technological. A virtual revolution in the technology of warfare occurred between 1830 and 1870.[3] However, the military and political leaders of Europe might have continued successfully to ignore its significance had it not been for Prussia's decisive victories in 1866 and 1870. The Prussian military, in contrast to their brethren elsewhere, understood and took advantage of the opportunities offered to them by the Industrial Revolution. A pernicious syndrome developed after 1871, as all the other Great Powers desperately sought to copy Prussia's behavior. Instead of small professional armies, conscripted mass armies became the norm. Larger armies of nonprofessional soldiers could mean: (a) that wars were bound to be more comprehensive in scope, affecting the whole society; (b) that new industries faced large demands; (c) that longer wars were likely since the soldiers might be less efficient, and their political demands less controllable; and (d) that since reserves had to be called immediately once a crisis erupted, enormous significance was attributed to the railroad in effectively mobilizing a country.[4] The country which mobilized

[2] See Gordon Craig, "The System of Alliances and the Balance of Power," in J. P. T. Bury, ed., *The New Cambridge Modern History* (Cambridge: Cambridge University Press, 1960), X, 271.

[3] B. H. Liddell-Hart, "Armed Forces and the Art of War: Armies," in J. P. T. Bury, *The New Cambridge Modern History*, Vol. X: *The Zenith of European Power* (Cambridge: Cambridge University Press, 1960), *passim*.

[4] *Ibid.* The railroad also made the use of reserves increasingly possible: i.e.,

first presumably achieved a decisive advantage over its enemies.

What effect did this have? Primarily it meant that the alliances of the period after 1871 would remain essentially war instruments, as they were from 1854 to 1871, rather than return to the earlier pattern of defensive ad hoc arrangements. Since speed of mobilization, the getting of reserves into position before the enemy by means of a tight railroad schedule, was assumed to be critical, it was no longer possible to wait out a crisis or to seek allies after a crisis emerged. If an ally was to be of any use at all, it had to agree to mobilize its forces simultaneously with the nation it was allied with. Ad hoc agreements were useless because success required too much preliminary planning and coordination of time tables. Alliances became more and more significant as they began to be more and more inclusive: the two factors operated on and reinforced each other. Wars which were no longer to be limited by virtue of limited means necessitated allies who guaranteed specific and immediate aid should a conflict arise. The alliances which developed after 1871, therefore, were provided with concrete military plans which clearly delineated friend and foe. They were aimed not at the defense of the balance of power but at aid in an imminent war.

Alliances so extensive and concrete were bound to rigidify, particularly in a period dominated by Franco-German hostility. The result, particularly after 1890 when France finally broke out of its diplomatic isolation, was the creation of two blocs which grew tighter after each crisis. The idea of the "European concert," always ambiguous and difficult to interpret, virtually disappeared as each bloc sought to achieve its own goals at the expense of the other.

These developments did not begin to mature until after 1890.

---

cause and effect are not clear in this instance. Some analysts indeed argue that it was the railroad which was the decisive factor—I have phrased the point somewhat differently to avoid an implication of technological determinism. But see Theodore Ropp, *War in the Modern World* (New York: Collier Books, 1962) p. 161: "Strategically, the most important of the new inventions were the railway and the telegraph, which made it possible to solve the practical problems of mobilizing, supplying, and commanding mass armies. . . . For the first time, a whole army could put its whole strength into the enemy's country. It was the railway, in short, which made mass armies practical."

From 1871 to 1890, the most pernicious effects of the technological revolution and Franco-German hostility were mitigated by
France's weakness and Bismarck's policies of peace and consolidation. Neither Bismarck nor the other European statesmen perceived
the full impact of Germany's industrial power: that was to occur
only after 1890.

In the years before then, a curious kind of politics predominated:
Germany was clearly the most powerful state in Europe, though
not powerful enough to defeat all the others, but she pursued a
policy aimed at maintaining the status quo, not altering it.[5] The
primary means which Bismarck employed were alliances: pre-1854
in that they were defensive and specific in terms of the *casus
foederis,* but post-1854 in that they were negotiated beforehand
and laid out explicit terms of cooperation. The anomaly of a system
of alliances which partook of features from two different eras could
be ignored until the linchpin of the system reversed its own policies.
That is, a system of defensive military alliances negotiated before
any crisis arose, delineating the details of cooperation should the
crisis occur, could persist only as long as all the Great Powers
favored the status quo or were too weak to do anything about it.
The system could avoid excessive rigidity by virtue of the fact
that the major conflict was momentarily quiescent. As long as
France remained too weak to challenge Germany directly, the
worst effects of bipolarity could be avoided. In fact, a good deal of
cooperation occurred between supposedly hostile states. After 1890,
when these conditions no longer held, the alliance systems lost
their defensive and specific nature and were replaced by more
aggressive, inclusive military blocs.

For the statesmen of the various European Small Powers, the
implications of these developments were hard to discern. They
stood to benefit from the increasing significance attached to the

[5] The range of permissible behavior foreseen by Bismarck can be inferred from
his comment on the struggle between Russia and Austria-Hungary in the Balkans
in 1876: "We could certainly tolerate our friends losing or winning battles against
each other, but not that one of them should be so severely wounded and injured
that its position as an independent Great Power, with a voice in Europe, should
be endangered." A. J. P. Taylor, *The Struggle for Mastery in Europe, 1848–1918*
(Oxford: The Clarendon Press, 1954), p. 239.

development of international law, democracy, and liberalism, developments which seemed to be crowned by the equality granted Small Powers at the Second Hague Conference in 1907. The years of general peace during Bismarck's extended tenure indirectly protected most of the Small Powers from the potentially dangerous effects of an undiluted power struggle. They could not alter their status by taking advantage of Great Power conflicts, but neither were they much threatened by Great Power aggressions. Obviously a Small Power may be protected not only by a real balance of power among its neighbors but also by the peaceableness of the leading Great Power.

In any event, the position of the Small Power from 1871 to 1890 varied little from its position up to 1854. Neither its advice nor military support were considered significant enough to warrant any concessions to it on the part of the Great Powers.[6] From the point of view of the latter, the military potential of the Small Power may even have seemed to decline. Even though no major wars were fought, all armies were rapidly being converted from small professional groups to large, nonprofessional units. In an era dominated by such armies, with their heavy reliance on an industrial base, the miniscule armies of partially industrialized Small Powers should have faded into insignificance—in theory. The situation in practice was considerably different: Europe converted its armies but not its thought patterns. Power continued to be measured by number of infantrymen, and not by number plus industrial base.[7] In any system which continued to think quantitatively rather than qualitatively, the Small Powers retained the possibility of increasing their influence in direct proportion to the extent that the numbers attributed to the Great Powers seemed to create a standoff. Before the last decade of the century, this possibility was of minor import, for Great Power alignments were still fluid enough to make it more worthwhile to concentrate on

---

[6] Thus, after the Balkan conflicts, Greece in 1878 demanded Crete, Thessaly, Epirus, and part of Macedonia as a reward for her efforts: her claims were ignored by the Great Powers.

[7] See Taylor, *The Struggle for Mastery in Europe,* p. 551; Liddell Hart, "Armed Forces and the Art of War," p. 302 ff.

shifting the position of another Great Power rather than a Small Power. The traditional pattern of thought was further bolstered by the lessons European statesmen drew from the wars of 1866 and 1870.[8] They assumed, with minor exceptions, that the next war would be as quick and relatively painless as the earlier ones. And for quick, limited wars, the Great Powers did not need to bargain for the support of Small Powers.[9] The latter's influence, perversely, could grow only in proportion to the assumption that the next war would be general.

As in the earlier system, alliance opportunities for the Small Power were few and generally disadvantageous. A bilateral Great Power-Small Power alliance was either unattainable or too dangerous. The Small Power had too little leverage over its larger ally to be anything but an exposed satellite.[10] A multilateral Small Power alliance had little chance of accomplishing its purposes unless the Great Powers lost all unity. In addition, it might be destabilizing if it did not include all the local Small Powers, since the pariah could always sell itself to an outside Great Power in order to establish an equilibrium. A multilateral Great Power-Small Power alliance was again the most acceptable alternative, but it was difficult to achieve. Rumanian ties to Germany and Austria-Hungary, which were initiated before 1890, nevertheless are more accurately treated as an aspect of the later political situation.

To repeat, the position of the Small Power in a world dominated by a status quo Great Power is not markedly different from its position in a fluid, balance of power system in which no power is

[8] Some sense of the extent to which traditional patterns of thought prevailed may, perhaps, be discerned by reading Disraeli's comments on the behavior of one of his ambassadors at a conference to impose reforms on Turkey: "Salisbury seems most prejudiced and not to be aware that his principal object, in being sent to Constantinople is to keep the Russians out of Turkey, not to create an ideal existence for the Turkish Christians." R. W. Seton-Watson, *Disraeli, Gladstone and the Eastern Question* (London: The Macmillan Company, 1935), p. 138.

[9] Richard N. Rosecrance, *Action and Reaction in World Politics* (Boston: Little, Brown and Company, 1963), p. 153 ff.; and Ropp, *War in the Modern World*, pp. 203–4.

[10] For example, by virtue of the Austro-Serbian treaty of 1881, the Serbs virtually became a satellite of the Empire. See William L. Langer, *European Alliances and Alignments, 1871–1890* (New York: Alfred A. Knopf, 1950), p. 328 ff., for a discussion of this alliance.

dominant. In both cases, the Small Power remains of peripheral significance. If satisfied, it is relatively content with its minor role; if revisionist, it hopefully awaits the dawn of Great Power conflict. The revisionists were given their great opportunity in the years after 1890 when the European system began to rigidify into opposing blocs, and the satisfied Small Powers were to be shocked out of their reverie by the increasing tensions and hostilities of a new kind of political world.[11]

Sometimes, too much is read into any discussion of early bipolar political systems in an effort to gain some insight into the contemporary world. A great deal of caution needs to be exercised in making the effort because of the significantly different factors which are operating within each system, even if there is an external similarity in terms of general patterns of behavior. The current debate about the relative stability of bipolar systems is indicative of the dangers.[12] The bipolar system now may be more stable than its critics presume because of the revolutionary impact of nuclear weapons. But that argument is specific, not general. Earlier bipolar systems were clearly less stable than balance of power systems.[13] In effect, then, one may feel the need of creating

[11] Some indication of their state of mind may be perceived by taking note of an incident in the Belgian Chambre in 1901: the majority of Senators left the hall in protest when one of their number suggested improving their army; they felt it would be an insult to their neighbors.

To be fair, it must be noted that not all Belgians were so naive. In fact, many diplomats and soldiers had serious doubts about England's intentions toward Belgium, particularly after the entente between London and Paris. These Belgians feared British intervention which might make Belgium the primary battlefield of the ensuing war—and above all, the Belgians wanted to remain out of the war. They did not want to be 'rescued' when that 'rescue' might involve their destruction. The similarity with Belgian fears in the late 1930s is quite apparent, except that it was the effects of French intervention which agitated them then. See Jonathan C. Helmreich, "Belgian Concern over Neutrality and British Intentions, 1906–14," *The Journal of Modern History*, 36 (December 1964), 416–27.

[12] See Kenneth Waltz, "The Stability of a Bipolar World," *Daedalus*, 93 (Summer, 1964), 881–909.

[13] That may be due, as Waltz suggests, to the fact that bipolarity based on alliance blocs is less stable than a bipolarity based on the power of two states; the latter, presumably, is more flexible, more unified, able to react more quickly, etc. *Ibid.*, pp. 899–901. One may also be permitted some doubt about Waltz's

a unique category in which to discuss current patterns of behavior, rather than attempting to assimilate them with earlier bipolar systems.

The necessity of making this distinction seems all the more evident when we consider the numerous differences between the state system which existed from 1890 to 1914 and the Cold War system. The existence of nuclear weapons is simply the most obvious, though not necessarily the most important. The earlier system contained no Superpowers, whereas the contemporary one does and would even if nuclear weapons were nonexistent. The earlier system was only incipiently worldwide, since it remained essentially Europe-oriented. The states which operated within it were homogeneous: all spoke the same political language, both literally and figuratively. More significantly, they possessed a shared pattern of expectations about the outcome of various political choices. Thus there was a general assumption that a war could be fought and won quickly, that it would not destroy the traditional state system, and that it was an acceptable and legitimate instrument of statecraft. None of these assumptions now hold, at least with any real force. The contemporary state system also is far more variegated in its relevant actors, extending from Superpowers through traditional Great Powers, traditional and very new Small Powers, and international and supranational organizations. War, at least major war, is perceived in an entirely different fashion, and there is no longer any significant amount of shared expectations about political events. Systems which possess such decisively different internal characteristics may be more profitably studied as different in kind, not merely degree.

In any event, the system which began operating after 1890—perhaps, more precisely, after the completion of the Franco-Russian entente—opened up a new kind of political world for Small Powers. The hypertrophy of their influence, so pervasive now, can be

contention that the contemporary system is stable primarily because of its bipolar character: this may attribute too much significance to structural characteristics and not enough to the nature of the primary antagonists and their weapons systems. For a different criticism of the Waltz position, see Richard N. Rosecrance, "Bipolarity, Multipolarity, and the Future," *The Journal of Conflict Resolution*, X (September 1966), 314–17.

traced back to developments in this period. The disunity and hostility of the Great Power blocs, the continuing influence of intellectual trends which sought to legitimize Small Power rights, and the willingness of various Small Powers to use their new opportunities to accelerate or continue instability created a new view of the role of Small Powers in world politics, a role which was to become increasingly prominent in the next decades.

The assumption that a general European war was likely became prevalent as the two blocs developed. It was still assumed that even a general war, in terms of the number of participants and the area of battle, could be kept limited in its ultimate effects. Nevertheless, the Small Powers began to be increasingly sought as military allies. It was true that the coming war was presumed capable of limitation in certain aspects, but in other aspects it might be impossible to do so. A Small Power might be able to tip the military balance in a local area, particularly if the opposing Great Powers were equally powerful. It might also facilitate an invasion, or prevent one, by controlling a strategic area. At the very least, it would deprive the other bloc of one potential resource base. These various strategic considerations, buoyed by the traditional notion of equating strength with numbers, led to a struggle among the Great Powers to establish predominance over centrally located Small Powers, particularly those in southeastern Europe.

The Small Powers in the previous system had rarely been sought as either military or political allies. Their influence was virtually nil, but so was their responsibility for events. They were not expected to carry part of the burden in maintaining the security of the system. They were merely to keep out of the way. If they did not, they might be neutralized or they might become buffers, but they normally survived, in one form or another. But now the immunity of irrelevance was taken away. By aligning with a Great Power bloc, or in opposition to it, Small Powers accepted all the implications of that role. The full weight of choosing unwisely would fall on them, as much as it might on their greater ally. In freely accepting an active role in international politics, in accepting all of the implications of having real choices, the Small Power gained influence but lost security.

That gain in influence was more illusory than real, at least in long-range terms. The Small Power was gaining influence in response to its willingness to commit itself to fight from the *start* in a Great Power war. It was sacrificing its traditional policy of waiting until the dust began to settle before it made a move. For minor immediate gains, such as its ally's support in a local dispute, it accepted the possibility of fighting in a war in which it could only be the first sufferer. It now became a legitimate target for the other Great Power bloc. Unless its own military strength was very high, or its Great Power ally felt itself strong enough to lend aid beforehand, it was likely to have to rely on its own power to repel the initial attack. And for most Small Powers, the initial attack was also very close to being the final attack.

Since the decision to ally involved so much more for the Small Power, it had to be made with great care. A study of some of the decisions, such as the Rumanian, indicates that the Small Powers seemed to have some realization of this. There was at least some nostalgia for the days of limited liability.[14] Nevertheless, the decision had to be made, for in most cases the probable penalties of nonalignment seemed worse than those of alignment. In other cases, the pressures of the neighboring Great Powers were so strong that some decision was imperative.

A bilateral alliance with a Great Power was almost out of the question once all the Great Powers joined one or the other bloc. Even if possible in a formal sense, substantively it involved a commitment to one of the blocs. Neutrality was attractive, but of limited significance. Successful neutrality required a favorable geographical position *and* a strong army. Once the Schlieffen Plan was adopted, an attack on Belgium was inevitable; but the Netherlands, in a slightly more favorable geographical position and with a slightly better army, managed to remain neutral. In any event, neutrality offered no protection against the victorious coalition. Unless one could be sure that the war would end in some kind of stalemate, it seemed wiser to gamble on choosing the stronger side. Of course, even a correct choice offered little real protection against

[14] See R. W. Seton-Watson, *A History of The Roumanians* (Cambridge: Cambridge University Press, 1934), pp. 361 ff.

the victorious Great Power, even if it happened to be your own ally. The hope that gratitude and/or satiation will induce the victor to be magnanimous is all that remains. Thus, for all practical purposes only two alternatives were relevant: a multilateral Great Power-Small Power alliance, and a multilateral Small Power alliance.

In theory, a Small Power allied with two or more Great Powers, particularly in a period when there is some tendency to value even minor accretions of strength, is in an advantageous position. By accepting an alliance it obviously relinquishes its opportunities to stand aside during a conflict. Presumably, the advantages outweigh the disadvantages. The Small Power can now play intra-alliance politics much as it previously played (or tried to play, as the case may be) the wider diplomatic game. It may be able to influence alliance policies in a favorable direction by playing one ally against another or by making effective use of any right it has won to state its own position or acquiesce in that of its partners. And it also benefits from the intrinsic advantages of an unequal multilateral alliance.[15] Some substance can be furnished to these observations by noting several aspects of Rumania's position in the Triple Alliance.

Rumania, like Belgium, was caught between two hostile Great Powers—Russia and Austria-Hungary. Alliance with either would expose the Rumanians to the retaliation of the other. The obvious solution was to seek the support of a third Great Power, in this case, Germany.[16] However, once Germany and Austria-Hungary negotiated the Dual Alliance, Rumania was forced to choose between its Great Power neighbors. Despite the fact that any agreement with Austria-Hungary would inevitably force the Rumanians to relinquish their demands on Transylvania, which was part of the Empire, they accepted the sacrifice.[17] The decisive factor which motivated Bucharest to opt for Vienna, and not Moscow, was clear. It was not simply the fear of isolation or the impos-

---

[15] See Chapter 3 above.

[16] See Langer, *European Alliances and Alignments,* p. 348 ff.

[17] L. S. Stavrianos, *The Balkans Since 1453* (New York: Rinehart and Company, Inc., 1958), p. 495.

sibility of neutrality (obviously none of the requisite preconditions were present), nor Russia's arrogance, ". . . but above all the fact that while Russia had no ally against Austria, the latter now definitely had Germany behind her." [18] Rumania chose to ally with what clearly seemed to be the stronger side. It was a tactic which, though sanctioned by all the canons of traditional diplomacy, merely increased the imbalance of power, a condition detrimental to Rumania's long-range interests. The Rumanians were too preoccupied with immediate problems to consider the long-range. However, even if they had, the imperatives of immediate security would probably have prevailed.

The Rumanians expected several perquisites from their decision, not the least of which was support for its demands on Bulgaria, to which its interests turned when the possibility of acquiring Transylvania disappeared. The Central Powers regarded Rumania's allegiance as significant. It contributed to Germany's refusal to renew the Reinsurance Treaty after Bismarck's fall, since alignment with both Moscow and Bucharest seemed incompatible, given their hostility.[19] True to their word, the Great Powers continued to offer the Rumanians both military and diplomatic support up to the outbreak of the war. In the Balkan Wars, the Central Powers supported Bucharest despite Vienna's reluctance. The latter favored Bulgaria over the Serbs, but was forced to acquiesce in Bucharest's pro-Serb policy.[20] Kaiser Wilhelm felt the Rumanian alliance was significant enough to justify full support, "even at the risk of temporarily offending Austria." [21]

The Rumanians clearly benefited from their alliance choice. They received general protection against Russia as well as local support against Bulgaria. Moreover, they were able to operate within the alliance to such an extent that Vienna's hostility was

[18] Seton-Watson, *A History of the Roumanians*, p. 361.

[19] *Ibid.*, p. 372.

[20] *Ibid.*, p. 450 ff. Thus Berchtold was forced to tell the Bulgarians that "given our relations with Roumania, a *rapprochement* between Austria-Hungary and Bulgaria was possible only on terms which took these relations into account." Quoted in Luigi Albertini, *The Origins of the War of 1914* (London: Oxford University Press, 1952), I, 492.

[21] *Ibid.*, p. 463.

controlled by Berlin's friendship. Bucharest also received some amount of military and economic aid to lighten its load. From the point of view of the Central Powers, the sacrifices noted seemed worthwhile: Rumania's strategic position in the Balkans, as well as its military and economic strength, were important factors in preventing the Entente from establishing a hostile Balkan League in the area.[22] Should war finally come, the retention of Rumania also opened an alternative route into Russia.

Rumania was constrained from taking full advantage of its bargaining position by one obvious fact. If it became too aggressive, or if it ignored the desires of its allies too often, they could always turn elsewhere:

They were fully alive to the possibility that if they drew away from the Central Powers, Germany might have to look for other allies in the Near East, and that after a decade of successful penetration in Turkey she might not look in vain.[23]

Even in a bipolar situation, in which both sides actively bargained for its support, Rumania never had carte blanche. Both sides had options which were unpalatable to the Rumanians. Nevertheless, the decision to join the Central Powers seemed to be both wise and profitable, until the completion of the Franco-Russian entente. The full implications of commitment to one side in a bipolar world, and one in which war was hardly proscribed, did not become clear until the years when bipolarity became a recognized fact and war an ever-nearer possibility. Then the Rumanians recognized that the concessions they had wrung from the Central Powers had been given in the form of an IOU which was soon to be collected. They were expected to carry part of the military burden against an overwhelmingly powerful neighbor. The degree to which the Rumanians desperately sought to dissociate themselves from their two allies in 1913 and 1914 was in direct proportion to their recognition of what that tie implied.

[22] For Austria-Hungary, this was a significant gain: Vienna very much feared a Balkan League not under its control for, after Turkey was eliminated from Europe, the League's gains could only come at the expense of the old Empire. See Albertini, *The Origins of the War of 1914*, p. 991.

[23] *Ibid.*, p. 375.

In sum, the multilateral Great Power-Small Power alliance was not an unmixed blessing in a bipolar world. It offered immediate aid in exchange for a commitment of full support in an ensuing Great Power war. Yet, in spite of its obvious dangers, it was probably a sound policy choice for some Small Powers, specifically, those that found themselves within the likely area of the war. For the latter, there was no legerdemain by which they could disappear from view. They were bound to suffer from the war. On balance, then, the wisest choice may have been to accept the full implications of this fact, choose the stronger side, and eke out as many concessions as possible. The Small Power in such a situation has no real choice between involvement and noninvolvement. It can only hope to influence the terms and nature of some kind of participation.

Small Power alliances in this bipolar political world were also of varying utility. As an effort to ward off Great Power military intervention, they were virtually useless. It is difficult to find any statement even suggesting that they might be so used. For the most part, they were constructed in an effort to achieve political goals, or limited military goals against local rivals. Thus the Balkan League was designed to deprive Turkey of part of its territory while Turkey's protectors were involved elsewhere, but not to work against those protectors themselves.

In a period preceding the rise of formal international organizations, and in which traditional patterns of thought still prevail, it is clear that one of the primary advantages of a Small Power alliance is lost. The political advantages which later generations of Small Powers earned by bartering their votes in an increasingly internationalist environment were simply not to be had. If, therefore, an argument can be made for the value of such alliances before 1919, it has to be made on grounds which are avowedly more realpolitik than would be necessary in later years.

The balance of power system worked most effectively according to the degree of consensus among the Great Powers. When they were united on methods and goals, the system was stable. But a bipolar system postulates a lack of unity between its Great Power constituents. From a system in which it had few, if any, real choices, the Small Power found itself thrust into a world in which many choices had to be made but in which the choices were of major significance. That considerably diluted the attractions of having to choose. One possible advantage of a Small Power alliance in this situation was that it gained time. The fact of commitment and the difficulty of decommitment increased the possibility of controlling and limiting Great Power pressures. Preliminary agreement among several local Small Powers also considerably increased the possibility of successfully altering a local status quo when the Great Powers were busy elsewhere or when they were so precariously balanced that they feared local intervention would serve as a catalyst for the major war all feared.[24] Presenting the Great Powers with a *fait accompli* and a unified front increased the likelihood that they would do nothing at all to reverse the new configuration.

The history of the Balkan League illustrates some of the problems noted. Unsuccessful in the 1860s, because the Great Powers were still unified enough to control their inferiors, the Balkan League suddenly registered several successes in 1912. With Europe divided into alliance systems, the common denominator of Great Power agreement was considerably lowered. Since it was necessary to consult one's allies, and since the Balkans were of different degrees of significance to each ally, it was much easier to agree to do nothing at all than to hammer out a common policy. Moreover, if both alliance systems intervened—and if one did, the other had to follow—the chances of war rose: but the wrong war, at the wrong time, and at the wrong place. The Small Powers recognized the immobility this situation forced upon the Great Powers, and attacked Turkey, "for they knew that the great powers would never be able to cooperate long enough and closely enough to enforce their threat of no annexations."[25]

Having grasped their opportunity, the Balkan states shortly thereafter lost it:

---

[24] Thus this was one case where preliminary agreement among *all* the local Small Powers was not necessary, since the Great Powers were too involved elsewhere to heed the pleas of any local Small Power left out of the agreement.

[25] Stavrianos, *The Balkans Since 1453*, p. 534.

Mutual trust or any conception of some sort of a Balkan federation never entered into the picture . . . once the war had started and the Turks had been defeated, there was nothing left to hold the League together and it dissolved into warring factions.[26]

They had understood the significance of the bipolar political situation insofar as it related to opportunities to act against the will of the Great Powers. But they had failed to maintain a unified front once they accomplished their immediate aim. The result was a political maelstrom, in which defeated or dissatisfied Small Powers sought the support of external Great Powers, and in which the latter dashed from capital to capital in an effort to construct a new alliance of Small Powers, but one under their own tutelage.[27] Kaiser Wilhelm in fact envisioned the Balkan League ". . . as the seventh Great Power, leaning on Austria-Hungary and the Triple Alliance." [28] The result was that no one achieved any significant goals.

In summary, the Small Power alliance in this period still could achieve political goals, though within a rather limited range. The critical problem concerned the difficulties of remaining unified in so unstable an environment. If a defeated, dissatisfied or ignored Small Power could appeal to a Great Power for support, and if the Great Powers valued Small Power support enough to respond to that request, the most likely result of a venture like the Balkan League was the creation of a microcosm of the whole system's instability. Given the additional fact that Small Power alliances had very little military utility against a Great Power (the forces were never integrated, and the *casus foederis* never committed the allies to fight against a Great Power), and that their use against another Small Power was bound to result in Great Power intervention, the verdict would seem to be that they are virtually useless instruments of statecraft in the kind of bipolar system which existed from 1894 to 1914.

[26] L. S. Stavrianos, *Balkan Federation* (Northhampton, Mass.: Smith College Studies in History, 1944), p. 170.

[27] *Ibid.*, p. 174; see also Albertini, *The Origins of the War of 1914*, Chapters VII and VIII.

[28] Seton-Watson, *A History of the Roumanians*, p. 449.

All in all, despite the spurious influence it conferred, the bipolar system which existed before 1914 constituted a very unattractive political world for Small Powers. The particular configuration of power induced the Great Powers to violate their traditional tactics, and to actively seek the support of Small Powers. But that quest rested solely on the assumption of imminent war. Small Powers were granted minor concessions in order to guarantee their participation in a general war. The fact that contemporary military technology actually made Small Powers more vulnerable than ever before and less useful in a large-scale war, illuminated the real significance of their new prominence. That prominence did not reflect any substantive change in their political position. Rather it reflected the existence of a unique and presumably transitory state of affairs, the elimination of which would find the Small Powers cast back into their traditionally peripheral role. In fact, only the revolutionary and wholly unperceived effects of the First World War, coupled with the continued development of an internationalist ethic, allowed the Small Powers to continue, and to improve, their new status in world politics.

CHAPTER 7

The Interwar Years: 1919–1939

IDENTIFYING the system of politics which predominated during the interwar years is extremely difficult. The root of the trouble, of course, is the abnormal power distribution created by the effects of the First World War. With Germany and the Soviet Union weakened, Austria-Hungary eliminated, and the United States withdrawn from world politics, the pattern of relations which emerged was bound to be unique. The situation was further complicated by the existence of the League of Nations, an institution which promised much but which lacked an operational history on which statesmen could base their policies. The result of the interaction of these factors was that the first ten to twelve years of the period were highly transitional. Until the power situation was clarified, and the League of Nations had a record which could be evaluated, no definite pattern of international relations could be established.

It would be particularly inaccurate to describe the early years of the period, let alone the later, in terms of the theory of collective security. Surely a version of the theory, imperfect but recognizable, was inscribed in the Covenant of the League of Nations. However, so many of the prerequisites for an effective collective security system were absent that it is illusory to assume that the policies of the members of the state system were based on its dictates.[1] The fact that France construed the security provisions

[1] For a discussion of the theory of collective security, see Inis Claude, *Swords Into Plowshares* (New York: Random House, Inc., 1956), Ch. XII.

of the Covenant as a license to create an anti-German alliance, and that Great Britain, the only other center of available power in the 1920s, construed them as an instrument to facilitate discussion and conciliation confused the matter beyond hope.[2] If any state had really wanted to base its policies on the imperatives of collective security, and there is very little evidence that any did, its desires were bound to be frustrated by the antithetical ways in which the two leading Great Powers interpreted its significance.

If the period cannot adequately be described in terms of collective security, neither can it be described in traditional terms. It was not a balance of power system nor was it a bipolar system. It could not be a balance of power system because the requirements of such a system had been destroyed by historical developments: the flexibility, moderation, ethical indifference, and simple power calculations of the old system were beyond recall.[3] It could not be a bipolar system because power simply wasn't distributed in the correct fashion. The two centers of available power were, despite their constant frictions, bound to be on the same side in a major crisis because they recognized that Germany was potentially more powerful than either alone.

The simple way out of the dilemma is semantic. One could describe the period as incipiently bipolar in the first decade, and actually bipolar thereafter. However, this is not particularly satisfying since the earlier years exhibited characteristics which are clearly out of joint with bipolar politics. One might also resolve the dilemma by accepting it. The period could be identified as being merely transitional, as one in which patterns of behavior normally identified with three different kinds of political systems intermingled. While this attempt to define the period by incorporating all its ambiguities in a definition is not wholly unsatisfactory, it sheds very little light on the actual politics of the period.

It is quite true that the first ten or twelve years of the interwar

---

[2] See Arnold Wolfers, *Britain and France Between Two Wars* (New York: Harcourt, Brace and Company, 1940), *passim*.

[3] For a discussion of these points, see Ernst Haas, "The Balance of Power as a Guide to Policy-Making," *Journal of Politics*, XV (August 1953).

period intermingled characteristics of different systems. But this theoretical confusion should not obscure the fact that the period possessed landmarks distinct enough to serve as policy guides. Amid the confusion about general patterns of behavior, there still existed shared perceptions about certain aspects of the actual political world. The most notable of these perceptions concerned the power position of France. Despite the fact that France was actually losing ground in its efforts to match Germany, her victory in the First World War seemed to have restored her primacy in Europe. France's rivals were defeated, eliminated, or ostracized—except for Great Britain. Since the latter was more and more involved in Commonwealth affairs, to the detriment of its European interest, and since its traditional policy of creating a balance in Europe suffered from the inevitable difficulties of strengthening and favoring a defeated enemy at the expense of a victorious ally, the result was that France was virtually the sole power factor in Europe until the 1930s. If Bismarck's Germany dominated Europe from 1871 to 1890, the France of Poincaré and Briand dominated Europe from 1919 to 1933. In effect, then, while the period was clearly transitional in terms of the pattern of politics which it would tend to foster in the future, it was predominantly unipolar in its own politics. European politics were still "world" politics. If a world war was to come, its origins would still be in Europe. And, despite the fact that the realities of power would shortly make this view anachronistic, France dominated European politics. That domination was obviously illusory: France's furious efforts to bolster its own security, in a period when she appeared more secure than anyone else, indicate that the illusion was more sharply perceived as true in other capitals than in Paris. To London, Prague, Warsaw, Rome, even Berlin, France's predominance in Europe seemed beyond dispute and its desperate efforts to achieve more security could never be adequately understood. Thus the period we are discussing is primarily unipolar, but uniquely so, for it was the seemingly decisive center of power which acted in the most distraught and destabilizing way.

As for Small Powers in this period, several factors should be emphasized. Clearly, their influence was on the rise, though their power position relative to the Great Powers was actually worsening. Public opinion now condemned the worst features of the nineteenth-century diplomatic game, one feature being the way in which Small Powers were treated. Collective security promised them, though it did not assure them, real protection against the Great Powers. The League of Nations itself guaranteed them equal status as well as an arena in which to discuss their problems. In addition, the sheer number of Small Powers had been so increased by the effects of the war that they were bound to seem more important, simply because they were more visible. Finally, the power vacuum in Europe assured them of a new role, however transitory it might be. As long as France or any other Great Power sought allies, and as long as Washington, London, Berlin, Moscow, and Vienna were unavailable, the only alternative was to ally with Small Powers. Conversely, it meant that any Small Power which sought a formal alliance with a Great Power had no viable choices other than France, or perhaps Italy.

The real power position of small countries was weakened, nevertheless, by the continuing development of modern arms. Only countries with large areas or with the most advanced weapons could possibly defend themselves. The banality of this conclusion was obscured until the second decade of the period. The war-weariness of the Great Powers, various unilateral and interstate disarmament policies, and the continual international discussions of disarmament created an atmosphere in which the lack of armed strength did not appear as significant as it once had. In any case, since it was clear that war was impossible for some time—the usual estimate was "at least ten years"—armaments seemed a long-range problem. In sum, many of the Small Powers which emerged from the First World War were militarily stronger than their predecessors, but were actually more vulnerable for a variety of reasons. The most significant of the latter centered on the nature of military technology. They had also lost the opportunity to balance between opposing sides, since only one center of power really counted. And they were internally weak states, a condition which had rarely affected earlier generations of Small Powers but was destined to affect future generations even more decisively (as Chapter 8 will note).

One particularly curious aspect of this period concerns the moral evaluation of Great Powers and Small Powers. No one would have described earlier generations of Small Powers as superior moral units. Yet, after 1919, they began to be conceived in this fashion, perhaps as a reaction to the effects of the Great Power war just concluded. For example, a liberal newspaper in Sweden declared in 1923 that "the world opinion which will gradually gather strength and rise up against the domination of the powerful, must have its origins in the smaller states . . . simply because the interests of the weaker always coincide with those of justice." [4] Arnold Toynbee illustrated the same point nine years later when he wrote that "the proposition that if there were no 'Great Powers' in the world there would be no danger to the peace of the world was a thesis which could hardly have been contested, in 1932, by any impartial student of public affairs." [5]

The new moral eminence of Small Powers combined with the moral disapprobation attached to alliances to create a security problem. Alliances were roundly condemned as the primary cause of the First World War. While they were not formally proscribed by the League of Nations or by collective security, it was clear that sentiment was strongly against them. If they were to be acceptable at all, they had to fulfill certain conditions. Alliances were to fit within the framework of the League which, in practice, seemed to mean that the League was to be officially notified of their provisions, and they were, in theory, to be open to all states. That is, they were not to be aimed against a specific state, but at aggressor "X," a ploy necessary to maintain the facade of collective security, even if all concerned knew X's real identity. Since keeping X's identity formally secret eliminated the possibility of preliminary military planning, such alliances were marginally more effective

[4] Herbert Tingsten, *The Debate on the Foreign Policy of Sweden, 1918–1939* (London: Oxford University Press, 1949), p. 63.

[5] Arnold Toynbee, *Survey of International Affairs, 1932* (London: Oxford University Press, 1931), p. 184.

for deterrence than defence. That is, they presumably deterred war by the threat of cooperative retaliation. The fact that preliminary planning about the ways in which to make that cooperation explicit was forbidden diluted the significance of such alignments as instruments by which to actually fight a war.[6] Alliances were to be instruments of peace, not war. The political advantages of alignment inevitably outweighed the military advantages.

Small Powers were caught in a dilemma. To retain their moral status, it was incumbent upon them to support the League fully, and to accept all the implications of the incipient collective security system in the Covenant. But to rely on nonalignment, or on alliances as ambiguous and uncertain as those which fit the requirements of collective security, was a dangerous gamble. It was an acceptable gamble only to the degree to which they felt secure in the immediate future. However, to revert to a traditional alliance involved, in addition to the usual difficulties, a significant loss of prestige.

The choice was difficult because most of the Small Powers recognized the long-range potential of an effective League and an operational collective security system.[7] But no one thought either would be immediately effective: that meant other means had to be adopted in the interim to guarantee security. The problem concerned the degree to which immediate and future needs impinged on each other. The dilemma was acute only for those Small Powers which felt threatened: Czechoslovakia and Poland, for example, but not Sweden or Canada. For the fearful, the only real option seemed to be an alliance of some sort even, if necessary, one which injured their moral status.

The cruelest dilemma was faced by the revisionist Small Powers. Hostile to the League and to collective security, they nevertheless

[6] See Sir James Headlam-Morley, *Studies in Diplomatic History* (London: Methuen & Company, 1930), p. 8.

[7] It should be noted that the Small Powers viewed the League from a different perspective than the Great Powers. They conceived it as a means to hobble and constrain the Great Powers from unilateral actions, not as a reinforced Concert in which the only restraints the Great Powers accepted were self-imposed. See Gwendolyn M. Carter, *The British Commonwealth and International Security* (Toronto: The Ryerson Press, 1947), p. 100.

lacked the power to alter their status. France, of course, supported the status quo. Their only hope was Italy. However, even after Mussolini converted to a revisionist policy, Italy lacked the power to effectively support a campaign against the status quo. It could only follow its traditional jackal policy, hoping to profit from whatever crisis emerged.[8] The revisionist Small Powers were forced to cultivate patience. Their antagonists, the various Small Powers supporting the territorial settlement, had much the better of it. They could ally with France (though no one else) or they could create a Small Power alliance which deliberately excluded Great Powers.

The power vacuum in Europe appeared to offer the Small Powers more opportunity to maneuver than it really did. It was surely true that the traditional restraints imposed by Great Power unity were gone. However, multilateral unity was replaced by unilateral dictation. Small Powers could maneuver to the extent that their actions did not conflict with France's defense of the status quo.

France's alliance policy, for the most part, determined the general pattern of alliances in this period. In an effort to devise an acceptable substitute for the traditional Russian tie and the repudiated Anglo-American guarantee, the Quai d'Orsay set out to construct an alliance system composed of like-minded defenders of the status quo. Bilateral agreements were negotiated with Poland, Belgium, Rumania, Yugoslavia, and Czechoslovakia. At a minimum, they provided for consultation in a crisis and military aid. At a maximum, they involved an automatic commitment to provide military support against aggression.

The Small Powers which committed themselves to France received various benefits in return. In addition to actual aid, usually in the form of a French military mission, their prestige was enhanced by close ties with the recognized leader of the European system. More significantly, the deterrent value of alliance with France increased their ability to frustrate revisionist designs on the territorial settlement. Yet, having conceded the advantages of align-

[8] See A. J. P. Taylor, *The Struggle for Mastery in Europe, 1848–1918* (Oxford: The Clarendon Press, 1954), p. 286.

ment with Paris, it remains to be said that, for the Small Powers, the balance sheet was negative. The costs of aligning with France outweighed the gains. The wisdom of traditional warnings against Great Power-Small Power alliances was aptly illustrated.

The primary advantage a Small Power gets from its larger ally is the promise of military support. It is primarily as a military alliance against an immediate threat that such agreements find justification. Without the existence of such a threat, the political costs of allying with superior power are exorbitant. The Small Power allies of France either misunderstood these factors, or chose to gamble on their ability to control them. Their errors were particularly egregious because they themselves recognized that they were not confronted by an immediate military threat. Their own arms, singly or in combination, were sufficient to defeat any aggression by local Small Powers, and none of the Great Powers was an immediate threat.

The effect of their error was compounded by virtue of the fact of France's predominance. If an alliance with unequal power was to be generally avoided, that dictum ran with even greater force in an essentially unipolar system. The Small Powers allied with France lacked even the minimal leverage achieved by threatening to bolt the alliance. They had nowhere to go, short of agreeing to revise the peace settlement. Once allied with France, they became virtual satellites.

If anything should have warned them of the doubtful wisdom of their choice, it was France's military policy. While the Quai d'Orsay committed itself to all kinds of support against revisionists, the General Staff built a wholly defensive army. That is to say, even the possibility of French military support in the future against a new threat was eliminated by the nature of France's army. For France, the alliance system served a variety of purposes. Her small allies could drain off German troops, allowing Paris time to mobilize; they were, in effect, a kind of distant Maginot Line. They also increased French prestige and influence as the hub of a ring of supposedly powerful alliances.

What should be clear is that France never intended to come to the military aid of her allies. They were one-way alliances, designed to buy France time and troops against superior German forces. But Paris had neither the intention nor ability to fight in eastern Europe. The Little Entente states discovered this rather belatedly in the 1930s, though they should have been warned by the debates on the Maginot Line.

To some extent, France's real purposes were obscured by the way in which it treated its military agreement with Belgium. That agreement stands as a classic example of a Great Power's ability to use an alliance with a Small Power for its own purposes. France insisted on maintaining secrecy concerning the nature of the agreement. But publicly, in particular to its eastern allies, it acted as if the agreement allowed France to use Belgian territory as a launching pad into the Ruhr the minute Germany attacked east-ward. France would protect its allies by the threat of striking Germany from the rear. However, the Belgian agreement con-tained no such commitment. Although its terms were ambiguous, they clearly did not extend to the contingency France had in mind. By insisting on secrecy, by the adroit use of carrot and stick, the French coerced the Belgians into silence until 1936. The price Belgium had to pay included internal crises because of Flemish opposition to any tie with France, political and military inter-vention by Paris, and the loss of prestige and influence attendant upon its dependent status. Germany, Great Britain, even Holland, regarded Brussels as a French satellite. In exchange, France offered economic concessions in Luxembourg and military aid against Ger-many—which she was in no position to deliver when needed.[9]

The other alternative open to Small Powers, which felt the need of external support but wanted to avoid the problems of an unequal agreement, was an alliance composed solely of Small Powers. If this period provides a classic example of the disutility of Great Power-Small Power alignments, it also furnishes an example of the utility of Small Power groupings. The latter are most likely to be effective in a period when war is unlikely and when the Great Powers cannot agree on a common policy. The first point is clearly appropriate. Another Great Power war was very unlikely in the 1920s. As for the second point, rather than the opportunities

[9] See Chapter 3 above.

created by Great Power disunity (e.g., the Balkan League successes in 1912), the opportunities created by agreement with the primary power center should be substituted. Small Power alliances are useful, that is, when there is no agreement between Great Powers or when their policies are in agreement with Great Power dictates. Thus an alignment, like the Little Entente, favoring the status quo was advantageous, but one attempting to overthrow it was useless because it ran counter to French wishes.[10]

The existence of the League of Nations added to the value of a Small Power alliance. By voting together and by developing common policies, the Small Powers could increase the prestige of their alliance and its bargaining potential. Moreover, by reaching agreement about a common policy in its area, by becoming its policeman, the alliance could limit the amount of Great Power intervention with which it had to contend. In addition, it might represent enough real force to defeat local rivals without external aid. In sum, an alliance like the Little Entente achieved more external prestige and influence for its members than they could have achieved singly or by allying with a Great Power. It left them with a significant amount of control over their own affairs, and it increased their opportunity to direct regional developments in a favorable direction.[11]

On the debit side, the alliance tended to freeze the status quo to the extent that dissatisfied local Powers never accepted its legitimacy. For example, the Little Entente was easily the primary power center in southeastern Europe. With France behind it, and the other Great Powers weak, its writ ran virtually unchallenged. But it became so powerful and influential that it did not feel the need of compromising its difficulties with Hungary, Austria, Poland, or Italy. The result was that the Little Entente, rather than solving the problems of its area, merely froze them until a new power configuration arose in the 1930s. In the new circumstances, the prestige and influence it had enjoyed in the 1920s would prove to be spurious. Nevertheless, in the short run the Little Entente did achieve a position of real influence: over a long period of time,

---

[10] See Chapter 4 above.
[11] *Ibid.*

it was given the opportunity of effecting to *some* degree the actual course of events. That the Little Entente failed in the 1930s was due to factors beyond its control. That it did not achieve as much as a theoretical analysis suggests was possible can be ascribed to its internal weaknesses. But that it achieved even as much as it did probably should be attributed to the effectiveness of the kind of alliance created. It seems clear that the same judgment could be made for other states in similar circumstances.

After 1933, Europe rapidly degenerated into a quasi-bipolar system superficially similar to the one which operated from 1890 to 1914.[12] The new system differed in three essential respects from the old. First, the injection of a tripartite ideological conflict enormously complicated the problem of creating two monolithic blocs. Any division of Europe into two blocs seemed inherently unstable, at least more so than had been true in 1914. The dictates of strategy now might run afoul of ideological affinities. If it did not prevent an alignment, it surely complicated its operation. Second, Europe still lived with the memories of 1914. Statesmen were very much aware of the inherent dangers of their situation. There was, particularly for the Western Powers, more of a tendency to seek a peaceful way out of each crisis. They knew, as their predecessors had not, that the next war would not be short and limited. Therefore appeasement seemed less of a danger than any alternative. Third, for the first time the European political system was forced to operate at a time when two of its leading members repudiated its legitimacy. Nazi Germany and Soviet Russia were too powerful for the old kind of politics to prevail; but they were also directed by men whose patterns of thought could not be compre-

---

[12] "Quasi-bipolar" is an obviously unsatisfactory term to employ as a description of the complex system which existed in Europe after 1933. However, it seems slightly more satisfactory than any of the alternatives: bipolar, tripolar, or multipolar. The system ultimately did become bipolar; but that result was not foreseen by very many commentators, primarily because of the difficulty involved in forecasting Soviet behavior. To many, it seemed as if the system *ought* to be bipolar in order to counter Germany's power; but the unattractiveness of aligning with the Soviets, and uncertainty about Stalin's willingness or ability to do so, made the system appear to be at least potentially tripolar.

hended by statesmen steeped in the diplomatic history of nine-teenth-century Europe.

The position of the Small Powers in this system was considerably worse than it had been before 1914. They were again sought as allies by the Great Power blocs, and they again faced the same choices: alignment with one bloc or the other (alignment with a single Great Power involved a tie to the bloc which that Great Power represented), Small Power alliances, or neutrality. How-ever the potential costs of each decision were much higher. Both Great Powers and Small Powers recognized, as they had not in 1914, that the military contribution a weak state could make was insignificant, that weak states might be military liabilities, not assets. Nevertheless, they were still sought either for strategic rea-sons or to forestall acquisition on the part of the opposition. Small Powers were truly defenseless in an age of mass, mechanized war-fare. The bargaining leverage they possessed was thus considerably reduced. They were not nearly as attractive as a prospective ally as they had once been. In fact, it was probably easier to defeat them militarily, unless they were protected geographically, than to satisfy them with extensive concessions.

Alignment with a Great Power bloc was an unattractive possi-bility. This was particularly true given the manifest superiority of the Axis before 1939. There was no point in allying with France and Great Britain, for they were too weak to protect even them-selves. To ally with Hitler promised immediate gains, but at the price of further aggravating an already unstable balance. More-over, it provided no guarantee at all against German victory and the revisions which were bound to follow. Belgium was most acutely caught in the dilemma. To remain tied to France antagonized Ber-lin, and probably insured another Schlieffen Plan. But to abandon the tie with France not only antagonized the only state which could offer aid against Germany but also left Belgium isolated in the coming crisis.[13] Was there a viable alternative?

The answer is probably not. Faced by Hitler and forced to rely on Daladier and Chamberlain, Brussels, Prague, Warsaw, and

---

[13] See Chapter 3 above.

other Small Powers needed a miracle, by way of geographical transplantation, to avoid disaster.[14] They did not get it.

However, the policies they did choose to adopt probably insured their demise beyond doubt. What the exposed Small Powers chose to do was to refuse to confront the real world. Instead of recognizing that they could not avoid participation in the war, and were inextricably involved with the course of events, they sought to isolate themselves, morally and politically, from events beyond their own boundaries. The mentality of the Small Powers may be illustrated by quoting a Swedish source in 1939: "As the determining factor must be the resources of men and material available, states with a small war potential had no hope of intervening effectively, and therefore no responsibility." [15] And a British diplomat warned London in 1938 that "however immoral Germany's next action may be, it would be the height of unwisdom to count on the cooperation of a single Small Power in Europe against her." [16] The European Small Powers opted for a policy which they called neutrality but which was in fact nothing more than a desperate attempt to avoid war.[17] As Winston Churchill noted, "Each one hopes that if he feeds the crocodile enough, the crocodile will eat him last. All of them hope that the storm will pass before their turn comes to be devoured." [18]

Perhaps the tendency is to be too harsh on the Small Powers, for their situation was indeed perilous. They could see little advantage in allying with one of the blocs: whichever won, they would be devastated in the course of ensuing war. They could not rely on a Small Power alliance because the situation required force beyond the capacity of such alignments. The Little Entente, for

[14] Note that I am not concerned with the ability of various peripheral states to preserve their neutrality during the war. For such a study, see Annette Baker Fox, *The Power of Small States* (Chicago: The University of Chicago Press, 1959).

[15] Herbert Tingsten, *The Debate on the Foreign Policy of Sweden, 1918–1939* (London: Oxford University Press, 1949), p. 220.

[16] G. B. D., Series III, Vol. I. p. 97.

[17] See Nils Ørvik, *The Decline of Neutrality, 1919–1941* (Oslo: Johan Gundt Tanum-forlag, 1953), pp. 187 ff.

[18] Winston Churchill, *Blood, Sweat and Tears* (New York: G. P. Putnam's, 1941), p. 215.

example, could win a few minor political victories in the 1930s, but it was neither designed for nor capable of handling a military conflict with a Great Power. Reliance on the League of Nations and collective security was also impossible, particularly after the Ethiopian debacle. And when Chamberlain declared that "collective security does not differ from the old alliances of pre-war days which we thought we had abandoned," [19] supporting the League simply meant joining the weak, Western states. Only a kind of schizophrenic neutrality was left. It was bound to fail, but at least it eliminated the necessity of making harsh choices.

No period was as unattractive for Small Powers as the one which existed in the 1930s. With all the advantages of the earlier bipolar system (1890–1914) diluted by technological and ideological developments, Small Powers found themselves without a single viable policy choice. Nonalignment, bloc alignment, and Small Power alignment were all disastrous. It seems likely that the best of the bad options still involved choosing the winning side. This created a truly cruel dilemma for the democratic Small Powers, like Belgium, which favored the West but knew that they were too weak to help them before it was too late.[20] In theory, of course, the Small Powers should have allied with the weaker bloc in order to try to recreate an equilibrium. Since that increased the likelihood that they would be attacked (or sold down the river by their allies to gain time: à la Czechoslovakia in 1938), it is hardly surprising that the long-range theoretical imperatives were ignored.[21]

[19] Ørvik, The Decline of Neutrality, p. 192.

[20] Still, in the period between March and September 1939, when it was very obvious that war was imminent, several Small Powers did in fact seek and accept guarantees from London and Paris, in spite of the evident weakness of the democracies. Poland, Rumania, and Greece accepted the guarantees, obviously, because they had no other viable alternatives. They were not unaware of the fact that the existing imbalance of power was mortally dangerous for them, nor had they forgotten the betrayal of Czechoslovakia at Munich. But they could not align with Germany and its allies because the cost was prohibitive: territorial revisions plus the effective loss of independence. The guarantees from London and Paris were grasped more in desperation than hope. The situation illustrates why status quo Small Powers are so fearful of disequilibrium among the Great Powers.

[21] The tendency to move toward the stronger side, and to ignore the necessity of recreating an equilibrium, was not confined to the European states. Thus Thailand joined Japan in 1940–41 because of the weakness of Great Britain and France; see Donald E. Nuechterlein, Thailand and the Struggle for Southeast Asia (Ithaca: Cornell University Press, 1965), p. 107.

PART III

The Contemporary World

CHAPTER 8

Alignment, Nonalignment, and
Small Powers: 1945-1965

A FUNCTIONING balance of power system, comparable to the one which existed throughout the first half of the nineteenth century, limits the ability of Small Powers to achieve their own goals. However, in compensation, it provides more real security for them—in terms of the maintenance of independence—than any other historical system, all of which offered the Small Power some elements of maneuverability, but to the detriment of long-range security. At first glance, the contemporary political system appears to contradict this generalization. Surely, one would presume, the new status of Small Powers reflects a system in which the weaker units of international politics have finally achieved both security and influence. Nevertheless, a closer examination of actual patterns of interaction substantially qualifies the latter point: the original generalization, that is, remains basically sound.

It is extremely difficult to characterize the present configuration of power, but it is necessary to do so if the degree to which the position of Small Powers has been altered is to be understood. For some years after the Second World War the transitory weakness of all but the two Superpowers combined with the relative quiescence of the non-Western world to create what seemed to be a bipolar system. The revolution in nuclear technology, whatever its ultimate effects, merely confirmed this state of affairs. The world was obviously bipolar in military terms, on both the conventional and nuclear level, and it was more bipolar than anything else in political terms. The monolithic nature of both blocs, as well as the early difficulties encountered by Yugoslavia, the prime defector, illustrated the point. Similarly, the tendency to regard nonalignment as "immoral," to divide the world sharply into friends and enemies, also reflected thought patterns consonant with a bipolar distribution of power. After all, in a *purely* bipolar world nonaligned states would not exist, and in a tight but not purely bipolar world their influence and power *ought* to have been nil: if "immoral" was an inapposite description, unwise would not have been.

The world still remains essentially bipolar at the nuclear level, and will probably remain so for several decades, unless the possession of a few primitive atomic bombs and an archaic delivery system is presumed to constitute an effective deterrent against the nuclear giants. However, on the political level (but not the economic) and on the level of conventional warfare, bipolarity has given way to multipolarity primarily in the ways in which states behave, if not in the actual capabilities they possess.[1] The reasons for the erosion of the earlier pattern are fairly obvious. The economic and political recovery of formerly weak allies, as well as the cumulative effect of the creation of so many new sovereignties, are most conspicuous. A gradually developing sophistication about the significance of nuclear weapons has also been critical: the assumption that the two Superpowers have reached a nuclear stalemate, however much the strategists put the notion in doubt, has affected allies and neutrals in somewhat similar ways. The allies, already stronger, demand more participation in their own defense; but also more freedom to pursue their own goals independent of Washington and Moscow. And the neutrals perceive the stalemate as an opportunity to maneuver at local levels; and care about the East-West struggle only to the extent that they do not want to see the stalemate destroyed by a war which would also injure them simultaneously.

It is impossible to characterize this confused pattern of interactions with a simple label such as bipolarity. Nor is it much more helpful to employ a mixture of labels: e.g., bipolar on the nuclear level, multipolar on the political and conventional levels, tripartite in policy (i.e., policy takes account of three centers of influence), dualistic in major conflicts (North-South, East-West).[2] Some of

[1] George Liska, *Nations in Alliance,* pp. 214 ff.
[2] *Ibid.,* for an attempt at this kind of clarification.

the labels are too simplistic—for example, conceiving the dominant conflicts in a dualistic sense dangerously slights the intra-bloc dissensions which have become increasingly prevalent. Moreover, even if the descriptions are accurate, so many levels of interaction are left that their relationships cannot be isolated.

In any event, the contemporary international system is so variegated and multifaceted that it confuses rather than compels clear policy choices. It might be argued, for example, that a balance of power system contains obvious policy imperatives which any actor in the system can ignore only at its own peril. The same argument could not be made now, at least since the relatively simple bipolar pattern of the earlier period has eroded. But if a statesman is limited in the directions he can draw from systemic patterns, what landmarks do in fact serve to orient his behavior? [3] The contention here is that a statesman operates with a set of loosely drawn "rules of thumb" based on his perception of the characteristics of the present configuration which are *both* salient and relevant to his immediate situation. That is, in lieu of the ordering principles attendant upon a systemic categorization which would encompass the relationships between the salient landmarks, he must perceive and order those landmarks himself. And he will do so within a context which is local, ad hoc, and parochial, not systemic.

Some of those characteristics are so obvious, so salient, that they have served as rough but constant guides throughout the years since the Second World War. The technological revolution in weaponry is clearly preeminent. By ruling out large-scale wars, except for ultimate threats, and by exacerbating the problem of controlling limited violence, because of the fear of escalation and the unsuitability of nuclear weapons for local conflicts, the new weapons have altered traditional security calculations for both Great Powers and Small Powers.[4]

[3] The extent to which assumptions about the nature of the international system actually influence decision-makers has never been determined—the supposition that they act in a certain way because they perceive that they are operating within one kind of system, and would therefore act differently in another kind of system, is still merely an analytical and *a priori* judgment. In fact, decision-makers may never make *systemic* judgments at all, but merely react, as the next sentence in the text suggests, to perceptions about the immediate impact of a range of considerations which constantly vary as problems vary.

[4] This point is discussed at greater length below.

Traditional behavioral patterns have also been altered because of the intrusion of a large number of actors who are not only new but also different in kind. NATO, the Common Market, and the Afro-Asian bloc have few, if any, *significant* parallels in earlier international systems. Even the development and policies of the United Nations in an era of nuclear weapons, rampant anti-colonialism, and East-West conflict have diverged from those of its predecessor. More significantly, the new states which have emerged since the war differ—this point will be discussed at greater length—in many essential respects from the traditional members of the international system.

Despite its virtual universality, or perhaps in part because of it, the contemporary system is also characterized by a large element of subsystem dominance. The fact that nuclear war is unlikely, or that it is presumed to be so, has tended to concentrate attention on regional conflicts to the extent that it is generally assumed that the most dangerous *systemic* threat is the escalation of a subsystem conflict, which accounts in some significant degree for the influence of many Small Powers.

Finally, it is clear that the value consensus which facilitated the process of politics in earlier years is no longer in existence. It would be difficult to repeat at least one of Neville Chamberlain's follies. While he could still presume, with very little opposition, that Hitler could be treated like a Birmingham (or was it a Manchester?) businessman, it is now clear that many actors in the present system not only reject the old tradition of European politics but also are willing to use virtually any means to alter the course of events in a favorable direction. Whether this is simply another way of noting the decline of Europe, or of a more than normal intrusion of ideological issues into politics, is uncertain. But its effect is to compound the confusion and suspicion created by the interaction of the factors already noted.[5]

One recent analysis of the contemporary scene has argued that its most salient characteristic is that *both* total war and limited war

[5] For a somewhat different attempt to list the basic features of the contemporary system, cf. Michael Brecher, *The New States of Asia* (New York: Oxford University Press, 1963), Chapter I.

are less likely than in earlier periods.[6] If true, it would surely dilute the significance of the preceding points, for a declining value consensus would be of minimal significance if it occurred in an environment dominated by a decreasing likelihood of all kinds of war. However, while very few analysts would dispute the contention that total wars are less likely, the proposition that limited wars are also less likely is clearly debatable, unless the proposition is assumed to refer only to direct conflicts between the Great Powers. At any rate, the contention that Small Powers have more maneuverability in our time can be argued without reference to the relative likelihood of limited wars.

The unique characteristics of the contemporary international system limit the extent to which it can be compared with earlier systems, even those in which the power configuration was more or less bipolar (e.g., 1891–1914; 1933–1939). For one thing, the thought patterns of the earlier "bipolar" systems, insofar as those thought patterns can be detected and isolated, remained within the old balance of power tradition. A self-conscious perception that the rules of statecraft had to be adjusted to a new kind of power configuration did not occur. For that matter, it occurred only fitfully and irregularly in the contemporary world and, as a tendency, has declined rather sharply in recent years. In earlier international systems Small Powers achieved a transitory maneuverability as a result of the power configuration per se, as well as the prevalent assumption that *general* war was imminent. In the contemporary system, the power configuration is not nearly so clear, and it is the assumption that general war must be avoided, not that it is imminent, which accounts in some degree for the new status of Small Powers. Superficial similarities in overt behavior cannot obscure the differing bases on which that behavior rests. Perhaps the differences, as well as the similarities, between the various systems which have been described as bipolar will be clearer if contemporary alliance policies are examined and contrasted with earlier examples.

[6] Herbert S. Dinerstein, "The Transformation of Alliance Systems," *The American Political Science Review,* LIX (September 1965), 590 ff.

The Creation of NATO

An initial distinction must be made between NATO and other contemporary alliances. The conditions which facilitated the creation of an alliance of such scope and power are no longer present. In a sense, in NATO's early years when the Soviet threat appeared very real and very immediate, NATO was analogous to the rigid blocs created in the decade before the First World War. In both periods, alliances were conceived primarily as elements in a war policy: the emphasis was on preparedness and on common reactions to external threats. Moreover, strategic responses based on mobilization schedules in the one case, and on massive retaliation in the other, tended to bind statesmen in a similar way. The necessity of striking first was so critical that it could accelerate the incipient destabilization created by any crisis. Membership patterns were also generally similar, emphasizing bloc solidarity even at the cost of national interests. And in both cases, regional and ideological affinities (the Franco-Russian case aside) reinforced a rigid bipolarity.

However, the two cases are not completely parallel. The Triple Entente and Triple Alliance Powers sought relatively limited gains (no one wanted to destroy the old system) but with the aid of all the means at their disposal (even if they did not understand just how destructive those means really were); the Cold War antagonists originally sought wider gains (in part because of ideological differences), but by much less than total means. Thus the pattern of politics which emerged in each case was bound to be different.

As the military threat represented by the Soviet Union (and by Germany from the other perspective) has seemed to recede, and as the allies of each Superpower have gained strength, the cohesiveness and integration of each alliance has tended to decline. The sense of permanence which once surrounded both blocs has dissipated; one hears ever more discussion, for example, of the possibility of imminent demise for NATO. The analogy with the blocs created before the First World War seems much less pertinent than it once did. The extent to which NATO will regain its original strength is debatable, and it is very unlikely that any other alliances will be created which parallel the early NATO in integration and scope. Therefore, NATO will be treated as a unique case, and not as an example of general alliance patterns in the Cold War.

To understand the latter, it is necessary to examine the policies of the new nations. Since those policies are normally described in terms of "neutrality" or "nonalignment," an examination of alliance policy may seem contradictory or useless. However the rationale for nonalignment also clarifies and illuminates the contrary case: the conditions which would foster alignment.

Chapter I indicated that differences *between* Small Powers would grow increasingly important. That statement is particularly true for the period since the Second World War, although it also has some relevance for the interwar years. It is no longer possible to use the term "Small Power," even with the explicit qualification that the concern is only with "Small Powers faced by a Great Power threat," without further identification: it is necessary to indicate which Small Power, or at least which group of Small Powers, is being discussed.

The distinction would not be necessary if it was assumed that the current status of Small Powers could be explained solely in terms of the impact of bipolarity and nuclear weapons. Clearly it cannot. The behavior of the nonaligned countries differs from the behavior of the older generation of Small Powers not only because the environment in which they live is different but also because they are, in many respects, a different kind of Small Power. It is not simply that they are weak, inexperienced, beset by regional conflicts, nationalistic, and unstable domestically; the same characteristics could be used to describe the first generation of "new" Small Powers, the successor states to the Austro-Hungarian Empire. The critical difference does not lie so much in their external circumstances as it does in the fact that many of the contemporary nonaligned states lack any identification with, or attachment to, the traditions of the Western state system. They tend, that is, to think differently than their Western counterparts (*both* the stable states like Belgium and the unstable ones like Rumania in the interwar years). Most significantly, perhaps, they do not have the *same* sense of what being a Small Power implies in terms of a range of acceptable behavior.

In theoretical terms, the point need not be carried to an extreme. There are still enough similarities between the two groups of Small Powers to warrant the assumption that they can be subsumed under the same general label. Most of the European Small Powers (except for Sweden, Finland, Austria, and Switzerland) belong to one or another of the Great Power blocs; very few of the new states do. However, both the allied and the non-allied Small Powers have at least the one identical systemic interest of insuring that both blocs survive. The allied Small Powers require the presence of the other bloc in order to maintain their value as allies.[7] The unaligned Small Powers require the presence of both antagonists in order to retain their maneuverability. The similarity noted merely reflects a commonplace: the lesser units in any bipolar or quasi-bipolar system prefer the dangers and advantages of bipolarity to the disadvantages a hegemonial system offers. Still, the point remains that all Small Powers have some similar interests imposed upon them by the nature of the environment. Their differences arise, primarily, from the fact that the nonaligned states possess a different political tradition and lack a stable organizational framework.

The remainder of this chapter will concentrate on the policies of the new generation of Small Powers. Inevitably, the policies of the older Small Powers will be slighted. This decision reflects a number of considerations which ought to be noted. The most significant is the implicit assumption that the behavior of the European (and most other aligned) Small Powers has not altered greatly and that their decision to join the bloc system after 1945 has little *theoretical* interest as they possessed few, if any, viable alternatives at the time. The inclination to concentrate on the new and nonaligned states also reflects their prominence and importance in the contemporary international system and the concomitant assertion that their new status symbolizes a fundamental revision of Great Power-Small Power relationships, a point of real theoretical import.

---

[7] Cf. Karl Deutsch and Morton A. Kaplan, "The Limits of International Coalitions," *International Aspects of Civil Strife,* edited by James N. Rosenau (Princeton: Princeton University Press, 1964), pp. 170–89.

The Advantages of Nonalignment

The deterioration of semantic accuracy in the use of the term neutrality can be traced back to the efforts of various European Small Powers to cloak their frightened reactions to the anarchy of the 1930s in familiar terms.[8] It is beyond dispute that neutrality traditionally referred to the rights and duties of nonbelligerents during the course of a war. Obviously, whatever else it may refer to, the current attraction of policies defined as "neutral" has nothing to do with legal rights. On the contrary, it reflects political, military, and psychological judgments about the opportunities and dangers of the contemporary political configuration.

The current policies of the new states are also not analogous to the status of guaranteed neutrality. In addition to the specific political requirements which had, or have, to be present to make any guarantee viable, it was presumed that the recipient of such status was being withdrawn from world politics—that the political system would operate as if the guaranteed state was no longer present. Contemporary neutrality does not necessarily envisage any such thing: the state so defining itself (a reversion of the past in itself) may do so in expectation of playing a more active role in world politics, not a less active one.

Nonalignment is thus a more acceptable term, at the very least, because it lacks the historical connotations of "neutrality" or any of its derivatives. In addition, it is a more descriptive choice, since it corresponds to what its advocates say they are doing, even if their policies reveal inconsistencies.

Some contemporary analysts regard nonalignment as a new departure in world politics. J. W. Burton argues that the nonaligned states are "not involved in the power dispute" between the United States and the Soviet Union, and that they have "a status and stability wholly unlike any previous form of noninvolvement in conflict."[9] He concludes that "nonalignment has become an institution, and moreover one which does not necessarily rest upon

[8] Nils Ørvik, *The Decline of Neutrality, 1919–1941* (Oslo: Johan Gundt Tanum-forlag, 1953), p. 187 ff.

[9] J. W. Burton, *International Relations: A General Theory* (Cambridge: Cambridge University Press, 1965), p. 115.

the continued existence of rivalry between two power group-ings." [10] If Burton's argument is substantially correct, then the role of the Small Power in international relations has indeed been altered, if not reversed.

It bears emphasis that the attractions of nonalignment are not new. As a tactical approach to the issues of foreign policy, and nonalignment ought not to be mistaken for a foreign policy as such, it has frequently appealed to the weaker members of an interna-tional system which has *bipolar* characteristics.[11] The virtues, and perquisites, of a position between or unattached to the Great Power blocs are hardly as new as Tito and Nasser apparently believe.[12] In fact, of course, everybody would prefer to avoid the onerous commitments of alignment as long as their security position seems unthreatened.

Nonalignment is thus attractive (and usually viable) in periods of "cold war," that is, when Great Power relationships have neither sunk to war nor risen to peaceful cooperation. In the circumstance, Small Powers find themselves the objects of competition but not the victims of war (or, perversely, of Great Power cooperation which would remove their bargaining leverage). The viability of nonalignment is, therefore, directly related to the power balance between the Great Powers. It is decisively affected by that balance, and it in turn exercises some influence over its operation.[13] Non-alignment is not only impossible in conditions of overt Great Power war or substantive cooperation; it is also nonviable for *Small Powers*

[10] *Ibid.*, p. 167. For another argument about the distinctive character of non-alignment, cf. Cecil Crabb, *The Elephants and the Grass* (New York: Fred-erick A. Praeger, 1965).

[11] The point ought to be emphasized to avoid misunderstanding: nonalignment is an entirely different kind of proposition in a balance of power system. In fact, it is unlikely that it would be viable in any system where the Great Powers com-peted for each others' allegiance directly, rather than concentrating on winning the support of a "third world."

[12] Thus Nasser has said "Tito is a great man. He showed me how to get help from both sides—without joining either." Quoted in Peter Lyon, *Neutralism* (Leicester University Press, 1963), p. 86.

[13] Coral Bell, "Non-alignment and the Power Balance," in *Components of De-fense Policy*, edited by Davis B. Bobrow (Chicago: Rand McNally & Co., 1965), p. 69.

in a balance of power system where the Great Powers primarily seek the support of their peers rather than their inferiors.

Nonalignment, in sum, is a tactical principle designed to extract the widest range of advantages from a particular kind of power configuration. Therefore Burton and others, including, of course, many spokesmen for the nonaligned states, overstate the case when they argue that nonalignment has become an institution of world politics unaffected by the vagaries of "power politics". Nehru himself was more analytically perceptive when he declared in 1954 that:

When there is substantial difference in the strength of the two opposing forces, we in Asia, with our limitations, will not be able to influence the issue. But when the two opposing forces are fairly evenly matched, then it is possible to make our weight felt in the balance.[14]

There is, however, a more substantial reason for doubting the presumed institutional permanence of nonalignment, irrespective of alterations in the distribution of power. Nonalignment is viable for a Small Power only so long as it is not threatened by a Great Power; once directly threatened, it is difficult to avoid alignment with another Great Power.[15] In a real sense, then, an explicit policy of nonalignment always involves an implicit *arrière-pensée* that, in effect, Great Power support will be available if needed. The future ally is disguised, but it is the presumption that he will be there, once called, which makes his disguise acceptable. And thus, once again, the contention that nonalignment is independent of power relations is incorrect. A recent statement by Raj Krishna, an Indian economist, is illustrative: "non-alignment has always been, in reality, an informal, unstated, unilateral alignment with unnamed Powers." [16] So, too, is an earlier statement of an avowed "neutralist," Prince Sihanouk: "In case of a massive Viet Minh invasion we

[14] Quoted in *ibid*.
[15] The situation is different if war has broken out. Cf. Annette Baker Fox, *The Power of Small States*, for a discussion of Small Powers directly threatened by the Great Powers during the Second World War.
[16] Raj Krishna, "India and the Bomb," *India Quarterly*, XXI (April–June 1965), p. 122.

will count on the aid—material and armaments—of the United States." [17]

Still, something must be conceded to those who contend that contemporary nonalignment policies differ from earlier versions. The difference is one of degree, rather than kind. But why has the situation changed at all? What has transformed a rather obvious tactical principle into, according to some of its advocates, an institution much venerated and much praised? Understanding can result only from an examination of the dynamics of nonalignment in relationship to the environment in which it must operate—for if contemporary nonalignment is, indeed, different even if only in degree, it is because of (and not in spite of) the nature of the prevailing configuration of power.

The general characteristics of nonalignment are relatively easy to detect.[18] Its proponents see it as an active policy designed to exploit the Cold War for their own ends.[19] Thus Nkrumah could declare in 1961 that "we have adhered strictly to our policy of positive neutralism and non-alignment and whatever we have done, we have always placed Africa first." [20] The benefits which non-alignment presumably confers range over a wide area. One study notes that it has been justified as: (a) ensuring freedom and independence; (b) keeping Small Powers out of larger conflicts of no concern to them; (c) a means of avoiding alliances which make local problems more difficult to solve; (d) a means of preventing the diversion of scarce resources to military obligations; (e) and as a means of obtaining foreign aid from both sides.[21]

[17] Quoted in Roger M. Smith, *Cambodia's Foreign Policy* (Ithaca: Cornell University Press, 1965), p. 53. And for Sweden's tacit assumption that Western support will be forthcoming even without an alliance, cf. James J. Robbins, "Recent Military Thought in Sweden on Western Defense" (Santa Monica: The RAND Corporation, 1955), pp. 80 and 84.

[18] Not, of course, to all people. A recent article in India has noted that in some circumstances "you would have found Nepal practicing non-alignment against us." M. R. Masani, "The Challenge of the Chinese Bomb," *India Quarterly*, XXI (January-March 1965), p. 15.

[19] The desire to extract some benefits from a relatively bipolar situation is not new: the Balkan states before 1914 and Poland after 1933 are indicative.

[20] Quoted in Arnold Rivkin, *The African Presence in World Affairs* (Glencoe: The Free Press, 1963), p. 196.

[21] Ernest Lefever, "Nehru, Nasser, and Nkrumah on Neutralism," *Neutralism*

It is surely true that the nonaligned states seek benefits from both sides in the Cold War, and that they assume that it guarantees them more independence and prestige than any other alternative. Yet this catalogue of advantages, true so far as it goes, obscures the decisive consideration: the underlying conditions which make the achievement (as distinct from the desirability) of any advantages possible. Small Powers, historically confined to a limited role, even locally, are now significant elements of the political process; in fact, in regional terms they are very close to being environment-determining actors, rather than mere objects of a game played by others. More than ever before, they influence the nature of Great Power involvement in local areas; and articulate their own desires and their own needs to a unique degree. It is absurd to suggest that they have actually reversed the traditional hierarchy of international politics, but they do exert a significant influence on the fate of their own regions, and they have even achieved something of a role in extra-regional conflicts.

It is the impact of nuclear weapons on world politics which is normally adduced as an explanation for this development. Insofar as they have made Great Power wars too dangerous, they have altered—and *perhaps* revolutionized—the relationship between members of the international system. Conflict, rather than being eliminated, has been concentrated in areas where nuclear weapons cannot be used effectively, or where the stakes involved would not justify their use. In addition, conflict has been transferred from the formal military level to the level of political, economic and paramilitary confrontation.

In the past, the influence of Small Powers rose only when they were sought as allies on the eve of a Great Power conflict. But now, with Great Power military conflict limited, they are still sought as allies or friends: but in place of, not because of, an imminent Great Power war. That is, Small Powers are now sought as symbols of victory in a political struggle which is never destined to erupt into Great Power conflict, at least, even according to Mao

---

and Nonalignment, edited by Laurence Martin (New York: Frederick A. Praeger, 1962), p. 95.

Tse-tung, for some long period of time. The basis of Small Power influence is thus different from any of its earlier manifestations, and since it rests on perceptions about a technological development which cannot be reversed, rather than a political development which can, it *may* be more permanent. After all, whatever its global significance, from the point of view of Small Powers, it is clearly advantageous to be sought as allies or friends in a political conflict which the Great Powers envisage as the only viable alternative to direct conflict. They are still targets of Great Power policies, but they have more means by which to defend themselves in a political conflict, and they are somewhat less exposed to direct Great Power military intervention. A reasonable fear that intervention will increase the dangers of escalation, that it will offend other nonaligned countries, and that it will not lead to a quick and relatively painless solution to the crisis which prompts thoughts of intervention have induced caution, though surely not abstinence, on the part of the Great Powers.

Stanley Hoffmann has noted that revolutionary periods, such as our own, tend to increase the influence of lesser units, since military power is only one dimension among several in such periods.[22] Deficiencies in material power no longer seem quite so critical. Mere possession of the formal accoutrements of sovereignty is enough to make a Small Power a worthwhile target of the political-symbolic struggle now underway. The military capabilities of Small Powers are significant only in a very limited sense, for they are usually inadequate even on a local level. On the global level, of course, the two Superpowers can more easily change the military balance in their own laboratories, or by increasing their own defense budgets, than by acquiring allies.

Clearly, then, the primary reason for the new status of Small Powers inheres, as it always has, in the nature of Great Power relationships. Since the latter have been altered by the impact of nuclear weapons, the position of Small Powers was bound to undergo some amount of transformation. However, the attractions of nonalignment cannot be attributed *solely* to the new military

[22] Stanley Hoffmann, "Restraints and Choices in American Foreign Policy," *Daedalus* (Fall 1962), pp. 692–93.

technology: it is a necessary but not sufficient explanation. By themselves, nuclear weapons would only make nonalignment a more attractive tactical principle. But nonalignment is more than that to its advocates: it has a *mystique* surrounding it which can only be understood in terms of the nature of the nonaligned states themselves. What would have been, to an earlier generation of Small Powers, a device to extract concessions has become, to a new generation, a state of mind presumably capable of ordering all questions of foreign policy in a meaningful way.

Nonalignment is especially significant now because it is psychologically attractive to its practitioners. For states only recently freed from dependence, any political stance which emphasizes independence and which rationalizes a unique role in world politics will gain adherents. Nonalignment, as C. B. Marshall has noted, simultaneously reflects a desire to avoid commitment to former rulers and yet to exercise real influence on the course of events.[23] The mere act of repudiating the traditional system of international politics—a system which excluded, ignored, or abused them—has its own peculiar "moral" appeal of somehow transcending "power politics".

The desire to take independent positions on general issues, to avoid identification with the Great Power blocs, thus rests on more than the tactical possibility of extracting aid from both sides. An analysis, even by a spokesman for the nonaligned states, which notes only the advantage of being courted, by all sides is too "classical". Raj Krishna's statement is illustrative: "The military significance of the policy of non-alignment is simply that it avoids a complete military alliance with any one Power in order to permit limited military agreements with all Powers".[24] Nonalignment is

---

[23] C. B. Marshall, "On Understanding the Unaligned," in Martin, *Neutralism and Nonalignment*, pp. 13–33. The psychological attractions of nonalignment suggest that it would have been an attractive policy to the new states *irrespective of the distribution of power*. Note, for example, some of the similarities in behavior between the United States in its formative years and the current generation of new states. However, it is worth reemphasizing that nonalignment, whatever its instinctive appeal, could not be a *successful* policy without a particular kind of power configuration.

[24] Krishna, "India and the Bomb," p. 122.

attractive not only because of the tangible benefits it promises, *and* not only because of the nature of Great Power relationships, but also because it grants status to those heretofore denied it by the hierarchical or quasi-hierarchical structure of international society.

The psychological attraction of nonalignment is reinforced by all the other environmental pressures which affect the behavior of emerging societies—nationalism, anti-colonialism, revolutionary attitudes, the imperatives of economic growth, and so forth. Very few of the underdeveloped countries have been able to contend with these forces in an effective way. The normal result has been domestic instability. A foreign policy of nonalignment can become, under the circumstances, a means of bolstering prestige damaged on the home front. The publicity engendered by playing a world role may compensate for domestic failures; at the least it may silence, or justify silencing, domestic critics. In fact, a rationale for nonalignment can be developed based solely on its significance in internal politics.[25] It ought not, however, to be overemphasized, for it is a successful domestic tactic only to the extent that it achieves external gains, and gains depend on Great Power relationships. But it does indicate, once again, why nonalignment has become something more than a tactical principle.

What relationship is there between public declarations of faith in nonalignment and the actual policies of the new states? How do proponents of nonalignment translate theoretical and practical desirability into substantive policy decisions?

In theory, nonalignment could serve as the basis for a real attempt to stabilize the Cold War; in reality, it has done quite the opposite. Most contemporary Small Powers have applied the general principles of nonalignment in an intensely egocentric manner. If nonalignment merely reflected felt security needs within a particular kind of power configuration the result *might* have been different. However, it also reflects an aggregate of emotional and

---

[25] Cf. the essay by Robert Good, "State-Building as a Determinant of Foreign Policy in the New States," in Martin, *Neutralism and Nonalignment.* This would have been an unlikely, if not inconceivable, rationale in the past when the *ethos* and imperatives of modernization did not prevail and when the Small Powers were, in general, more viable creations.

psychological factors which inevitably affect the quality of the policies pursued.

The new states have been concerned with the East-West conflict and its derivatives only to the extent that they hope to benefit from it. Since they assume that their position is strongest when the two blocs are stalemated, and that such a stalemate exists in fact, their only concern with East-West issues has been to insure that no crisis gets so out of hand that it leads to war. Thus their efforts have been directed at facilitating any settlement which appears to reduce tensions, irrespective of the quality of the settlement.[26] A consistent indifference to the terms of any settlement has been supplemented by an increasingly prevalent assumption that both Great Power blocs are immoral, that the only moral policies in this world are those practiced by nonaligned states, and that the nature of a settlement between immoral parties is clearly not of great import.[27] What they hope to do, of course, is to maneuver expedientially in one major conflict in order to enhance their position in the conflict which they feel is dominant.[28]

The result could have been different if the new states were stable and viable constructions. As it is, they face too many pressures, particularly domestically, to indulge in the kind of thoughtful, long-range security policies *occasionally* practiced by European Small Powers of another generation. The situation could also have developed differently if the Small Powers perceived the Soviet Union and China as a security threat, but for the most part they do not. Their own inexperience, the oft-noted "appeals of communism," and an understandable reluctance to forsake the advan-

[26] Cf. William C. Johnstone, *Burma's Foreign Policy* (Cambridge: Harvard University Press, 1963), for numerous examples with respect to Burma.

[27] *Ibid.*, pp. 113–15.

[28] A Ghana memorandum for a meeting of the nonaligned states in 1958 reflects both the sense of moral superiority and the desire to use the East-West conflict expedientially: "It would be unwise, therefore, to implicate ourselves by artificial ties in the ordinary vicissitudes of European policies. Our detached position invites us to pursue quite a different course . . . why, by interweaving our destiny with that of any part of Europe, entangle our peace and prosperity in the toils of European ambition, rivalship, interest, humor or caprice?" Quoted in Thomas Hovet, Jr., *Africa in the United Nations* (Evanston: Northwestern University Press, 1963), p. 27. Warner Schilling has reminded me of the striking similarity between the Ghanaese language and that of Alexander Hamilton.

tages of nonalignment account for an apparent indifference to Soviet designs. Communism is by Lenin's definition nonimperialistic; aggression is always by imperialists; *ergo,* the Communists cannot be aggressors. In any case, even if the threat is perceived, there are too many perquisites attached to nonalignment to abandon it easily. The excessively optimistic assumption that the elimination of Great Power conflict has *completely* transformed the nature of the struggle in the underdeveloped areas, so that it will always take a nonmilitary form, merely confirms the tendency to slight or ignore security questions; they are by definition and conviction, or by hope, of secondary importance.[29] The willingness of the United States to come to the aid of those new states, such as India, which guessed wrong and remained nonaligned in the face of a threat which should have sent them beseeching aid has not facilitated early appreciation of the security problem—why ally if you can get all the benefits without doing so?

The end result is a series of nonalignment policies justified in the most principled terms, but in reality resting on very pragmatic and instrumental judgments about the best way to take advantage of contemporary events.[30] Ironically, there is a sense in which nonalignment policies based solely on expediential calculations are ultimately destructive of real independence for Small Powers: their vaunted flexibility turns out to be nothing more than the traditional scavenger policy of Small Powers in new clothes. They have the freedom, that is, only to react to and take advantage of Great Power rivalries.[31]

It is doubtful that nonalignment can ever be very much more than a tactical principle. However, its advocates maintain that it is more than that. Thus they can fairly be blamed for not even attempting to develop nonalignment policies which rest on wider

---

[29] Cf. Liska, *Nations in Alliance,* p. 210 ff.

[30] Cf. Lefever, "Nehru, Nassar, and Nkrumah on Neutralism," p. 96.

[31] Cf. Johnstone, *Burma's Foreign Policy,* p. 76, where he notes Burma's "growing dependence upon the vagaries, sudden changes, and swift developments in the struggle of the giants." Cf. also Pierre Hassner, "La Montée des Jeunes Etats et les Relations entre les Deux Blocs," *La Communauté Internationale Face Aux Jeunes Etats,* edited by J. B. Duroselle and J. Meyriat (Paris: Librairie Armand Colin, 1962), p. 399.

and sounder considerations. That refusal assures the continuation of a large gap between theory and practice: a theory which asserts the constructive role of nonalignment in world politics but a practice which turns it into a device to extract and extort minimal gains.

The emergence of Communist China as an independent threat, and as a new policy option, may alter the pattern of the first two decades of the Cold War. That pattern has, in any event, been in the process of evolution. In the first decade when the blocs were cohesive and the level of tension and enmity was high, the Small Powers were actively courted by both sides, but as converts. Tactically speaking, nonalignment was extremely attractive since the Small Powers could gain very little from joining either side. Neither the United States nor the Soviet Union appeared to be a very attractive ally; not choosing either, insofar as it remained possible, was clearly the wisest course. In addition, as a group, the nonaligned states were relatively unified by virtue of common agreement on the relevance of the anti-colonial issue.

The situation began to change in the mid-1950s. The cause and effect relationships are extremely difficult to untangle, but several points can be made with some assurance. Intense pressure to join either bloc began to relax. In fact, the blocs themselves began to lose cohesiveness, though this was not the decisive consideration. The military factor was undoubtedly critical. Aside from the problem of bases, which affected a limited number of new states, Small Powers became increasingly less significant (if not actually a hindrance) in terms of security. If security was to come via a "balance of terror," and if the Small Powers were therefore no longer needed as allies or outposts, they could safely remain nonaligned, but neither more nor less. Their allegiance was still symbolically significant and neither bloc willingly countenanced overt commitment to the other.

Some decline in tensions between the United States and the Soviet Union and a concomitant shift in psychological attitudes toward nonalignment were also significant. Nonalignment became progressively less "immoral" as the overt allegiance of Small Powers became less important. In certain circumstances, nonalignment even began to appear as an optimum alternative. In situations where the major powers were reluctant to intervene because the potential dangers seemed too high—as in the Congo and Laos—particularly since one intervention would prompt another, some form of "neutralization" seemed clearly preferable.[32] Intervention was also bound to cause trouble between the rest of the nonaligned states and the two Superpowers, and as their votes and political support on a wide range of issues became increasingly more important then their military contribution, this too became a consideration.

The reduction of tensions was not entirely beneficial to the Small Powers. Nonalignment was neither as wise nor as advantageous as it had been in the earlier power configuration. It was, to a significant degree, simply harder to extract concessions in a less intense conflict. The image of the "enemy" was not so clearly drawn. The relative decline in the colonial issue, and a relative increase in domestic difficulties, also contributed to the emergence of a new pattern. In addition, the rapid proliferation of new states tended to decrease the bargaining potential of any single state (or group). It clearly provided the Great Powers with leverage they previously lacked. Differences *between* the nonaligned states began to emerge. Significantly, some discussion developed about what role they could or ought to play in world politics. The discussion was unnecessary in the early period when the role was imposed by external circumstances; the possibility or wisdom of creating a bloc of nonaligned states began to be seriously discussed only when the conditions which *might* have made it possible were being eroded. Nonalignment, in sum, was not disavowed nor did any major alternatives to it appear, but it had to be both justified and practiced in a more sophisticated manner.

The emergence of China has created, or may create, an entirely new pattern of relationships. At the moment, the impact is more theoretical than practical, but it is hardly likely to remain so for long. China's refusal to accept the legitimacy of nonalignment harks back to an earlier era of the Cold War. Some similarities with the first decade of the Cold War are striking. The argument, for example, that India is not nonaligned but rather aligned with the

[32] Cf. Bell, "Non-alignment and the Power Balance," pp. 70–71.

United States and the Soviet Union recalls the simple dichotomy which seemed so compelling to John Foster Dulles and, perhaps, to Stalin. And China's "have not" position recalls earlier versions of Soviet policy: as the state with less to lose in any confrontation, it can afford a revolutionary policy which justifies overbidding the status quo powers.[33] There is, however, an obverse side to this in that the Chinese are not only a threat but also a potential, very potential, source of aid and support. The emergence of a new center of power goes some way toward creating a tripolar balance which could, in theory, provide more security for the Small Powers than could be found in any bipolar situation. At any rate, the historical record suggests that the security of Small Powers increases (though not their opportunities to improve their position) as the balance of power widens. Unfortunately, that may not be the case in a situation where at least one of the major powers is determined to destroy the system itself. And it is not absolutely clear that a tripolar system, because of its inherent instability, is actually more advantageous than either a bipolar or multipolar world. It may depend on the extent to which conflict within it remains on an essentially nonmilitary level.

The decisive factor in the years ahead may well be the attitude the Soviets assume toward the Chinese challenge. They could choose to pursue a conservative policy in the developing areas, concentrating on stabilizing pro-Soviet and "neutralist" regimes against the revolutionary threat from Peking. That might, as Manfred Halpern has suggested, provide the nonaligned states with two options against the Chinese: the support of the United States against the threat of external aggression, and the tacit but important support of the Soviet Union against internal subversion.[34]

The problem, of course, is that the Soviet Union may respond by reviving their revolutionary ardor and attempting to outbid the Chinese. In that case, the compromises implicit in mutually acceptable "neutralization," as in the Congo and Laos, will be undermined by the aggressive behavior of *both* the Chinese and the

---

[33] *Ibid.*, pp. 73 ff.

[34] Manfred Halpern, *The Politics of Social Change in the Middle East and North Africa* (Princeton: Princeton University Press, 1963), pp. 410 ff.

Soviets. This suggests that the Sino-Soviet split is essentially tactical, and that its primary result will be a competition to see which Communist power is more Communist, i.e., revolutionary.[35]

Which choice the Soviets will make is clearly uncertain. They may, in the grand tradition of Western statecraft, merely muddle along until events impose a choice. However, whatever ultimately happens, in the short run some provision must be made to handle the worst possible contingency of two revolutionary regimes intent on disrupting an already precarious stability.

It is possible to argue that Chinese behavior will be constrained by the fear of driving the United States and the Soviet Union together, though it seems an overly optimistic assumption. The kinds of things which the Chinese are capable of doing in the immediate years ahead are not likely to be dangerous enough *to the Soviet Union and the United States* to force the two together; the Chinese threat may have to be direct before it compels a true "reversal of alliances." For the interim, therefore, policy-makers cannot assume Soviet support against the Chinese. The best that can be hoped for is a kind of tacit acquiescence in United States efforts to thwart Chinese designs, and even that may not come to pass.

The aggressive and revolutionary nature of the Chinese threat will undoubtedly increase the importance of fundamental questions of security. Nonalignment will have to be justified not only in psychological and economic terms but also in military terms. And for states which suddenly realize that they confront a real threat to their security, it may not appear sufficient. They may feel compelled to consider the virtues, and defects, of alignment in a new perspective, and it thus seems appropriate to conclude this chapter with a few words about alliances and nonalignment.

Complete commitment to a policy of nonalignment involves a repudiation of any alliance involving Great Powers. The latter, in an effort to attain or sustain influence, have been compelled to il-

[35] Thus one analyst argues that the Sino-Soviet split "obliges each side . . . to intensify its efforts to demonstrate its superiority over rivals." Brian Crozier, "The Struggle for the Third World," *International Affairs*, XL (July 1964), 451.

lustrate their good faith by offering aid shorn of strings and by pledging nonintervention. In an atmosphere in which alliances are, or have been, regarded as symbols of virtually all of the worst aspects of traditional "power politics," [36] Small Powers have been forced to rely on the UN, some form of inter-area agreement, or the exhaustion of minimal resources to settle their disputes. The cost of overt attachment to one of the blocs (but particularly the Western) merely to pressure a local enemy has seemed excessive: it may in fact amount to ostracization by the other nonaligned states.

In psychological terms, alignment constitutes a serious derogation of independence and a loss of prestige and status. However, there is also a range of traditional assumptions about the evils of an alliance with a superior power which buttresses the decision to remain unaligned. Nonalignment thus appears to be the only way to limit Great Power intervention: once one Great Power allies with a local state, inevitably its opponent follows suit (or tries to, which leads to the same result). The Little Entente and the Arab League illustrate the point. Both were designed, at least in part, to exclude or limit the extent of Great Power intervention in each area. And in a system with ideological undertones, alignment guarantees that a state will become a prime target for subversion, whereas nonalignment offers some possibility of avoiding it, particularly when both blocs accept nonalignment as a legitimate tactic.

Some of the standard arguments against alliances are also still significant—e.g., a loss of independence and flexibility, an increase in outside intervention, and so forth. Moreover, to the extent that we appear or appeared to be relying on nuclear weapons to honor our alliance commitments, any desire to align with us was vitiated: the prospect of defense by nuclear weapons being much worse than the prospect of no defense at all. A live satellite lives to fight, or at least to maneuver, another day.

Despite the disadvantages, some of the new states have entered alliances with the United States or its Great Power allies. They have done so reluctantly and only when the perception of an

[36] Cf. Liska, *Nations in Alliance*, pp. 206–07.

external threat has been very high, or when it has seemed to be the only way to counterbalance a superior local state (e.g., the case of Pakistan and India). While the theoretical distinction between a bilateral Great Power-Small Power alliance and a mixed, multilateral alliance still holds, in practice the distinction has been diluted. In substance, multilateral alliances like SEATO and CENTO really constitute unilateral Great Power guarantees.[37] For the most part, it has been the superior power, the United States, which has insisted on the multilateral form in an effort to decrease the political losses attendant upon alignment. The Small Powers, conversely, once recognizing a situation grave enough to justify an alliance commitment, *may* prefer a bilateral agreement. The latter is likely to offer more opportunities to increase aid: the pie will be cut into fewer slices. Moreover, the commitment to act undoubtedly will be diluted in a multilateral alliance. It may, for example, be easier for the United States to evade its commitment in SEATO than in a bilateral pact such as the United States-Formosa agreement.[38] On the other hand, a multilateral alliance still gives the Small Power more intra-alliance bargaining leverage and more opportunity to advance its own views. It may also cost less in terms of external prestige and domestic discontent.[39] The decision

[37] Cf. Modelski, *SEATO—Six Studies* p. 8, where he describes SEATO as "a great power association for the support of certain small nations. . . ." The Small Power, at any rate, may try to extend and strengthen the commitment of a multilateral alliance to compensate for its lesser degree of credibility.

[38] Thus a study of all the crises faced by SEATO shows "in all cases the decisive event at issue had been the actual or potential joint or individual intervention of the Western great powers on behalf of a small state of South-East Asia." *Ibid.*, p. 15.

For Philippine efforts to extend and improve the nature of the U.S. Commitment in SEATO, cf. Roger M. Smith, "The Philippines and the Southeast Asia Treaty Organization" (Ithaca: Cornell University Southeast Asia Program, 1959), pp. 12 and 18. And for the efforts of Thailand to strengthen SEATO, and for fears that the U.S. commitment to it was weakening (particularly after the events in Laos in 1960 and after), cf. Donald E. Nuechterlein, *Thailand and the Struggle for Southeast Asia* (Ithaca: Cornell University Press, 1965), Chapters IV and V.

[39] It might also be noted that SEATO conferred some benefits on states which remained out of it. Thus "Communist China knew that too great a pressure on Burma involved the risk of forcing her into SEATO." Modelski, *SEATO—Six Studies* p. 9. Although India stayed out of SEATO, which in any case could not

on form will be heavily conditioned by perceptions concerning the degree of immediate danger: if high, a bilateral alliance is clearly wiser.

Ultimately, the primary advantage of an alliance with a Great Power involves recognition of the fact by all concerned that the Small Power has the ability to commit its ally: the latter presumably cannot accept the losses attendant upon its weaker partner's defeat. This can be a significant advantage, given the mutual fears of the major powers. In contrast to the past, where there was a relative advantage in committing oneself last, *ceteris paribus,* and thus tipping the scales decisively, the advantage now tends to lie with the side which commits itself first.[40] The opponent must then decide whether the stake is worth the risk of escalating the conflict by intervening. The Small Power which can force one of the Great Powers to intervene on its behalf, or appear ready to, may thereby be able to achieve some kind of local stalemate. In particular, if the losses incurred by accepting the situation seem smaller than the potential losses of escalating the conflict, the benefits of alliance may be high.

Even if the other Great Power intervenes, it is likely to do so at a minimal level, i.e., below the threshold of direct Great Power conflict. Traditionally, when the Great Powers fought, Small Power allies simply became a target of attack. Now, with the response set at a level below war, the Small Power may not suffer as much from being the weakest link. The enemy response may be an effort to persuade it to change its alignment, or an increase in internal subversion, but not an overt attack.

The preceding arguments primarily reflect the pressures of an international system in which nuclear weapons have forced the Great Powers to walk very softly just because they are carrying a very big stick. The impact of nuclear weapons on Great Power-Small Power relationships obviously increases when the military

---

offer support in the north where India was threatened, it might have benefited from Chinese concessions there, in response to the southern threat represented by SEATO. Cf. Rosemary Brissenden, "India, Neutralism, and SEATO," in *ibid.,* pp. 217 ff.

[40] Cf. Liska, *Nations in Alliance,* p. 76. I have qualified the point somewhat.

aspect of that relationship comes to the fore. But there is also a sense in which nuclear weapons may restrict the freedom of Small Power allies, at least at its outer limits, where that "freedom" appears to be causing a crisis which might involve the Great Powers. The "mindlessness" and drift which characterized an earlier generation of relationships between unequal allies, and which in certain circumstances gave the weaker partner significant leverage to achieve its own ends, is now too dangerous to countenance. The Great Powers may be forced to control the behavior of their weaker allies when it becomes too aggressive (particularly, of course, if the spread of nuclear weapons continues). In sum, while the existence of nuclear weapons has tended to lessen the chances of general war, and has thus transformed the role of Small Powers, it has done so only within certain clear limits. The freedom to maneuver is high, but the freedom to start a Third World War, to be another Serbia, is very low.[41]

The fact that the Great Powers may be forced to control the behavior of their weaker partners when it becomes too destabilizing merely reinforces a tendency which has been developing since this century began. From the point of view of Small Powers, alliances have increasingly become instruments designed to achieve non-military goals. In theory, this would seem to suggest, as Herbert Dinerstein has argued, that Small Powers have more freedom *within* an alliance to achieve their own goals since the necessity of worrying about preparations for war would be considerably relaxed.[42] However, in practice the point is not so clear. The non-Western Small Powers have tended to join an alliance with the Western powers *only* when confronted by a military threat, and are hardly in a position to ignore military considerations. And they are free to maneuver within an alliance only to the extent that

---

[41] Thus Thornton Read has noted that: "The weaker member of an alliance is less able to commit its stronger ally to a course of action that the latter is reluctant to undertake. For example, in 1914 Austria was able to commit Germany to war, while in 1956 the United States not only dissociated itself from the British-French Suez adventure but even subjected its allies to pressure." "Military Policy in a Changing Political Contest" (Policy Memorandum No. 31, Center of International Studies, Princeton University, 1964), p. 41 *n.*

[42] Dinerstein, "The Transformation of Alliance Systems," p. 593.

their actions do not precipitate or exacerbate a crisis. In general, the point that alliances are increasingly becoming nonmilitary instruments still holds, but with much less force for a bilateral alliance between a Great Power and a Small Power than for other forms of alliance.

It is clear that an argument for the increased utility of alliances composed solely of Small Powers can be made. In the past, their greatest advantage has been in the political sphere, their weakness in the military realm. But in a period when the primary conflict is carried on by political means and for symbolic victories, the military weakness of Small Power alliances is less important and their political strength more important. In addition, the significance which both blocs have attributed to parliamentary victories in the United Nations has given even more influence to groups of Small Powers able to vote together.

However, rather than full-fledged Small Power alliances, akin to the Little Entente or the Balkan League, a number of very loose voting blocs have emerged involving very little cooperation outside the UN.[43] One reason for the failure to develop real alliances is, of course, the inability of the new states to agree on anything but a mutual dislike of colonialism. Since the regions they inhabit are territorially unsettled, there is no internal consensus concerning the status quo. They can agree on the negative task of evicting the Great Powers, but on little else.[44] Any regional arrangement would have to involve a commitment to accept previous boundaries—but since many of the new states are revisionists (or threatened by revisionists), regional agreements have proved to be tenuous and unproductive. A good many of the revisionists also feel they can strike a better bargain with the Great Powers in bilateral rather than regional negotiations. Still, even though the record of the few regional groups which have been formed scarcely justifies optimism, at least one recent study of the Arab League contends that its

[43] Cf. the books by Hovet and Rivkin, previously cited, for a discussion of these blocs.

[44] Peter Calvocoressi, *World Order and New States* (New York: Frederick A. Praeger, 1962), p. 66, notes that regional arrangements would have to be defensive, since agreement could not be reached on an offensive project.

failures have been caused by external factors beyond the League's control and that it has had *some* success in dealing with internal crises:

The Arab League states have effectively policed their own region during most of the League's history. Despite bitter propaganda exchanges between rival Arab states, there have been surprisingly few breeches of the peace by Arab League members.[45]

While it would be absurd to suggest that that assessment validates the theoretical proposition that the significance of Small Power alliances is on the rise, it does at least suggest that the judgment that Small Power alliances are worthless ought to be reconsidered.

[45] Robert W. Macdonald, *The League of Arab States* (Princeton: Princeton University Press, 1965), pp. 292–93.

CHAPTER 9

Nuclear Proliferation and
the Prospects for Small Powers

SMALL POWERS exert more influence and receive more attention in our time than they ever have in the past. Nevertheless,
a reasonable argument could be made for the proposition that their
role in international politics has *not* altered nearly as much as
appearances suggest. It is surely true that they possess a much
wider latitude within which to seek their own goals. But the extent
of that latitude is still dependent on a factor beyond the control
of any Small Power: the nature of Great Power relationships. In
reality, the Small Power tail does not wag the Great Power dog
very much more now than it did in the nineteenth century. The
difference resides in the fact that the dog, as it has grown ever
more powerful and dangerous, has found it increasingly difficult
to employ its strength in a rational manner. True independence,
an independence which is assured whatever the status of Great
Power relationships, still escapes the grasp of Small Powers. If
anything seems capable of altering this condition, it is the dispersion of nuclear weapons to more and more states, or so it seems.

Introduction

In a historical perspective, it becomes increasingly clear that the
most important variable affecting Great Power-Small Power relationships concerns trends in the distribution and nature of military
power.* For the greater part of the nineteenth century, number

* Other factors are obviously also of great significance. Small Powers have bene-

of infantry remained the criterion by which Great Power or Small Power status was determined. Moreover, the wars which were planned and fought were limited in terms of the goals sought and the means employed. As a result, the contribution which any Small Power could make was minor. A Great Power in need of additional power could either increase its own strength or bargain for the support of one of its peers (a possibility which remained open as long as the system remained fluid).

This situation changed as the European system was transformed at the end of the century. As war became increasingly likely, and as the possibility that it might be an all-European war emerged, the Small Powers were sought as potential allies. Retrospectively, it is obvious that their military contribution was bound to be worthless or irrelevant in a general war: but the habit of equating numbers of troops with actual power continued, and even minor increments of manpower assumed some significance. The apparent equilibrium between the two major blocs intensified the quest for Small Power support. In a conflict which appeared so even, any amount of assistance was welcome. The bipolar nature of the situation accentuated the struggle for allies. By definition, one side's failure was the other side's success. The fact that Small Powers were becoming military liabilities was obscured by the failure to appreciate the impact of the new technology, and they were able to maneuver and bargain to an unprecedented degree. Their new status rested on the existence of a unique power con-

---

fited from the growth of norms prohibiting the use of force; from the general revulsion against war itself (a revulsion probably stronger in the West than in the non-Western areas which it indirectly protects); from the general *ethos* of the time, which condemns imperialism and intervention and justifies national self-determination and domestic revolution against the forces of the past; and from the apparent tendency of advanced, industrial states to concentrate on domestic concerns and to intervene abroad with reluctance. For a good discussion of many of these points in the context of the decline in the utility of military force in our time, see Klaus Knorr, *On the Uses of Military Power in the Nuclear Age* (Princeton: Princeton University Press, 1966), *passim*. No one, of course, argues that military power is useless: rather that its general utility has gone down and that the forms of military power which have retained significance have also altered from the past. These changes, needless to say, have had a positive impact on the position of Small Powers.

figuration as well as on a monumental misunderstanding of the relationship between war and technology; nevertheless, that new status was not temporary.

In the decade immediately after the First World War, Small Powers became increasingly influential. A number of factors accounted for this condition: specifically, the presence of the League of Nations, the emergence of a theory of collective security, and the peculiar power configuration in Europe. However, there can be very little doubt that the latter factor is most significant. With Austria-Hungary, the Soviet Union, and Germany permanently or temporarily outside the pale of European politics, the Small Powers could influence the conduct of world politics in an unparalleled way as long as they did not antagonize France. In fact, the Small Powers which supported the status quo served as virtual surrogates for the absent Great Powers. That condition was obviously temporary. As the European situation deteriorated in the 1930s, the influence of Small Powers proved to be as fragile and illusory as their power. No one made quite the same mistake which had been made before 1914. The impact of technology was well enough perceived so that the military utility of Small Powers was regarded as negligible. A new kind of perception emerged in an inchoate and rudimentary form: alliances with Small Powers involved guaranteeing their existence more so than it involved receiving their support. Alliances with Small Powers could still be justified, but not (or not solely) because of the military support they could provide.

In the period since the Second World War, Small Powers have regained and increased the influence which they exerted on international relations in the 1920s. Their military weakness relative to the Great Powers has increased substantially, but, paradoxically, their political influence has also increased. The bipolar characteristics of the present situation accentuate the extent to which they are sought as allies—not, however, as military allies but as a kind of symbol of victory in a struggle conducted primarily on nonmilitary or very limited military grounds. This is hardly to deny that several Small Powers have benefited from possession of a military asset which a Great Power desires: for example, the military bases in the Azores or Turkey. But this situation reflects a rather fortuitous geographical placement rather than a contradiction of the generalization that Small Powers are sought for primarily nonmilitary reasons. The extent to which the struggle for their allegiance has been conditioned by the inhibiting effects which nuclear weapons have produced on the two leading Powers is difficult to discern. The nature of the problem presented by the new Small Powers might have produced a similar struggle, with or without the presence of nuclear weapons. In any event, nuclear weapons have undoubtedly affected the extent to which the competition between the two blocs has focused on areas where the use of extensive amounts of force is difficult to justify. The point to be noted is familiar: the role of Small Powers is once again heavily conditioned by the nature of and the distribution of military strength among the Great Powers.

Certain inferences from the preceding argument have been drawn in previous chapters. The relative military disparity between Great and Small Powers has continually increased since the latter part of the nineteenth century. If anything, Small Powers have become more and more vulnerable against a Great Power attack. Even allied with a Great Power against another Great Power, they stand a very good chance of being overwhelmed before aid arrives. Thus a *military* alliance with a single Great Power has become an increasingly dubious instrument of statecraft for Small Powers. The military condition of Small Powers has become so parlous that it is virtually beyond the power of any alliance to correct unless, of course, that alliance promises to perform the function of deterrence to an extraordinary degree. The extent to which it is likely to do just that obviously cannot be predicted in the abstract. Still, it is fair to note that for a Small Power faced by a Great Power threat the political rationale for allying has come to outweigh the military. Insofar as the Small Power faces other threats, the point may need qualification. Even in this instance the disadvantages, already noted, of a military alliance may outweigh the advantages.

The temptation to conclude by suggesting a number of tactical principles which Small Powers ought to observe is inevitably very strong. Nevertheless, it should be resisted, since any tactical principles which could be inferred from the substance of this analysis are as ambiguous and tenuous as the prescriptions and maxims of previous commentators. If any insights have emerged in the preceding pages, they do not relate to specific actions. Rather they relate to a very general level of analysis, suggesting the kinds of actions which are likely to be more or less successful, *ceteris paribus,* in particular kinds of political systems.

The limited relevance of various tactical principles may perhaps be illustrated by a very brief discussion of several principles whose obviousness appears to put them beyond dispute in *any* circumstance. Small Powers have been warned to ally only with states exposed to the same threat. Failure to do so presumably involves the possibility or probability that the threat confronting the Small Power will be ignored or downgraded. This advice clearly overlooks the fact that an alliance commitment per se may have some utility, even if the allies seek different goals, and that willingness to ally only with states confronting identical threats limits the range of potential allies, and the range of maneuverability, to an excessive degree. Small Powers have also been warned to avoid an ambiguous commitment because it is normally the weaker ally which suffers most severely when a commitment is left open to continuous interpretation. The commitment may be so extended or so narrowed that the Small Power finds itself accepting a degree of risk far beyond its original intention. The advice is generally sound, but it can hardly be denied that ambiguity can serve more than one master; in some cases, it may well be the Small Power which benefits most from uncertainty.

Finally, at least one other suggestion ought to be discussed, even though it is rarely mentioned: the threat to fight a Great Power enemy even if a Great Power ally explicitly refuses to help. The Small Power, in effect, threatens to commit suicide in the hope of forcing its ally to change its mind. At bottom, this suggestion rests on the assumption that a Small Power about to be sacrificed by its erstwhile ally is under no obligation to accept its fate silently and gracefully. In threatening to fight, or in actually serving as a catalyst for the start of a war, it may force a reluctant ally to come to its aid despite the ally's desire to avoid conflict. The ability of the Serbians to precipitate war in 1914 and the probable ability of the Czechs to do so in 1938 illustrate the point. Nevertheless, the situation is hardly as clear as the examples suggest. Threatening to commit suicide was a considerably less dangerous expedient before the advent of modern technology. As a tactical principle, this suggestion has become increasingly less relevant as suicide has come to imply not the limited losses of the nineteenth century but the total losses implicit in modern warfare. "Better red than dead" has been offered by some as political wisdom in an age of nuclear weapons, even for a Great Power; but accommodation rather than courage may have become a wise principle for Small Powers several decades before the advent of nuclear weapons. After all, as Beneš pointed out in 1945, the decision of the Czechs to yield in 1938 had something to do with the relatively unharmed condition of the country to which he returned in 1945.

Historically, Small Powers have always confronted one virtually insoluble dilemma. Whatever the political system, the necessity of insuring short-run security by supporting the strongest power conflicts with the necessity of bolstering long-run security by supporting the weaker Powers. The desire to foster equilibrium too often yields, as it must, to the more basic desire to survive. The tactical principles which have been offered as palliatives in this situation are banal and commonplace. Even so, the situation itself is so much at the root of the difficulties confronting Small Powers that the most perceptive of these principles ought to be mentioned. The security of Small Powers is always in danger. There is no policy option open to them which does not create *nearly* as many difficulties as it avoids. Thus a policy of deliberate and calculated procrastination, aimed at delaying commitment to the stronger side until the last possible moment, incorporates much of the political wisdom which Small Powers can glean from the historical record. If this seems no more satisfactory a principle of action than any of its predecessors, one point at least ought to be clear: the impossibility of devising specific principles for Small Powers short of knowing all the circumstances affecting their situation.

Nuclear weapons have been proliferating since 1945, but the

"problem" of proliferation is relatively new. The five states which have actually developed nuclear weapons are all Great Powers. Thus, as two French commentators noted, proliferation seemed to be occurring in tune with "a sense of normal order."[1] The problem of proliferation, in terms of an issue which provokes debate and arouses fears, began to emerge only when we were forced to contemplate the possibility of Egyptian, Israeli, or Indonesian nuclear arsenals. In the circumstances, that "normal order" clearly began to break down.

The presumption that proliferation will become increasingly dangerous rests on something more than the "statistical" dangers of a world inhabited by an increasing number of nuclear powers. It also reflects the fear that several of the potential nuclear powers will be more irrational and irresponsible than their predecessors. The United States, for example, would undoubtedly deplore a Swiss or a Swedish or a Canadian nuclear deterrent, but not much more than we deplored the French decision to build the *force de frappe*. We implicitly presume that their decision-making process is as "rational" as ours. But the mind balks at the thought of Sukarno or Peron with any kind of nuclear arsenal.[2]

This chapter is designed to serve a twofold purpose. The next section attempts to illustrate the extent to which Great Power-Small Power relationships will *not* be decisively altered by the proliferation of nuclear weapons. It can be shown that properly "read," the advantages which Great Britain and France have received because of their independent deterrents will *not* come to Small Powers who attempt to follow in their steps. The analysis is interesting, but only theoretically, since it is almost irrelevant in terms of understanding the actual decision-making process in the potential "nth" countries.

[1] The phrase is from Christian de la Malène and Constantin Melnik, *Attitudes of the French Parliament and Government Toward Atomic Weapons* (Santa Monica: The Rand Corporation, 1958), p. 14.

[2] On Peron's efforts to produce a cheap bomb, see Hedley Bull, *The Control of the Arms Race* (New York: Frederick A. Praeger, 1965), p. 153. Assumptions concerning the presumed irresponsibility of future nuclear powers may rest not merely on the "non-Western" nature of their political processes but also on the imperatives of operating with a weak and exposed nuclear force.

The British and French experiences are examined in the following section in an entirely different fashion, that is, the question is asked: What is it in those experiences that will actually appear significant to a potential nuclear power? The Indian reaction to the Chinese nuclear explosion in 1964 is discussed, and will be followed by discussion of some policy proposals in the light of the preceding material. In effect, the last third of this chapter is designed to serve a somewhat different purpose than any of the earlier parts of this book: it concentrates on illuminating the policy dilemmas which confront the United States as it attempts to devise a consistent approach to the problem of nuclear proliferation.

Before turning to the analysis, it may be helpful to summarize certain aspects of the previous discussions of proliferation. A significant proportion of the early literature perceived the problem in terms of its presumed effect on the international system. Given the initial assumption of a relatively stable strategic balance, the potential effect of an intrusion of X number of new nuclear powers was not difficult to forecast. There was obviously a high probability that it would be intensely destabilizing. The list of potential dangers is as familiar as it is chilling: an increase in the possibility of accidental, irrational, or catalytic nuclear wars; the danger of preventive war by one Small Power to forestall asymmetric dispersion to another; a decline in conventional strength; the fragmentation of alliance systems and an increase in intra-bloc frictions; the complication of disarmament negotiations; and a general increase in tension.[3]

A focus which emphasized international stability was bound to be somewhat misleading. It inevitably led to a blanket condemnation of any kind of proliferation, for a multinuclear world was obviously potentially far more dangerous than the relatively stable world which existed. The fact that the rate, the pace, the extent and the kind of proliferation which occurred would determine the way in which the problem affected the international system was

[3] For relevant analyses, see Leonard Beaton and John Maddox, *The Spread of Nuclear Weapons* (New York: Frederick A. Praeger, 1962), pp. 201 ff.; Robert W. Tucker, *Stability and the Country Problem* (Washington, D.C.: Institute for Defense Analyses, 1961); Herman Kahn, *Thinking About the Unthinkable* (New York: Avon Books, 1964), Ch. VII.

either ignored or underemphasized. The systemic perspective also normally produced one practical suggestion which has become a recurring feature of the public debate. Policymakers were urged to concentrate on negotiating a nonproliferation treaty not only because the dangers were so significant but also because the United States and the Soviet Union manifestly shared a common interest in maintaining that aspect of the status quo.

However, the necessity of forestalling proliferation collided with one overriding technological consideration. It was simply becoming too easy to become a nuclear power. The list of states which can, irrespective of whether they will, develop their own nuclear arsenals is rapidly increasing.[4] And since we tend to presume a kind of "chain of falling dominoes" process, the pessimistic conclusion emerges that once one current nonnuclear power crosses the great divide, the others will have to follow.

Pessimism can be somewhat qualified if the discussion is broadened to include all the problems which would confront a fledgling nuclear power. Merely exploding a nuclear device or possessing a few primitive bombs might not be *very* destabilizing. As one very good analysis notes, new nuclear powers would have to pass through a number of stages before they began to have an adverse effect on international stability:

First, there must be a dissemination of the ability to build or acquire nuclear bombs; second, a capability of creating or obtaining a delivery, command, and control system must be present; third, there must be a resolute national will to create a nuclear weapons capability; fourth, possible counteraction by major powers must not be permitted to nullify the advantages of nuclear status; fifth, and finally, the nuclear system developed must actually be used in such a fashion as to endanger local or international peace. Failure to pass through each of the given stages means that nuclear diffusion does not attain to international signifi-

[4] Lists abound and some indication of their effect may be inferred from a recent dispatch in The New York *Times*, Nov. 4, 1965 (p. 21) which, in describing recent efforts to negotiate a nonproliferation treaty, noted that:
The eight nonaligned countries have been laboring in a compromise atmosphere made urgent by warnings that as many as twenty nations may acquire atomic arms in the next few years if agreement is not reached to prevent this possibility.

cance; it does not pose an independent problem to world stability and peace.[5]

Since the remaining "nth" countries, barring certain exceptions such as West Germany and Sweden, are relatively poor and weak, the possibility that they could fulfill all of the preceding conditions is clearly small. It is not very difficult to explode a nuclear device, but it is extremely difficult to become an *effective* nuclear power.

If the perspective is reversed, and the problem of proliferation is examined from the point of view of specific states, the limited relevance of the preceding analysis is easily understood. It is obvious, for example, that the apparent value of stabilizing the existing international system has rarely, if ever, affected the calculations of very many states (unless they already have all they want, or expect they can get, from any system). Moreover, it is very doubtful that the remaining nonnuclear powers are "rational" enough to worry about the difficulties of becoming an effective nuclear power, particularly if becoming *any* kind of nuclear power seems to offer advantages. In sum, by analyzing proliferation in terms of categories too abstract and rationalistic, an understanding of the problem may have been obscured and confused.[6]

Any analysis of the problem of nuclear proliferation involves some degree of prediction about the likely course of future developments. As such, it ought to be read with a great deal of caution. Moreover, any predictions ought to have their biases and assumptions clearly labeled.

Prediction normally involves isolating what are considered to be the relevant aspects of past experiences and projecting them into the future. There is no theory or method offering a better alterna-

[5] *The Dispersion of Nuclear Weapons,* edited by Richard N. Rosecrance (New York: Columbia University Press, 1964), p. 293. The quotation is from Rosecrance's conclusion.

[6] Growing recognition of, or assumptions about, the imminence of proliferation have led to several recent efforts which urge concentration on controlling the effects of the spread rather than on fruitless efforts to halt it. Cf. Roger Masters, "What about a Nuclear Guarantee for India?" *The New Republic,* CLIII (Dec. 25, 1965), 9–10. For an interesting early article which pointed out some of the ambiguities in the argument that proliferation inevitably increased the chances of war, see Fred Charles Iklé, "N[th] Countries and Disarmament," *Bulletin of the Atomic Scientists* (Dec. 1960), pp. 391–94.

tive, and there are obvious dangers in this kind of enterprise. Undoubtedly the most significant is that it is implicitly assumed that the future will differ from the present in much the same way as the present differs from the past: in effect, that change is linear and "unchanging".[7]

There is, therefore, a conservative bias in most predictions. It is assumed that predictions are made within a wider context, which will remain constant for the period of time within which predictions are offered.[8] It is only in this sense that the "past," an elusive concept in itself, has any meaning at all for predicting the future. If truly revolutionary futures are predicted, the observer's experiences become irrelevant.

The remainder of this chapter presupposes an international system very similar to the one which currently exists. The critical assumption is that, aside from the question of nuclear weapons, no other major changes will occur which invalidate initial premises.[9]

A recent study has suggested that, *inter alia*, systems change when the members of the system are able to do different things to each other (in terms of scale of force, etc.).[10] In this sense, nuclear proliferation could transform international relations, and it ought

[7] See Bertrand de Jouvenel, *Futuribles* (Santa Monica: The RAND Corporation, 1965).

[8] See Daniel Bell, "The Study of the Future," *The Public Interest,* I (Fall 1965), 130. Mr. Bell's article offers several insights into the problems of prediction, all of which may be worth further study.

[9] I would very much like to avoid another of the proliferating efforts to describe the current international system in terms of some set of interacting polar opposites: hetero-symmetrical, hetero-asymmetrical, tripolar, multipolar, bipolar, polycentric, etc.—and, of course, all on different levels, for different functions and purposes, etc. I expect that, in terms of policy concerns, all these labels are irrelevant; and, in terms of theoretical concerns, they are either ambiguous or so general as to be platitudinous. Perhaps one key to understanding this situation is its very confusion: members of the system see very few clear paths, and no consistent conceptual framework, by which to orient their actions. And thus we find ourselves in another of those systems in which the sense of transition and the awareness of complexity imperil any attempt to suggest the way in which policy *ought* to reflect existing patterns—which patterns? Analysis of policy is thus, even more than normally, forced into close examination of the specific and parochial conditions which condition choices, rather than presumably perceived systematic constraints.

[10] Stanley Hoffmann, "International Systems and International Law," *World Politics* (Oct. 1961), p. 207.

to be discussed in terms of the new kind of system which is emerging. All of this *may* be true. Nevertheless, a contrary assumption prevails here. The analysis assumes a period of time in which no major technological revolution in weaponry will occur (very roughly, *perhaps* the next fifteen years). The corollary assumption is that, within that period, the impact of nuclear proliferation will not be extensive enough to drastically transform the conduct of international relations.

Theoretical Calculations and Nuclear Weapons

The British and French decisions to develop their own nuclear weapons can be used to illustrate several different propositions. The economic and political difficulties which both countries have encountered might serve as an illustration of the futility of independent deterrents, at least when the deterrent is designed to influence either Superpower.[11] It might also serve as a more general indication of the need for wider and more integrated security arrangements. Conversely, an analysis cast in terms of British and French priorities, rather than American or NATO priorities, might illustrate the degree to which the creation of an independent deterrent, whatever its immediate costs, is a wise policy if only as insurance against the future.[12]

However, this section and the next will concentrate on two other aspects of the British and French experience. The first involves an abstract analysis of the different kinds of calculations which motivate Great Powers (like Great Britain, France, West Germany, and perhaps China) and Small Powers when they decide to become (or not to become) members of the nuclear club. While the analysis is relatively effective in indicating that Great

[11] For example, see H. A. De Weerd, "The British Effort to Secure an Independent Deterrent, 1952–1962," in Rosecrance, *The Dispersion of Nuclear Weapons*, p. 100 and *passim*.

[12] For an imaginative and important effort to point out some of the virtues of the European strategic position, from their point of view, see Hedley Bull, "Strategy and the Atlantic Alliance: A Critique of United States Doctrine" (Policy Memorandum No. 29, Center of International Studies, Princeton University, 1964).

Powers and Small Powers do (or ought to) calculate differently, it is also a negative illustration of the virtues of abstract analysis. The "logic" of the analysis is of little utility in understanding the actual factors which may ultimately condition a decision to develop nuclear weapons, though it provides a useful intellectual framework for the remainder of the chapter. The next section will examine the British and French experiences in an entirely different fashion. Whatever theoretical relevance those experiences may or may not have, they constitute virtually the only cases which a potential nuclear power can ponder. Thus an effort to speculate on the ways in which a nonnuclear power might "read" those experiences may yield some insight into the problem of proliferation.

General Pierre Gallois has argued that:

Thermonuclear weapons neutralize the armed masses, equalize the factors of demography, contract distance, level the heights, limit the advantages which until yesterday the Big Powers derived from the sheer dimensions of their territory . . . It is easy to prove that countries as different as Switzerland and Communist China are in the same boat when it comes to the nuclear threat.[13]

Very few serious political or military analysts would accept General Gallois' conclusions. It hardly needs to be emphasized that they are exaggerated, ambiguous, and unproved. Nevertheless, they cannot be ignored for they reflect a reaction to nuclear weapons which however spurious the reaction may seem when viewed from the perspective of the nuclear Superpowers, many weak states, great and small, may find increasingly attractive. Objective analysis can cast grave doubts on the Gallois thesis, or any of its derivatives, but it cannot completely dispel its seductiveness. For after all, even if nuclear weapons cannot reverse the "natural order" of things in world politics, they *might* be able to alter it just enough to make their possession worthwhile. For weaker states, that potential with all its uncertainty may be more appealing than the certainty of continued insecurity in the world as it is.

It is, of course, becoming increasingly simple to develop nuclear weapons. Conversely, it is becoming increasingly difficult to de-

[13] Quoted in Raymond Aron, *The Great Debate: Theories of Nuclear Strategy* (Garden City: Doubleday and Company, 1965), p. 102.

velop effective means of delivery, at least against the nuclear giants. However, the last point is hardly decisive. Nuclear weapons seem to offer a number of advantages to weaker states whether or not they are coupled with a modern delivery system. Moreover, against any state except the three original nuclear powers, virtually archaic means of delivery still suffice, for without advanced air defense systems in the defending state the airplane remains effective.

In any case, the decision to become a nuclear power is rapidly becoming transformed. For a wide range of states, the question is no longer can I become a nuclear power? but, rather, should I become a nuclear power? In the abstract, the kinds of factors which will determine or condition the choice are easy to enumerate. They differ hardly at all from the factors which traditionally affected the choice of one weapons system rather than another. Nevertheless, the decision to become a nuclear power appears to be unique. It is qualitatively different from traditional decisions, for though the questions asked in order to make the decision remain constant, the answers received are fundamentally different. The consequences involved in becoming a nuclear power appear far more extensive and complex than those which are normally associated with a choice of military means.

In the circumstances, a general and abstract analysis of the decision to become a nuclear power is not likely to reveal a great deal about the actual decision-making process. For policy purposes, detailed case studies are needed indicating the degree to which nuclear decisions differ from traditional security decisions; for theoretical purposes, an abstract analysis is more useful. It may indicate whether Great Power and Small Power decisions differ in kind as well as in degree, and whether they each possess a unique perspective. If they do differ, a weak Great Power like France ought to perceive the problem of becoming a nuclear power in a manner clearly different from a Small Power such as Switzerland or Egypt. If they do not differ, we are dealing with only one category of states, and the British and French experiences ought to be generally relevant.

For France, or more accurately, for some French leaders, the decision to become a nuclear power was uncomplicated. As Premier

Debrè said, "We might even say that we simply have no other choice unless we are prepared to surrender all political autonomy, all influence in international life, all scientific ambition in the world of tomorrow, and all military defense in general." [14] Much the same kind of reasons also justified Great Britain's earlier decision to become an independent nuclear power. But for a Small Power, Debrè's argument is too concerned with the long-run, perhaps even too hypothetical. Whatever considerations finally determine a Small Power's decision, they are bound to be more (but not completely) short-run and more specific. Great Powers can afford, or rather must afford, to buy a piece of the future on speculation. Small Powers, virtually by definition, can not. The point may become clearer as the considerations conditioning the decision to become a nuclear power are examined.

The impact of nuclear weapons on international politics has been so extensive that the decision to become a nuclear power can be justified in a variety of ways. Ultimately, however, that decision must at least appear rational on military grounds. A state might invest in a nuclear arsenal only to influence its allies or to enhance its prestige, but if it cannot simultaneously endow its decision with a military rationale, it is unlikely to achieve any of its purposes. Clearly then, whatever the range of other reasons underlying the debate, it is the contention that nuclear weapons somehow augment security which is *analytically* predominant.

Yet it is the impact of nuclear weapons on security which is most ambiguous and uncertain. Presumably they are designed to deter any enemy from aggressive actions. But, under the circumstances, the only certainty results from their failure, for the relationship between successful deterrence and nuclear weapons is unclear. Obviously the enemy might never have intended to attack at all or, conversely, could have intended to attack but been deterred by other factors present in the situation. The security argument is thus entirely hypothetical. It concerns what the defender thinks he has achieved in felt security, not what he actually has achieved.

Still, this is hardly a decisive argument against nuclear weapons.

[14] *Ibid.*, p. 103. The decision, of course, was not quite that obvious, as will be noted as below.

Even if their effects are indeterminate, it remains true that they seem to offer certain security benefits to weaker states. Gallois, for example, contends that the proliferation of nuclear capabilities simultaneously ensures peace and dissolves alliances.[15] Peace is ensured because it simply becomes too costly to attack a state armed with nuclear weapons, and alliances become unnecessary if all states can defend themselves. Both propositions rest upon one absolutely critical hypothesis: that the nuclear forces of the weaker state achieve complete invulnerability against an enemy disarming first strike.

In effect, then, Gallois conceives a world in which at least one kind of war—a deliberate premeditated nuclear attack—is proscribed by virtue of the fact that all states possess invulnerable deterrents which can inflict unacceptable damage on the aggressor after he attacks. Rational leaders presumably will read the signs clearly and not attack. In addition, they will not need allies, nor will they want them since the cost of supporting them in a nuclear war could be prohibitive.

The Gallois thesis, as well as certain similar propositions, is occasionally summarized in terms of a theory of proportional deterrence. The idea seems simple. A weak state, in a conflict with one of the nuclear giants, obviously cannot count very much in the Superpower's calculations. To deter that Superpower it needs only a force capable of inflicting more damage on the Superpower than it itself is worth to that Superpower. Belgium, in theory, ought to be able to deter the Soviet Union by developing an invulnerable nuclear capability which, say, could destroy Kiev and Leningrad. However, the theory is really more subtle. The harm which the Small Power's retaliatory force can inflict on the Superpower is only one part of the equation; the other part concerns the effect that that retaliatory strike might have on relations between the Superpowers. If the strike carries enough weight, it might appear significant enough to tilt the overall strategic balance.[16] In reality, then,

---

[15] *Ibid.*, pp. 100 ff.

[16] A certain similarity to Tirpitz's "risk theory" vis-à-vis the British navy suggests itself. He assumed substantial concessions from the British by virtue of possessing a fleet which could do just enough damage to the British fleet to make

the smaller state might be protected by virtue of its ability to affect relations between the Superpowers.

An analysis of the potential utility of proportional deterrence rests, at least initially, on the question of invulnerability. Developing an invulnerable second strike force is obviously an enormously difficult task, even for the most powerful states.[17] It may, in fact, be so difficult for weaker states to accomplish, especially against a more powerful state, that they will always seem to possess a force whose primary utility resides in striking first.

Suppose, however, it is presumed that a weak state does develop an invulnerable deterrent. If the weaker state is not a Small Power, if it is, say, France or Germany, its security may very well be enhanced. The potential aggressor's belief in the credibility of the deterrent is not likely to be very high, except in the case of a massive attack, but it is likely to be high enough to deter all but the smallest actions. If the defender has a powerful ally, the deterrent effect may be augmented. The small force might be able to inflict enough damage by itself to upset the strategic balance. The fear that it will serve as a catalyst for the launching of its ally's forces might also deter a wide range of actions. Even here the nuclear deterrent would have to be supplemented by conventional forces capable of handling limited contingencies. A small nuclear force in the hands of a weak Great Power is not likely to be very credible against anything short of a major attack. The weak Great Power is also likely to find its nuclear force of limited utility against nonnuclear states. Once again, short of indulging in nuclear blackmail, it will need to invest in conventional forces.

Whatever its ambiguities, and whatever its destabilizing effects in terms of an international perspective, from a national point of view the decision to become a nuclear power, justified solely in

---

it inferior to the combined fleets of its two largest competitors. When Britain established friendly relations with those competitors, the "risk theory" became an absurdity—it may, in fact, have been the critical factor in creating the very ententes which undermined it. This may not be an entirely irrelevant analogy. The fact that the Germans kept both the theory and its navy long after it became a dangerous anachronism is also worth noting.

[17] See Albert Wohlstetter, "The Delicate Balance of Terror," *Foreign Affairs* XXXVII (January 1959), 211–34.

terms of security, may be rational for some Great Powers. This is particularly true if the possibility of developing an invulnerable force increases. Since the latter possibility is uncertain, the whole question might appear to be academic. However the military rationale is not the only, nor even the most critical, aspect of the decision to become a nuclear power. Even a weak deterrent, in a world in which at least several states do have nuclear weapons or the ability to produce them relatively quickly, may make a state feel psychologically more secure. It grants a kind of status, even if it is no more than a minimally shared perception of standing on the edge of a precipice, which is denied to those who seek security by other means.

The argument appears to run in much the same way for Small Powers such as Belgium or Egypt as much as for Great Powers such as France or Germany. Yet the two cases are somewhat different. A Small Power will obviously have an even more difficult task than France or Germany in achieving an invulnerable deterrent. In fact, it can probably be presumed, with some degree of safety, that the costs of invulnerability will remain prohibitive for most Small Powers, especially against the Superpowers. However, the basic difference lies in the area of purpose. Great Powers and Small Powers hope to achieve different kinds of goals by virtue of possessing an independent nuclear force.

The French and British deterrents, for example, are aimed primarily at deterring certain actions on the part of one of the nuclear Superpowers. They are designed, that is, to deter a certain range of actions, with some debate about the limits of the lower range, by threatening strategic retaliation either alone or in company with allies. But the deterrent is not designed to be used against very limited contingencies within Europe nor against any contingency outside of the European area.[18] Since the enemy to be deterred possesses *superior* nuclear forces, the essential requirement for French and British deterrent is invulnerability.[19] In addition,

---

[18] That may not be entirely true at some future time, in particular if nuclear weapons do spread to more and more countries. If they do spread, it surely appears advantageous to have a head start on potential enemies.

[19] This is not meant to imply that a vulnerable and unsophisticated nuclear

it ought to be large enough and sophisticated enough to appear capable of playing an important role in a strategic exchange.

The case is significantly different for Small Powers, particularly those outside the NATO area.[20] For them, the deterrent is not really designed to be used against the United States or the Soviet Union. A direct military threat by either Superpower is a remote contingency, at least of the kind to which a small deterrent force would be applicable.[21] It is difficult to conceive a Small Power even desiring a nuclear capability if its presumed purpose is to deter either Superpower by a threat of suicide, for protection against one Superpower can come only from the other. Moreover, the Small Power has much less hope of serving as a catalyst for the release of either Superpower's nuclear forces, whereas the catalytic function may at least remain open to Great Powers like France and Great Britain.[22] Thus Small Power deterrents are essentially local instruments. Their targets are neighboring states who either completely lack a nuclear capability or have only a very weak and vulnerable one.[23] As long as it stays out of trouble with the Soviet

---

force is useless. It may, as the argument below notes, induce significant concessions from a Superpower ally. However, in military terms, or in terms of security without considering impact on allies, invulnerability is the most significant requirement. Without it, against superior nuclear forces, the military rationale is undermined.

[20] Being in an alliance which already promises nuclear support may significantly alter the nature of a decision taken in isolation, as will be noted below.

[21] Again, the statement requires dating: future developments—e.g., the easy acquisition of invulnerable forces or a more sophisticated Chinese nuclear force —might increase the attractiveness and/or relevance of the idea of proportional deterrence. And there are a few states which, even now, might hope to use their deterrent against a Superpower, at least in theory (e.g., Cuba and Turkey).

[22] The Small Power's force is unlikely to be able to "tear an arm off" either Superpower, to borrow de Gaulle's phrase. The vulnerability and weakness of its nuclear force, comparable to even Britain and France—at least in the current stage of technological development—obviously lowers its effectiveness, perhaps to the point where either Superpower would prefer riding out the attack (and destroying the Small Power alone) rather than launching a total war: i.e., the strategic balance could not be tipped by a Small Power deterrent. In addition, it is unlikely that either Superpower would commit itself very closely to a Small Power armed with a highly destabilizing nuclear force: more likely, considerable effort would be expended to indicate to the Small Power that it was on its own.

[23] The contention that a Small Power's force is designed only for deterrence

Union and the United States, the Small Power's nuclear force need *not* be invulnerable since, theoretically, none of its competitors possess a force equal to it or capable of destroying it in a disarming first strike.[24]

In other words, a very rudimentary nuclear force can be an extremely persuasive military instrument against a very wide range of states. To possess such a force, by oneself, may be a very appealing prospect, and a very necessary prospect if achieved by others. Some of the economic and technological constraints which have inhibited this development are obvious. The most critical restraint is probably the political one of realization that the decision to develop a nuclear capability will force enemies to do the same, or at least to launch a preventive war before the capability is achieved. It seems valid to conclude, then, that Small Powers may not need a nuclear force as sophisticated as the one required by Great Powers seeking to influence the existing strategic balance and who, at least in the future, may contemplate using their nuclear forces in some form of "extended deterrence." Calculations which point out that the Small Power's deterrent is virtually useless against the Great Powers are not likely, by themselves, to inhibit the dispersion of nuclear weapons.

In sum, a Small Power armed with a vulnerable nuclear force is unlikely to be able to achieve any significant *military* goals against a large state armed with a more sophisticated deterrent. Whether it could achieve any political goals remains to be seen (and it is here that a reading of the British and French experiences may be crucial). The threat and necessity of striking first in order to inflict any damage at all upon the large state, and at the cost of national suicide via the retaliatory strike, is hardly credible. Worse

---

of direct attack and not for "extended deterrence" is slightly ambiguous. It is not designed for deterrence of a direct attack by a large state, and it may have "extended" uses against local states, at least in my analysis. For an apparently contrary view, see Edmund Stillman, Herman Kahn, and Anthony J. Wiener, *Alternatives for European Defense in the Next Decade* (Croton-on-Hudson, N.Y.: Hudson Institute, 1964), pp. 33 ff.

[24] Obviously this is not meant to suggest that the force would not be more effective if it was invulnerable: rather, the point is that it can still be relatively effective even if quite vulnerable.

yet, it is so potentially destabilizing that a threatened Great Power or Superpower might be forced to demand or carry out the nuclear disarmament of the Small Power—the Cuban missile crisis is, in part, illustrative.[25]

The argument does not change significantly if the Small Power's deterrent is invulnerable. It is obviously less destabilizing, since it does not necessarily have to be used only in a first strike, but it is not substantially more credible since the cost of using the force against a larger state remains national suicide. For a Great Power intent on influencing the strategic debate between the Soviet Union and the United States, or concerned with ensuring the future, *some* of the preceding calculations are identical. The Great Power, too, is ensuring its own destruction in a strategic exchange. But the Great Power seeking different goals and operating within a different kind of political tradition requires a different kind of nuclear force. Consequently, its evaluations of costs and benefits will differ because of its different estimation of its role and relationship to the overall strategic balance.

Impact of Alliance Commitments on Nuclear Decisions

If a Small Power actually developed nuclear weapons in the hope of deterring certain actions on the part of the Superpowers (or Great Powers possessing sophisticated deterrents), these calculations might be decisive.[26] However, the rationale for a Small Power's nuclear force comes essentially from its impact elsewhere: militarily on its weak neighbors, and politically and psychologically, on its neighbors and allies, both large and small. There are, therefore, apparently clear advantages involved in becoming a nuclear power, even a weak and vulnerable nuclear power,[27] *if* becoming

---

[25] It remains true, and is undoubtedly worth some emphasis, that Cuba did achieve some very significant military and political gains out of the missile crisis, despite the reaction of the United States, or perhaps because of that reaction.

[26] It hardly seems necessary to point out that Small Powers are unlikely to indulge in the kind of academic analysis herein employed: some discussion of this point follows.

[27] Much more so for a Small Power seeking local advantages than for a Great Power seeking to affect the overall strategic balance or seeking goals within an

a nuclear power is economically and technologically feasible, *if* it does not promise to fragment valuable alliance ties, and *if* the Great Powers and the Superpowers do not intervene to veto the action.

The latter point could be decisive. The larger states might perceive enough mutual interest in delaying or preventing the proliferation of nuclear weapons to take some sort of common action. But the prospect of effective common action is surely unlikely. Inertia on the part of the Superpowers, conflict or disagreement between them, or deliberate policy choices by all the current nuclear powers, will undoubtedly guarantee some degree of immunity to various Small Powers bent on developing a nuclear capacity.

Nevertheless, a Superpower feeling significantly threatened by the prospect of a Small Power neighbor armed with nuclear weapons, or worried about the possibility of escalation in a regional conflict, *might* be prompted to take unilateral action. Thus Raymond Aron has argued that:

If even a few missiles in the hands of a minor power can frighten a major one, as has been stressed time and again, then it follows that no small country will be able to acquire such missiles *unless it be under the protection of a big one.*[28]

Aron's point may be overstated, but it does indicate the extent to which calculations about alliance policies and nuclear policies have become intermingled.

The precise way in which the development of an independent nuclear arsenal by a weak state will affect its alliances is uncertain. Obviously it depends on the reactions of its allies and its enemies and, of course, on the way in which the weak state attempts to exploit its capabilities. Any discussion is hypothetical. But it is pertinent to point out, once again, that the argument runs somewhat differently for Great Powers than it does for Small Powers.

From the point of view of either Superpower, the dispersion of

---

area which both Superpowers consider vital enough to justify the use of their strategic forces; in the latter circumstance, the Great Power's force may be intensely destabilizing. It may, however, have some utility anyway, as the ensuing discussion will point out.

[28] Aron, *The Great Debate,* pp. 114–15 (my italics).

nuclear weapons to any other state is bound to appear dangerous and perhaps even potentially disastrous. The argument goes beyond the fact that the process of dispersion is likely to have intensely destabilizing effects on the strategic level. It also involves a clear appreciation of the increased dangers and difficulties of controlling allies armed with nuclear weapons. In fact, a projection of current trends, or more accurately an extrapolation from them, seems to suggest the obvious conclusion that alliance commitments will be diluted and disavowed as the weaker partners achieve deterrents which they assume enhance their independence but which also drastically increase the possibility of accidental, irrational, catalytic, or miscalculated wars.[29] It is worthwhile to point out that this contention is not quite as obvious as it seems. The extent to which alliance commitments will be diluted remains dependent on a range of calculations and developments which cannot be evaluated simply by projecting logical reactions to the continuation of current trends.

The primary calculation which remains ambiguous concerns the manner in which the Superpower balances its desire to retain the support and allegiance of its ally against the increased dangers of any commitment at all. And it is in this calculation that the differences between Great Powers and Small Powers emerge most clearly. On a commonplace level, a Great Power is obviously a more significant ally than a Small Power. On a more sophisticated level, the different purposes, and probably character, of Great Power and Small Power deterrents may alter the Superpower's calculations in a significant way.

France and Great Britain seek, at least in part, to influence the strategic debate between the United States and the Soviet Union. By developing nuclear forces powerful enough "to tear the arm off" an aggressor, and perhaps even serve as a probable catalyst for the launching of its ally's forces, the Great Powers create a substantial dilemma for their more powerful ally. The Superpower, in an effort to indicate to its peer that the launching of either Great Power's deterrent is a unilateral action which will *not* lead to the

[29] For a discussion of these and other effects of nuclear proliferation, see Kahn, *Thinking About the Unthinkable,* Ch. VII.

unleashing of its own force, may disavow or dilute its alliance commitment. But that action hardly proves that the Superpower will not reverse its decision in a crisis, in particular because it has sound reason to do so. The annihilation of a Great Power ally would involve enormous political and psychological losses. In addition, the "spiral" effect might determine both Superpowers' reactions. The aggressor, not believing its peers' disavowal of responsibility, might feel that it could not afford to *not* simultaneously attack the other Superpower (especially if the retaliatory effect of the Great Power's deterrent had the potential of upsetting the strategic balance). The other Superpower, knowing its disavowal disbelieved and aware of the thought process of the enemy (or, rather, substituting its own for its opponent's), may feel compelled to strike. Some awareness of this dilemma, and an ambiguous effort to avoid it, may be inferred from the Soviet reaction to the French *force de frappe*:

. . . there has been a notable avoidance of specific threats to the effect that the Soviet Union would retaliate automatically against United States' territory if the French attacked alone. In fact, there have been occasional suggestions from the Soviet side . . . that only if the United States were "itself to carry out . . . an attack" against a Soviet bloc member would the Soviet Union be impelled to deliver a retaliatory blow at the United States. This hint of an endeavor to avoid the automatic escalation of possible third-power conflicts in Europe may have been limited to a situation involving the two German states, but it would also seem applicable in some circumstances arising out of an individual initiative by the French force de frappe.[30]

However, even loosening the alliance commitment may not achieve the desired results. The Superpower's apparent willingness to stand by idly while a Great Power ally is destroyed simply cannot achieve the necessary credibility. The Great Powers may thus achieve a good part of their aims because the Superpower has no viable alternative. At the cost of integrating their deterrents with that of their larger ally, they may receive substantial benefits in terms of a voice in the discussion of how and when that wider deterrent will be used, and in terms of greater influence within the

---

[30] Thomas W. Wolfe, "Soviet Commentary on the French 'Force de Frappe'," (Santa Monica: The RAND Corporation, 1965), pp. 8–9.

councils of the alliance. In sum, from the point of view of the Great Powers the development of an independent nuclear capability *might* force a Superpower ally to withdraw its commitment of support. It is just as likely, perhaps even more likely, that the unattractiveness of that alternative might force the Superpower not only to continue its commitment but actually to adapt it more closely to the interests of its weaker partners.[31] And this is aside from whatever other advantages the Great Power may achieve in terms of prestige and psychological support against an uncertain future.

The argument is considerably different if we are concerned with Small Powers and not Great Powers. A Small Power with an independent nuclear force might hope to induce its larger ally to come to its aid in a crisis or during an actual isolated attack on its territory. In reality, however, the calculations which led it to create a nuclear force are likely to have rested on an entirely different foundation. If it sought to achieve primarily local goals with its new forces, the effort to serve as a catalyst for the forces of its ally is likely not only to be unsuccessful but also to be disastrous, if successful. The Small Power might be attacked or threatened by one of the Superpowers, but the *military* support of the other Superpower succeeds only in insuring the devastation of the Small

---

[31] This argument also illustrates another point: the extent to which invulnerability is primarily a *military* requirement. It is a decisive factor for a Great Power only if it hopes to use its deterrent to achieve primarily military purposes (like deterrence). If it seeks other goals, invulnerability, while still desirable, is not nearly as significant. Thus, as the argument contends, a weak nuclear force might be enough to convince an ally of the need to make extensive concessions.

It may be appropriate to point out that the addition of a new factor, the impact of nuclear forces on allies and alliances, has considerably altered the conclusions which emerge from concentrating solely on the relationship between nuclear weapons and national security (i.e., without benefit of alliances). This should become clear in the next few pages. The essential point is that a Great Power's weak nuclear forces may still have an advantageous impact on its allies' behavior; whereas a Small Power's weak force may antagonize allies and dissolve alliances. In sum, the advantages of a nuclear capability are not symmetrical in the two instances: that is, when discussing its impact on security alone or on alliances and security. And the Great Powers seem to have a much better cost-gain calculation when alliances are counted.

Power. The latter can only hope to deter a Superpower by virtue of the protection inherent in an overall strategic balance. If that balance is tilted enough to warrant aggressive action by one of the Superpowers, the Small Power gains virtually nothing by possessing a nuclear force which is too weak to adjust the overall balance and which, simultaneously, is powerful enough to ensure that the aggressive Superpower will be required to destroy it in a strategic exchange. A Small Power, in contrast to a Great Power, also cannot hope to buy a nuclear deterrent as a means of staying out of war and sparing its homeland. It may in fact do quite the opposite.

Moreover, the Small Power is obviously not as valuable to the Superpower as one of the Great Powers. If it develops a nuclear capability, particularly one which is vulnerable and destabilizing, its Superpower ally may very well disavow its commitment and leave the Small Power to fend for itself. The Superpower might even attempt to exert pressure on the Small Power to dismantle its nuclear forces. Another calculation may also be of some significance. If its large ally disavows its commitment because a vulnerable nuclear force is too destabilizing, the enemy Superpower may take advantage of that disavowal to destroy or threaten to destroy the force. After all, it is bound to appear an even more dangerous and destabilizing weapons system to an unfriendly state.

The Small Power may find itself in something of a dilemma. It undoubtedly desires a nuclear capability to enhance its local position, and not to achieve any gains at the expense of the Superpowers. But one or both of the Superpowers may find that capability so dangerous that elimination of it will be insisted upon. Indeed the Small Power may not even be able to achieve local gains by virtue of its nuclear arsenal because it will inevitably force the Superpowers to intervene in each crisis or to offer some kind of nuclear guarantee to the threatened Small Power.[32]

Two points (again, in the abstract) seem clear, and both indicate the extent to which Small Powers, even with nuclear weapons, remain dependent upon the actions of larger states. The pre-

[32] Thus President Kennedy once noted that the dispersion of nuclear weapons may lead "to an increased necessity for the great powers to involve themselves in otherwise local conflicts." *The New York Times,* July 27, 1963, p. 2.

sumed "equalizing" capacity of nuclear weapons may be nothing more than a very dangerous myth. In the first place, the destabilizing effect of nuclear proliferation is such that it may force one or both Superpowers to intervene to prevent it. If this proves true, Small Powers can only develop a nuclear capability with the active support or, at least, the tacit protection of one of the Superpowers. It is only in this manner that the other Superpower can be deterred from hostile action. The Small Power may actually be more in need of its Superpower ally, rather than less, when it seeks to become a nuclear power, if only to protect it on the strategic level while it seeks goals at the local level.[33] It hardly seems likely that either Superpower would accept an alliance commitment of this nature.

The second point rests on the assumption that, despite the inherent dangers, neither Superpower intervenes to halt the spread of nuclear weapons (and that, of course, the Small Powers feel that the advantages of becoming a nuclear power clearly outweigh the disadvantages). As a result, both Superpowers might withdraw all military commitments from Small Power allies possessing, or threatened by, a nuclear force because of fears of escalation, miscalculation, and the like. However, it may be just as likely that the Superpowers will actually do just the opposite: intervene quickly and decisively in local quarrels to inhibit their effects. In particular, they might offer guarantees of support to non-nuclear states threatened by a neighboring Small Power armed with nuclear weapons.

This promise of support might appear too contingent and ambiguous to the threatened Small Power. If France and Great Britain doubt the will of the United States, how can it be assumed that India or Pakistan would find it credible? The Small Power may feel compelled to develop its own nuclear weapons, with further destabilizing effects. In this circumstance, the Superpower may actually be induced to *give* nuclear weapons to the threatened Small Power in an effort to maintain a local balance. Consequently, the advantages which the nuclear Small Power hoped to achieve by virtue of its monopoly will be eliminated. Moreover, its freedom

---

[33] It might also need other kinds of aid, economically and technologically. Cf. Albert Wohlstetter, "Nuclear Sharing: NATO and the N^{+1} Country," in Rosecrance, *The Dispersion of Nuclear Weapons*, p. 196.

of movement may be sharply curtailed by the Superpowers. The critical variable in this situation is, of course, the existence and credibility of a guarantee by one of the larger states. If one, or both, of the Small Powers does not believe in the guarantee, or in the promise to turn over nuclear weapons, both Small Powers will undoubtedly be forced to seek an independent capability.[34]

A Theoretical Conclusion and a Practical Objection

The preceding analysis suggests several conclusions. First, the argument that Small Powers will not or should not seek independent nuclear capabilities because those capabilities are bound to be vulnerable and destabilizing is not likely to be decisive. Small Powers seek nuclear weapons to achieve goals not dependent on the possession of an invulnerable and sophisticated deterrent. A difference in degree, if not in kind, exists between Great Powers and Small Powers. Second, if an inferior nuclear force appears advantageous, Small Powers can be dissuaded from developing them only by the intervention of the Superpowers or by a clear perception on their part that the presumed advantages of an independent nuclear capability will disappear, because the large states will be forced to either guarantee threatened nonnuclear Small Powers or to constantly intervene to limit the effects of local conflicts, or both. Once again, significant differences between Small Powers and Great Powers, not only in the rationale underlying the decision to become a nuclear power but also in terms of expectations concerning the possible reactions of the nuclear giants, are apparent. The last point is not as academic as it may first appear. An effort to impress on any potential nuclear power the fact that the advantages which have accrued to Great Britain and France need not come to them may be salutary. Finally, it ought to be emphasized that the preceding analysis at least suggests that nuclear weapons are unlikely to alter

[34] The actual conditions under which a Small Power would prefer an external guarantee of nuclear support to the creation of its own nuclear capability seem too dependent on specific circumstances to justify any extensive *abstract* analysis of the problem; the last section of this essay will discuss a few of the practical aspects of this situation.

the traditional relationship between Great Powers and Small Powers. Contrary to a number of simplistic appraisals, they may actually reinforce or revive the tendency of the larger states to control the conduct of international politics.

If the discussion could stop here and remain content with treating Small Powers, Great Powers, and Superpowers as monolithic entities, each determining its behavior in the light of a particular set of rational calculations, the problem of nuclear proliferation might seem less pressing. Correctly "read," the analysis would suggest that Great Powers and Superpowers should agree to a compromise arrangement in which the Superpowers yield absolute control of nuclear weapons, even to the extent of accepting independent deterrents, only if the Great Powers agree to centralized control or coordination of those deterrents or, at the very least, to an effort to make them invulnerable. And thus the urge to create MLF's, ANF's, community deterrents, and the like. Conversely, Small Powers ought not invest in any nuclear capabilities at all, for they could not expect the Superpowers to react in the same way and to proffer political concessions in exchange for nuclear control.

It is unfortunate, but undoubtedly true, that few if any Small Powers are likely to evaluate the decision to become a nuclear power in the foregoing manner. All of the arguments about the dangers and difficulties of becoming a nuclear power are apparently true, surely to some convincing degree. They are enormously expensive; so much so for most Small Powers that they may foreclose the possibility of conventional defense. In addition, nuclear states become the targets of other nuclear states. One may only be buying the certainty of devastation in any future conflict. In addition, allies and enemies may be forced into some form of extreme behavior. Yet for those Small Powers economically and technologically capable of producing nuclear weapons, it is difficult to avoid the impression that the attractions or necessity of joining an ever-expanding and ever-cheaper nuclear club will easily outweigh the objections.[35]

---

[35] For a contrary, and somewhat more hopeful, analysis of the problem, see Morton H. Halperin, *China and the Bomb* (New York: Frederick A. Praeger, 1965), especially pp. 107–8. Halperin argues that "The generally left-wing and

However spurious or ambiguous the arguments supporting the acquisition of an independent nuclear capability may be, and however obvious or decisive the arguments against achieving such a capability appear, it remains true that the situation is very uncertain. An analytical examination of probabilities, based on an extrapolation of current trends, and assuming a means-ends kind of rationality, hardly yields definitive answers. At best, it merely sets the framework within which the actual decision will be made. And that decision, of course, will be based on idiosyncratic factors beyond the ability of abstract analysis to isolate.

Before more specific considerations are discussed, it seems appropriate to point out one very general factor that ought to be kept in mind, namely, the nature of Small Powers. Forced to exist in a situation of continuous insecurity, dependent for survival on the vagaries of Great Power behavior, Small Powers have tended to develop a unique pattern of response to developments in world politics. That response, reflecting dependence on virtually uncontrollable external developments, has been the essentially ambivalent one of exaggerated emphasis on formal and ceremonial status, alternating with unrepentant Machiavellism. These remarks refer only to Small Powers which feel threatened by an existing power configuration, but the numbers thus distinguishable are numerous enough and significant enough to justify analysis.

---

to some extent pacifist orientation of most political groups in the Asian countries makes them to some extent uninterested in the achievement of national nuclear power and uneasy about the acquisition of nuclear weapons from an ally." (p. 107). He also notes that the French experience may persuade many of these states of the wisdom of not getting nuclear weapons. But the opposite conclusion *may* actually be more appropriate, since it is not so clear (at least to me) that France will not achieve substantial gains by virtue of possessing its *force de frappe*. For further discussion of the way in which the French and British experiences might be "read," see below.

Mr. Halperin also argues (pp. 107–8) that the political motives to get nuclear weapons are likely to be fewer in Asia than in Europe, but that the security motives may be stronger since these states lack the commitment of support which we have given to the Europeans—conversely, the U.S. risk in providing deterrence for various Asian states against Communist China's nuclear bomb is less than the risk involved in countering the more sophisticated Soviet arsenal (i.e., risk on a strategic level). While I am in general agreement with these points, I believe they need to be supplemented by the observations which follow.

That political style contains characteristics which may tip the balance in favor of becoming an independent nuclear power. Development of a nuclear capability involves obvious dangers, but the *potential* advantages of nuclear power involve the *possibility* of altering the worst features of the Small Power's position in world politics. They may someday be a deterrent against even the Superpowers. Not to develop them now may foreclose the possibility of benefiting from that situation. They may be the decisive factor in local conflicts, both military and political, by inducing the larger states to withdraw rather than risk escalation. They are, once possessed, a strong bargaining element in any diplomatic confrontation. Moreover, they confer both prestige and status: prestige in terms of possessing the most advanced weapons and status in terms of membership in a relatively limited group. Both considerations weigh heavily in Small Power calculations. Finally, they may reduce military expenditures. The evident fallaciousness of this argument undoubtedly will not be perceived any more quickly by Small Powers than Great Powers. The extent to which any of these considerations is true is just the extent that any purely rationalistic analysis of Small Powers and nuclear proliferation falls short.

It cannot be denied that these considerations are abstract and hypothetical, and that several of the disadvantages of becoming a nuclear power are very real and tangible. The decision to become a nuclear power involves a dangerous gamble on possibilities which very clearly might not come to pass. Yet the possibility that any one of them might is inordinately attractive to a group of states whose political behavior reflects a history of insecurity and dependence. The fact that analysis seems to indicate that the acquisition of a nuclear arsenal may actually make Small Powers more, not less, dependent on the actions of the Great Powers is not a decisive consideration, for acceptance of the status quo involves the same thing. The gamble, then, may very well be taken, if only because the calculation that continuous insecurity as a weak nuclear power is far more dangerous than continuous insecurity armed only with conventional weapons is rarely made by Small Powers. And, if made, it is not as impressive or compelling as the possibility, or rather the hope, that nuclear weapons may, now or someday, actually transform the security problem for Small Powers.

The British and French Experiences from a Small Power Perspective

A purely abstract perspective suggests that the British and French experiences are relevant only for other Great Powers. However, if the tendency is to plan for the future by means of a projection based on a selective culling of past experiences, selective in terms of what presumably will remain relevant in that experience, the British and French decisions to develop an independent nuclear capability also constitute the most valuable available body of material for any practical study of nuclear proliferation, at least until more knowledge is available about the Communist Chinese decision or other experiences which appear even more relevant. The fact that the British and French experiences appear unique may not be as significant as the fact that they are really the only cases which a prospective nuclear power can examine. That examination will undoubtedly be highly selective, centering on a quest for points of salience and affinity which appear relevant to a state studying the possibility of developing its own nuclear weapons. Thus the next few pages will examine the British and French cases in a peculiar fashion, with the intention of isolating certain factors which appear to be salient and which also may bear some affinity to future decisions.[36]

The British and French decisions were both conditioned by something which might be called the "Great Power syndrome". In traditional terms, a Great Power was a state which could insure its own security against all comers. But being a Great Power involved something more. A Great Power was also distinguished from its inferiors by a set of tangible and psychological apprecia-tions which affected its perception of what constituted "normal" behavior. It took hardly any reflection, but rather simply a reflex response, for a Great Power to seek any weapon which its peers

[36] We are very much in need of case studies in depth on this subject; lacking them, any general analysis is bound to be superficial.

had obtained; even Austria-Hungary built Dreadnoughts. Prestige ("grandeur") and status demanded it, even if the security function of the weapon was uncertain.

That the British were affected by this syndrome after 1945 has often been indicated.[37] But it is worthwhile to point out that the French were equally affected long before de Gaulle returned to power in 1958. For example, Pierre André, a right-wing deputy, argued in 1954 that without nuclear weapons France would be nothing more than "an ally of the second rank".[38] And a study of the attitudes of the French Parliament and Government toward nuclear weapons indicated that the French leaders in 1954–55 were reassured by the fact that a "sense of normal order" prevailed: the United States, the Soviet Union, and Britain had the bomb, and it was thus "normal" for France to get it next.[39]

The Great Power syndrome involves something beyond the necessity of enhancing prestige and status by all available means. It also involves, perhaps more significantly, the assumption that buying insurance against contingent futures is a normal part of the policy-making process. Thus one study of the French decision contends that the necessity of providing for "unforeseeable eventualities" was the critical factor in seeking an independent capability.[40] And the British fear that the United States' deterrent might not hit certain targets which London felt were important has been a constant theme from Churchill to Gaitskell. In effect, too much dependence meant too little flexibility in meeting future threats. To illustrate, Macmillan argued in 1955 that relinquishing the Bomber Command "deprives us of any influence over the selection of targets, and the use of our vital striking forces," and Gaitskell argued in 1960 that "the real case for our having our own inde-

[37] See Alfred Goldberg, "The Atomic Origins of the British Nuclear Deterrent," *International Affairs*, XL (July, 1964), 427.

[38] Quoted in George Kelly, "The Political Background of the French A-Bomb," *Orbis* (Fall 1960), p. 293; see also C. E. Zoppo, "France as a Nuclear Power," (Santa Monica: The RAND Corporation, 1962).

[39] De la Malène and Melnik, *Attitudes of the French Parliament and Government*, p. 14.

[40] C. E. Zoppo, "France as a Nuclear Power," in Rosecrance, *The Dispersion of Nuclear Weapons*, pp. 115 ff.

pendent nuclear weapons is fear of excessive dependence upon the United States . . . [which] might force upon us policies with which we did not agree. . . ." [41]

If it is indeed true that the preceding factors are salient enough to attract the attention of any state considering a nuclear future, can the impact they might have be foreseen? It must be emphasized that the point at issue does not concern whether Small Powers also seek prestige and status—they obviously do—or whether they also worry about the future, for to some degree, they must. Rather the question is whether Great Britain or France has actually achieved either of these goals by virtue of its nuclear capability, or enough so to impress a potential nuclear power.

No definitive answer is possible, and that may be just the point. Surely the possibility that the two Great Powers will enhance their position in world affairs by possessing an independent deterrent remains open. In fact, it is difficult to refute the contention that they have already done so. A state intent on achieving similar kinds of goals will hardly be inhibited by the historical record.

It is true that though a Small Power and a Great Power can seek the same kind of general goals, the scale is considerably different. The "unforeseeable eventualities" which may confront a Great Power are not any more intrinsically significant than those likely to confront a Small Power, but they surely may be more extensive. De Gaulle, for example, worried about worldwide commitments which required a strategic posture of the first rank.[42] The Small Power's fears involve threats which are more immediate in terms of time and more local in terms of area, but survival can be at stake in either case. The argument, therefore, cannot be read in the following manner: Great Powers develop nuclear weapons as a response to extensive threats; Small Powers face less extensive threats, and thus will not require nuclear weapons. The point is that the definition of "extensive" shifts as the perspective is altered. A certain comparability in motivation and a willingness to read the British and French experiences in a manner justifying acquisition of

---

[41] Both quotations are from Richard Gott, "The Evolution of the Independent British Deterrent," *International Affairs* (April 1963), pp. 243, 248.

[42] Zoppo, "France as a Nuclear Power" (The RAND Corporation), pp. 1–3.

nuclear weapons may be presumed. The same argument holds, in general, if the question of prestige and status is examined. Despite differences in degree, the British and French experiences appear relevant and lead to the same conclusion.

It is perhaps worth emphasizing that it is at this point that theory and practice most clearly intersect and conflict. The sharp theoretical distinction between Great Powers, who seek "grandeur" by nature and by necessity, and Small Powers, who desire "grandeur" but must be content with survival, breaks down before the obvious fact that in practice the difference is one of degree rather than kind. If nuclear weapons yield substantial benefits in terms of status and prestige, the fact is true, though not equally true, for both groups of states. The qualification may, however, be significant enough to justify a limited degree of optimism. Nuclear weapons are not an *intrinsic* necessity for Small Powers (a factor which tends to reestablish the theoretical dichotomy), since their more limited quest for prestige may be satisfied short of procuring all the accoutrements of Great Power status. As long as diffusion does not become widespread, substitute gratifications are at least conceivable, though not likely.

A second aspect of the French and British decisions which stands out concerns their essentially political and nonstrategic nature. Neither country developed a national strategy which clearly indicated the need for nuclear weapons, and then set out on a development program. On the contrary, they developed nuclear weapons and *then* sought a strategy which would justify their acquisition.

The British, as Richard Rosecrance indicates, never examined the premises underlying their decision.[43] In some sense, of course, the environmental context in which the original decision was made explains the failure to analyze advantages and disadvantages in a coherent fashion. The extent to which atomic weapons were revolutionary was not clearly perceived, nor was their impact on Britain's defensibility. In addition, the decision was made although no enemy against which the bomb might be used was evident, and without any clear appreciation of the likelihood or need for an

[43] Rosecrance, "British Incentives to Become a Nuclear Power," in Rosecrance, *The Dispersion of Nuclear Weapons*, pp. 58–62.

American strategic umbrella. In sum, none of the familiar liabilities and costs of becoming a nuclear power, such as vulnerability, delivery problems, costs, and the like, were recognized.[44]

The original British decision to build a bomb is, therefore, of less interest than either London's later experiences in living with the effects of that decision or the French experiences in developing a nuclear arsenal in a more relevant strategic environment. The context in which the British made the decision is simply too unique. No other state will be able to become a nuclear power without at least recognizing the existence of a range of problems which the British ignored. The fact that the British merely continued a nuclear program which had begun during the war is also significant. It took considerably less effort, intellectually and technologically, to proceed with that program than it would have taken to create an entirely new program. That program was also already oriented toward military ends. The extent to which this experience is relevant for other states may depend on their progress in presumably peaceful nuclear research: on how close they are to the point where producing a bomb is one simple step forward, and not producing it necessitates a major and formal decision.

Though the French showed very little public concern with nuclear weapons before 1955, their decision was made within a context of increasing self-consciousness about the significance of nuclear weapons.[45] Even so, it was a political decision, unmotivated by strategic considerations.[46] More precisely, it was a decision which took shape soon after the defeat in Indochina,[47] and within an environment in which the French seemed to be increasingly isolated in diplomatic terms.[48] The degree to which the decision, at

[44] *Ibid.*

[45] See de la Malène and Melnik, *Attitudes of the French Parliament and Government,* pp. 1–10.

[46] "There is no doubt that the motive of the trend toward nuclear armament in France has been, not 'to produce a modern and powerful army,' but 'to make France politically respected,' 'to enable France to carry on an independent policy.' " *Ibid.,* p. 67; see also Wolf Mendl, "The Background of French Nuclear Policy," *International Affairs* (Jan. 1965), pp. 22–36.

[47] See Kelly, "The Political Background of the French A-Bomb," p. 303.

[48] De la Melène and Melnik, "Attitudes of the French Parliament and Government," pp. 32–33.

least in part, reflected bitterness about a lack of support by its primary allies is also of interest:

The Parliament members gradually acquired the conviction that American policy in North Africa and the Near East was pursuing objectives that were entirely different from, not to say opposite to, those of France. This explains why, little by little, French possession of atomic weapons came to be regarded almost as an anti-American measure, rather than as a measure of deterrence.[49]

Thus France's nuclear mindedness grew in direct proportion to the extent to which it felt frustrated in achieving its own ends and abandoned by its allies.[50]

Still, the French, who had become increasingly aware of some of the liabilities of seeking an independent nuclear deterrent, might have held back had it not been for the effect of the "Great Power syndrome," which seemed to justify the acquisition of nuclear weapons as "natural," and a growing awareness of certain other considerations:

The fear of the responsibilities involved in the creation of an arsenal has tended to diminish with the growing recognition that (1) atomic armament is the low-price armament of the weak; (2) atomic armament is the only possible means of deterrence and a means adaptable to the scale of the country in question; and (3) for lack of atomic armament the defense of French interests in the world is becoming very difficult.[51]

The first consideration may very well influence all potential nuclear powers; the second will undoubtedly grow in attractiveness; and only the third seems relevant solely for Great Powers (e.g., West Germany).

There is nothing in either the British or French decision which

[49] *Ibid.*

[50] A very recent major study of the French experience notes: "Not only could she not act effectively on her own, as the Suez incident in 1956 so dramatically demonstrated, but she also seemed incapable of exercising any degree of influence on her allies." Lawrence Scheinman, *Atomic Energy Policy in France Under the Fourth Republic* (Princeton, N.J.: Princeton University Press, 1965), p. xxii. Mr. Scheinman emphasizes the impact of external factors in several places, e.g., pp. xvii, xxiii-xxiv, 186 ff.

[51] De la Malène and Melnik, "Attitudes of the French Parliament and Government," pp. 63–64.

justifies optimism about the possibility of preventing nuclear proliferation. Neither a description of the potential dangers of diffusion nor a discussion of the presumed costs and liabilities of becoming a nuclear power are sufficient, by themselves, to induce nuclear abstention. Proliferation only appears dangerous when produced by *other* states; costs and liabilities yield to the vision of potential benefits. It is not merely that the British and French decisions were reflexive and "thoughtless," and that they were not narrowly rational in terms of some set of military criteria but rather reflected political frustrations. It is also that those decisions have not led to disaster and may yet prove wise and provident.

It may also be relevant to point out that the democratic political structure of Great Britain and France did not in the least inhibit the decision to develop a bomb. In both countries, public concern and political debate was limited and governments (or even strategically placed nongovernmental groups) left, right, and center were able to do as they pleased. As Lawrence Scheinman notes, "Indeed, one of the most singular features of atomic policy in the Fourth Republic was the almost total lack of parliamentary discussions of the implications of atomic power for France in either a peaceful or military context." [52]

The lack of public debate is not surprising. The extent to which complex military decisions are primarily executive in nature is well known. But two further points are clearly worth emphasizing. The first concerns the fact that nuclear policy in France, though only to a much lesser degree in Britain, was developed and determined by a small and essentially extraconstitutional group:

The action of responsible political leadership was the last in a long chain of events. . . . Guidance and direction for nuclear policy came not from the French Government or the French Parliament, but from a small, dedicated group of administrator-technocrats, politicians and military officers whose activities centered on and emanated from the C.E.A. [53]

The second point concerns the fact that, even when discussed and debated, each specific decision appeared to be nothing more than

[52] Scheinman, *Atomic Energy Policy in France,* p. xv.
[53] *Ibid.,* pp. 214–15.

a limited and logical extension of an ongoing program. Thus it is difficult to isolate an early date on which a major decision to become a nuclear power was made. Rather, the procedure was a series of discrete steps leading to the same end.[54]

Certain inferences may be drawn from these points. In the large, it is unlikely that the political structure of any other country will be any more effective in inhibiting a Government which has decided to take the plunge. Moreover, the fact that the decision can be taken and implemented secretly, and by a small group of people, ought at least to qualify whatever optimism exists about the possibility of knowing what a country engaged in nuclear research has in mind. Finally, the nature of the process—discrete steps rather than a single, specific decision—illuminates the danger of freely passing out information about the peaceful uses of nuclear energy. The point at which the decision to become a nuclear power is not merely technologically easier but also politically and psychologically inevitable merely advances more rapidly.

It should, of course, be reemphasized that the British and French experiences cannot be taken literally. The specific kinds of concessions which the British and French might get, or the scope of the threats they might have to face, are very different from those confronting the remaining nonnuclear states (except for West Germany and perhaps Japan). The available experiences are relevant only in the very general sense that they indicate something about the factors which might influence potential nuclear states, and in the more limited sense that examination reveals that it is possible to "read" them in a way which suggests that becoming a nuclear power is not wholly disadvantageous.

The Emerging Prospect

All of the critical questions involved in an examination of the problem of nuclear proliferation remain ambiguous. Whether and by whom the process of diffusion will continue is unknown. What kind of nuclear weapons will become available and what effect they will have on international politics is unknown. Whether the

[54] *Ibid.*, pp. 94–95.

process can be stopped (or if it ought to be stopped), or whether it can be controlled if it cannot be stopped is unknown. What policy ought to be adopted toward the problem, and whether any single policy is possible toward a problem which has both discrete and general manifestations, either of which may conflict with the imperatives of the other, is also unknown.

Examined solely in terms of military security, analysis suggests that, on the margin, the utility of nuclear weapons for the remaining nonnuclear powers is not likely to be high. But when political and psychological factors are added to the analysis, the calculus of utility has to be adjusted. In an atmosphere of great uncertainty, buying nuclear weapons, or taking out the option of doing so, looks increasingly attractive. And insofar as the British and French experiences are relevant, they are more likely to reinforce than inhibit an incipient desire to become a nuclear power.

Nothing in the preceding pages suggests that proliferation can be prevented. Even a nuclear disaster so compelling that visions of Soviet-United States cooperation become realistic might be insufficient unless it occurred before proliferation had proceeded very far. Inevitably, just as disarmament discussions turned into arms control discussions when the possibility of verified disarmament disappeared, the nature of the discussion is becoming transformed. The dangers of diffusion and the necessity of preventing it are no longer emphasized, but rather the "realism" of accepting its inevitability and concentrating on controlling its worst effects. But the transformation is not complete, for there is still much discussion of the possibility of United States or Soviet guarantees in exchange for promises of not developing an independent nuclear arsenal. As trite as the metaphor may be, the world is indeed at a crossroads. If the options still available are not carefully scrutinized, undoubtedly, there will be none to choose from in the decade ahead.

It is a commonplace to point out that the adoption of any hypothesis about the likely course of future events may by itself lead to behavior and policies which make those events inevitable. Nonetheless, it may not be entirely irrelevant to emphasize the degree to which the adoption of either point of view about the inevitability of nuclear proliferation may condition what actually happens. It is not yet impossible that a concerted and consistent policy aimed at preventing proliferation, and/or punishing those who actually develop their own nuclear weapons, could be successful. Conversely, if it is in fact believed that proliferation is inevitable in the decade ahead, the policy imperatives are considerably different. The difficulty is that neither assumption is clearly right nor wrong. But it may also be true that failure to choose between them could be disastrous.

It is very unfortunate that the evidence on which to base a choice is sparse. Very few of the potential nuclear powers are yet at the point where public discussion is meaningful or necessary. Moreover, many, like Israel, see (and will see) an advantage in calculated ambiguity. A choice between speculations remains.

Certain nonnuclear states appear to have a "threshold" character. A decision by any one of them to become a nuclear power may very well serve as a catalyst for a similar decision by other states. For the most part, these are states locked in conflict with a neighbor (e.g., India and Pakistan, and Israel and Egypt) or at least desirous of matching the gains of a neighbor (Argentina and Brazil). On the other hand, certain states may possess the ability to become nuclear powers without fundamentally affecting the process of proliferation (Canada, Sweden, Switzerland, Australia). The rationale is not merely reversed. These states are not locked in conflict with a neighbor, but more significantly it is presumed that they would be more "rational" in their choice of strategies (and, perhaps, rich enough to build or buy an effective and invulnerable force).

The acquisition of a nuclear capability by China, as well as its aggressive behavior, has forced India to reappraise its nuclear policy. A brief examination of some aspects of that reappraisal may be illuminating, particularly if India is indeed a threshold country in terms of the proliferation problem. The Indian case may not, of course, be any more generally relevant than the cases of Great Britain and France. However, something very near the opposite may well be true. The Indian arguments and the Indian decision may be carefully examined by many states, because India is neither a Great Power nor an aligned state. And, in any event, the Indian case provides an interesting contrast with the previous discussion of the French and British cases.

The Significance of the Nuclear Debate in India

In technical terms, India could become a nuclear power more quickly than virtually any other state including Japan, West Germany, and Canada.[55] In the past, India has rejected the possibility of developing nuclear weapons in the most unqualified terms. The combination of technical facility and political avoidance presumably yields certain advantages:

Having an unused option which could have produced a bomb by 1963 may give India certain psychological-political advantages. With this ability, an anti-bomb attitude is more likely to be respected, and India could become a leader in test-ban and disarmament negotiations. If others, such as the Chinese, try to gain prestige by brandishing bombs, the fact that India can build one is at least a partial answer.[56]

Nevertheless, while no one could deny that it is more impressive to renounce that which one could actually have, India's position has been increasingly complicated by the recognition that China is a military threat. India could respond to that threat by merely continuing its traditional policy, on the presumption that any radical change would provoke the Chinese into further aggression.[57] But the attractiveness of doing nothing rapidly declines as its deterrent value diminishes: while developing a nuclear arsenal may be provoking, it is possible that not developing one might be even more provocative.

It should not be presumed that very many Indians have thought through the problem and emerged with a clear and logical position. As the scientific correspondent of an Indian journal noted, the Chinese bomb "caught us napping": "We had heard that they were going to do it but there had been hardly any serious attempt to

[55] See Beaton and Maddox, *The Spread of Nuclear Weapons*, pp. 141–42.
[56] Michael A. G. Michaud, "India as a Nuclear Power" (Los Angeles: U.C.L.A. National Security Studies Program, 1963), pp. 41–42.
[57] For evidence of such fears, *Ibid.*, p. 47.

anticipate its effects or examine in advance its possible implications. Inevitably, the explosion itself caught us napping. . . ." [58] Some preference for a desire to avoid thinking the problem through is understandable. The situation is so uncertain and complex that even detailed analysis yields only very tentative conclusions. Still, at least some serious discussion of India's nuclear policy has begun to appear in journals, and even the government's public position underwent some modification when Shastri announced that India would not build the bomb "at present". [59]

The Chinese bomb was bound to create some movement in India's position, but the degree of movement suggested varied widely. For example, R. K. Nehru, India's delegate to a number of disarmament conferences, argued for a policy of minimal adjustment. He advocated continued nuclear abstention but supplemented by some sort of guarantee against a nuclear threat:

Well, the United States has made a general statement that its assistance will be available to any country which is threatened by nuclear attack. That is good enough. It is not necessary to go further and ask for a formal declaration that the United States shall protect us, because that means a deviation from our basic policy of non-alignment. [60]

The ultimate, and most satisfactory, solution according to Mr. Nehru would be a "collective guarantee". In the interim, President Johnson's "general statement" would have to suffice. Nehru's position had one very obvious appeal: India would not have to do anything that it was not already doing.

M. R. Masani, a right-wing member of Parliament, adopted a minimal position in terms of favoring nuclear abstention, but his position on the matter of an outside guarantee was extreme. He wanted a United States (or a United States–Soviet) promise to launch a first-strike "if any one threatens to drop a bomb on one

[58] Amalendu Das Gupta, "A Nuclear Policy for India," *Conspectus*, I (1963), 3.

[59] *Ibid.* Shastri also said "I do not know what may happen later, but our present policy is not to build an atom bomb, and it is the right policy." *The New York Times*, Jan. 9, 1965, p. 2.

[60] R. K. Nehru, "The Challenge of the Chinese Bomb," *India Quarterly*, XXI (Jan.–March 1965), 10–11.

of these [nonnuclear] countries. . . ." [61] He did not examine the credibility of the aforesaid guarantee nor the probability that it would actually be offered.

In any event, whatever their difficulties, the positions of Nehru and Masani share a desire to avoid the dangers of nuclear abstention by virtue of some kind of outside guarantee. It is not altogether unlikely that similar responses will occur among other nonnuclear states when confronted by a nuclear threat (or perhaps even a very superior conventional threat). Thus the possibility or probability that a guarantee will actually inhibit the process of nuclear dispersion is worth examining, although any examination is bound to be tentative and ambiguous. After all, if the United States opts for a policy designed to prevent, rather than to control, proliferation, it appears inevitable that one aspect of that policy will be a series of guarantees to states faced with a nuclear threat. Before turning to that examination at least one other Indian suggestion ought to be discussed.

Raj Krishna, a government economist, argued that a strategic deterrent was beyond India's means, but that it could afford a *tactical* nuclear force. The latter, *inter alia*, would presumably create a local balance of power and would also counter Chinese nuclear blackmail. The sense in which he was using the term "tactical" was not perfectly clear. Apparently he had in mind a small nuclear force which would be capable of deterring a large-scale Chinese conventional and/or limited nuclear attack, and perhaps also forestalling nuclear blackmail. However, to handle a strategic threat, India would have to rely on Western nuclear forces:

The only real choice, therefore, is that the West, including Russia, provides strategic, long-range cover which it alone can do, and we provide tactical, short-range capability which we can and must have to match similar capability on the Chinese side . . . the burden of deterrence on land, the burden of defense against tactical and short-

---

[61] M. R. Masani, "The Challenge of the Chinese Bomb—II," *India Quarterly*, XXI (January–March 1965), 23.

range atomic warfare on land and in the air must be regionalized as soon as possible.[62]

What Krishna wanted, thus, is "a division of labor in deterrence" which, he assumed, would avoid the dangers of "linking total escalation with every limited engagement." [63] A tactical nuclear capability which would match the Chinese capability was within India's means. However, technical aid would facilitate its creation and might also provide a small stockpile of weapons and an aircraft delivery system.[64]

Krishna's plan contains several ambiguities and disadvantages. The economic costs, while lower than those involved in a full-scale effort to develop an independent deterrent, would still be high. In addition, the moral and psychological costs of India's decision to become a nuclear power, even if we grant the presumption that there is a substantive distinction between strategic and tactical weapons, might be even higher. Finally, the assumption that the West would be willing to extend a strategic guarantee to India involves two problems. If granted, it might not be very credible; and the likelihood of it being given at all might decline if India possesses a tactical nuclear force which gives it the possibility of escalating a local conflict into a general war. If nuclear guarantees are to be offered, it is not inconceivable that the United States would prefer to do it under conditions where it controlled *all* nuclear responses.

Nevertheless, the idea is not without value, particularly if the United States wants to concentrate on controlling the process of proliferation.[65] If nuclear weapons are going to be diffused, a case can be made for trying to channel that diffusion in a tactical direction. It would not eliminate the dangers of proliferation, but it

[62] Raj Krishna, "India and the Bomb," *India Quarterly*, XXI (April–June 1965), 127–28.

[63] *Ibid.*, p. 128.

[64] *Ibid.*

[65] I have not discussed the whole range of responses in India to the Chinese bomb: e.g. suggestions to build an independent deterrent, or to rely on a moral appeal to the world, are ignored here on the assumption that the responses discussed are more immediately relevant.

would offer some possibility of ameliorating or limiting them. And a tactical force in the hands of a local power might have a relatively high level of credibility.[66] The degree of credibility will depend on the existence of a *strategic* guarantee as well as on the nature of the nuclear forces which the potential aggressor possesses.

A policy of extending nuclear guarantees to states which promise not to develop their own nuclear weapons can ultimately work only as part of a larger policy whose purpose is to prevent any proliferation at all. A policy which only attempted to control the spread would undermine the attractiveness or credibility of a guarantee. As more and more states developed nuclear weapons, the willingness to do without them, and gamble on the word of a protector facing ever more dangerous threats, will decline. An unhappy choice must be faced. Can dispersion be prevented by guarantee? Or should concentration be focused on directing proliferation into less dangerous channels (e.g., by aiding in the creation of invulnerable and/or tactical forces, by cutting economic losses via technical aid)? The choices are not as stark as the question may suggest, but as an analytical device the question at least illuminates a distinction which has to be kept in mind.

Before discussing these alternatives, several things remain to be said about the Indian case. For one thing, the Indian decision may not serve as a very realistic paradigm for the problem of proliferation in the future because some Indians implicitly assume that they will be granted outside support if they are attacked. Thus Krishna maintains that "non-alignment has always been, in reality, an informal, unstated, unilateral alignment with unnamed Powers." [67] The degree to which this opinion prevails is uncertain, but

[66] It must be admitted that the suggestion to channel diffusion in a "tactical direction" is not without ambiguity. Obviously "tactical" nuclear weapons are usually of lower yield than "strategic" weapons, but this need not be true: it depends on how and against what they are used. Still, it is clear that some weapons and some delivery systems are, in relation to a specific area, *more* tactical than strategic, or at least more likely to give that impression to the states concerned. An Indian delivery system which would have great difficulty in reaching beyond the Himalayan mountain passes is illustrative; it could be supplemented by concentration on defensive measures, such as the acquisition, if possible, of an anti-ballistic missile system.

[67] Krishna, "India and the Bomb," p. 122.

the fact that it is held at all by influential spokesmen is significant. It tends to place India at least partly in a category with states like Sweden and Canada whose nuclear decisions are also heavily conditioned by underlying assumptions about the inevitability of outside support.[68] While this hardly indicates that India will not build bombs, it does imply that in psychological terms it possesses a slightly wider margin of error. It places the decision to become a nuclear power within a context where the Indian Government may assume that it has time to make a nuclear decision that is not merely a reflex response to the next crisis.

That does not mean that India has a great deal of time nor that it will use whatever time it has wisely. Great Britain and France developed nuclear weapons without any clear ideas concerning the ways in which they might be used nor, for that matter, against whom they might be used. There are reasonable doubts that either the British or French developed nuclear weapons because of any serious intention of using them in a conflict against the Soviet Union. The rationale rested primarily on the "Great Power syndrome" and its behavioral imperatives. But the Indians, whatever they assume about the likelihood of external support, must make their decision in a context dominated by the existence of a real enemy armed with nuclear weapons. Their case, in this sense, differs radically from the British and French cases. And this clearly implies that the Indians must worry about the *military* rationale for a nuclear arsenal, more so in any event than their Great Power predecessors did. A real enemy with real nuclear weapons demands an attention to military details which Paris and London could ignore. Since proliferation appears most likely in just such a circumstance, at least until nuclear weapons are as common as jet fighters, the Indian experience may have its widest relevance in instances within the next decade where a state confronts a major threat to its existence.

It is too soon to predict the course that India will actually follow. Yet the fact that a debate has begun which at a minimum questions the wisdom of the "no bomb under any circumstances" policy

[68] For Sweden, see James J. Robbins, *Recent Military Thought in Sweden on Western Defense* (Santa Monica: The RAND Corporation, 1955), pp. 80, 84.

may be important, for it reveals the very weak hold the "no bomb" policy actually has. It is unlikely to last much beyond the point where external threat and internal capability to produce a bomb at an acceptable cost intersect. As noted earlier, one hope of avoiding this outcome rests on the potential ability of a policy of guarantees to serve as a satisfactory substitute for an independent nuclear capability.

Credibility of Nuclear Guarantees

The decisive factor may very well be the degree to which the United States can make any guarantee that it offers credible to itself, to the recipient, and to a potential aggressor. The guarantees which have been discussed thus far are too ambiguous to satisfy any threatened state since the commitment of support remains uncertain. President Johnson's statement, shortly after the Chinese explosion, merely declared that: "Nations that do not seek nuclear weapons can be sure that, if they need United States support against the threat of nuclear blackmail, they will have it." [69]

But what kind of support, under what circumstances? If the United States commitment to its NATO allies is uncertain, how can it possibly assume that a commitment which will undoubtedly be drawn in an even looser fashion, and granted to states with fewer historical ties to the United States, will possess sufficient credibility? Even if honored in the breach, the primary purpose of the commitment would have been destroyed.

An alternative suggestion is to offer a guarantee but to sweeten it with peripheral benefits. Representative Chet Holifield's (D., Cal.) recent proposal is an illustration:

The United States should explore, together with other nuclear nations, the possibility of arrangements whereby all nations who agree to not develop their own independent nuclear weapon capability will be guaranteed assistance in the event of a nuclear attack by others.

In addition, the United States could make a particular effort to furnish economic and social aid to those nations who are willing to deny themselves independent nuclear capability. . . .[70]

[69] *The New York Times,* Oct. 19, 1964, p. 1.
[70] *The Baltimore Sun,* Nov. 16, 1965, p. 11.

However, it is surely more likely that a state which does not intend to build its own nuclear forces, because it does not feel threatened, will find the offer of economic and social aid more attractive than will a state actually confronting a nuclear threat. Peripheral offers of aid can be attractive only to states which feel that their chances of survival to use it are reasonably high.

An attempt to gain some insight into the problem of guarantees by examining the historical record yields few significant insights. For example, a long analysis by Sir James Headlam-Morley, at one time historical adviser to the Foreign Office, concludes with the rather trite observation that guarantees have worked only when definite in character and limited in scope to areas where the guarantor has real interests.[71] A more recent attempt to assess the factors which make a guarantee to a small power credible is somewhat more helpful, primarily in trying to place successes and failures in categories, but its conclusions are also commonplace; in effect, that credibility depends on the existence of some degree of economic, political, and military interdependence between guarantor and recipient.[72] The conclusion amounts to saying that we are more likely to defend areas to which a greater commitment has been made, not merely a political promise but also economic and military aid. Nonetheless, while it is hardly surprising that the promise of support has been challenged most often in cases where the commitment has been limited to words or treaties, it ought to be kept in mind that extensive commitments have also been challenged, and the guarantor found wanting.[73] The Czech case of 1938 provides an illustration. And, to reverse the proposition, the decision to support South Korea was made without much interdependence between the United States and Korea.

[71] Sir James Headlam-Morley, *Studies in Diplomatic History* (London: Methuen & Co., Ltd., 1930), pp. 105–192.

[72] Bruce M. Russett, "The Calculus of Deterrence," *The Journal of Conflict Resolution*, VII (June 1963), 97–109.

[73] Some guarantees obviously mean more than others: and the commitment which symbolizes the guarantee, no matter how limited or extensive, is clearly not as important as the assumptions and perspectives of the guarantor—which accounts, in part, for the fact that the use of overt and tangible ties to indicate credibility is not always a very good indication of real interest and intentions.

The point, of course, is not that the analysis is bad (it is, in fact, interesting), but that the historical record is inherently ambiguous. It is very difficult to go much beyond the generality that the credibility of a United States guarantee is likely to go up in proportion to the degree that the United States accepts more and closer ties on all levels. But in a nuclear age where the guarantor may be making a promise which endangers his own survival, even extensive integration may not be very credible (and, conversely, very little integration *might* be just credible because the costs of miscalculation are so high).

In any event, the proposition that a United States guarantee must be supplemented by extensive military and economic aid seems sound enough to constitute a valid starting point. But practical difficulties abound. What kind of aid ought the United States to give and for what purposes? The question is particularly acute in military terms. Military aid must simultaneously convince the recipient and the target that promises of the United States are sincere and yet be nonprovocative and a contribution to felt security needs. The relationship between conventional strength and the credibility of a guarantee is significant here. The United States can promise support against a nuclear threat, but it neither wants that promise to be challenged nor to have the recipient confronted by so overwhelming a conventional threat that it has no choice but to seek its own nuclear weapons (or demand that the United States use its weapons). Whatever stability the nuclear guarantee imparts may be undermined by the spiraling effects of serious conventional inferiority. Thus India's conventional weaknesses against China may ultimately be even more dangerous than its nuclear weakness. At the very least, it may create renewed demands to invest in nuclear hardware.[74] The point is that the military aid given by the United States (or economic aid which releases funds for military purposes) must be designed to maintain a conventional balance.

[74] Thus one commentator has noted the dangerous effects of the proliferation of conventional weapons: "Yet in at least two big confrontations, between India and Pakistan and between Israel and her Arab neighbors, this has directly influenced consideration of national nuclear weapons." Alastair Buchan, "Arms Nobody Wants to Control," *The New Republic*, CLIII (Nov. 6, 1965), 17.

The nuclear umbrella does not shield the United States from all storms, nor even against the most likely ones.

However, even a political commitment and extensive aid may not provide sufficient credibility. It may actually be necessary to station some portion of the nuclear forces which the United States promises to use *within* the boundaries of the guaranteed state. The apprehensiveness of West Germany concerning the withdrawal of United States troops from Europe provides an illuminating analogy. An American presence, complete with missiles and/or planes, would undoubtedly have a very salutary effect, particularly in psychological terms, on the credibility problem. The weapons, of course, would still remain under United States control (the more securely the better, especially from the point of view of the enemy), although some dual-key arrangements might be possible, and the weapons would, presumably, be sufficiently protected against a first-strike attack. Whether the weapons would be used against both a nuclear and a conventional attack is uncertain. If conventional inferiority is great, they may very well have to be so used (or promised).

A guarantee implemented in the foregoing manner may have some chance of success, more so than one limited to a political statement without an actual military presence. That it has many problems can hardly be in dispute. Some countries may not accept a United States presence for fear of loss of prestige or status among the nonaligned or for fear of an adverse domestic reaction. It may only be acceptable to a country which confronts a serious threat, recognizes its existence, and is unified enough to accept the costs of a foreign military presence. Not many countries will qualify. More significantly, having thought about it, the United States may not want to accept the costs and liabilities of so extensive a commitment. The chances of nuclear war may increase; the United States might become hostage to the host country, and forced to support it; the nuclear forces may be subject to sudden attack and use by the hosts, perhaps initiating a war; and, finally, the domestic difficulties of operating such a policy may be extensive. In sum, the United States may lose flexibility and increase the chances of accidental or miscalculated wars. But the proliferation of independent nuclear deterrents may have effects which are even more pernicious. Therefore, if the assumption that an effective guarantee requires an actual presence holds, the United States faces a very difficult decision. But the other alternatives may be even more unpalatable.

Guarantees do no more than increase the probability of future support; they do not make that support certain. Under the circumstances, if a state feels threatened, and if it has the technical means to do something about it, the guarantee can only have an interim significance until it can build its own nuclear capability. The guarantee, in effect, would become a device to control or ameliorate the worst features of a process of (inevitably) asymmetric diffusion. But it might not be effective enough; and the end result could be an arms race in primitive nuclear weapons.

Perhaps the United States could add some degree of stability to the situation by offering guarantees which included a specific promise to *give* an equivalent (or substantial) nuclear force to a country suddenly threatened by a nuclear power. The guaranteed state, if it believed the promise would be fulfilled, would not have to develop its own nuclear forces, and it could (in theory anyway) concentrate on improving its conventional forces. More critically, the promise might inhibit the whole process of proliferation. Any state intent on developing its own nuclear forces for security, prestige, to steal a march on its enemies, or whatever would presumably be extremely reluctant to do so if it knew that its competitors would simultaneously receive a nuclear force of its own, and a more effective one at no cost. George Liska has suggested that, while many of the nonnuclear powers are reluctant to develop nuclear weapons first (though the point remains in doubt until more of them are rejecting a *real* option), all of them want to be "assured seconds".[75] A promise by the United States might provide that assurance. It might succeed in deterring certain nonnuclear powers from "going" nuclear. Moreover, if compelled by circumstances to honor our commitment, its implementation might elimi-

[75] George Liska, "Problems of United States Defense Policy in a World of Nuclear Proliferation" (Mershon National Security Program, Ohio State University, 1965), pp. 95–96.

nate some of the dangers implicit in asymmetric diffusion. Finally, it ought not to be overlooked that the nuclear weapons which the United States might give to a threatened state could be less destabilizing than the weapons which it could build on its own. The latter point assumes that a limited number of relatively invulnerable weapons are given which are as defensive in character as possible.

As a policy, the preceding propositions suggest several problems. For one thing, they accept the necessity in certain circumstances of *deliberately* proliferating nuclear weapons as the lesser of several evils. It would, therefore, be necessary to create a political climate in which a policy as dangerous as the one suggested could be accepted and understood. It is also obviously not altogether clear whether such a policy would be wiser than doing nothing and leaving the threatened state to its own devices (or to some other source of support). A good deal would depend on idiosyncratic factors which cannot be specified beforehand. Assumptions about the intentions of the potential nuclear aggressor would be significant. The condition of the total military relationship between the two states would also be important. Nuclear superiority which bolsters an already existing conventional superiority may be more destabilizing than nuclear superiority and conventional equilibrium (i.e., the first might compel outside nuclear support for the weaker state; the second might not). The extent and pace of proliferation in the preceding years would also be significant. In a world in which several more states already have nuclear weapons, and in which the cost of procurement is declining, the necessity of giving nuclear weapons to various states might increase. In addition, the remaining nonnuclear states might feel compelled to "discover" or "invent" a nuclear threat to themselves in order to demand nuclear aid from the United States, or even threaten to turn to other potential donors. The analogy with the economic and military aid programs of the past, while perhaps somewhat overdrawn, is suggestive.

It may very well be that what the foregoing remarks imply is that the policy of promising to give states nuclear weapons in certain circumstances ought to be considered as a discrete and not general proposition. We ought to limit that part of the guarantee (though not necessarily the policy of guarantees as such) only to states who face a real nuclear threat and who could build their own bombs and would do so if we did not offer an alternative.

The credibility problem remains. How could a state which fears an imminent nuclear threat or an overwhelming conventional threat actually rely on a United States promise to give them nuclear weapons? Confidence might be bolstered to some degree by stationing nuclear forces in the guaranteed country under some form of double-key control, with the promise that full control would be turned over to the host country in the event an enemy developed (or received) nuclear weapons. The fact that United States forces could be overwhelmed by the host country might induce a kind of negative confidence that the United States commitment would be honored. It is also a reason why the policy ought to be limited in scope to states which are valued highly, and trusted at least somewhat. An alternative possibility might involve giving the guaranteed state all the *accoutrements* of nuclear power, short of the explosives themselves: e.g., missiles, bombers, perhaps even submarines.[76] If anti-ballistic missiles become a practical possibility, giving them to a guaranteed state might be considered. However reliable the ABM's turn out to be, they are defensive in nature and may increase confidence in the threatened state. It might be more difficult for the United States to renege on a promise having already made so extensive a commitment.

Policy Alternatives: A Summary and a Prospect

An element of fatalism is beginning to characterize many analyses of the problem of nuclear proliferation. But proliferation is *not* inevitable, though it may indeed be very probable. And if it occurs, it need not take a form which is intensely destabilizing.

However, it is surely difficult to avoid pessimism about the possibility of actually preventing an uncontrolled diffusion. Optimistic analyses of the problem tend to overstate the relevance of the Canadian, Swedish, and Indian examples. It is true that each has

[76] *Ibid.*

rejected, to this moment, a real option of developing an independent nuclear capability. The fact that, to varying but still significant degrees, each assumes the availability of external support in case of attack, and the fact that until very recently none confronted an immediate threat beyond its own means, limits the lessons which can safely be drawn from their cases. The beginnings of serious debate in India on the possibility of acquiring nuclear weapons, as the Chinese threat has grown, ought further to qualify optimistic assessments. Moreover, while Small Powers do not require all the arms which Great Powers possess, they must surely possess what their peers and subordinates acquire. The likelihood that Canada, Sweden, and India along with Italy, Japan, Belgium, Norway, and the Netherlands (none of this second group are yet confronting a threat not also a major threat to the United States) will continue to refuse the nuclear option when Egypt, Indonesia, and South Africa have exercised it is not very high. Nevertheless, some time remains before Egypt and the others can become nuclear powers. It is not impossible that five to ten years remain in which to develop and apply a policy designed to prevent proliferation. It might even work, in particular because the states which have the capability of becoming nuclear powers before the next five years are up are those least likely to take up the option, even if threatened, *assuming* the United States can provide a credible guarantee. These states are also, in general, the states least likely to serve as catalysts for a process of uncontrolled diffusion and least likely to use their nuclear weapons, if acquired, in an unsettling manner.

The list of disincentives which, in theory, ought to inhibit a rational state from seeking a nuclear capability are very familiar: economic costs, the risk of becoming a target in a nuclear exchange, the inevitable decline in conventional strength, the dangers of increasing proliferation, the loss of moral status, the possible fragmentation of alliance ties, and the like. They are not compelling, for the decision to become a nuclear power occurs, or will occur, in a perspective dominated by the potential virtues of nuclear status and the potential dangers of nuclear abstention.

Therefore, if proliferation is going to be stopped it will be by a concerted policy combining stringent controls designed to make nuclear production increasingly difficult with a series of guarantees bolstered by tangible evidence of interdependence. Neither controls nor guarantees, by themselves, appear likely to be successful. Combined, the increased difficulties of production may balance or dilute the inevitable relative incredibility of a guarantee.

The elements of the first aspect of this policy are well known. They include agreements to prohibit nuclear testing, production cutoffs, and extensive controls on peaceful uses of the atom.[77] Other suggestions include agreements prohibiting the export of nuclear weapons, some forms of nuclear sharing, and the creation of denuclearized zones.[78] The attractiveness of these is, however, heavily dependent on the degree to which proliferation has already occurred. If it is in fact occurring rapidly, the United States may be compelled to export certain kinds of nuclear weapons, or to share them in various ways (and even to create certain kinds of nuclearized zones) rather than to continue to try to implement a policy which has lost its rationale.

How likely are these measures, combined with the kind of guarantee already discussed (involving some form of nuclear sharing), to be successful? Optimism would clearly be out of place, but so would fatalism. The potential effects of proliferation are so disturbing, even if they do not lead to nuclear war, that an attempt to prevent it, rather than merely to control or ameliorate it, is surely worthwhile. Unfortunately, even a concerted effort may fail, for technological difficulties will undoubtedly decline and the other inhibitions may disappear or be ignored. The United States also cannot control the policies of all the other current nuclear powers. Recent reports of French aid to Israeli missile development are illustrative. The assumption that the newer nuclear powers (from France onward) will be as conservative as their predecessors in selling or dispersing nuclear capabilities may be overly optimistic. As more nuclear powers emerge, and as they come from states

---

[77] Bull, *The Control of the Arms Race,* p. 156; see also Arnold Kramish, *The Emergent Genie* (Santa Monica: The RAND Corporation, 1963).

[78] *Ibid.* We could also use economic and diplomatic sanctions or benefits in conjunction with this policy.

with extensive economic problems and less commitment to stability, inhibitions against selling or sharing capabilities *might* decline.

It is, therefore, appropriate to conclude with a few observations on the immediate effects of failure. The states most likely actively to seek a nuclear capability in the next few years are those locked in a fundamental conflict with an equally powerful neighbor. Once proliferation becomes widespread, states may seek nuclear arms in much the same way that Great Britain and France sought them— without a strategy, without a declared enemy in sight, but simply as a form of insurance. For the moment anyway the United States is in a different situation, and nuclear weapons will be sought *against* someone and within a local context which may parallel certain aspects of a classical arms race.

Samuel P. Huntington has argued in a notable article that the likelihood of war in any arms race varies inversely with the length of time it has been going on. In effect, war is more likely in the early stages before peaceful patterns of action and reaction have been established.[79] This conclusion may very well correspond to what could occur in the next few years. Diffusion to one hostile neighbor leaves the other with very few viable alternatives. It can surrender, or it can start a preventive war to forestall nuclear blackmail (or devastation). Of course, it can also increase its own arms level. But in contrast to traditional races, it may be impossible or unwise to do so, for the enemy with nuclear weapons may attack or threaten to attack if a nuclear program is begun. The crux of the difference concerns the fact that an inferiority in nuclear weapons cannot be balanced by superiority on other levels. In this case, as he himself notes, Huntington's second conclusion, that a qualitative arms race is less dangerous than a quantitative one, clearly may not be valid for a nuclear arms race. It is true that nuclear arms merely form one part of an armaments spectrum, but they are a part which may be more than the whole if the whole does not also include nuclear weapons.

[79] Samuel P. Huntington, "Arms Races: Prerequisites and Results," *Public Policy*, edited by Carl J. Friedrich and Seymour Harris (Cambridge: Graduate School of Public Administration, 1958), VIII, 41–86.

The only other alternative is to seek outside aid. But it is in just this situation of intense hostility combined with a qualitative arms race (which is secret in nature) that the policy previously enunciated, of rigid controls on production plus a guarantee involving nuclear sharing, is least likely to be successful. Perhaps the United States could offer a guarantee involving nuclear sharing until the hostile state explodes a nuclear device, and then promise to turn over the nuclear weapons previously shared to the host state. The commitment gains in credibility if the weapons are promised when the other state sets off its first explosion, for the threatened state still retains the possibility of preventive war in the interim if the United States revokes (or it can attack United States personnel). Moreover, by giving only reliable, defensive, and invulnerable weapons one small element of stability may be added to an otherwise extremely precarious position. As noted earlier, this kind of guarantee *might* succeed in deterring a prospective nuclear power. But it is also very dangerous. The best that can be said for it is that it may be the least dangerous alternative in a situation where hostile states confront each other.

In any event, Lewis Richardson's contention that an increase in the level of arms inevitably increases the probability of war must be qualified in these circumstances. The chances of war may actually increase if arms levels do *not* go up. Conventional instability is obviously more dangerous when one or both local states possess nuclear weapons, and a potentially one-sided nuclear confrontation may be more destabilizing than some form of mutual deterrence. The difficulty is insuring that the nuclear weapons available are used to enhance deterrence, rather than aggressive intentions. And that may be more difficult to accomplish in the years ahead when the prospective nuclear powers are heavily involved in deadly quarrels.

The dangers of giving states nuclear weapons, or any weapons, are frequently noted. It is difficult, and in the short run virtually impossible, to control their use once given. But it may be even more difficult to control the use of weapons which are home-grown and unsophisticated. It hardly needs emphasis that the United States should adopt a policy of transferring control only in limited instances, when the alternative is an immediate local war or an uncontrolled arms race. In other circumstances, the United States ought to try to prevent proliferation at all costs. And it is not absolutely certain that it will be impossible to implement both policies together. The United States could offer to give nuclear weapons in an attempt to control the worst effects of immediate crises, and it could, in all other circumstances, concentrate on preventing indiscriminate proliferation by a combination of guarantees and stringent controls on production.[80]

[80] It strains the imagination—mine, in any event—to believe that the United States Government would adopt a policy as extreme as the one I have suggested. This is particularly true in light of the current emphasis on the "inevitability" of proliferation and the tendency to point out that the current nuclear powers will still be dominant and that a Small Power which "goes" nuclear will hurt only itself without compensating disadvantages. The "first" nuclear war, so the argument goes, will only destroy the Small Power(s), leaving the Superpowers unaffected. In addition, adoption of a policy as extreme as the one I have outlined would necessitate harsh actions against some of our allies and some neutrals who refuse to remain nonnuclear. Since the dangers of proliferation are relatively far off, and the losses attendant on antagonizing allies and neutrals immediate, it is hardly surprising that the Government has begun to hedge even on so limited a measure as the current nonproliferation treaty.

The point, it seems to me, is just how dangerous one imagines the process of proliferation will be. If one assumes that it is inevitable, and *hopes* that it can be managed in much the same way that the state system integrated technological innovations in the past, than the measures I have suggested are extreme and unnecessary. If one believes, as I do, that proliferation is the most critical problem of our time, and that it cannot be handled by pious affirmations about the adaptability of the state system or by vague allusions to the successful control of gunpowder, dreadnoughts, tanks, etc., then the measures I have suggested are the minimal conceivable ones if a "world of nuclear powers" is to be prevented. This is not meant by way of apology for suggesting extreme measures; rather, it is an affirmation that they are seriously meant. Nor is it an argument against trying to "manage" the process if it begins: obviously there would be no alternative.

Index

Date Due
